THE YUGOSLAV PEOPLE'S AGONY

*To my children
Tatjana, Stefan and Igor*

The Yugoslav People's Agony

The role of the Yugoslav People's Army

MIROSLAV HADŽIĆ

ASHGATE

© Miroslav Hadžić 2002

All rights reserved. No part of this publication may be reproduced, stored in a retrieval system or transmitted in any form or by any means, electronic, mechanical, photocopying, recording or otherwise without the prior permission of the publisher.

The author has asserted his moral right under the Copyright, Designs and Patents Act, 1988 to be identified as the author of this work.

Published by
Ashgate Publishing Limited
Gower House
Croft Road
Aldershot
Hampshire GU11 3HR
England

Ashgate Publishing Company
Suite 240, 101 Cherry Street
Burlington, VT 05401-4405 USA

Ashgate website: http://www.ashgate.com

British Library Cataloguing in Publication Data
Hadžić, Miroslav
 The Yugoslav people's agony : the role of the Yugoslav
 People's Army
 1. Yugoslavia. Jugoslovenska narodna armija 2. Yugoslav War,
 1991-1995 3. Yugoslavia - Politics and government -
 1980-1992
 I.Title
 949.7'024

Library of Congress Cataloguing in Publication Data
Hadžić, Miroslav
 The Yugoslav people's agony : the role of the Yugoslav People's Army / Miroslav Hadžić
  p. cm.
  Includes bibliographical references and index.
  ISBN 0-7546-1642-8 (alk. paper)
  1. Yugoslavia--Politics and governement--1980-1992. 2. Yugoslavia--Politics and government--1992-3. Yugoslavia. Jugoslovenska narodna armija--Political activity. 4. Yugoslavia—History, Military. 5. Civil-military relations--Yugoslavia. I. Title.

DR1309.H33 2002
322'.5'09497--dc21
                                                                                    2002074725

ISBN 0 7546 1642 8

Printed and bound in Great Britain by MPG Books Ltd, Bodmin, Cornwall

Contents

Abbreviations	*vii*
Author's Note	*xi*
Introduction	1
PART I: THE ARMY'S ROAD TO WAR	33
1 The Army Fails to Acknowledge Reality	38
1.1 The Political Milieu of the Yugoslav People's Army	39
1.2 The Army's Defense of Socialism	47
1.3 Ideological Entrenchment	57
2 The Army's Rejection of Reality	71
2.1 The Political Disintegration of Yugoslavia	73
2.2 The Army's Ideological Arbitration	80
2.3 Illusory Monolith	85
3 The Army's Destruction of Reality	102
3.1 The Political Dissolution of Yugoslavia	103
3.2 The Army Abandons Yugoslavia	110
4 The Destruction of Yugoslavia By Common Consent	132
4.1 War by Arrangement	136
4.2 War in Doses	140
4.3 Introduction to a Bestial War	147
PART II: THE JNA'S WARFARE BALANCE	163
5 The Essence of the Yugoslav War	165
5.1 The Trill of Striking Motives	167
5.2 The Yu-War's Social Energy	171
5.3 Cumulative Effect of the Legacy	176

6 The Powerlessness of the Military's Might	187
6.1 Irrevocable Submission to State Control after the Dissolution of SKJ	190
6.2 Alliance of Reform with the Federal Government	193
6.3 Independent Putsch	195
6.4 Accepting and Supporting the Recomposition of Yugoslavia	197
6.4.a Support for turning Yugoslavia into a confederation	197
6.4.b Support for the creation of a new 'Pan-Serbian' state	201
7 Foundations of the Army's Powerlessness	206
7.1 The JNA's Systemic Protection from the People	207
7.2 Social Profile of the JNA	211
PART III: CHANGING WITHOUT CHANGE	223
8 New Model of an Old Gun	225
8.1 Hidden Traces of the Legacy	227
9 Self-Transformation of the Yugoslav Army	239
9.1 Shortage of Prerequisites	240
9.2 The Yugoslav Army's Capacity for Transformation	246
9.3 The DOS Dividing Line	248
Conclusions	256
Bibliography of Cited Works	273
Index	286

Abbreviations

ABH	Muslimanska Armija BiH – Muslim Army of Bosnia-Herzegovina
AP	Autonomna pokraijina – autonomous province
B-H	Bosnia and Herzegovina
CK	Centralni komitet – central committee
CK SKH	Centralni komitet Savez komunista Hrvatske – Central Committee of the League of Communists of Croatia
CK SKJ	Centralni komitet Savez komunista Jugoslavije – Central Committee of the League of Communists of Yugoslavia
DEMOS	Demokratska opozicija Slovenije – Democratic Opposition of Slovenia
DOS	Demokratska opozicija Srbije – Democratic Opposition of Serbia
DSZ	Društvena samozaštita – Social Self-Protection
EU	European Union
FNRJ	Federativna Republika Jugoslavia – Federal Republic of Yugoslavia
FRY	
GŠ	Generalštab – General Staff
HDZ	Hrvatska demokratska zajednica – Croatian Democratic Union (Croatian nationalist party)
HINA	Hrvatska informativna novinska agencija – Croatian New Agency
HVO	Hrvatsko vjeće odbrane Herceg-Bosne – Croatian Defense Council of Herceg-Bosnia
IPO	Ideološko-političko obrazovanje – ideological-political education
JNA	Jugoslovenska narodna armija – Yugoslav People's Army
JUL	Jugoslovenska Udružena Levica – The Yugoslav United Left
KLA	Kosovo Liberation Army
KNOJ	Korpus narodne odbrane Jugoslavije – Yugoslav People's Defense Corps

KONO	Koncepcija opštenarodne odbrane – Concept of Total National Defense
KPJ	Komunistička partija Jugoslavia – Yugoslav Communist Party
KPSS	Kommunisticheskaya Partija Sovietskoga Soyuza – The Communist Party of the Soviet Union
MPS	Moralno-političko stanje – moral-political state
MUP	Ministarstvo unutrašnje poslove – Ministry of Internal Affairs (after 1990) – the police
NATO	North Atlantic Treaty Organisation
NOR	Narodnooslobodilački rat – War of National Liberation (World War II)
ONO	Opštenarodna odbrana – Total National Defense
OS	Oružane snage – Armed Forces
OSCE	Organisation for Security and Cooperation in Europe
OSH	Oružane snage Republike Hrvatske – Armed Forces of the Republic of Croatia
OSK	Organizacija saveza komunista – Organization of the League of Communists
OSKJ	Organizacija saveza komunista Jugoslavije – Organization of the League of Communists of Yugoslavia
PO	Političko obrazovanje i vaspitanje vojnika – soldiers' political educational and training
PU	Politička uprava (SSNO) – Political Administration (of the Ministry of Defense)
RH	Republika Hrvatska – The Republic of Croatia
RIV	Republičko izvršno veće – Republican Executive Council (government)
RK	Republički komitet – Republican Committee
RSK	Republika Srpska Krajina – the Serb Republic of Krajina
RV I PVO	Ratno vazduhoplovstvo i protivvazdušna odbrana – the Airforce
SANU	Srpska akademija nauka i umetnosti – Serbian Academy of Science and Arts
SAO	Srpska autonomna oblast – Serbian Autonomous District
SDA	Stranka demokratske akcije – Party of Democratic Actin
SDS	Srpska demokratska stranka – Serbian Democratic Party
SFRY	Sociajlistička Federativna Republika Jugoslavije – Socialist Federal Republic of Yugoslavia

SIV	Savezno izvršno veće – Federal Executive Council (Federal Government)
SK	Savez komunista – League of Communists
SKH	Savez komunista Hrvatske – League of Communists of Croatia
SKJ	Savez komunista Jugoslavije – League of Communists of Yugoslavia
SK-PJ	Savez komunista – Pokret za Jugoslavia – League of Communists – Movement for Yugoslavia
SKP(b)	Vsesoyuznaya Kommunisticheskaya Partyia (Bolsheviki) – The All-Union Communist Party (Bolsheviks)
SPS	Socijalistička partije Srbije – Socialist Party of Serbia (Slobodan Milošević's party)
SR	Socijalistička republika – Socialist Republic
SSRN	Socijalistički savez radnog naroda – Socialist Alliance of the Working People
SRVS	Savez rezervnih vojnih starešina – Alliance of Reserve Army Officers
SSNO	Savezni sekretarijat za narodnu odbranu – Ministry of Defense
SSOJ	Savez socijalističke omladine Jugoslavije – Union of the Socialist Youth of Yugoslavia
SSRNJ	Socijalistički savez radnog naroda Jugoslavije – Socialist Alliance of the Working People of Yugoslavia
SUBNOR	Savezno udruženje boraca Narodnooslobodilačkog rata – League of World War II Veterans' Associations
SUP	Sekretarijat za unutrašnje poslove – Police Department
TO	Teritorijalna odbrana – Territorial Defense
TOS	Teritorijalna odbrana Republike Slovenje – Territorial Defense of the Republic of Slovenia
UDB	Uprava državne bezbednosti – State Security Administration (secret police)
UJDI	Udruženje za jugoslovensku demokratsku inicijativu – Association for a Yugoslav Democratic Initiative
UN	United Nations
UNPA	UN Protected Area
USA	United States of America
VJ	Vojska Jugoslavije – Yugoslav Army
VPI	Vojnopolitički informator – Military-Political News

VRM	Vojska Republike Makedonije – Army of the Republic of Macedonia
VRS	Vojska Republike Srpske – Army of Republika Srpska
VRSK	Vojska Republike Srpske Krajine – Army of the Republic of Serbian Krajina
VSO	Vrhovni savet odbrane – Supreme Defense Council
VUR	Veće udruženog rada – Chamber of Associated Labor

Author's Note

In mid-1989 I was given an opportunity to study firsthand the operations of the top generals in the JNA (Yugoslav People's Army). At that time Admiral Šimić, the Army's communist party leader, engaged me unofficially as a consultant on the matter of party pluralism, since the military leaders had to take a political stance in this regard. I quickly discovered that the professional and realpolitik arguments that Šimić acknowledged were empty before the dogmatism and messianic arrogance of General Kadijević. The true proportions of the generals' ignorance and rejection of the new, undesired reality, however, became clear to me when preparing the Army's delegates for the continuation of the 14th Congress of the Yugoslav League of Communists (January 1990) and at the conference on expanding the Concept of Total National Defense (May 1990). The sudden opportunity to present my findings to the top JNA generals on two occasions easily neutralized the intimate impression of futility and powerlessness, particularly since the rare generals with reasonable views were pushed aside by the aggressive readiness of most of their colleagues to use bombs to preserve socialism and Yugoslavia. There was little consolation when these same generals later began with even greater fervor to demonize other ethnic groups in the name of protecting their own.

    This brief encounter on the fringe of the generals' circle pushed me for the first time to seriously question the nature of the Army which I had joined at age 15 (1961) and in which I had already served for twenty-five years. During that period I spontaneously began to put together a mosaic consisting of my personal experience and incidental literary knowledge about the Army. My previous disinterest in the JNA necessarily followed from my basic lack of adjustment to the military's organization. I found a way to escape from the troop by being a part-time student of political science. This enabled me as a corporal in 1973 to become a teacher at the JNA's Military Political School. The subjects I taught (Modern Socialism and Modern Society) and the surprising academic atmosphere in the School kept me at a decent distance from military reality. Friendships with colleagues from the IV Department gave me additional affability and protection. Thanks to this, my forced encounter with the real JNA was primarily devoid of strong sensations. But there was a sudden rise in the number of questions for which I could not find sufficiently valid answers.

My search for coherent answers gave rise to the first outline of this study at the end of 1991. Chance meetings with civilian colleagues who had held onto their level-headedness provided direct incentives. Regardless of the fact that I was no longer surprised by the daily, dangerous inanities of the top generals, I was quite surprised by the fact that prominent professors and researchers had an insufficient understanding of the JNA's social being; particularly since most of them were convinced that the generals could have prevented the disintegration of Yugoslavia in the war by means of a military putsch. This brought certain topics and dilemmas within my field of vision.

The need to explain to myself above all the fundamental reasons for the disintegration of the second Yugoslavia as an introduction to examining the JNA's share in the war led me to a classical methodological mistake. I was fortunate that the broad undertaking was balanced by the initial intention to provide only a model for future research on the JNA's role in the war. The desire to summarize the key factors behind the state's self-destruction nonetheless took a year of work, which gave rise to what I would find out was 150 pages of text written in vain. I spent the next year reconstructing the Army's road to war in order to obtain a factual base for the final discussion of the reasons for the destructive actions and final collapse of the JNA. At this point sufficient conditions were reached that forced me to leave the Army and give myself over to the charms of struggling for my family's and my own survival.

Once I reached the Institute of Social Sciences, I returned several times to the study, which had already grown to 350 pages. In the process I had a hard time shaking off the impression that the archiving of the JNA and my unfinished study were leading to my own personal archiving, particularly since those years I had derived and published several essays from the raw text and this had satisfied my need to present the professional public with a summary of my findings. Intending to collect new material to strengthen and refresh my views, in 1996 I tried to survey 42 key JNA generals who had retired. This attempt failed owing to the objections of the chief of the VJ (Yugoslav Army) General Staff at the time, Momčilo Perišić, and the unwillingness of potential respondents.

A new delay arose from my reorientation towards researching civil-military relations in the third Yugoslavia. Within this context all my attention was turned to the concept of the democratic control of the Army (Armed Forces). What followed was a logical move towards the problem of security in Southeastern Europe. When I was already on the verge of stopping all work on this study, a concurrence of happy coincidences led me to the Copenhagen Peace Research Institute (COPRI) in the fall of 1999. Professor Haakan Wiberg, director of the Institute at the time, not only encouraged me to finish my work but also included COPRI in its publication, which has taken over the expense of translating the text from Serbian into English and preparing it for printing. With the support of their fine reputation, Prof. Wiberg and COPRI had a crucial impact, I feel, on the well-known Ashgate publishing house, which accepted to publish this book. I would like to thank them especially on this occasion for their help and support. The most important gain, of course, came from my friendship with the dear Viking, Haakan.

I would also like to express my gratitude to Ms. Anita Elleby and Ms. Mette Lykke Knudsen at COPRI for their patient and collaborative efforts in transforming my raw manuscript into a Camera Ready Copy.

I would not like to miss this opportunity to give special thanks to my esteemed colleagues from Belgrade who encouraged me directly and indirectly in this work. With the risk of offending someone, I would single out Dr. Nebojša Popov, Prof. Vojin Dimitrijević, Prof. Vlado Goati, Dr. Vesna Pešić and Prof. Milan Podunavac. Dr. Mihajlo Basara, a colonel, is also part of this group; he has been willing all these years to read my attempts and help me resolve numerous quandaries. I would also like to thank Mrs. Alice Copple-Tošić whose translation skills have made this text available to readers from English speaking areas.

I will never know how much the ten years of work on this study cost Tatjana, Stefan and Igor, my children, and my wife Jasna. Thanks to their love and care, I was able to overcome every crisis and finally put the last period at the end of the manuscript. The support of my brother Miodrag was of invaluable importance on this road.

In the end, all that remains is for me to confront and shoulder the drawbacks of this work, for which I alone am responsible.

Miroslav Hadžić, Belgrade

Introduction

The history of Yugoslavia is full of symbolism and paradox. All previous Yugoslav states rose and fell in wars: they were created by war and destroyed by war. The country was always the stakes of war and the army was the main protagonist. By winning and losing wars, armies created and lost states, and could not escape their fate. In the warfare constantly surrounding Yugoslavia, all that changed was the sequence of states and armies that rose and fell, replacing each other, changing in accordance with historical and territorial conditions.

The Serbian army's victory in the First World War gave rise to Yugoslavia, but Serbia and Montenegro disappeared.[1] With the creation of the new state, the Serbian army was replaced by the Yugoslav army. The army's collapse in April 1941 began the final destruction of this first Yugoslavia. The end of the king's army was the beginning of the Communist Party's army and this new army dealt the final blow against the old state. Ending the first Yugoslavia by means of war, the new army founded the second Yugoslavia. Fifty years later, all that was left of Yugoslavia was the army. Rescuing the country only led to the army's destruction; by destroying the country's defense, the army destroyed itself. The new states that arose from the second Yugoslavia formed their own armies; it remains to be seen how these states and their armies will fare.

After 70 years, Yugoslavia's military-state circle closed with a paradox. Everyone is at the beginning once again, and nothing is the same. Serbia, and Montenegro through it, put both their states and their armies into Yugoslavia. They came out without either. All that remains is the rump (third) Yugoslavia and its renamed army. There are insufficient guarantees that what remains of the state of Yugoslavia will last very long. The other states created out of the former Yugoslavia instituted both their states and their armies in Yugoslavia and the JNA (Jugoslovenska narodna armija – Yugoslav People's Army), but in order for these new states to become viable they had to break up the former Yugoslavia. A prerequisite to this was destroying the army. Objectively and against its will, the JNA wholeheartedly assisted in both undertakings.

Yugoslavia's history cannot be understood without the history of its armies, and this has yet to be written. The collapse of the king's army waited 40 years for a worthy interpreter.[2] In the same vein, scholars have yet to make a reliable judgement on the disintegration of the first Yugoslavia, thus there are little prospects that anyone in the near future will give serious consideration to why and how the second Yugoslavia was destroyed.[3] What is certain, however, is that the JNA cannot be avoided in any such undertaking. Without investigating its role and contribution to the destruction of its own state, the covers on the book of Yugoslavia's recent history cannot be closed.

Yugoslavia's history is also swathed in a mystical veil. Historical truths are hidden under a multitude of myths. The historical awareness lacking among the Southern Slav peoples has been substituted by myths,[4] produced without interruption by an endless number of mythmakers. Myths have collided, replaced and destroyed each other, but the awareness of myths has survived. The path towards the ideological production of reality is paved with this attitude towards myths.[5] For this reason, former and current power-holders, old and new aspirants to power in the states that arose from the second Yugoslavia, are issuing newly composed myths and ideologies every day. The nonexistent future and disastrous present are perceived and justified in terms of the shining past. The former future has become the past, and the former past threatens to become the only future. Forces from the past have fought and are still fighting in the name of this uncertain future. The past is being used to nullify the future of the present, and historical and heavenly peoples are being produced by force to suit the needs of the pasts that are arising. The people are embedding themselves in this mythical path towards the past. The remains of the people are being forced into armies and refugee camps.

From the moment it was created in 1941, the JNA was part of the mythical and ideological triad REVOLUTION – PARTY – ARMY. Created by the Party in the name of the Revolution, the Army alone served it to the end. When the Party disappeared, the Army started to serve itself. Earning its colors through antifascism, the JNA soon put on a revolutionary uniform. Since its boundaries were set by ideology, its value was measured by ideology as well. For the needs of ideology it was mythicized; the old myths about manly virtues and bravery, strength and invincibility were then relocated in new myths. New ideological and mythical elements were woven into the mythical essence of the Army. Rooting itself in reality, the new Army was constantly entangled in this myth; in its efforts to convince others, over time the Army itself came to believe the myth. It lived continually in three separate and intertwining worlds: turning into a myth, the JNA grew into a supernatural being – the standard for and refuge of the real yet ideological Army that was constantly being manufactured from the mythical Army. This ideological Army tailored the real Army to its liking. Shackled by the myth and tailored by ideology, the Army lived parallel to reality.

Unable and unwilling to perceive the real limits of its social and political power, the JNA was gradually seduced by the illusion of the military's omnipotent power. That it was named 'people's Army by the Party also convinced many people of this omnipotence. The ideologically tailored and repressed people equated this mythical Army with the real Army; the ideological content was completely overlooked. By playing along with this game, the people produced their last safe haven. The prince on the 'white tank' was saved, intimately and publicly, for the final showdown with all existential, national and state adversities. With the support of the people, the JNA turned itself into an icon for them, reserving the right to prohibit nonbelievers from approaching it. The circle of those who were prohibited widened over time; undesired reality was prohibited too. But the road from prohibition to abolishment was short; what followed was the autarchic production of reality tailor-made to the Army's narcissism.

The self-management, socialist and non-aligned mirror of the JNA was placed in the Total National Defense framework of self-protection. The only one who reciprocated love steadily from that mirror was the eternal Leader. Already cracked, the mirror was constantly glued together and polished. When the mirror finally shattered, the JNA responded with gunfire, but the shots shattered it as well. This caused the already ignited fast-burning fuse of the social bomb to burn even faster. When the Army was finally forced to confront reality, the result was necessarily disastrous for everyone. Reality, already apocalyptic, laid bare all the powerlessness of the military's mythicized power.

When the JNA and its self-reflecting awareness finally faced reality and society, the result was devastating for them both: neither was society such as the Army had imagined and hoped for, nor was the Army such as it had presented itself and been imagined by society.

Dismayed by this undesired truth, society and its Army, hand in hand, rushed into even darker despair. The pace at which they were fleeing reality suddenly intensified. But now it was every man for himself, each in a different direction. The great love between the Army and the people quickly turned into mutual hatred. The icon was broken and the believers turned into heretics. Their meeting with reality, long in the preparation and constantly postponed, lasted but a moment. With Pavlovian speed, the instinct for survival and self-deception prevailed among them all. Already nicely divided up and accommodated in nationalistic cubbyholes, the peoples started to judge the Army using newly acquired criteria. Going from a Yugo-communist and Serbo-communist army to an occupying force and Serbo-Chetnik army, the JNA reached the appellation of Serbian army at which point it disappeared, with no one ever satisfied with it. Everyone used the Army, and the Army offered itself as it saw fit. Some claimed it had destroyed everything, others claimed it had not destroyed enough and thus should crumble. The Army soon became the standard for incompetence, obesity and privilege. Driven into the open where it had senselessly rushed by itself, everyone put the blame for the outbreak of war on the JNA, although for opposing reasons. As they stripped the Army naked, they all actually wanted to cover themselves and hide.

The Army met the challenge of the truth with 'special war' instincts acquired through long years of ideological drilling. Everyone and everything in and around it was blamed for the war and the Army's failure. The top generals were constantly discovering old and new, international and internal conspiracies. Not only was the state wicked, but its inhabitants were wicked as well in the guise of malicious attackers of the JNA or as cowards and deserters. Then, on the wave of universal and internal paranoia, there was a succession of purges and promotions, jeering and congratulations.

As everyone fled, unwelcome reality was the first to be discarded. No one wanted to face the truth about himself. The people did not want to accept the fact that the JNA was their own product and their highly sharpened and unretouched picture, so they broke the glass and started tearing up the picture. The Army could not understand that those who were shooting at it were part of what had once been its people. The Army thus rejected them and went searching for its own true people of Israel who belonged to it, and were as beautiful and powerful as the Army. And the peoples went out in search of armies of their own, leaving the Army no other alternative but to find or create a people that suited it. Linked by birth, the peoples and the Army could not part in peace. And thus began the wartime rape and destruction of their sole, common reality.

In the general free-for-all war, the only ones to suffer defeat, as expected, were the ordinary people. Everyone else was a winner. The problem is there is no one to celebrate. As they rush towards their bright future, the victorious and the new/old military commanders want to escape from their common womb – Yugoslavia's past. They don't want to know that their new states and armies come from the same litter and have the same genetic mistakes as the mother-state. They think they have rid themselves of the mistakes along with Yugoslavia and the JNA, losing sight of the fact that in order to correct hereditary mistakes one first has to discover the reasons for their origin and the conditions for their later reproduction.

In the spirit of the mythical-ideological understanding of their own history, all those participating in the Yu-war have easily resolved this problem. They simply conclude from Yugoslavia's collapse that it never should have existed. In the process they want to make someone else pay the price for their historical blindness, discovered in hind sight. Since Yugoslavia was a prison for them all, each leader led his people out of it. Then they all joined forces and destroyed the prison, but preserved the cells. The path to their ethnically cleansed freedom was therefore paved with the people; what remained of the people was then placed in the repainted and freshly decorated cells with new guards.

For their services in the (self)destruction of the JNA, those who took part in the war bestowed laurel wreaths upon themselves. In the process, each one took from the JNA as much as he wanted and was able. But none of them suspected that the Army officers, both those who left and those who remained, traitors and patriots, assumed part of their being along with their weapons. Since the Army's nature and spirit are so tenacious, it is highly likely they will reappear and continue their interrupted existence, but in a different guise. They continue to be in great abundance in the vital juices of the Yu-states and peoples.

The myth of the Yugoslav People's Army has been shattered for good, although today we still don't know much more about its true nature than we did yesterday. Its nature, and thereby its competence, could only be shown in war. Shattering the myth of the power of military might did not, however, do away with the military's myth of the power of might. The armies that arose from the JNA continue to have a monopoly over armed force in their states. Until they are put under democratic, civil control, it might not be a bad idea to look once again at the key issues in the Yugoslav war and the JNA's role in it.

I

After the eastern Serbian remains of the JNA were renamed the Yugoslav Army (Vojska Jugoslavije, VJ) the new states arising from the former SFR Yugoslavia dropped all interest in the fate of what had recently been the Army of all the Southern Slav peoples. Furthermore, any need to establish the reasons for its collapse during the war disappeared along with it. The real wartime results of the JNA have also been left outside the limelight; there are few reasons to expect anyone will ever again want to examine its wartime role and evaluate its contribution to the disintegration of Yugoslavia.

This is in spite of the fact that the JNA was the center of attention of the warring parties, the local and the world public before and during the war. It was one of the key subjects of political analyses, as well as the main target of propaganda campaigns. For preventive measures and/or in order to increase their influence, all interested parties tried to forecast the Army's (pre)war reactions, even then they had neither the desire nor the need, nor the knowledge, to understand the essence of the JNA's being. This is shown by countless newspaper articles on the personal composition of the General Staff that wanted to forecast the JNA's behavior based on analyzing the ideological, national, educational and family profile of the key generals. It would have been easier and more useful to take a look at the manifest side of the Army's implosion.

The dilemmas surrounding the JNA and the fundamental problems of the disintegration of Yugoslav society have been absolved with seemingly self-explanatory, critical insight. They have thus remained primarily on the level of the stereotype and empty abstraction. For example, regardless of their side in the war, everyone accused the JNA of Bolshevism; it was a constant, self-explanatory and generally applicable argument. Indeed, at the time it fit in nicely with the process of general, and primarily feigned, de-Bolshevization. The widespread production of stereotypes certainly had its purpose, for everyone used them, each according to his needs, to offer the various ethnic groups a clear-cut answer to the question of the Yu-war and the collapse of the JNA.

Although no one has catalogued, let alone analyzed, all the local articles about the JNA in the war years of 1991/92, a brief glimpse indicates that the Army and its activities were the most frequent topic in the press. In spite of this, there was a visible lack of interest in uncovering the real reasons for the ideological and national bias of the JNA's behavior, and thus the disastrous results that ensued.

On the eve of war, the JNA was used in the west of the Balkans as the crown argument to prove Yugoslavia's damaging effect on the Slovenes and Croats. The JNA's public treatment was contingent on these republics' intention to secede, and was thus determined by it. All aspects of the Army's organization and operations were given orchestrated criticism; the widespread odium that was created towards the JNA culminated in the severance of its financing and the cessation of new recruits from these republics.

Immediately after the beginning of conflicts in Slovenia and warfare in Croatia, the JNA was declared the aggressor. From that moment on it was the sole target of their psychological, propaganda and armed attacks. All attention was directed towards destroying the Army, both its military competence and its morale. There were parallel efforts to make the Army lose face, particularly in the foreign public; great pains were taken to prove that the JNA, working in conjunction with Serbia's leaders, was primarily to blame for the war. Behind the all-out propaganda campaign was the accusation that the JNA was a Serbo-communist army. Soon the Chetnik argument was raised, thus inserting into the propaganda trauma from the Second World War. By combining countless variations of the JNA's Serbian, communist and Chetnik characteristics, fuel was added to the Serbophobia and nationalism that had already been created in the local public.

When the JNA left these republics, political interest in it drastically declined. The propaganda that continued, primarily in the international public, was intended to maintain and strengthen the thesis of the Serbo-Army's responsibility for the outbreak of war and its expansion to B-H (Bosnia and Herzegovina). The intention was to bring about even harsher international sanctions and to call in armed intervention against Serbia (FRY – the Federal Republic of Yugoslavia). Therefore, the reasons for the JNA's collapse and destructive actions in the Yu-war were not analytically scrutinized in Slovenia and Croatia, which was to be expected, one might say, since the JNA was the alleged aggressor. This maneuver was actually intended to hide the part played by Slovenia's and Croatia's leaders in inciting and waging warfare. If and when these states come out of their nationalist-authoritarian framework, they, too, will have to examine their own culpability for the war that broke up the Yu-republics; they will have to weigh their decades-long contribution to transforming the JNA into a Party army that was outside of public and parliamentary control.

In Serbia in the east, the JNA was long considered the key instrument of pro-Yugoslav and then pro-Serbian policies and was evaluated and questioned from this viewpoint. In the political home stretch of the crisis, the JNA had the full support of Serbia's official authorities and the public. The first critical reexamination began during the war, caused by the Army's lack of military success and snowballing disintegration. It was noted that the Army's propaganda self-criticism and the official Serbian criticism were based on the same cliche. The Slovenes, for example, immediately reduced the trouble to disloyalty among Army and Federal state leaders.

It was not until the war in Croatia that the Army's 'black box' was partially opened. At that time a more rigorous analysis began of the military performance of what remained of the JNA. Problems were noted with its war goals, fighting efficiency and full battle complement. Direct and indirect requests were made to rename it the Serbian army and openly subordinate it to Serbia's interests. At the same time, retroactive and basically sensationalistic discoveries began of numerous weaknesses in the JNA – from the poor selection of its leading officers to corruption, privileges and incompetence among part of the officer corps. Once again, the depth and scope of the criticism was dictated by daily and war-related reasons, thus fundamental issues regarding the JNA were left untouched.

On the eve of and during the war, of course, the least that could be expected of the JNA was to be self-critical. Obstacles to this included the political dilettantism and ideological rigidity of the military leaders, which were clearly exhibited in the final stage of the crisis. From the campaign against Slovenia to the point when the JNA disappeared, the top generals were constantly in a retroactive position. Since most of their judgements proved inaccurate, they were constantly lagging behind events. The generals thus directed all their efforts to finding arguments to justify themselves before the Army and the domestic public. The anthology of stupidity includes the military leaders' attempt to justify their professional failure in Slovenia by claiming that the JNA had been caught off guard, betrayed, offended and humiliated, and had been the victim of conspiracy and a plot. The silence that surrounded the JNA in Serbia/FRY was then extended to its successor, the Yugoslav Army. Then the old generals of the new army immediately rushed to dissociate themselves from the JNA and release themselves from any responsibility for its fate.[6]

The brief inspection provided herein points to a lack of proper insight into the JNA's wartime collapse and its role in the breakup of Yugoslavia. Were we to judge only by the consequences, it would be easy to conclude that even though the JNA waged war, it failed to accomplish a single one of its tasks. In particular, it did not carry out its constitutional obligation to preserve the territorial integrity of SFRY; it did not preserve the constitutional order, which was also one of its constitutional obligations; to make matters worse, it did not protect the Yugoslav population from war and the destruction of their property. Moreover, the JNA made its own great contribution in this regard. It thereby destroyed all of society's previous, enormous investments in its own defense and in peace.

The above-mentioned is already quite sufficient for the preliminary calculation of a cost-benefit analysis of JNA's involvement in the Yu-crisis. The conclusion that all warring sides would have agreed upon at the time, for mutually exclusive reasons of course, would read: the JNA is to blame. Accepting this final judgement without question, however, does not provide a satisfactory answer. There is still not enough information regarding how and why this happened. Although the consequences of the JNA's wartime excess cannot be changed, there is reason to ask how this was possible, i.e. whether it was inevitable. In order to measure the JNA's role in the war, an entire series of preliminary and parallel questions must be answered.

The first and most difficult question reads: Was the country of Yugoslavia at all possible anymore? If not, then: Did it have to be consumed by war? This opens up a new set of questions: Was the JNA an independent factor in the production of war, a participant on equal footing or simply the executor of someone else's political will? All of this requires us to establish whether the JNA entered the war voluntarily or was dragged into it, i.e. whether it could have ignored the coercion and acted differently in the crisis. This brings us to the inescapable question: Could the JNA have prevented the crisis from leading to war? The fact that it did not imposes a new question: Once it had already entered the war, could the JNA have been militarily more effective? And also: Should the JNA have immediately declared itself the protector of the Serbian people, and if so why didn't it? And finally: Why and how did the JNA collapse, and how much of the price for this was paid by the inhabitants of the former Yugoslavia?

II

A comprehensive investigation of the JNA's participation in the war requires consideration of the following crucial points:

- In spite of the fact that the JNA's constitutional position and assigned tasks obliged it to safeguard the second Yugoslavia and its inhabitants at any price, the Army became one of the destructive participants in the crisis and war. Its blame for and participation in the war are in principle proportionate to the amount of destructive power at its disposal at the beginning of the war. At the start, in June 1991, the JNA had the greatest destructive power.[7]
- The JNA was the sole participant to have been training and preparing for war for decades at the expense of the whole Yugoslav society. Later claims by the generals that the Army was not preparing for internal warfare can be contested for several reasons. It necessarily follows from the JNA's constitutional obligation to protect the legal system that the Army had to be prepared to defend the system from any internal menace. This is testified by the decades-long elaboration of the doctrine of a 'special war' in the JNA, and elevation of the battle against so-called internal and external enemies to a strategic level. By consistently modifying the special war, independent of any valid premises and arguments, the military leadership warned of such a possibility. Therefore, the JNA was the only actor that was expected and also obliged, at least on the war-plan level, to have procedures developed and forces prepared to protect Yugoslavia's constitutional system and territorial integrity. Furthermore, it was the sole actor in the political finale of the crisis to equate its fate with the country's, claiming that the JNA was the sole guarantor of Yugoslavia's survival. In addition, for years the JNA had been assuring the public that it was militarily prepared to respond completely to all provocations of war.
- Had it acted differently, the JNA was a factor that could have had a crucial influence on the resolution of the Yugoslav crisis. And *vice versa*, its behavior hastened Yugoslav society's entrance into warfare and spiraling death. This gives rise to the need to discover why the top generals chose and/or agreed to the alternative of war. For this purpose, we must discover why the military leadership kept making wrong decisions based on bad judgements and unattainable goals.

- There was an enormous discrepancy between intentions and results in the JNA's military-political activities. This makes it harder to establish objectively the real reasons and targets behind its destructive operations. At the same time, the paths leading to crucial decisions on the use of military power are still unknown. This is shown by the frequent change in strategic goals: during 1991-1992 the JNA went from being the protector of Yugoslavia and socialism, to being an occupying (paramilitary) formation, and then a nonexistent army.
- Among all those taking part in the war, it is most difficult to discover the internal logic of the JNA's military and political activities; at the same time it is easiest to prove that the JNA did not stick to the basic practices of its profession, and that it failed on its own premises.
- In conjunction with other, internal and external, military-political factors, the JNA's activities had the worst consequences – heavy casualties and material loss. These same results were delivered to the JNA's own soldiers and officers in no smaller quantities.
- The JNA was the sole participant to take part in destroying its own state, either voluntarily or by force; allegedly in order to save the state, the JNA destroyed itself in the process.
- In conjunction with the state leaders of SFRY, the JNA was the only participant to invalidate its own legitimacy and legality. It was the first and only one of the participants to be left without a social and political stronghold; for this reason, following its own interests, the Army was forced to enter a military-political coalition with other participants in the Yu-war.
- The JNA had a relatively free hand in the initial and crucial phases of the political resolution of the Yu-crisis. It had attained what might be called unlimited political freedom owing to a combination of circumstances and the political ambitions of its leaders. In spite of this, the JNA's freedom to act was restricted by the circumstances at hand and the newly arising political constellation. Initially, this seemed to be the military leaders' freedom to choose among the alternatives for the political and/or military use of the JNA. Therefore, it can be reasonably established that if the JNA did not exactly choose military intervention in the Yu-crisis, this is what it preferred.
- All during the war the JNA was in the most difficult military and political situation. It was waging war without clear goals, without a legal supreme command, without social support and sufficient political backing. Therefore, the JNA was the only participant, under the given circumstances, with no way to win the war.

- The JNA was one of the participants to have its operations internationally condemned; then UN Security Council Resolution 757 declared it together with the Serbs as being primarily to blame for the outbreak of war in B-H.
- The JNA was the only participant, together with SFRY and its (rump) presidency, to have disappeared from the political scene. This participant, however, multiplied by dividing and for a long time created the nucleus of all the armies on the territory of the former Yugoslavia. Therefore, even postmortem was present on the political scene and continued indirectly to complicate the drama of the Southern Slav peoples.
- The JNA was the only army to test its doctrine of a total national war of defense on its own people and its own self. Waging war against the citizens, it repudiated and nullified the ideological postulates of the concept of ONO (Opšenarodna odbrana – Total National Defense) and brought down the accompanying system, but in a paradoxical and tragic manner it also proved their operational-tactical validity.

The above list by no means exhausts all the reasons for investigating the JNA's participation in the war. It does, however, provide convincing arguments that an analysis of the JNA's social, political and military being is needed in order to determine the basic reasons for its collapse. In the same vein, the reasons for the JNA's destructive actions should be sought in its social and political status in the former Yugoslavia. Then, provided with such information, we can analyze the JNA's interaction with the circumstances that surprised it. Whether or not the JNA could have acted otherwise in the Yu-crisis and war can only be proved or refuted within this framework.

Establishing the points of departure to investigate the JNA's participation in the war entails the resolution of numerous methodological and practical problems. The JNA's participation in the war is empirically visible and proven, but it is not easy to establish the determinants, causes and logic behind its wartime involvement. Since these are the subject of the analysis that follows, we will only note some of them here.

The first problems arise when using the apparently self-explanatory term 'JNA'. It says all and nothing about the subject of the analysis. This term is immediately associated with the systemic characteristics – hierarchy, subordination, etc. – of every military organization. It implies an understanding of the JNA as a monolithic and unequivocal organization, and reduces its members to one-dimensional, impersonal and automated individuals. Moreover, since it is empty of real content, it allows analytical manipulation of the JNA as depersonalized and generalized.

It is interesting to note that before and during the war this term was used almost equally by all participants in political communications, including the military leaders. The top generals used this collective term to demonstrate the allegedly high ideological-political and military unity of the JNA's members. The Army's political allies thought along the same lines. In order to obtain public support for the Yu-Serbian option, they constantly bandied about the abstract term 'JNA'. The secessionists made use of the nonspecific term 'JNA' in a negative context to achieve several effects. Disqualifying the whole Army as Serbo-communist, they encouraged national (ethnic) differentiation in the JNA, while putting their own ethnic group *en bloc* against the Army at the same time. The return effect was to increase social and propaganda pressure on its members. Giving national-ideological proscription to the whole JNA, the leaders of the northwestern republics removed any prospect of the Army having a constructive influence on the Yu-crisis. Above all, this forced the Army leaders to choose a (pre)war side as soon as possible.

The polyvalent meaning of the term 'JNA' argues all kinds of complexities in the Army's being. Overemphasizing the Army's complexity and lack of transparency might produce the same results, however, since it offers the idea that the JNA cannot be investigated *in concreto*. What logically follows is the blanket and stereotypical formation of a judgement on its participation in the war.

The term 'JNA' indicates who actually carried out the destruction in the war, but also hides their identity because it says nothing about the distribution of power within the Army. It covers up the military organization's specific social structure and dynamics, giving no insight into the military and political behavior of different Army people involved. It thus becomes an obstacle to discovering or at least investigating the attitude of sub-army groups – officers, noncommissioned officers, soldiers and civilians – towards the crisis and war, and the use of the JNA. At the same time, this term says nothing about the tangle of interpersonal, self-interest and other relations in the Army. This makes it hard to discover the basic motives of its members to (not) participate in the war. It says almost nothing about the internal causes and reasons behind the JNA's national/ethnic disintegration.

Isolating and emphasizing the top generals also has limited analytical value. Focussing attention on the generals only provides a partial answer. They were certainly an important center of decision making about the war and how the JNA was used. But using the term 'top generals' is limited by virtue of the fact that they formed a heterogeneous, power-holding subgroup, with military power unequally distributed within its framework. This resulted in constant conflict among the JNA generals regarding supreme military power, which was mediated by personal, national (birthplace), professional and self-interest factors.

We would also add that singling out the generals removes from the analysis the nature of the military organization from which they arose. Under the given circumstances, the statement that there was little likelihood of the top JNA generals being very different from generals Kadijević, Brovet and Adžić is not far from the truth. They were only one of the products of this military organization and its society taken to the extreme by the war. In any case, most of the war generals – both in the Yugoslav Army and in the armies of the former republics – had their origin in the same military 'nest'. They were all, directly and indirectly, participants, co-creators and implementers of the JNA's pro-war policy. In addition, the number of mistakes that were made before and during the war shed doubt on their ability for rational – political and professional – judgement. At the same time, it was an indication of their unconscious-intuitive ability to recognize and protect their partial and group interests regardless of the cost.

The across-the-board treatment given the generals during the war was also induced by the JNA, and not by accident. It was an indirect expression of the servicemen's rising dissatisfaction with the generals' poor command and unsuccessful warfare. The men's anger was further inflamed by the high (personal and family) price they paid for the wartime (mis)use of the JNA, which was only possible, of course, with their support. In addition, the rising resentment was an indicator of the clashes that had begun within the general corps over the new redistribution of power. To this effect, the national (ethnic) criterion was crucial in the orchestrated Army criticism of some generals. As the war moved about the Yu-republics, there was a rise in the number of ethnically unsuitable generals, or generals to blame for the JNA's failure. There was a corresponding rise in the number of Serbian and Montenegrin generals who were suitable for higher positions, and colonels deserving of the general's star.

A key difficulty in investigating the JNA's participation in the war is discovering the substance, nature and purpose of the political-interest connections existing between (part of) the General Staff and other actors in the Yu-war. The constitutional-systemic status of the JNA does not offer sufficient answers for a proper understanding of its military-political actions then and later. All key arrangements between military and political leaders were concluded far from the eye of the public, who then received only the consequences. For this reason, we should check once again whether and to what extent the JNA acted independently in the home stretch of the Yu-crisis. That is, whether its arbitrary behavior resulted from the key generals' illusions about the autonomous role and power of the JNA or was only the product of a previously established alliance with Serbia's leaders; particularly since the deepening crisis and drawn-out war made the JNA increasingly dependent on external factors that it could not control. Thus even within its own sphere – waging war – it soon lost all independence.

Direct damage had already been made to the Army's military independence when its federal financing was suspended and no new recruits were sent from the secessionist republics. Although the top generals had already teamed up with Milošević's regime at the beginning of 1991, they feigned subordination to Federal state leaders during the immediate preparations for war and the 'Slovenian adventure'. Their false presentation reached a peak in the first phase of the war in Croatia. Operations based on the Serbian regime's goals were hidden behind alleged battles against neo-fascism (the Ustashe) and protecting the Serbs. The impression of the JNA's independence was enhanced by Kadijević's frequent negotiations with Tudjman and representatives of the EU and OSCE regarding the cessation of hostilities. Soon, however, the Serbian-military joint alliance of interest reached the light of day and the question of who was doing what, for whom and why, became immaterial. After the war began in B-H and changes were made in the military leadership, what remained of the JNA submitted publicly and totally to Serbia's political leadership.

This brings us to a new problem that is important for an understanding of the collapse of the JNA: were the reasons for its collapse political or military? In other words, did the political ambitions, illusions and incompetence of the military leaders professionally disable the Army or did the war bring to the surface basic insufficiencies in the JNA, which were only multiplied by the military leader's activities. The need for a military-professional analysis of the JNA's activities before and during the war is supported by the fact that its mechanisms did not function as planned and/or expected in a single one of its segments.

The first obstacle in this regard is the lack of theoretical and empirical material on the JNA's social and military essence. Prewar literature on the JNA consists of quasi-scientific considerations of military problems. An entire library of ideological-apologia books has been produced on the JNA,

ONO and DSZ (Social Self-protection).[8] All that distinguishes the authors are their meticulous pretensions, and the epigonic and indoctrination-like scope of their writing. Such a library is unusable for any scientific understanding of the JNA's nature. It is, however, an inescapable source for the study of its ideological super-determination. The rare critical inspections of civil-military relations in SFRY do not, however, result from the scope of Marxist (ideological) thinking on the army and defense, but are directed towards perfecting KONO (the Concept of Total National Defense).[9] What little scientifically-based research was conducted in the JNA remained outside the public eye.[10] Even greater importance lies in the fact that the military leaders paid no attention to it, since it had only been conducted to provide proof for their convictions.[11]

It is therefore not surprising that no one in the JNA used scientific methods to monitor, analyze and forecast the course of events before and during the war. Individual partial investigations were initiated at one time, but there was no comprehensive undertaking.[12] This is because warfare, although a 'bloody laboratory', does not provide a suitable atmosphere for scientific research. In spite of this, the JNA leadership had a moral and professional duty to collect all relevant factors about the Yu-war and their own Calvary. Nonetheless, it is hard to expect a disintegrating army to want to get involved in the anamnesis and diagnostics of its own dissolution. A valid investigation of the JNA's being and its participation in the war is prevented above all by the legal protection of military secrets. The Yugoslav Army has continued this protection, thus the JNA's internal documents on the Yu-war remain inaccessible.

III

Numerous domestic and foreign researchers have endeavored to explain the ten years of war among the peoples gathered in the second Yugoslavia. The products of political propagandists on the Yu-war and the JNA, whose services were used continuously by all domestic and foreign participants, are naturally excluded. By 1996, domestic bibliographers counted 2,654 units that had been published on the crisis and war in former Yugoslavia.[13] Only ten works are strictly devoted to special studies of the JNA's role in the war. This numerical disproportion does not allow any conclusion regarding the (small) role of the Army, rather indicates the insufficient research that has been conducted in this regard. Furthermore, as the Yu-war moved around former Yugoslavia, professional interest in the JNA declined. A new wind rose of war finally shifted the focus of analysis to the Serbian-Macedonian-Albanian triangle. There was a parallel rise in NATO's mediation of the Yu-war, crowned by aggression against FRY.[14] The new course of events covered up the original reasons for the outbreak of war in this area, and the JNA was necessarily pushed into the background.

Thus the available reading material on the JNA's wartime role is insufficient to reach any final conclusions. For example, James Gow, the only author of a special study on civil-military relations in SFRY, does not treat the final phase of the crisis and JNA's role in it until the last third of his book.[15] He devotes more attention to analyzing the sources and course of the JNA's (self) legitimization during Josip Broz Tito's reign than to the process and reasons for its (pre)war de-legitimization and willing participation in the destruction of its own state. The author's valid intention to look at how the JNA was constituted and operated in order to find the reasons behind its participation in a war against its own citizens is pushed into the background, however, by situational circumstances and the course of the Army's pro-war involution. The JNA's behavior at the end of the crisis was determined by its Party origin and client status, but the top generals made crucial decisions under the pressure of situational circumstances and the actions of all the national-republican actors. Although this author submits an abundance of data on the JNA and shows an enviable understanding of civil-military relations in Yugoslavia, he is nonetheless unable to go beyond the political cliche at the time whereby Serbia's and the military's leaders were unilaterally responsible for the outbreak of war. The reason for this might lie in the fact that the book was completed and published near the end of the Slovenian and Croatian episodes of the Yu-war, during which the author could not or did not want to dig deeper under the surface of events.

Since our intention here is not to evaluate the numerous writers on an individual basis, we will limit ourselves to an aggregate impression of the prevailing treatment given to the JNA's wartime results. A partial inspection of the literature by foreign authors[16] confirms that the JNA's actions were an inescapable item in their analyses of the Yugoslav crisis and war.[17] However, most authors' desire to understand the crisis and war *in toto* has placed the JNA on the margins of their interest. The result is the prevalence of generalizations and simplified evaluations on the course and motives of the Army's war activities. A comparative look at these works cautions that a uniform pattern has been outlined to easily interpret and qualify the JNA's wartime activities.

The fulcrum of such approaches is the Party origin and ideological being of the Army. Its client status and decades-long loyalty to Tito take on an axiomatic status, whereby the reactions of the top generals to the intensification of the Yu-crisis become self-explanatory and understandable. Contextual arguments are then produced by easily adopting the initial propaganda cliche on the alleged (pre)war conflict between the Slovenian-Croatian democrats and the Serbian Bolsheviks. As soon as the inter-Yugoslav conflict has been placed within the national-religious framework, the same standard is used to judge the JNA.

The central argument is therefore built on the unequivocal concept of (pre)war symbiosis between the military's and Serbia's leaders. The high percentage of Serbs among the recruits and officers in the JNA is often cited for this purpose. Then, in order to strengthen their arguments, parallels are drawn with the army of the Kingdom of Yugoslavia, intending to show continuity in Serbia's domination of the army, and thereby of Yugoslavia. Selective evidence is prepared to back the claim implicitly and explicitly that it was inevitable that Serbia and the JNA would join forces on the eve of and during the war. The next step is merely to show the Serbo-Army's aggression against Slovenia, Croatia and B-H. Then, using the same procedure, Yugoslavia's recent and distant past is presented in order to prove that the country was untenable.

The whole story of the JNA is thus formed around Slobodan Milošević, so the misuse of the Army for the greater state goals of the Serbian elite can be used as a premise, but also as a conclusion. In this process, the first (pre)war product of the crisis – the alliance between Milošević and the top JNA generals – is then submitted as the inevitable and fatal cause of war. This excludes from the analysis all the others who drove the Yu-peoples to fight each other; their contribution to the fact that the generals joined forces with Milošević has thus been insufficiently recorded.

Two constants can be discerned in the prevailing approach to the JNA's performance in the war. Most of the analysts' efforts stop at the gateway to the JNA and lack any serious inspection of its social and military-political essence. Then, without any greater delay, an equal sign is drawn between the military leaders and the entire Army. Using an *en bloc* approach, the formal and informal course of the Army's (re)distribution of power is excluded from the analysis, allowing Kadijević's triumvirate to misuse the JNA and most of its members for their own purposes. These analysts have thus relieved themselves from having to investigate the contradictory processes that originated in the JNA during the political finalization of the Yugoslav crisis. This gives them no insight into the social, ideological, political, national and value system repercussions of the crisis and war preparations on the members of the Army. The individual and collective loss of the old identity, and the JNA (noncommissioned) officers' search for a new identity, forced upon them by existential reasons, is easily translated into their natural alignment with the new leaders and nationalistic ideology. Consequently, counting on the Serbian majority in the JNA, the need is removed to investigate all sides of the thesis about the Serbian predetermination of the Army.

Foreign writers, but all others as well, must take into consideration the extenuating circumstance of the lack of prewar research on the JNA's being, which was hidden additionally by ideological mystification. The fact should also be borne in mind that the JNA's wartime impact redirected attention to the visible consequences and their destructive scope, which reduced any interest in discovering the fundamental reasons for the harm that was inflicted by the Army on the Yu-battlefields.

The manner in which the great majority of researchers, journalists and memoirists from the Serbian circle understand the Yu-war and the JNA's wartime activities has directly encouraged the widespread production of methodical and propaganda stereotypes. The fact that writers in the newly-arising Yu-states have interpreted the war using the same equation, but with the opposite sign, does not justify them in the least. Both groups have one thing in common: there is no special investigation of the JNA's war role, and not a single comprehensive study on this topic has been published in the former Yugoslavia today.[18] Admittedly, in 1992 Anton Bebler published the rather long essay 'The Yugoslav Crisis and the JNA' in which he outlines the rather correct point of departure for an initial understanding of the JNA's role in the war that finalized the Yu-crisis.[19] Here again, however, the JNA's treatment is determined directly by the manner in which the author understands the causes of the crisis and the political revocation of the second Yugoslavia. This is why Bebler tries, between the lines, to pardon Slovenia and to some extent Croatia for any responsibility for what the JNA did(not) do; first, from responsibility for the decades-long joint production of a client army outside of democratic civil control, and second, responsibility for Kadijević finally siding with Milošević.

In Serbia (FRY), the lack of research on the Yu-war and JNA's wartime role has been substituted with retrospective texts by individuals who directly decided the fate of the second Yugoslavia and its army; and through them, of course, the fate of the citizens who were caught up in the war and turned into refugees. This has given rise to a special (sub)genre of alibi books. Contrary to this, books of triumph have arisen in the new states, created by the local military leaders and their executors in their own honor.[20] The founders of the alibi discourse are Borisav Jović, former president of the SFRY Presidency, during whose mandate the immediate preparations for war were made, and Veljko Kadijević, the last Federal Minister of Defense and (self)appointed chief of the Supreme Command Staff, thanks to whom the crumbling JNA ended up the wartime instrument to implement Milošević's ambitious plans.

Although the intentions of both Jović and Kadijević are to offer their views on the disintegration of SFRY and describe its last days, both authors have surpassed their own expectations. Instead of providing an alibi for themselves and Milošević, and thereby the war-crazy Serbian majority, they inadvertently wrote historical and political bills of indictment against everyone. The Hague Tribunal might soon start to weigh the criminal-law potential of this writing. Jović not only discloses part of the behind-the-scene games to force the Serbs across the Drina River into war with their neighbors, but vividly shows how the Serbian leaders, relying on the JNA, rushed to modernize the Yu-federation by systematically doing away with it.[21] Kadijević prepares the public for this type of revelation, showing that under his command the JNA carried out its constitutional role by giving rise to three wartime Serbian armies.[22] In the process, he cynically overlooks the fact that this task was not in the constitutional description of the JNA's obligations, and that he and his closest associates (Stane Brovet and Blagoje Adžić) used the Army autocratically in accordance with the interests of the Serbian power-holding center concentrated in Milošević.

Numerous contenders to both hindsight and foresight quickly joined the ranks of this literary genre. It is interesting to note that most of them come from high circles in the JNA.[23] The investigations of these (para)writers are therefore reduced to the more or less unsuccessful justification of JNA and its top generals.

Branko Mamula, for example, recently declared[24] that he has always been for democracy and reforms; Milošević was his political opponent and if it weren't for his retirement he would have dethroned him with the Army. The author does not trouble readers with any proof, leaving them free to take him at his word, and his 332 pages are supplied with only a few quotations. He also spares readers from the knowledge that he was the first to use the JNA to protect his own life and work, as well as his villa in Opatija. He avoids mentioning that afterwards, under his leadership and that of his personally chosen successor Kadijević, the military leaders interfered in the political complexities of the Yu-crisis and then, working together with the national (ethnic) leaders, successfully turned it into war.

Serbs with foreknowledge that the second Yugoslavia would collapse in the war weave a wreath of stories emanating from the kitchen of the 'New World Order', the CIA, the Comintern and the Vatican.[25] Hence, there are no essential differences between the method and contents of the propaganda approach that was used to draw the Serbs into war and today's approach that is allegedly getting them out of it.

A variety of epigones of Milošević's policies used and are still using the conspiracy theory to explain the Serbs' (self)deception and defense.[26] Based on the supposed geopolitical and geostrategic importance of Serbia and other areas inhabited by the Serbs, they use this theory to explain the Serbs' (mis)use of the JNA.[27] The central point of this narcissistic self-reflection is built on the worn-out metaphor of the 'house built in the middle of the road', whereby Serbia, in their opinion, was and remains the target of all types of conquerors. Preoccupied with the underground work of world history, these writers overlook the fact that this enterprising ethnic group has always built its house 'in the middle of' or right next to the road, in order to take advantage of it. If they happened to be far from the main road, their interests led them to build roads to reach it.

The wartime and ideological functionality of seeing a conspiracy behind the historical heritage and current processes cannot be disputed. Disclosing a conspiracy and those who are behind it makes the war self-explanatory for everyone, and justifies all national goals. For this purpose, the war is shifted from real time to history, and the reasons it was waged become unquestionable. This results in numerous manipulative derivations. Conspiracy covers up and pardons the leading political and military leaders' participation in the war. People threatened by a conspiracy have additional wartime integration and motivation.[28] At the same time, the masses of voluntary and involuntary participants in the war are offered (ir)rational shelter in the name of saving the nation from the conspiracy. Narcissism flares up among a people that is lagging behind the rest of civilization; since they are the target of all kinds of conspiracies, they become more self-important; they must be worth something special because they are the constant object of others' desire.

The key problems in the political and ideological self-justification of the primary Serbian participants in the Yu-war spring from their unwillingness to suffer the consequences of their opinions and actions. When these consequences started to arrive of their own accord, all forces were used to reject them and a new manipulative circle of the conspiracy theory began; it was proven that the consequences were undeserved and that an alliance had been formed once again between malicious external and internal enemies. It is therefore no wonder that the Serbs using the conspiracy theory to explain the causes, essence and goals of the Yu-war stubbornly avoid facing the consequences of their actions.

Maneuvering to avoid the consequences, first the reasons and main actors in the Yu-war are renamed, and then responsibility for the outbreak of war is shifted to external meddlers (the international community) and their local collaborators (Slovenia, Croatia). However, giving precedence to external factors in the destruction of Yugoslavia and the downfall of Serbia's (Milošević's) policies, and particularly claiming that the scenario had been elaborated long ago, gives these conspirators supernatural powers. It is claimed, perhaps unwillingly, that the conspirators had been able long ago to forecast, calculate and guide international and internal events towards the destruction of the second Yugoslavia, everything to the detriment of the Serbs and Serbia.

At this point other consequences appeared whose unpleasant conclusions have been adamantly avoided by all Serbian advocates of the conspiracy theory. If we accept that there was a valid scenario and people capable of carrying it out, then the question logically follows: why didn't the Serbian people (politicians, leadership) warn of and/or prevent the conspiracy? Ignorance is not a valid answer since the entire story rests on the claim that previous proof existed of a plot against the Serbs. What is left is incompetence and/or stupidity.

The effects of incompetence, however, cannot be restricted. If incompetence is acknowledged, it must include at least the part of Serbia's history spent in all three Yugoslavias (from Nikola Pašić to Ćosić's Pašić – Slobodan Milošević). Then an answer is needed regarding how much Serbia is to blame for ruining the Yu-project. That is, whether and how much the Serbs and Serbia's policies contributed to the strivings of the other Southern Slav partners to leave the common state. To make matters worse for them, even if Serbia's conspiracy lovers admit their ignorance and incompetence, they will necessarily have to face the collective stupidity of their national elite. Discovering with a delay of 70 years that Yugoslavia is (was) Serbia's great mistake, and that the others, in particular the Slovenes and Croats, entered it for selfish reasons and not for pan-Slavic love (towards the Serbs), deserves no other epithet.[29] And stupidity necessarily leads to aggressiveness and arrogance: knowing about a conspiracy and not preventing it, or knowing that you are the target of a plot and not preparing to defend yourself against it, are a sure sign of stupidity. If we were to call that foolishness, we would be complimenting an entire pleiad of Serbian politicians and writers who sprouted from the conspiracy theory. This conclusion cannot be contested by citing the Serbs' lack of power, for gaining knowledge of the limits of one's own power, or one's lack of power, is already a rational act that can give rise to a rational national and state policy.

The conspiracy theory would have become/remained the private affair of its creators if, at the end of the 1980s and beginning of the 1990s, arriving directly from the previous (19th) century, they had not reached the very center of Serbia's political power-holders, and the military power-holders not long afterwards. Raising this blind-eyed view of the world to the rank of official national ideology, Serbia's war leaders succeeded in ten years in ruining and destroying everything they undertook. Of course they did not even try to offer coherent answers to the sufferings of the Serbian people and the Army, let alone the sufferings of other peoples who found themselves in the middle of their war operations and artillery range.

The logical conclusion ensues that Serbia and the Serbs cannot extricate themselves from warfare until they get rid of the sources and mainstays of their war policies. When this happens, the Serbs and the citizens of Serbia (FRY) will finally have a chance to see what lies behind their mirror. But what has happened since October 5, 2000 repudiates such hopes. The first results of the intervention in the crisis by the citizens and DOS have remained below their joint expectations and real possibilities. Indeed, the moment DOS was inaugurated, the citizen's responsibility for the new government's (in)activity became indirect and secondary.

There is increasing proof in favor of the claim that there was no revolution on October 5.[30] The rupture with the old regime remained on the personal, rhetorical and symbolical level. We are witnessing the discontinuing continuity of a system that is proceeding according to the tenets and prescriptions of the disempowered regime. It is therefore no wonder that the Yu-war, the JNA and its successor the Yugoslav Army continue to be outside the critical inspection of the new power-holding elite. The president of FRY Vojislav Koštunica made his own contribution to shifting the war story from cause to effect by noting that 'handing over the former president of Serbia and FR Yugoslavia Slobodan Milošević has many implications, one of which is fear among the leaders of the Yugoslav Army (VJ) regarding the fate of professional officers, bearing in mind their participation in the wars waged on these lands'.[31] Instead of inquiring about the sources of and reasons for fear among the military leaders, the President wants to remove the fear itself. Instead of ordering an individualized approach and punishing any possible war crimes committed under the aegis of the VJ/JNA, both armies are let off the hook as he takes under his protection (rightfully so?) the frightened, unnamed members of the top military leaders.

Certainly many reasons can be cited to justify DOS's momentary silence regarding the wartime contribution of the Serbian community and the Serbian part of the JNA in the disintegration of the second Yugoslavia by means of war. But arguments can also be forwarded whereby a democratic and modern state cannot be formed on the rotten and/or underlying foundation of the previous state. A healthy foundation needs a modern and professional army that will be under democratic civil control. The inherited Yugoslav Army will be unable to come close to this model until an inventory is made and the war baggage received from the JNA is unloaded. And this requires an investigation of the JNA's role in the war, and of the role of its eastern Serbian remains, condensed in the Yugoslav Army, in its decade-long support of Milošević's regime.

IV

The subject of this study arose from the JNA's participation, which has yet to be measured, in the wartime dissolution of the second Yugoslavia. Regardless of how evident this was at the beginning of 1991, and seems incontestable today, the generals' rushing headlong into war on behalf of Milošević raised dilemmas that still have no valid answers. The claim has been intentionally avoided that they did this 'on behalf of the Serbian side', because the consequences of the generals' stupidity and arrogance were felt by the Serbs at least as much as by the others. Only the order of the consequences was reversed. This could have been forecast with high probability if not as early as 1987, then in 1990 for sure.

The need to discover the Army's road to war grew rapidly along with our conviction that the Yu-peoples' conflict had turned into ten-year-long ethnocide owing to the generals' easy (mis)use of the JNA. The initial reasons for our interest in the JNA's political behavior arrived daily from the conflict-ridden developments of the Yu-crisis finale. They were supported by our private astonishment at the amount of political stupidities, blunders and failures committed at the end of the 1980s by the leading generals. However, it quickly became clear there was nothing to be learned from the 'personal equations' of this or that general. It was evident that they and their henchman did not reach those positions by chance. They were the fifth generation of mediocre military officers distilled from the smoothly operating Party-police procedure into the JNA. Additional confirmation is provided by the parading gallery of national-political leaders – the nth clones of their Bolshevik fathers and step-fathers. The terrifying results necessarily had to follow from the fact that they, each of them individually and all together, produced and brought to power a horde that was even worse than themselves.

Our initial inspection quickly brought us to the timeless view defined long ago by Alexis de Tocqueville: the remedy for defects in the army is not to be found in the army but in society. After finding additional information about the JNA's participation in the war, which is enclosed, we might supplement the above by stating that once defects reach the army they can become malevolent and then, should a crisis arrive and the army be outside of civil control, the army can make an about-face and destroy its own society.

In order to remain faithful to this point of departure, all our considerations of the military-political impact of the JNA and then of the VJ had to be made within a specific social context. Wherever space for this is lacking, we have indicated that the context was at least borne in mind. Our intention is to investigate how the JNA reconciled and internalized both the achievements and the defects of Yugoslav society. This required that we emphasize its social and professional characteristics on every suitable occasion. After the achievements of Yugoslav society were invalidated with the wartime involution of the crisis, all that was left to analyze were the defects.

The cumulative effect of these defects revealed the long-hidden weaknesses of the JNA that reached a peak when it entered the internal war. Therefore, wherever possible and justified, we have included in the analysis internal processes or at least their visible consequences. What logically follows from this is a graduated approach to the process of evaluating responsibility for the (in)activity of the JNA and VJ. We then designate the top generals, as the central military power-holders, as the most responsible for the (mis)use of their subordinates in the Army. This, of course, does not release the other (noncommissioned) officers in the JNA and VJ from responsibility, but at least requires they be given different treatment. In any case, our intention is not to judge anyone, but to present one more understanding of the reasons why the Army, which called itself the people's, took part in a war against its own creators and providers.

Our findings are presented in nine chapters which are then placed in three sections related by topic and time. A chronological approach to the processes and events is not of paramount importance. By placing the analysis in a framework of time, we wanted to create the contextual prerequisites for an understanding of the fundamental – social and political – processes in Yugoslav society and the JNA. We have focussed on the interactive link between society and its Army. First, a concise examination is given of the effects that the radicalization of the crisis in Yugoslav society had on the JNA. Then the Army's political and military reactions to the crisis are analyzed. In this context, using available information, an examination is made of the measures and proceedings that the military leaders undertook within the JNA in order to bring its members over to their side, by hook or by crook.

Concentrating on the JNA's activities required that we first take a look at its formal disappearance (May 1992). This is why the war in B-H and the wartime performance of the western Serbian remains of the JNA – the Army of the Republic of Srpska Krajina and the Army of Republika Sprska – are not thematically treated. An additional reason for this is the fact that an analysis of that war would raise new challenges which we could not respond to properly without turning the study into a set of voluminous monographs. This would also make us redefine our initial concept.

Instead, a separate (third) section follows the fate of the eastern Serbian remains of the JNA gathered under the name of the Yugoslav Army in the third Yugoslavia, in particular because it was the logistical base of the western Serbian armies, as long as they existed. Our decision was certainly influenced by the fact that we were in a position to monitor directly and authentically the new phase of the old army's extended existence within the unchanged coordinates of Slobodan Milošević's regime.

The first section of the study '*The Army's Road to War*' consists of four chapters and is thus the most voluminous. The first three chapters '*The Army Fails to Acknowledge Reality*', '*The Army's Rejection of Reality*', '*The Army's Destruction of Reality*' present in parallel the main prewar developments of the crisis and the military leaders' reactions to them. The section ends with the chapter '*The Destruction of Yugoslavia by Common Consent*' which analyzes the contents and meaning of the 'War by Arrangement' in Slovenia, and the 'War in Doses' in Croatia. This is followed by a brief examination of the main reasons for the Yu-war in Bosnia and Herzegovina 'Introduction to a Bestial War'.

The second section entitled '*The JNA's Warfare Balance*' is devoted entirely to a discussion of the dilemma as to how and why the JNA went to war. It seemed advisable before this, in the fifth chapter '*The Essence of the Yugoslav War*' to offer our views on the war between the Southern Slav peoples of the second Yugoslavia. We did this because, in our opinion, the frequent emphasis of individual dimensions, for example national-religious or the manifest sides of this war, covers up the real reasons why the Yu-peoples went to war against each other.

We felt this would provide the suitable framework for a concise evaluation of the reasons for the JNA's biased and unsuccessful intervention in the crisis and war. For this purpose, the sixth chapter *'The Powerlessness of the Military's Might'* constructs different variations for the Army's prewar intervention in the crisis, and we investigate whether the JNA could have prevented war and under which conditions. The fact that the military leaders readily rushed into the wartime finale, which climaxed in the defeat of the JNA and the disappearance of the second Yugoslavia, led us to search for reasons in the social being and systemic status of the former army, chapter seven *'Foundations of the Army's Powerlessness'*.

The striking similarity between the regimes of Slobodan Milošević and Franjo Tudjman was the reason for the third section *'Changing Without Change'* and an investigation of the nature of the armies that arose or remained in the new Yu-states *'New Model of an Old Gun'*. Using the JNA as the standard, we wanted to make a parallel analysis to check whether and how much the Yugoslav Army and the Croatian Army have distanced themselves from their source. This gave us a chance to compare them as well. The final chapter *'Self-transformation of the Yugoslav Army'* examines the prospects of transformations taking place in the inherited civil-military relations in FRY. With this in mind, we tried to measure the transformation capacities of the VJ, i.e. to establish the weight of its wartime and Party baggage. We end the discussion 'The DOS Dividing Line' by considering the Yugoslav Army's prospects, after Milošević's dethroning, of finally being put under democratic civil control.

The concluding remarks are used as an opportunity not to repeat what has already been said but to communicate some of our understandings and, wherever possible, take them to their final consequences.

Two reasons were instrumental in determining our attitude towards the literature and sources. Our intention to monitor and analyze the JNA's road to war and collapse in the specific context led us to use secondary sources – civil and military newspapers and periodicals. And primary sources were outside our reach in any case. The purpose of the facts, views and findings that are cited is to support, illustrate or justify what has been said.

Fidelity to our initial idea released us from the need and/or temptation to polemize with other authors, otherwise few in number, on the JNA's participation in the war. Wherever necessary (the first chapter), we relied more on the insight of others, but tailored it to our own understanding of the source and essence of the Yugoslav crisis' wartime finale.

Notes

1 By decision of the Podgorica Assembly, Montenegro joined Serbia and for all practical purposes entered into the state with 'three tribes'; compare: Decision of the Great National Assembly in Montenegro, Branko Petranović, Momčilo Zečević, Yugoslavia 1918-1988, thematic collection of documents, *Rad*, Belgrade, 1988, 128-129.
2 Compare: Velimir Terzić, Slom kraljevine Jugoslavije 1941 (The Collapse of the Kingdom of Yugoslavia in 1941), Narodna knjiga, Belgrade, 1982, Vol. 1, preface.
3 A comparative analysis would show that there are no essential differences between the long years of the Party's interpretation of the history of Yugoslavia and the current national interpretation, particularly its nominally socialistic development. They can be used as an illustration of the prevailing approach to their own and other's history, but not a sufficiently reliable source.
4 'For mankind the myth is the oldest form of legalization through genesis. More succinctly, the basic function of the myth is to give genesis legitimacy,' Agnes Heller, *The Theory of History*, Rad, Belgrade, 1984, 30. (quote translated from the Serbian).
5 'There is no doubt that comparing ideology to a myth is crucially important for its understanding (...) In the very least, this perspective makes it easy for us to realize how well ideology goes with myth, how proper and justified it is to link ideology with myth, how truly modern is the need to understand ideology by means of myth.' Mihajlo Djurić, *Mit, nauka, ideologija* (*Myth, Science, Ideology*), BIGZ, Belgrade, 1989, 129.
6 'The political leadership of the former Yugoslavia (...) was the most responsible for our tragedy. It is already an ugly and painful past, and we have turned towards the future,' Života Panić, chief of the Yugoslav Army General Staff, in an interview in the weekly 'Vojska', 03.09.1992, 4.
7 According to data from the International Institute for Strategic Studies, during 1990-1991 the JNA had 180,000 men, of which 101,400 were recruits. Its weapons included: 1,850 tanks, more than 2,000 various types of artillery, 4 frigates, 15 rocket launching boats, 14 torpedo and 30 patrol boats, 25 coastal batteries, 455 fighter and training aircraft, 198 helicopters, etc. In: *The Military Balance 1990-1991*, London, 1990, 95-96.
8 This is shown by book titles in the selected bibliography of Total National Defense prepared by Radmila Protić. Compare: *Strategijski problemi,*

godššnjak 88 (*Strategic Problems, Almanac 88*), COSSIS, Belgrade, 1988, 234-238.
9 Compare: Anton Bebler, Razvitak jugoslovenske vojne doktrine, (Development of the Yugoslav Military Doctrine) *Politička misao* no. 4/85, Zagreb, 123-141. The author criticizes the military leaders, analyses the disputes surrounding the concept of ONO, and the monopoly of Josip Broz Tito, but does not question the fundamental validity, and especially the social and political meaning and contents of KONO.
10 Their mainstay at one time was the Center for Adult Education, Psychological and Sociological Research in the JNA which, at the bidding of the top generals, was discontinued in 1973 owing to disagreements over projects that the Center proposed (for example: Social Relations in the JNA) and their dissatisfaction with the results obtained.
11 In autumn 1990 a pilot study was made for the SSNO in the Rijeka Corps, and its results clearly warned of future national/ethnic and professional ruin in the JNA, caused among other things by the poor policies of the top generals. The report ended up in a drawer and the research was suspended.
12 For example, in the Military Medical Academy psychological-psychiatric research was conducted using former prisoners of war returning from Croatia.
13 Compare: Dobrila Stanković, Zlatan Maltarić, *Svetska bibliografija o krizi u bivšoj Jugoslaviji* (*World Bibliography on the Crisis in Former Yugoslavia*), International Policy and a group of publishers, Belgrade, 1996.
14 This is illustrated by two volumes of the special edition 'Serbia and NATO' (The Serbian Discourse of War and World Debate), *Nova srpska politička misao*, Belgrade, 1999.
15 Compare: James Gow, *Legitimacy and the Military, The Yugoslav Crisis*, St. Martin's Press, New York, 1992.
16 Owing to the long years of international sanctions, the Serbian scholarly public, including this author, had no access to numerous studies on the Yu-war.
17 See, for example: Susan Woodward, *The Balkan Tragedy*, Filip Višnjić, Belgrade, 1997.
18 The bibliography 'Yugoslav Authors on the Crisis and the Disintegration of Yugoslavia' (Bojana Vukotić, *Sociološki pregled*, Vol. XXIX, no. 565-579) registers only one work on the JNA.
19 See: Anton Bebler, *The Yugoslav Crisis and the Yugoslav People's Army*, Forschungsstelle fur Sicherheitsoikutuj und Konfliktunalyse, ETH Zentrum Zurich, 1992.
20 These include, among others, Janez Drnovšek, Stipe Mesić and Janko Bobetko.
21 Compare: Borisav Jović, *Poslednji dani SFRJ* (*The Last Days of SFRY*), Kompanija Politika, Belgrade, 1995.

22 See: Veljko Kadijević, *Moje vidjenje raspada* (*My Views on the Disintegration*), Politika, Belgrade, 1993.
23 The following have published their views to date: generals Pavle Jakšić, Nikola Čubra, Ilija Radaković and Milutin Kukanjac.
24 Branko Mamula, *Slučaj Jugoslavije* (*The Case of Yugoslavia*), CID, Podgorica, 2000.
25 In the military-publicist circle, the meticulous duo Vilić-Todorović was the prizewinner, easily reporting from all centers first anti-Yugoslav and then anti-Serb conspiracies; compare, for example: *Razbijanje Jugoslavije 1990-1992* (*The Breakup of Yugoslavia 1990-1992*), DIK Književne novine, Belgrade, 1995, in particular 33-201.
26 'The policy of using the situation in Yugoslavia to gain influence was first started by the USA with the construction of a strategy to attack communist forces and countries. The strategy of Brzezinski was especially important in this regard, as shown during the World Congress of Sociologists in Upsala in 1978, which proved to be very effective. (...) Analyzing the situation in Yugoslavia, he maintained the possibility existed of influencing internal developments owing to: (a) the economic situation (...), (b) international relations (...), (c) the situation in the League of Communists (...), (d) the state of defense possibilities...', Momir Stojković, Novi geopolitčki položaj Balkana i Jugoslavije (New Geopolitical Position of the Balkans and Yugoslavia), *Vojno delo* no. 6/91, 59-60; the author does not explain why Yugoslavia's political leadership did not discover the 'critical points' in the security of their society and state, i.e. why nothing was done to prevent this scenario from being carried out. At the same time, he loses sight of the fact that for decades the communists had declared their basic goal to be the destruction of world imperialism, thus there is nothing surprising or abnormal about the fact that the USA had elaborated a strategy to bring down communism.
27 'The greatest danger to Yugoslavia's security (...) comes from the so-called low intensity strategy (...) which might be motivated by direct strategic interests in Yugoslavia coming exclusively from the West. Their basic goal would be to transform Yugoslavia into a Western type of civil society, and if that doesn't succeed, then to break it up and transform it again, or at least some of its parts, into the desired system,' Blagoje Adžić, Očuvanje jedinstva oružanih snaga – preduslov opstanka Jugoslavije (Preserving the Unity of the Armed Forces – Prerequisite to Yugoslavia's Survival), *Vojno delo*, special issue, Belgrade, August 1990, 23.
28 'The danger lies in the fact that the (conspiratorial –M.H.) view of history is never completely false, rather it always contains an ounce of truth and must contain it to appear convincing (...) My thesis is that in politics wherever there is affective identification with the leader (i.e. Caesarian), the masses and

the leader have this image of history: the misfortune that has befallen the masses is exclusively owing to the conspiracy of certain individuals or groups against the people..' Franz Neumann, *Demokratska i autoritarna država* (*Democratic and Authoritarian State*), Naprijed, Zagreb, 1974, 238.

29 'If we speak about today's Yugoslavia and its reality, we cannot avoid the Serbian question. The Serbs are undergoing extreme regression in Yugoslavia (...) That regression is ongoing: it is reflected in the economy, in civil liberties, in political democracy, in the destruction of the Serbian people's ethnic entity, in the nonexistence of a Serbian state, in the loss of the grandiose medieval culture. The Serbs are the only people in Europe to lose their ethnic territory, reduced by the 1974 Constitution to the borders defined by the Berlin Congress, and an ideology has annexed the entire Middle Ages and destroyed its wars of liberation.' Dobrica Ćosić, Uslovi demokratske budućnosti (Conditions for a Democratic Future), *Književne novine*, Belgrade, 1988, No. 766-767, 8.

30 For initial findings on this, see: Miroslav Hadžić (2001), Critical Security Points of Serbia/FR Yugoslavia, in: Ten Years After: Democratization and Security Challenges in Southeast Europe, P/P Consortium, National Defense Academy of Vienna, Faculty of Philosophy, Institute of Defense, University of Skopje, Vienna, March.

31 Exclusive interview with the president of FRY, Politika, www.politica.co.yu/2001/07/01_01.htm.

PART I
THE ARMY'S ROAD TO WAR

The Army's Road to War

It is impossible to understand the finale of war to the crisis in the Socialist Federal Republic of Yugoslavia (SFRY) without analyzing the political activities of its military commanders that preceded it. While Josip Broz Tito was alive, one of the first tasks of the JNA (Jugoslovenska Narodna Armija – Yugoslav People's Army) was to protect the absolute rule of their Leader and the Communist Party. Even after his death (1980), the Army's primary concern was to protect Tito's 'life and work' and his 'revolutionary legacy'. After the crisis became public knowledge, JNA's political involvement was no longer clear-cut and straightforward, but neither was it consistent.

The Army's policies were determined all along by two groups of factors. The first group resulted from the changing political and inter-ethnic constellation in Yugoslavia, and a set of contradictory international factors soon joined it. This group of factors created the Army's working environment that directly and indirectly determined its leaders' behavior. The second group of factors was of an internal nature. The Army leaders' behavior was determined at all times by the basic characteristics of the JNA – social, political and military. Measuring the degree and orientation of the interactive effect of both groups of factors thus requires an analysis of the Army's reaction to the crisis in society and in the government.

At the end of the 1980s, the Yugoslav crisis entered its final phase. The constitutional-systemic blockade and disintegration of the SKJ (Savez komunista Jugoslavije – League of Communists of Yugoslavia) encouraged JNA leaders to become directly involved in ongoing political clashes. The predominantly partial approaches to solving the crisis enabled military commanders to autocratically adopt the role of the only pro-Yugoslav actor. Army leaders therefore endeavored at all times to legalize and authenticate their activities.

The generals compensated for their lack of legality with an excess of ideological legitimacy, but to no avail. Army leaders sought and primarily received cover for their political activities from the SFRY Presidency. In the beginning, the generals justified their involvement with JNA's duty to defend the interests of the 'working people and citizens'. Later events forced them several times to change and reduce their legitimacy. This chronic lack of legality and legitimacy was a permanent handicap for the military commanders and had a negative effect on their key decisions.

Herein lies one of the main reasons for the Army leaders' reactive behavior. Aiming to act within the law, in a system that was already deregulated and had lost its legitimacy, they constantly reacted to events with delay. Their delayed response, caused by the lack of legality, increased the military commanders' dissatisfaction, so their ability to accurately evaluate situations and make optimal decisions was inevitably diminished. Adding to this the ideological nature of the premises upon which evaluations were made, it becomes clearer why the Army's ignorance of and failure to acknowledge reality, combined with its leaders' frustrations, produced an explosive mixture.

The Army carried out its public political activities through several well organized channels. The first were state and parliamentary institutions. On such occasions military commanders acted like the heads of a state body. Federal SKJ forums were another, much more frequently used channel. Army leaders appeared at them as an ideological symbol. The JNA had additional influence on the public through the work of active and retired generals in Party transmissions – the SRRN (Socijalistički savez radnog naroda – Socialist Alliance of the Working People), SRVS (Savez rezervnih vojnih starešina – Alliance of Reserve Army Officers), SUBNOR (Savez udruženja boraca Narodnooslobdilačkog rata – League of World War II Veterans' Associations) – and the military youth in SSOJ (Socialistički savez omladine Jugoslavije – Union of the Socialist Youth of Yugoslavia).

Another channel, parallel to the previous, was the military branch of the League of Communists – the Army's OSKJ (Organizacije saveza komunista Jugoslavije – Organization of the League of Communists of Yugoslavia). Military commanders used this forum to expound authoritative views, but in a much sharper form. Everything which, for reasons of political opportunism, the generals would not say in state and civilian Party forums reached the public through the military's Party forums.

The intensification of the crisis spurred military commanders to find new ways to influence the public. A spokesman was designated for SSNO (Savezni sekretarijat za narodnu odbranu – the Ministry of Defense) and public communiqués were issued. This gave the generals the opportunity to react to political events on a daily basis. The military media had the same purpose – in particular 'Narodna armija' (People's Army) and VPI

('Vojno-politički informator' - Military-Political News), controlled by the Political Administration of SSNO. The main task of these media was to gain the support of active and retired officers and noncommissioned officers.

Changes in JNA activities were dictated by the tempo with which the crisis intensified and expanded. Since the military commanders were just one of the components entangling the crisis, the real meaning of their actions can only be discovered within the constitutional, systemic, ideological and national whirlwind that arose. The best way to properly evaluate the aim and scope of the military commanders' activities is thus within the framework of a comparative analysis of the reactions of federal and republican actors to the crisis.

Understanding the substance and phases of the Army's policies requires that we consider them within the context of key events at the end of the crisis. We will therefore follow the military commanders' activities during three periods:

- May 1988 - January 20, 1990 – beginning with the proclamation of the 'three reforms'[1] at the First Conference of the SKJ and ending with the Congress[2] at which the SKJ disintegrated.
- January 1990 - January 1991 – beginning with the Party's self-dissolution and ending with the SFRY Presidency Decree on disarming paramilitary formations.[3]
- January 1991 - May 1992 – beginning with finalizing the preparations for war, continuing with the wars and ending with renaming the Yugoslav People's Army the Yugoslav Army.[4]

Notes

1   Held May 29-31, 1988; for introductory remarks by Boško Krunić, president of the Presidency of the CK SKJ and a discussion by JNA representatives, see: VPI 7/88, 7-26.
2   Held January 20-22, 1990 in Belgrade.
3   Issued January 9, 1991, for the text of the Decree see: VPI 2/91, 7-9.
4   See: the Tanjug communiqué on the decision by the Presidency of Yugoslavia regarding the reorganization of the JNA into the Yugoslav Army (Borba, 21.05.1992, p.2).

Chapter 1
The Army Fails to Acknowledge Reality

The period between the League of Communists of Yugoslavia's First Congress and its 14th Emergency Congress was crucial for the fate of SFR Yugoslavia. At this time the contradictions in society that had been suppressed and left unresolved emerged in an extremely heightened form. Several important, interdependent but destructive social processes took place at the same time. When the source and essence of the crisis was brought out into the open, preparations were initiated for the disintegration of Yugoslavia. At the same time, however, several possibilities were presented for its democratic reform. So the later breakup of Yugoslavia by means of war was only the ultimate consequence of everything that was politically conceived and prepared during this phase. Hence there are grounds for the allegation that the fate of Yugoslavia was decided before the war. War only tragically multiplied the price of the country's political disintegration.

Yugoslavia is an example that confirms the fact that an authoritarian system, even when it calls itself self-managed, does not have sufficient capacities and instruments for the peaceful resolution of a crisis. It was shown here once again that when the authoritarian essence of society is compressed into a system, it heightens any crisis and antagonizes its contradictions. For this reason, there were greater chances that the central authoritarian model would divide and multiply into (new) national states than that democracy would triumph over it.

Objectively speaking, the communist power holders in Yugoslavia were certainly not about to strip themselves of power. Yugoslavia's disintegration through warfare was thus the ultimate product of the communist oligarchy's inability to solve the crisis peacefully during this period. War was likewise the product of their refusal to include the mainstays of other ideologies, programs and interests in the crisis solving process. Instead of finding a platform upon which to establish a consensus for extensive reforms in Yugoslavia, the communist leaders started to settle accounts with each other. Transferring their conflicts to society, they incapacitated it and made a positive solution to the crisis impossible. Bringing down their own regime, they brought down the state and devastated society, leaving the population to the destructive power of politics and war.

1.1 The Political Milieu of the Yugoslav People's Army

At the end of the 1980s, the crisis in Yugoslavia's government and society came to a head. The critical points, current and historical limits of the Communist Party's socialism were made public. Hindsight would show that during this period the settlement began of socialist Yugoslavia's historical accounts. It quickly turned into balancing the accounts of the Southern Slavs' seventy years of living together in a joint state.

The destructive effects of the crisis first appeared in the sphere of economics. Previous attempts to stabilize the economy and supplement the political system had not produced expected results. The Party's feigned changes temporarily removed the crisis from center stage, but then it returned with a vengeance. The system's dysfunctional economic and political characteristics became more and more visible every day. It was no longer possible to stabilize the economic system. The economy's structural problems were left unresolved and what followed was a new wave of inflation.[1]

Social dissatisfaction was increasingly widespread. Germs of pre-civic and pro-civic social and political differentiation were noted. Initial awareness of the existence of social layers, spurred by the difficult economic situation, resulted in more and more strikes. The population's political dissatisfaction was also on the rise.

Owing to differences in the development levels and economic positions of the republics and provinces, the crisis did not have the same impact everywhere and was therefore understood differently. There were fundamental differences in opinions on how to solve it. At heart there was certainly a conflict of interests. Nominally everyone advocated a modern and efficient economy. In spite of this, conflicts began between republics that wanted to preserve their favorable economic position and those that demanded radical changes in economic relations, even at the price of redistributing poverty.

The Government's policy was hotly disputed in Slovenia owing to that republic's concentration of economic and political authority, which it wanted to preserve. There were disputes about the budget and financing the JNA.[2] Demands to change the Government soon arrived from Slovenia's and Croatia's parliaments. This was followed by a verification of the Government's two years of work, at which time demands were made to accelerate constitutional changes and adopt systemic laws before the other amendments were passed. Although the amendments were passed, the Government did not succeed in carrying out its plans and achieving visible results, and at the end of December 1989 it resigned. Financing the federation and the JNA[3] was settled once again with a provisional law which was not accepted by Croatia, while Slovenia disputed its constitutionality.

The task that Mikulić's Government was supposed to resolve was objectively unsolvable in the given circumstances. Although many of the Government's economic measures[4] went against the ruling system, its program as a whole did not go outside the bounds of the ideological framework. Theirs was an attempt to reform the system on unchanged Party postulates. But neither was the Government successful in reconciling the conflicting demands of the republics and provinces, nor was the system provided with the means to get out of the crisis.

A new Government followed with a program that relied on the Party's three reforms. Its concept of 'new socialism' announced the gradual removal of the groundwork of a Party state and Party society. Extricating itself from the vicious circle of self-management, the new Government was later able to develop a program that was essentially solid.

Confirmation for this is found in the fact that the new Government's program was immediately subjected to political and ideological criticism. The newly undertaken reforms immediately submitted economic invoices, certainly not equal, for preceding activities. Following what was already standard procedure, everyone refused to pay their share of the cost of reforms or tried to shift it to others. There thus began an unsynchronized but joint campaign by republican power holders against the Government. When the Government put the package of anti-inflation and initial reform measures into effect, the balance of power had radically changed.[5]

The scope of both governments' reform programs was directly limited by the republics' demands to reorganize Yugoslavia, particularly since the proposed projects were mutually exclusive – confederal[6] and federal. It might be said that as the Government's programs increased the chances for reform and the reconstitution of Yugoslavia, there was a simultaneous decline in the political will of the central actors in this regard. The Government's ability to devise a valid program was in counter proportion to and phased delay with the political will of the republican elite. A closed feedback system arose in which it was not easy to determine the direction or timing of destructive initiatives.

The Government's reforms prescribed a return of macroeconomic jurisdiction to the federation, along with part of the political jurisdiction. This was interpreted in Slovenia and Croatia as a violation of the existing relations among the republics and provinces, and led to a rejection of this concept of reform. Under additional political pressure from Serbia and the federal leaders, Slovenia and Croatia finally responded with the demand for a confederation. This in turn gave further legitimacy and spurred even greater pressure in favor of Yugoslavia, although it necessarily increased the feedback which rejected Yugoslavia in a (modern) federal form. Thus, the moment it became clear that without changes in the political system there could be no economic reforms, the economy took on secondary importance. Economic interests became eminently political and were determined on a national (ethnic) basis.

The economic crisis undermined the overall structure of society and threatened the existing division of power, announcing its institutional and non-institutional redistribution. The main political battles were waged over the relationship of power between the federation and the republics, while the same battle was being fought between SKJ and various opposition pretenders to power and rule.

All of this took place during discussions about changes to the Federal Constitution and successive changes to republican constitutions. The situation was highly dynamic in Slovenia and Serbia; Croatia soon joined them. The Federal Government was the first to request changes to the Constitution since it linked curbing the economic crisis with regulating the jurisdiction of the federation within the economic system. The proposal to change the SFRY Constitution received initial support from all relevant political entities except those in Slovenia.[7]

The Slovenian leadership's resistance to constitutional changes began with opposition to the manner in which amendments were adopted, as well as their political scope. They were not prepared to accept a single solution that went below the level of the provisions in the 1974 Constitution. All proposals for a Yugoslav referendum were also rejected, but a Slovenian referendum on constitutional changes was announced should the amendments Slovenia did not accept be included in the block.[8]

Slovenia gradually acquired sovereignty with synchronized activities in two directions. Any changes to established relations in the federation were prevented at all times. The constitutional evolution of the Slovenian leadership proceeded simultaneously, made to order by pressure from their own and the Yugoslav public. The constitutional 'peak-1974' was quickly abandoned in favor of an asymmetrical federation. Although any thought of secession was publicly denied,[9] the restriction of Yugoslavia's sovereignty in Slovenia actually began in the fall of 1989. In spite of this, the Slovenian leadership tried hard all the while to show that they were firm advocates of Yugoslavia and socialism.

At that time Serbia, on the groundswell of the 8th Session of CK SKJ (Centralni komitet Savez komunista Jugoslavije – the Central Committee of the League of Communists of Yugoslavia), was preoccupied with its own constitutional reconstitution and comprehensive political differentiation. In Serbia's political processes, the topic of Yugoslavia was only present in the beginning with regard to the 1974 Constitution, which had been identified as the key reason for the Serbs' unfavorable position.[10]

In spite of this, principled accord on the need to change Serbia's Constitution had already been reached at the federal level. The leaderships of all the republics gave declarative support to such changes.[11] During preparations for the passage of Serbia's new constitution, Slobodan Milošević locked political horns with the leaderships of Vojvodina and Kosovo. Along with a rise in the provinces' resistance to Serbia's constitutional centralization came a rise in non-institutional pressure against the provinces.[12] On the wave of the so-called anti-bureaucratic revolution, the Party and state leadership changed in both provinces. Crossing over Serbia's borders, this 'revolution' elicited the same results in Montenegro.[13] The massive outpouring of Albanians into the street in the fall of 1988 was the introduction to February's 'underground strike' by miners in Stari Trg. The federal state introduced emergency measures that temporarily anesthetized the Kosovo problem. Once the new constitution was passed, Yugoslavia returned to the center of the Serbian leadership's political activities.[14]

The reaction of Serbia's government and public to the autumn demonstrations by ethnic Albanians and the ensuing solidarity meetings were considerably instrumentalized in the western republics. Their media immediately declared the Serbian leadership's policies to be an obstacle to Yugoslavia's democratic evolution and reforms.[15] This was the overture to an organized campaign that created public odium towards Serbia (and the Serbs). This process necessarily reactivated all the old inter-ethnic animosities and phobias.

Although it had led to the crystallization of different visions of Yugoslavia, Kosovo was soon politically marginalized. Relations among the three 'axis' republics – Slovenia, Croatia and Serbia – became the central topic. Key political and ethnic conflicts arose within this space. Carried away by the successes of the 'anti-bureaucratic revolution', the Serbian leadership started to follow the same pattern of behavior towards Yugoslavia. A series of meetings – from the meeting for Yugoslavia[16] to the meeting in Gazi Mestan and the announcement that 'meetings of truth' would be exported to other republics – additionally aggravated political relations. In this phase the conflict was consummated by a break in economic links between Serbia and Slovenia.

Events in the other republics proceeded at a somewhat different pace and with somewhat different components. Croatia's official 'silence' was broken regarding several matters. The question of the constitutional definition of language started up again.[17] Sensitivity to happenings in Serbia was constantly on the rise among Croatia's public officials. The appearance of the nationalistic party HDZ (Hrvatska demokratska zajednica - Croatian Democratic Union) radically stirred up the political scene in Croatia. This could not pass without reverberations in Serbia as well. The celebration of the 600th anniversary of the Battle of Kosovo in the Knin area denoted the beginning of public complications in the dispute between Serbia and Croatia. This finally brought the conflict out of Party forums and resulted in the political and ethnic polarization of these republics and their inhabitants.

Constitutional-systemic and political disputes between the republics were actually a reflection of both fundamental and ongoing processes in Yugoslavia. The crisis announced a variety of changes in the political, social, national (ethnic) and ideological environment. Above all, it encouraged and enabled a political pluralism in society.

Discussions and conflicts within the SKJ took over the public scene. Irrevocable political and ideological pluralism emerged in the SKJ, thus bringing conflicts of interest. The first catalysts were the 'Slovenian spring' and the 'anti-bureaucratic revolution'. The sequence of events revealed that conflicts about Yugoslavia's state organization were actually hidden behind the 'spring' and 'revolutionary' communists' discussions on democracy. Minimum initial agreement only existed regarding the need to preserve the SKJ's leadership position. This required Party unity in the common battle against so-called anti-socialist forces. Party unity, however, was also interpreted differently in Party centers in Serbia, Slovenia and Croatia.

There soon came a pluralism and ramification of alternative scenes – political, ideological and spiritual. The many years of sporadic, minority opposition to the communist regime became politically articulated and gained in mass. Alternative youth movements[18] and committees on human rights and freedoms gave rise to the first political organizations outside the system. Although issuing from criticism of Yugoslavia's style of socialism, most of these movements were politically placed within the national (republican) framework. This built a bridge for the later juxtaposition and joint actions of nationalistic communists and anticommunist nationalists.[19] They were soon joined by the reactivated Diaspora.

During this period an atmosphere of fear was created all over Yugoslavia. The media were crucial in this regard, initiating a so-called media war. They reacted to all the Party-state leadership's attempts at democratization and pluralization with an ideological campaign against those who were not like-minded. For example, discussions about the JNA during the 'Slovenian spring' were used to accuse Slovenia of counterrevolutionary activities. The same method was then used in Kosovo.

Owing to its political monopoly, the SKJ had already undertaken measures to solve the crisis. The program of 'three reforms' was announced at its First Conference. After the initial consensus on the need for reforms, digressions and conflicts began among the SKJ leadership regarding their extent, scope and goals. The following series of CK SKJ sessions brought to light all the conflicts of interest, ideological and other differences that resulted in the collapse of the SKJ, thus laying bare its political infirmity and ideological insufficiency.

During Party discussions, the foundations of the system and the project of socialism were not questioned in the least and the deflection towards social democracy proposed by the SK Slovenia sparked strong opposition. The prevailing view was that the deformations at work resulted from systemic weaknesses, caused by a poor cadre policy, thus the disunited leadership. The crisis became highly personalized. Numerous economic scandals were used to kindle the illusion in the public that all the problems could be solved by simply replacing censured individuals and leaderships.

Divisions in the SK leaderships nominally started because of different understandings of how socialism should further develop in Yugoslavia. The socialism that existed was countered by 'humane socialism', or 'socialism with a human face'. Regardless of its justification, this countering only provided additional factors for internal Party polarization and pluralization. The real reasons were much deeper – the communist model of Party imposition over the state and society was worn out permanently.

Conflicts and schisms quickly crystallized around the key questions: was Yugoslavia still possible and acceptable as a common state, and if so, how should relations among the republics and ethnic groups within it be organized? The answer was urgent, since everyone was dissatisfied with the former Yugoslavia and relations with each other within it. Since both questions and answers were beyond the power of the SKJ, other political actors took part in resolving Yugoslavia's fate.

Three prevailing, but differing, approaches crystallized with regard to the attitude towards Yugoslavia, the social system and the status of the republics (nations): conservative, reform-minded and radical.

The conservative approach was concisely expressed by 'either-or': either Yugoslavia would be a socialist and modern federation, or it would cease to be. The reform-minded group moved within the space of 'both': Yugoslavia and its society would be both reorganized and modernly reformed. The radical approach was also an 'either-or' view, but with the opposite indication: either socialism and Yugoslavia would cease to exist or the original ethnic groups would never reach their desired sovereignty.

The conservative viewpoint was held by communist forces wanting to keep the status quo. Their basic goal was to feign changes using a tried and true method in order to keep their monopoly of power. Extensions of this group arose with regard to different understandings of the relationship between the federal and republic (communist) authorities. The conservative viewpoint was thus divided into federal communists (advocates of strengthening the central government) and republican communists (advocates of the republics' sovereignty).

The social and political nucleus of the federal groups were the former and current holders of central party and state power. They had been forced to accept reforms, albeit in word only. They conditioned their support for reforms with preservation of the ideological foundations of society – socialism, self-management, brotherhood and unity, non-alignment, national defense and the monopoly of the League of Communists. They saw controlled reforms as a chance to increase the efficiency of the system and also preserve their position. They hence reduced the reform project to the return and constitutional guaranty of central state intervention.

The group of republican conservative communists consisted primarily of young members in the second line of Party command. Their goal was to take over power in their republics, since power had already been shifted there.

The alleged battle for equal footing and their republic's independence led them into alliances with forces of national provenance. Thus began the two-sided misuse of Bolshevism and nationalism, whereby the question of who would get the upper hand became immaterial. Since they arose from and were reproduced by the same social and mental makeup, the communists and nationalists merged in the end. The communistic republicans immediately put on a nationalistic mask and the nationalists in return handed over their intact authoritarian being and makeup.

Groups of amorphous social and political composition were initially gathered around the reform-minded viewpoint. Discouraged communist believers went along with the slogan about a 'new socialism' but also with the idea of a provisionally convertible dinar. The reformers' positive attitude towards Yugoslavia had the same effect, since they treated the country as a desired and necessary state framework for their intervention in the crisis.

The Yugoslav framework of reforms brought the reformists the initial support of the federal conservatives. Conflicts arose between them regarding the concept of the federation. The reformists countered the speculative antinomy 'federation-confederation' with the concept of an efficient state as an instrument to reconcile general, special and individual interests and goals. The Government's announced plan to privatize enterprises was a good opportunity for the federalists, and not only them, to shift to the ideological terrain. They immediately saw in the reforms the danger of Yugoslavia being colonized by capitalism, which would lead to the destruction of socialism in accordance with the scenario that was already taking place in Eastern Europe.

Having turned into confederalists in the meantime, republican conservatives quickly replaced their initial support for the reforms with obstruction, because of the Yugoslav framework. Only the Serbian communist leadership was not able to find its bearings in this confusion. Led by the desire for power, Serbian communists waged the battle for Yugoslavia in their own way from an anti-reform platform.

The communists' combined obstruction to reforms played right into the hands of those in favor of radical changes. In the initial phase of Yugoslavia's decomposition, the radical forces leisurely relinquished the leading role to the communists, who then did the job for them. They prevented reforms from taking place and finished all preparations for the corrosion of the Yugoslav state.

Among those in favor of radical changes, differences were noted immediately between two groups of political forces. The first was based on the radical civic-minded criticism of socialism, with the proclaimed goal of the civic and democratic reconstitution of the state. They wanted Yugoslavia to come out of its pre-civic and pre-political state and join the European civilization and modern society.

A dividing line within these civic-democratic forces arose regarding the dimensions of the state framework of change. A smaller number of parties and movements took all of Yugoslavia as the space within which they were active. This group drew closer to the reformists owing to the Government's reform program that detached itself from socialist symbols and presented itself as a path to possible modernization. But, in the same vein, owing to the tempo with which reforms were eroded and the political space was divided up, the Yugoslav civic initiative was left without support. Soon it adjusted to the republic framework, in which ethnic groups had already gained the upper hand.[20]

The policies of the second, stronger group of the radical wing were founded on nationalistic criticism of socialism and Yugoslavia. Their first and foremost goal was to create or restore nation-states; in support of this they presented proof that their nation (ethnic group) in Yugoslavia was constantly being deprived of its rights, and was economically and politically exploited. They considered that conditions for isolated, national (ethnic) intervention in the crisis could only be achieved with the breakup of the common Yugoslav state.

The anti-reform approach was necessarily close to conservative and nationalistic forces. In order to preserve their power, the communist conservatives concentrated on preserving power in the republics. Hence they rushed to dismantle the federal government. Seeing a chance for themselves, the nationalistic forces heartily supported the communists as they broke up the country.

1.2 The Army's Defense of Socialism

The contradictory reactions of Party and state bodies to the crisis created political confusion. The least to be expected was for Army leaders to find their bearings in it. Professionally detached, and constitutionally-systemically protected from reality, the knowledge that Army commanders, and all of the JNA, had about what was going on was ideological at heart. The Army's lack of knowledge combined with the military commanders' support of socialism necessarily resulted in the aggressive disavowal of reality.

Ideological sanctities were being torn down before the military's eyes. For the first time, the generals faced the danger of not receiving the money they asked for the Army. The first breaches appeared in what had previously been an inviolable prohibition – the military and the organization of society's defense. The social and political status of the JNA started to undergo public scrutiny.

Confederal-federal disputes implied a change in the state and territorial sphere of the Army's operations. Economic decline and the political obstruction of reforms quickly corroded the JNA's economic power. Successive contesting of the budget and the introduction of provisional measures put the JNA in a situation of uncertain survival.

The destructive effect on the Army, albeit delayed, resulted in the collapse of its ideological foundations. The JNA's political and ideological inviolability was breached from two directions. The communists-republicans were behind the front attack. With this in mind, first Slovenia and then Croatia started to economically and financially bind the Army. Side attacks were made by alternative movements with demands that the Army be de-ideologized and depoliticized. Through the opposition's work behind the scenes, JNA myths about the revolution, the Party, Tito and socialism started to crumble. This irreversibly undermined the Army's central political support.

Destructive changes also took place within the Army's milieu. Interethnic conflicts and the rising influence of extreme ideologies had a twofold negative effect on the JNA. Owing to these changes, the Army's social reputation and influence were constantly on the decline. Its members were increasingly exposed to different pressures, particularly on a national (ethnic) basis. In accordance with this, the JNA's multi-ethnic harmony started seriously to crumble, and the officers began the process of secretly dividing up power.

The JNA's political inviolability was first corroded by alternative movements in Slovenia. They opened up a public discussion on the political and professional autonomy of the Yugoslav People's Army. The topic was then broadened to the social role of the Army and its political position in the system.[21] A reexamination began of the rationalization behind the system and concept of ONO (Opštenarodna odbrana – Total National Defense). Demands appeared to discontinue the subject of ONO and DSZ (Društvena samozaštita – Social Self-Protection) at the university.[22] Alternative forces were particularly interested in changing the recruitment system. They demanded that the mandatory military service be carried out in home republics, and the right to civil service and conscientious objectors be recognized. The military commanders understood this as an attack on the state, socialism and the Army[23] and presented it as such to the public.

The generals' political offensive was first directed against Slovenia, since the greatest challenges came from there. As political pressure had not given the expected results, the military commanders resorted to force: two

The Army Fails to Acknowledge Reality

journalists from 'Mladina' and two members of the JNA were arrested for allegedly revealing military secrets.[24] This was only the overture to new ideological and political pressure against the Slovenian leadership. There soon arose an ideological-joint interest group of opponents to announced changes in Slovenia and to changes in its relationship towards Yugoslavia. Military commanders and new party leaders in Serbia comprised the axis of the group.

This group was held together by fear of any change, particularly any radical inquiries into the merits of the communist regime. Their offensive attack against Slovenia was primarily intended to bring order within the ranks of their own ideological circle. They counted on a possible renewal of the monolithic Party to guarantee victory over anticommunist and other opponents.

In public discussions, the military commanders, together with the federal bodies of the Party and state, constantly forwarded ideological and not constitutional-legal and state arguments. The Army's evaluation of the country's situation was expressly supported by the new federal Government, which concluded its Analysis with the opinion that the 'ultimate goal of attacks against the JNA is therefore its 'dismantling' as a Yugoslav category and its complete invalidation. The ultimate consequence of the goal is to negate the essential function of the federal state in the domain of defense and social self-protection which would be a decisive step towards its breakup.'[25]

The Army leaders' alibi for their increasing public presence was the citizens' growing fear of intensification of the crisis. The military commanders countered the general anxiety with assurances that 'the Yugoslav People's Army, through its presence and behavior, will continue to be a cohesive force in the Yugoslav socialist self-management society and the guarantor of its free, undisturbed and democratic development.'[26]

At that time, the generals linked the security of the citizenry, Party and state to maintaining the JNA's current position. They claimed that 'any change in the social role of the Army would lead to the breakup of SFRY as a state and social community, and such attempts are being made. This is the general conviction of most working people and citizens.'[27] It can be seen from this message that the military commanders relied on the positive disposition of the citizens with regard to their political interventions. In order to instill confidence in the population, the military commanders constantly declared that the crisis had not decreased the JNA's battle readiness, since 'the systems of total national defense and social self-protection, particularly of the Armed Forces, hold part of the autonomous defense mechanisms that defend them from the effects of the crisis.[28] As proof it was cited that the activities of the SKJ in JNA based on Yugoslav, and socialist, patriotism were morally and politically educating the JNA in an organized fashion, and thereby immunizing it from the crisis.[29]

Since the military commanders were suffering dramatically from the changes in society, they made even more dramatic warnings about their meaning. It was first claimed that 'our revolution, the SKJ and our country, SFR Yugoslavia, are at a great historical crossroads.'[30] And the generals claimed that there was not a big choice at that crossroads, since 'it only leads in two directions'. In such an interpretation, choosing the first meant 'continuing the victorious path of the revolution and socialist development of the country, continuing the great work of comrade Tito, the work of the KPJ (Komunistička partija Jugoslavije – Communist Party of Yugoslavia) and the SKJ and of the great majority of all the peoples and nationalities'[31] Choosing the other path would mean 'letting our further development be marked out by those who condemn the socialist revolution and qualify it as a civil war and historical mistake.' The generals' message was clearly intended for the multitude of the population that had been raised on the ideology of the revolution without any knowledge of the revolution itself. The illustrations used were the key points of political self-legitimization by the military commanders in this phase of the crisis. Using a combination of ideological (NOR – Narodnooslobdilački rat (War of National Liberation - World War II) and the revolution) and existential reasons (preserving the state and socialism), the generals presented themselves as the only remaining protector of Yugoslavia and socialist life within it.

The manner in which the military commanders understood the reasons for and essence of the crisis clearly revealed the direction, as well as the limits, of their later policies. The generals built their coordinates for interpreting the crisis on the 'conspiracy theory' and an evaluation of the situation as comprising 'special' warfare. They never looked for the cause of the crisis in the very essence of the revolution and in the Party that resulted. The military's diagnosis was founded on the view that processes were going on 'that endanger the basic values of the revolution and socialist structures and threaten to break up Yugoslavia as a social community.'[32]

These increasing statements by the military commanders could not pass unnoticed in the public. In spite of varied criticism of the JNA and the ONO system, most of the republican leaders at that time were flirting politically with the generals. The regime's media, particularly in Serbia, revived the citizens' hopes in the Army as their unfailing defender.

Between the lines, the media often predicted, and even invited, more decisive actions by the Army. At the same time, there was a rise in the number of demands for the depoliticization of the JNA and its exclusion from the political resolution of the crisis.

The military commanders' reactions to such challenges followed a tried and true method – first the opposing arguments were twisted, then substituted for the original, and finally rejected. For example, dilemmas regarding the legality of the Army's political interference were reduced to two theses: 'One whereby the JNA should play a special role in resolving the Yugoslav crisis, including taking over power in a military putsch. And the other whereby the JNA officers should be excluded from the political life of the country and the barracks closed.'[33]

Focussing on the thesis of a putsch,[34] the military commanders wanted to achieve several effects. When bandying about the 'dose of a putsch' every other smaller 'dose' seemed less painful. Thereby the real problem – the crisis – was marginalized. Devising the story of a putsch, the generals simultaneously penetrated the political-psychological barrier and lowered the public's sensitivity threshold, because rejecting the idea of a putsch did not remove the possibility that the JNA might still carry it out. Opponents were thus indirectly sent the message that any decision about a putsch would be decided by the military commanders and not the public. At that time, the other thesis about depoliticizing the JNA seemed benign compared to a putsch, and so few were able to oppose it, particularly since the military commanders justified this with the legalistic claim that 'both theses are not only incorrect but malicious (...) although (...) they both recommend the same thing: changing the character, place and role of the JNA and its personnel, as established in our socio-political system by the SFRY Constitution.'[35]

During this period, interethnic relations were one of the central themes of the JNA generals. They drew special attention to the fact that 'for a long time now the ominous burden of nationalistic specters and elemental forces has stood over our society.'[36] Insisting on their Yugoslav viewpoint, the military commanders constantly tried to remain equidistant from both separatist and unitarian nationalism. The generals' main problem was how to criticize unitarianism without annulling their demand for a stronger central state. Or, how to package their demand for a modern federation without being accused of unitarianism. So they called upon their external authority, since 'in accordance with Tito's concept of Yugoslav national feelings and Yugoslav socialist patriotism, the Army's composition is explicitly against every nationalism – separatist as much as unitarian (...)

and is simultaneously against all tendencies that proclaim positive social trends that strengthen the country's unity as being unitarianism.'[37]

Not long afterwards, in the echo of Party discussions on relations in the federation, Army leaders launched the slogan that 'Yugoslavia can only exist as a true federation; otherwise, in our opinion, it will cease to be.'[38] The slogan unfortunately portended the approaching war that would break up the second Yugoslavia.[39]

Since the 'three reforms' did not give the expected results, the military leaders lodged complaints. Their approach to the crisis became a bit radicalized and they judged that 'time has shown that this serious social crisis cannot be surmounted the way others have been in the past. In order to supercede such a state, the assumptions upon which we have built some of our mistakes must be changed, and above all, measures must be passed that will separate the workers from the shirkers.'[40] For the first time, the generals' opinion of the crisis indicated that an awareness had been reached of some errors and mistaken notions. In spite of this, the military commanders concluded that 'today in Yugoslavia two prevailing processes are taking place simultaneously with completely opposite ideological and socio-political goals: (...) one, with the goal of leading the country out of the crisis through three reforms (...) and the other, with the goal of destroying Yugoslavia and its federal, socialist and self-managed system.'[41]

It is not surprising that the generals were unable to extend their suspicions about the source of the errors and mistaken notions to the ideological postulates of the JNA. Furthermore, it was stressed once again that the military commanders' priority tasks in building the Armed Forces, and the JNA above all, would be 'maintaining and strengthening the moral and political unity of the Army based on the program of preserving and further developing the heritage of the socialist revolution and the revolutionary ideas of Josip Broz Tito.'[42]

The frequent CK SKJ meetings increased the public's impression that the crisis had intensified to the ultimate limit and that the moment of truth was at hand. The military and Party leadership of the JNA made an additional contribution to this impression. Remarks made by members of the military at the 20th CK SKJ meeting summed up the Army leaders' previous views and sharply delineated their attitude towards the crisis. The accent was placed on relations in the SKJ and the federation. The point of departure was the opinion that 'the situation in Yugoslav society is rapidly reaching the culmination of the crisis. The League of Communists is losing battle after battle as never before in its history and cannot extricate itself from the vicious circle of its contrived and essentially powerless ways of thinking and acting.'[43]

It was noted with resignation that 'overall efforts by the SKJ Organization in JNA to build unity in the SKJ as a whole have clearly been insufficient since the factors eroding that unity are stronger and many of them outside our scope.'[44] It was then underscored that 'the opponents of our country and our socialistic, self-management system abroad, together with hostile Yugoslav emigrants and hostile forces within the country, are using every possibility and method to break up Yugoslavia.'[45]

Searching for the reasons behind the SKJ's powerlessness and the system's dysfunction, the Army leaders established that 'disunity on all levels of leadership is one of the greatest obstacles to stabilizing the country's situation (…) and in conditions of disunity, the lack of real attributes in the state and the federal state leadership is brought even more sharply to light.'[46]

The maneuver of substituting arguments was carried out this time too. Instead of discussing the real causes of the crisis and how to solve it, the generals spread the conviction that all the problems would be easily solved if unity was reestablished in the leadership. Then, in the second part of their view, they suggested that since unity was no longer possible, it ceased to be important, since everything could be compensated for by installing 'real attributes' in the federal state. In this spirit, attention was directed to the fact that 'the efficient functioning of the federation is one of the prerequisites to the survival of our country, but general Yugoslav interests continue to be suppressed, and decisions by the federation are ignored or even openly attacked.'[47]

The generals sent a crucial message to the public when they announced the fight for Yugoslavia: 'If the fight for Yugoslavia has already been declared, it cannot be waged without the Yugoslav People's Army and with it millions of working people who have Yugoslavia in their hearts much more than the individual, blinded and bureaucratically dulled groups and individuals who are either power hungry or want to break up this country.'[48] Owing to its multiple meanings, the message was very indicative. It was immediately obvious that the generals disqualified those who disagreed with them in the still joint Central Committee, and elsewhere,[49] and proclaimed them their enemies. Then they announced that the Army, independent of the SKJ, would resolve the crisis together with 'millions of working people'. Third and most important, by announcing this battle the Army leaders confirmed their attitude that Yugoslavia would not exist unless it was a (modern) federation. So at the 20th session of the CK

SKJ, the military commanders were actually announcing the battle for a federal Yugoslavia tailor-made to suit them. In this phase of the Yugoslav crisis, the military commanders' 'belligerent federalism' summarized all the political strategies and tactics of the JNA.

In the meantime, the military commanders could not avoid taking sides in the problem about party pluralism. After considerable hesitation, the Army announced that all democratic institutions in society must be based on law. In the current Yugoslav conditions and with Yugoslavia's historical experience, 'returning to a multiparty system would be a big step backwards.'[50] All the dilemmas regarding the Army's attitude towards pluralism were removed at the end of 1989 at the 9th Conference of the League of Communists in the JNA. A multiparty system was countered with pluralism 'within the system of socialist self-management', with the justification that 'in the current phase of social development, any form of institutionalizing political pluralism in the form of a multiparty organization is unacceptable.'[51] The penultimate argument was the claim that agreeing to a multiparty system 'would be doing a favor to further ethnic and nationalistic divisions in Yugoslavia.'[52]

Discussions on a multiparty system immediately opened up the problem of depoliticizing the JNA, Even mentioning the problem was unacceptable to the military commanders. In particular, they did not agree with the first consequence of pluralism and depoliticization – doing away with the SKJ in the JNA.[53] Rejecting a priori the legalization of political pluralism, the military commanders greatly contributed to aggravating the political situation.[54] Indeed, it was illusory to expect that the Army leaders would voluntarily renounce the military's SKJ branch, which allowed it to have a direct impact on society. In addition, the military's Party was an additional instrument to be used by the generals in the ideological and political disciplining of JNA members.

At the end of 1989, final preparations were made for the conclusive political differentiation of the SKJ. All signs indicated that the upcoming emergency SK Congress would probably be the last. The republican parties' views were already on opposite ends of the spectrum, and a compromise was nowhere in sight. Along with a noisy media campaign, starting and ending positions were taken and consolidated. The military commanders did not lag behind in this regard, and so a joint meeting was organized of the Military Council and the Presidency of the OSKJ Committee in the JNA.

The unusual composition, as well as the topic, gave the meeting the required dramatic element. All ambiguities were removed regarding the appearance of the joint state that the JNA would advocate. The message was clearly sent that the new 'SFRY Constitution should be the highest political and legal enactment. The constitutions of the republics should be coordinated with the SFRY Constitution', and therefore, 'any view is unacceptable that gives primacy to the republics' constitutions, whereby these constitutions should be passed first and only then the SFRY Constitution, with the SFRY Constitution depending on the constitutions of the republics.'[55] Based on this it was concluded that 'the state of SFRY can only function as a modern legal and sovereign state if the federation and its bodies carry out the jobs and tasks within their jurisdiction in a smooth, responsible and efficient manner. For this reason, the federation and its bodies must have at their disposal all the necessary authority and means to carry out their functions as defined by the SFRY Constitution.'[56]

In principle, it is hard to deny the military commanders' consistent espousal of a modern federation, which they supported with reform-minded undertakings.[57] However, it was no longer a question of the accuracy of the viewpoint but of the constellation of political forces in Yugoslavia. Once again the military commanders foresaw several important factors. First, the fundamental lack of integration in the Yugoslav community was being shown on a daily basis by constitutional and systemic crises. Second, the 1963 and 1974 constitutions legalized centrifugal tendencies and established the republics as independent power centers. Third, the 1974 Constitution practically prevented every change in relations between the federation and the republics, whether desired by one or several parties. Fourth, every rational argument collapsed because constitutional disagreements were passed through partial and nationalistic filters. And fifth, maximalist demands could not lead to an optimal solution acceptable to everyone. If the influence of rationalized JNA interests can be perceived in the military commanders' views, then their intolerance showed poor judgement of the political constellation.

Our understanding is supported by the manner in which the military commanders defended themselves from the accusation that they had already taken sides in the political conflict. Forwarding the argument that they were consistent, they wanted to show the JNA's political independence, since 'the Army's evaluations and views on the causes of the social crisis in Yugoslavia and the paths to overcoming it have a continuity of many years and have not changed essentially in the last several years.'[58] Once again, the military spokesman said more than he wanted. Emphasizing the continuity and constancy of the Army's views could be taken more as proof of the generals' dogmatism and lack of understanding of the crisis than as proof of their consistency.

The Army leaders' propensity to change was directly refuted by the explicit claim that 'there can be no discussion regarding the tasks of the Armed Forces in defending the lands established in the SFRY Constitution and federal laws, or any doubts about their readiness and ability to effectively carry out these tasks as precisely established in the SFRY Constitution and the Law on the People's Defense.'[59]

These views by General Veljko Kadijević, Minister of Defense, had the nature of a political platform, which is shown by the fact that JNA delegates to the Emergency Congress faithfully represented them,[60] with minor variations. Before that, the military communists' views had been brought in line at the 9th Conference of the OSKJ in the JNA. On that occasion, just before the Emergency Congress, the document 'Program of the Ideological-Political Tasks of the SKJ Organization in the JNA' presented the JNA leaders' views on basic social problems, elaborating them in detail.

The constant use of the already deceased Josip Broz Tito provided a decorative side to the military commanders' ideological and political activities. Tito was used in the Army as a model, a theoretical and methodological standard, as legitimacy, supreme evidence, an ideological and political whip, and also a totem.[61] The crescendo was reached at the 9th OSKJ Conference in the JNA, when the delegates pledged in chorus that they would not turn off 'his path'.

With their pledge to the late supreme military commander, the military commanders also expressed their mourning for the 'good old days' in which the JNA was protected from social crises. Since the military commanders judged the crisis all along by socialist standards, in their own interpretation, they clearly could not renounce their original criterion – Tito. Particularly since everyone was (mis)using him in the ongoing political conflicts. The generals expected their loyalty to Tito and ideological beliefs to strengthen their political position. Titoism, however, came right back to the military commanders like a boomerang. Accusations against the JNA that it was bolshevist were actually based on Tito's iconography which was easy to prove in the Army's activities.

An important indicator of how the generals accepted reality was their understanding of the failure of 'real-socialism'. The top generals immediately accepted the evaluation that socialism had failed owing to a world anticommunist conspiracy. In accordance with the implanted illusion that Yugoslavia was unlike other countries, they rejected every similarity between domestic socialism and real-socialism. The generals interpreted every analogy as a form of external and internal pressure on 'trends in our country, particularly on the contents and direction of our reforms.' This intention, naturally, was immediately ascribed to those who were the mainstays of non-socialist and anti-socialist changes in Yugoslavia. The public was therefore warned that 'today those forces encouraged by the 'defeat of socialism' are more open in their activities and they propagandize the destruction of socialism, the division of Yugoslavia and the restoration of capitalism.'[62] In spite of such reactions by the military commanders to the crisis, it would be hard to prove that their militancy at the time was directly motivated by fear of losing power. Their concern for the JNA's status was stated all the while within the scope of their worries about the revolution, socialism and Yugoslavia, and was most likely not a skillful or Machiavellian maneuver on their part. In addition, it will never be known whether the top generals truly experienced the crisis in the manner they presented to the public. It is indisputable that they developed rationalization mechanisms, both ideological and psychological. It seemed at moments, particularly in the case of General Kadijević, that some of them were caught up in messianism. The fact is far more important that the JNA's political views from this period clearly showed its top generals' mental confusion, ideological xenophobia and political aggressiveness.

1.3 Ideological Entrenchment

Although the military commanders were highly involved in political battles, during this period they devoted great attention to the situation in the Army. By means of Army commands and the Party, they undertook numerous measures to maintain the desired MPS (moralno-političko stanje – moral-political state) and the JNA's battle readiness.

The military commanders used political influence on their subordinates to achieve several desired effects. Their first intention was to protect them and ideologically immunize them from conflicts in society and the Party. By imposing their views, the generals wanted to keep their officers and noncommissioned officers on the 'correct' ideological course, but also prevent any possible political turmoil within the Army. In order to increase the JNA's public influence, they required the officers to become more involved in the current situation, along the lines of the military commanders' policies.[63] Thus, all the military commanders' efforts during this period were directed towards achieving, in official terminology, 'high ideological and political unity' of the OS (oružane snage – Armed Forces) and the JNA. References to making a monolith of the JNA members were even contained in the statements by Army leaders at state and Party forums.

The goals, tasks and contents of the Army members' situational indoctrination can be perceived through an analysis of the program for the ideological-political training and education of officers and soldiers at that time.

This is first offered by the Program for the ideological-political education of officers and civilians working in the OS SFRY IPO (ideološko-političko obrazovanje – ideological-political education). Regardless of the scope of changes undertaken in society, and particularly those that were announced, the main goal of IPO during this period did not change. The political administration of SSNO had defined the goal of 'teaching the Program, i.e. becoming familiar with the basic characteristics of the social-political situation in the country and the world,' in particular 'from the viewpoint of strengthening the ideological-political unity of the members of the Armed Forces'. All of this was to be 'in accordance with the platform and policies of the SKJ and the development of brotherhood and unity in Armed Force collectives' for the purpose of education in the spirit of 'Yugoslav socialistic patriotism' and training for direct 'political work in the units and institutions of our Armed Forces ... whose role, it is generally believed, will continue to rise.'[64] It is immediately obvious that this formulation of the goal makes no mention of the state duties of the OS and the JNA, or of the obligation to prepare their members to successfully carry out these duties.

In addition, the military commanders had not renounced their ambitions to shape the recruited soldiers in accordance with their own ideological model. This is shown by programs for the political education and training of the soldiers (PO – političko obrazovanje i vaspitanje – Political Education and Training). It was established that the basic goal of the 'soldiers' political education and training is to strengthen their moral and ideological-political awareness through Marxist-based scientific knowledge about society and man, the working class as the mainstay of revolutionary changes, NOR and the socialistic revolution, about building a self-managed society as a community of equal peoples and nationalities and about total national defense and social self-protection.'[65]

The fact that such goals were excessive and for a mediocre ideological school is beside the point. Through their political work the officers were obliged, during the recruits' 15 months of mandatory military service, to form 'ideologically and politically aware, morally unshakable, loyal and resolute fighters for the development and defense of freedom, independence and the constitutional order of SFRY. Implementing the PO Program (should – M.H.) develop Yugoslav socialistic patriotism and loyalty in the interests of the working class and working people, and brotherhood and unity of the peoples and nationalities of Yugoslavia.'[66]

The fact should be emphasized that the soldiers were being prepared to defend the state and constitutional order, while the officers who commanded them were acting according to the SKJ platform! Owing to ongoing processes, a new Program for the soldiers was adopted in 1988. Compared to the 1985 Program, however, the only changes were in the number of topics and their contents,[67] for the invariable ideological accents remained the same.

The system of evaluating the MPS (moralno-političko stanje – moral-political state) of units and institutions, and the political educational level of the soldiers was an important means with which to ideologically discipline and indirectly repress the JNA members. Officers were evaluated based on two criteria: as commanders/commanding officers and as individuals. The evaluation of a unit's battle readiness, and thus the quality of the officer corps, crucially depended on the state of MPS, which was even evaluated using ideological-political criteria. At the same time, the officer evaluation process, which was the basis for every officer's status and prospects for further promotion, separately judged the ideological-political attitude of the officers towards official social and military values.[68] A similar model was used to evaluate soldiers and the 'basic indicators of the success of the soldiers' political education and training' were 'the demonstration of thoughts, beliefs and views on essential socio-political questions and problems and the degree of the soldiers' involvement in carrying out their duties as soldiers.'[69]

So that nothing was left to chance, the process of the ideological entrenchment of the JNA members was completed with a parallel Party tutorial. Everything that was 'taught' within the IPO education program was repeated in Party organizations.[70] Debates in the military Party organizations had an additional function, however, since communists in the military were allowed to criticize the Party-state leadership of the republics and the federation. This was actually a surrogate safety valve where the soldiers let out their dissatisfaction for the poor state of society. Above all, by directing criticism outward, the danger was removed of inquiries being made into the activities of the JNA, the desire being to thereby increase the military commanders' political rating.

In principle there was a high level of agreement between the public and internal policies of the Army leaders. However, in their internal statements they were much more severe in evaluating political events and actors. By the same token, they were uncritical when (self) evaluating the merits of the system and concept of ONO, JNA organizations and formations, and the Army's political and social roles. Furthermore, in internal communications they constantly insisted on the need to strengthen the political role of the JNA. For this reason, the generals reduced the scope of the political views that obliged the Army's members. Just a little while before, all the information that arrived from the military commanders contained the obligation for JNA members to follow the policies and views of the presidencies of the SKJ and SFRY. After the announcement of a schism at the top of the SKJ, these obligations were immediately narrowed to the views of the SFRY Presidency. The views of the military commanders soon received the same status. In a later phase, when the generals became dissatisfied with the actions of the federal presidency, military members were only obliged to respect the views of the military commanders.

Mental paralysis of the officer corps was induced by constant demands from the military commanders to increase the ideological-political vigilance and security in the JNA. A key role in this regard was played by the omnipresent Military Security Service that operated in the spirit of the doctrine of special warfare. Their constant pressure on the officers was intended to increase their – individual and collective – sensitivity to 'hostile moves'. Thus, the positive views of some officers or civilians in the JNA towards a multiparty system, for example, were immediately qualified as a hostile act.

In this period it seems that the Army leaders were truly convinced that the JNA, and particularly the officer corps, had a high level of ideological-political unity. This conviction was maintained by systemic mechanisms of window-dressing reality in society and the military. In this regard, the military commanders regularly received data on the moral-political state in the JNA through command and Party channels. The parallel organization of the military and the Party, however, made these reports identical. The reports were window-dressed hierarchically, since they were made at every level in accordance with the needs of each command, i.e. its prognosis of the expected and possible reactions of higher commands. Thus every report ended with the evaluation that MPS was good, and that the unit was able to carry out its assigned tasks. The military commanders also made a significant contribution to warping the picture of reality with their hostility towards researching, monitoring and evaluating MPS. The top generals were ready to accept only those evaluations that corresponded to their ready-made notions on social and Army reality.

In spite of all their efforts, the Army leaders did not have full control over internal processes. With the crisis, especially during this period, came direct attacks against the Army's system of views, beliefs and values. Behind its monolithic illusion, there was a gradual erosion and dissociation of the social and political fiber of the Army. This is reliably shown by the results of polling the views of Army communists on social reforms in 1989.

The researchers' attention was directed at the views of the Army communists on social reforms that were presented in the Party platform of 'three reforms'.

An analysis of the Army communists' views of the socio-political system indicates that they 'basically corroborated their support of reforms', although at the same time they were quite dissatisfied with how the system operated. The most radical reform-minded views were shown by the Army communists in their evaluation of relations in the federation and how the federation operated; they were thus in favor of a stronger federation. In accordance with this, they primarily advocated the introduction of a Chamber of Associated Labor (Veća Udruženog rada – VUR) in the SFRY Assembly[71] as well as the reduction of consensual decision making there.[72] A great majority of those polled in the military favored the consolidation of a large number of jurisdictions and functions on the federation level, to the detriment of republican/provincial independence.[73] This was particularly evident regarding the constitutional status of the provinces at the time (Vojvodina and Kosovo), which most people thought should be rescinded. The fact that they were not just inclined towards a stronger federation but were greatly influenced by the ideological heritage is confirmed by the majority's readiness to maintain the socio-political councils[74] and introduce the VUR, in spite of the fact that those polled felt they had not proven useful for the working class.

Those polled made the democratic leanings of their reform-mindedness explicit with agreement to radical changes in the electoral system. However, their democratic potential was shown to drop along with the consequences of democratic elections. Competition among individual candidates was accepted for the most part, but it was not considered essential to have competition among their electoral platforms. Those polled accepted the free political organization of the people but only as nonparty organizations within SSRNJ,[75] thus rejecting the multiparty version of political pluralism. Finally, the Army communists clearly favored political repression, i.e. prohibiting the foundation and existence of new organizations and preventing their access to the media.[76]

In terms of the scope of the Army communists' reform-mindedness, they remained within the borders of the existing political and ideological concept of socialistic self-management. They basically wanted and demanded an increase in the efficiency and democracy of the existing system through reforms, while not touching the basic postulates – the rule of the working class, the SKJ in the leading position, self-management and 'nonparty pluralism'.

Based on survey answers dealing with Party problems, it can be concluded that the Army communists clearly sought changes in numerous areas of Party life. Their dissatisfaction with past and current SKJ activities at the time were the grounds for these demands.

The Army communists' answers supported changes in the SKJ in two directions. One was denoted by demands to change the manner in which the highest bodies and forums were elected. In this regard, the Army communists were in favor of discontinuing the parity principle to fill them. In this case, they clearly lost sight of the fact that the parity basis of the SKJ bodies and forums was analogous to the constitution of the political system, and in the prevailing conditions changing the Party system without simultaneously changing the parity system was politically unfeasible.

In addition, the communists in the JNA saw a way out of the crisis in strengthening the ideological and operational unity of the SKJ, as shown by their explicit demands to restore democratic centralism, along with permanent internal selection.[77] In this case as well they lost sight of the fact that transforming the SKJ into an alliance of independent republican and provincial parties would remove the possibility of democratic centralism being effectively applied, and so Party decisions arose by agreement or compromise among the leaderships. The Army communists were insufficiently prepared to face political reality, and relapses of monolithic consciousness were shown by their restrictive approach to the rights of minorities to be active in the SKJ.

Based on survey results, it can be concluded that at the time the majority of the Army communists supported the market concept of economic reforms. Nonetheless, they often abandoned their principled accord for the restrictive and selective treatment of individual elements and segments of a market economy. This might have been a sign of their unfamiliarity with the essence and consequences of this model, but also an expression of ideological-political inertia.

A comparative analysis of survey results from the JNA and republics/provinces on two dimensions of the basic views – federalism (strengthened, firm vs. elastic, loose) and reformism (restrained, moderate vs. marked, radical) – indicates that the views of the communists in the JNA during this period were neither atypical nor extreme. On the contrary, regarding both dimensions the mean value of those polled in the military gravitated around the Yugoslav average. However, it should be emphasized that the 'national orientation of the Army communists' primarily determined the political orientation of their views of federalism.[78] The results clearly lead to the conclusion that the Army communists at the time were neither a stronghold of unitarian views nor a conservative core of the SKJ, rather they expressed moderate views during a time of deep political divisions.

Research has shown that the reform concepts of all the republican/provincial leaderships did not suit the Army communists equally. Most of them at the time were impressed by the policies of the SK Serbia leadership and the policy of the SK Montenegro which was complementary to it. This is why the so-called Serbian option had the greatest number of adherents in the JNA. Its preponderance corresponded approximately to the percentage share of Serbs in the Army and in this sample. The results also showed that the Slovenian option did not enjoy substantial support in the Army, except partially with regard to economic reforms.

In spite of this, there is not sufficient proof that the political dichotomy, which was characteristic of the political scene at the time, had already gained stronger expression in the views of the communists in the JNA. However, when the views of those polled in the Army are observed in light of their national affiliation, it can be seen that the tendencies established based on the sample truly existed,[79] although in a considerably milder form. It was shown that those polled chose as the most perspective policy either that of 'their' (ethnic group) republic or one of the two prevailing: Serbian or Slovenian. In any case, in this analysis, after the Serbian option, the Slovenian option was proportionally the most represented in the Army communists' preferences.[80]

In their further political commitments and attitudes towards members of the JNA, there is no proof that the military commanders bore in mind the tendentious changes indicated in the survey. This can be said in particular about the initial, hidden, political and ideological differentiation of active members of the Armed Forces on an ethnic (national) basis. The military commanders simply disregarded everything that these polls indicated regarding internal trends and changes in the views of those in the Armed Forces. Furthermore, it seems that they did not even try to predict the proportions of the internal stratification and evaluate all the possible consequences that the negative development of the crisis would have on the battle readiness of the JNA. Thus there is reason to suspect that they did not even evaluate the negative repercussions that a possible schism within the Army would have on political processes in society.

The military commanders certainly used all available means and established channels to maintain control over the Army's opinions. Furthermore, they acted as though they had 'produced' these views once and for all and could shape them however they wanted. This is why the means they used with the members of the JNA were exclusively ideological, tailored after their own ideological goals. It can thus be concluded that during this period the military commanders were not able to understand the depth of the crisis and its negative consequences on JNA. Moreover, the generals showed with their arrogance, particularly in internal statements, that they were indifferent to the real state of opinions in the Army.

Notes

1 'Inflation quite clearly, rapidly and unerringly warns that society is not prepared for changes, that the root of instability is located in worsening economic structures, and its cause is to be found in the economic system itself. The economy lost its accumulation with inflation, and without that it was not able to initiate a new development cycle. That is actually the key indicator of the crisis' Korošić, Marjan, *The Yugoslav Crisis*, Naprijed, Zagreb, 1989, 295.
2 This led to the Law on Provisional Financing of the Federation (Borba, 04.01.1988, 3).
3 Amendment XXXIV proposed the introduction of special income and sales taxes to provide stable financing for the JNA, but the representatives from Slovenia refused (Borba, 17.10.1988, 4).
4 Including the Draft Enterprise Law that envisaged all forms of ownership to be treated on equal footing (Borba, 26.10.1988, 1).
5 Since the Government's package had not received sufficient support, the SFRY Presidency adopted it as a provisional measure (Borba, 22.12.1989, 1).
6 Prof. Ivan Kristan from Slovenia advocated the 'principle that the republics have jurisdiction and that sovereign power is primarily and authentically exercised in the republics, and the federation receives its jurisdiction from the

republics, and not vice versa', and therefore 'the principle of the parity composition of deciding federal bodies should be preserved along with the principle of consensus when making decisions regarding our most important common interests' (Borba, 08.03.1989, 7).

7   The document from the First Conference of SK Slovenia says: 'We will only allow the passage of a constitutional document that is based on the following postulates: Yugoslavia is a community of peoples that are linked by joint decisions; it is not based on erasing differences between peoples (...) and the basic principle of organizing affairs is independence in the republic and equal footing in the federation' (Borba, 1-3.05.1988, 3).

8   Compare: M. Potrč's speech cited above, ibid.

9   In an interview in 'Pobjeda', Janez Stanovnik, president of the SR Slovenia Presidency, confirming Slovenia's allegiance to the people's right to self-determination, stated that Slovenia's secession from Yugoslavia would be tantamount to suicide (Borba, 10.04.1989, 4).

10 Arguments in favor of Slobodan Milošević's policies were presented at various official discussions. At a meeting in SASA (Borba, 19-20.11.1988, 7) the 1974 Constitution was pronounced the basic cause behind the Serbs' problems; later Milošević emphasized this in an interview in 'Le Monde' (Borba, 13.07.1989, 1 and 10).

11 For example, at a session of the CK SK Croatia, principled support was given to constitutional changes in Serbia but disagreement was also expressed regarding the methods and contents of the Serbian leadership's policies (Borba, 15-16.10.1988, 7); the discussion at the CK SK Bosnia and Herzegovina had a similar intonation, ibid., 8.

12 The first larger meeting of this type was the protest of the Serbs and Montenegrins from Kosovo in Novi Sad on July 9, 1988 (Borba, 11.07.1988, 3); the aftermath in October was the resignation of the leadership of SAP Vojvodina (Borba, 07.10.1988, 4-7).

13 During the first meeting in Titograd on October 7, there was no change, and the Presidency of the CK SK Slovenia sent a telegram of support to the Presidency of the CK SK Montenegro (Borba, 10.10.1988, 3); however, repeated demon-strations forced the Montenegrin leaders to resign (Borba, 12.01.1989, 3).

14 The CK SK Serbia specified the tasks in the 'battle for socialism and Yugoslavia', announcing a campaign for the passage of a new SFRY constitution, systemic reconstruction in order to strengthen the federation's jurisdiction, and the creation of an integral economic and political space tailor-made by reforms and the citizens' rights and freedoms, and against all confederalization tendencies (Borba, 14.07.1989, 1).

15 In an interview in 'Večernje list', Josip Vrhove, member of the CK SKJ from Croatia declared the Serbian leadership's policy to be the basic cause of the crisis (Borba, 16.10.1989, 7).
16 Held at the confluence of the Sava and Danube rivers in Belgrade (Borba, 21.11.1988, 4-5).
17 Amendment 41 of the SR Croatia Constitution was intended to change the name of the official language with the introduction of the formulation 'Croatian or Serbian' instead of the 'Croatio-Serbian or Serbo-Croatian' language (Borba, 20.03.1989, 4).
18 See: Alternative Trends in Yugoslavia, Revija za sociologiju (Sociological Review), 4/88, 425-467.
19 This can be confirmed by a comparison of the ethnic lines along which opposition and official policies met in Slovenia and Serbia. In both cases the communist government gradually adopted the opposition's goals, with minor modifications. The difference lies in the fact that the communist leadership in Slovenia carried out the goals of 'New Review no. 57' while the Serbian leadership did not carry out those in the SASA Memorandum.
20 This is best viewed through the metamorphosis of UJDI which disappeared from the Yugoslav scene before the disappearance of SFR Yugoslavia, and its Serbian branch transformed into the Civic Alliance of Serbia.
21 Ljubljana's 'Delo' organized a discussion on the JNA's role in society, at which time discussions were held on the degree of the JNA's political independence and the possibility of its intervening in the crisis independently of legal bodies of authority. At that time S. Soršak, member of the CK SK Slovenia Presidency, forwarded the view that the Army would not and could not act politically independently (Borba, 09.02.1988, 1).
22 Students at Ljubljana University first started the initiative to discontinue this subject, which was opposed in 'Borba' by professors V. Vujačić and B. Jevorović from the Zagreb Faculty of Political Science (Borba, 13.06.1988, 4-5).
23 The list of basic demands and Army counter-arguments was concisely presented by General Milan Daljević, undersecretary in the Ministry of Defense, on the Coordinating Committee of SK SSSRJ for ONO and DSZ, at which time he said that it was 'very indicative that they appeared during an intensified emergency warfare against SFRY and aggressive attacks by right-wing and other enemy forces against the SKJ and our system in general, and even against the JNA', see: VPI 2/1987, 20-26.
24 The communiqué from the Military Court explained that an investigation had been undertaken against them since there was 'reason to believe that they committed the crime of revealing military secrets pursuant to Article 224 of the SFRY Legal Code' (Borba, 07.06.1988, 3).
25 For an analysis of the reasons for and evaluation of the attacks against KONO and the JNA see: Borba, 30.03.1989, 14; the Analysis contested and rejected

The Army Fails to Acknowledge Reality 67

   every demand, point by point, to change the concept and system of ONO, such as demands for republican armies, civilian military service, democratization of relations within the Army, changes in the financing of the JNA, discontinuing emergency military industries, equal footing of the languages, etc. (Borba, 27-28.03.1989, 10).
26 See: General Stevan Mirković, commander of the JNA Headquarters, discussion at the First Conference of the SKJ, VPI 7/88, 30; Stipe Šuvar repeated a similar opinion in his introductory remarks at the 17th session of the CK SKJ, VPI 11/88, 42.
27 Mirković, S., VPI 7/88, 30; see also the discussion by Bunčić, S, op. cit. 34-38.
28 Mirković, S., discussion at the 17th session of the CK SKJ, VPI 11/88, 59.
29 Ibid.
30 General Veljko Kadijević, Minister of Defense, VPI, 8/89, 7-8.
31 Ibid.
32 Mamula, B., address before the SFRY Assembly, 17.12.1987, VPI, 2/88, 13.
33 Kadijević, V., discussion at the 17th meeting of the CK SKJ, VPI no. 11/88, 53.
34 The cure for this was given by M. Kučan and his reaction to manipulations in the Slovenian public about a military putsch; compare his address to the CK SK Slovenia (Borba, 29.06.1988, 4).
35 Ibid.
36 Admiral Petar Šimić, president of OSKJ in the JNA, discussion at the First Conference of the SKJ, VPI 7/88, 31.
37 Mamula, B., report, VPI 2/88, 11; see also Simić, P., introductory remarks at the OSKJ Conference in the JNA, VPI 8/88, 7-14.
38 This slogan seems to have been first launched by the military commanders; compare: Kadijević, V., discussion at the 17th session of the CK SKJ, VPI 11/88, 53.
39 The Army's view was soon answered by the Slovenian Party leadership, whereby 'either Yugoslavia will be democratic or it will cease to exist' (Borba, 24.01.1989, 3).
40 Kadijević, V., interview on Army Day 1988, VPI 1/89, 11.
41 Kadijević, V., address before the SFRY Assembly, December 1988, VPI 1/89, 34.
42 Kadijević, V., VPI, 1/89, 16.
43 Šimić, P., discussion at the 20th session of the CK SKJ, VPI 3/89, 13-14.
44 Ibid., 13.
45 Kadijević, V., VPI 3/89, 10.
46 Admiral Stane Brovet, Deputy Minister of Defense, discussion at the 20th session of the CK SKJ, VPI 3/89, 18-19.
47 Ibid.

48 Šimić. P., discussion at the 20th session of the CK SKJ, VPI 3/89, 15.
49 'In addition, the JNA communists disassociated themselves from the statements of some retired generals and admirals who have recently on a variety of occasions contributed to divisions in this country and the SKJ.' Šimić, P., discussion at the 20th session of the CK SKJ, VPI 3/89, 16. These were the first signs of cracks among the elite generals (active and retired).
50 Kadijević, V., VPI 8/89, 15.
51 9th Conference OSKJ (Organization of the League of Communists of Yugoslavia) in the JNA, document, VPI, 1/90, 25.
52 Ibid.
53 In answer to the question, 'Can you, as a political man in these times, imagine the JNA without a SKJ organization?' the Army Headquarters commander said, 'No. Our Army was created in the flames of war and revolution, under the leadership of Tito and the Party, and since then the SKJ has been an inseparable part of its being and force.', Adžić, ibid.
54 Although even then most of the republican SK were in favor of 'nonparty pluralism'.
55 Kadijević, V., VPI 11/89, 11.
56 Kadijević, V., VPI 11/89, 13.
57 Ibid., 10-11.
58 Kadijević, V., VPI 11/89, 9.
59 Kadijević, V., address at the joint meeting of the Military Council and the Presidency of the OSKJ Committee in the JNA, VPI 11/89, 8.
60 Compare: discussion of the JNA delegates at the 14th Emergency SKJ Congress, VPI 2/90, 35-100.
61 Compare: Kadijević, V., remarks at the 21st session of the OSKJ Committee in the JNA, op. cit., 11-12.
62 Adžić, B., VPI 1/90, 9.
63 The soldiers were to direct their political work to 'specific political and educational activities' and thereby become capable of 'successfully recognizing and actively fighting against counterrevolutionary ideas and activities (nationalism, clerical-nationalism, dogmatism and others)'; Program POiV (političko obrazovanje i vaspitanje vojnika – soldiers' political education and training) of PU (Politička uprava (SSNO)) – Political Administration (of the Ministry of Defense)), 1988, 9-10.
64 The IOP Program for officers and civilians working for OS SFRY, SSNO, PU, November 1987, p. 2; the goals in the Program for 1989 left out the final remark on the growing role of OS, and added learning 'social-political trends and relations in our country and the world' from the viewpoint of 'building MPS and the battle readiness of the Armed Forces'; IPO Program, op. cit., November 1988, 2.

65 The Plan and Program of the Political Education and Training of Soldiers-Sailors in the JNA, SSNO, Political Administration 1988, 9; it is indicative that there are no essential differences between the goals of this program and the 1985 program; compare: Program POiV Soldiers-Sailors, SSNO, Pu, 1985, 9.
66 Ibid.
67 The 1985 Program had four thematic units: (1) Socialist self-management in Yugoslavia – nine topics; (2) The basic principles of ONO and DSZ – five topics; (3) Revolutionary traditions of the peoples and nationalities of Yugoslavia – 25 topics; (4) Current problems (information). The new Program had three units: (1) Socialist self-management and defense – nine topics; (2) Revolutionary traditions of the peoples and nationalities of Yugoslavia – 25 topics; and (3) Current problems (information); op. cit.
68 A separate set of indicators for evaluating the officer corps dealt with their moral-political qualities which were established with regard to: Marxist and socio-political knowledge, political activity in the unit – institutions, political activity in society, Interpersonal relations, Critical attitude and self-criticism, General and political future; compare: Rulebook on Evaluating Military Personnel, SSNO, Personnel Administration, 1980, 30.
69 Instructions for the Organization and Implementation of PO Soldiers-Sailors in the JNA, Plan and Program of POiV (1988), op. cit., 57.
70 During 1988, the SKJ Organization within the JNA had almost 76,000 members (soldiers and cadets 12%, civilians 33%, young officers 24% and officers 31%), divided into 2,543 basic SK organizations; compare: Documents on the Ninth Conference of OSKJ in the JNA, Belgrade, November 1989, Appendices 1 and 2, 125-126.
71 48.7% of those polled favored this solution, op. cit., 9, Table 1.
72 Almost half those polled were in favor of majority decision making in the Assembly, and around one-third were in favor of reducing consensus (Table 2); ibid. 10.
73 As many as 84.3% (Table 6) preferred this solution, whereby nationality was the only characteristic that distinguished those polled,; ibid., 12.
74 A considerable majority (64%, Table 5) of those polled felt that it was justified, but favored a detailed description of their authority; somewhat less than one-fifth (16.5%) felt that Socio-political Councils (houses in parliaments on every level) were unnecessary, i.e. that they were an expression of the undemocratic features of the system and the inequality of the citizens within it; op. cit., 11-12.
75 72.5% favored maintaining the existing system with the SKJ having the leading role, and 23.7% of those polled were for a nonparty model within SSRNJ (Table 20); ibid., 20.

76 46.1% favored prohibition, and 48% of those polled were for multiparty activities but under control (Table 22); 41.6% were in favor of prohibiting new parties' access to the media, and 54.1% of allowing only those who operated within SSRNJ (Table 23); ibid., 24.

77 56.7% of those polled supported permanent internal selection and 30.3% supported periodical differentiation in order to clarify relations in SK (Table 37); ibid., 36.

78 Additional analyses, conducted separately for active members of the Armed Forces and civilians working in the JNA (Table 76) indicate that within both categories there is a link between the attitude towards federalism and both national and republican affiliation. It can be seen from the Table that those with high results, i.e. advocating a strong federation, belong to the Serbian nationality and those who declare themselves Yugoslavs; owing towhere they are stationed they are doing their military service in AP Kosovo, ibid., 72.

79 See Table 69; 'Extreme results of the dimension 'federalism' are shown in SK Slovenia, as opposed to results from Montenegro, Serbia and Vojvodina. The Slovenian communists also stand out glaringly with their high values for the dimension of 'reformism'. On the opposite extreme of this continuum are typical results from those polled in SK Macedonia and SK Kosovo. The communists of SR Croatia have a high rating, in second place, on both dimensions', ibid., 61.

80 Ibid., 64-65. Reformism was less connected with essential characteristics, particularly nationalism, but 'views that referred to the other basic dimension (federalism, Table 75) were only significantly connected to the national (ethnic) and republican affiliation of those polled. (...) The national affiliation of being not only a Yugoslav but also an Army communist remained, or perhaps became, the main generator of differences of political views in which Yugoslav federalism was the common denominator'', ibid., 73.

Chapter 2

The Army's Rejection of Reality

The 1990s saw a fatal reversal of political positions in Yugoslavia. All those actively participating in events responded to the collapse of (real) self-management and demands for modernization[1] from pre-civic and pre-political positions. Instead of the democratic reformation of society, it started to split along ethnic lines. The main direction of the attack was not communism itself, but the form of the communistic state. Instead of changing the authoritarian nature of their common country of Yugoslavia, local leaders started to create separate and potentially ethnically pure nation-states.

Ethnic tensions, induced by political tensions, continued to rise during these years following their own inherent logic. Since Yugoslavia had no mechanisms that would systematically amortize and/or peacefully resolve ethnic conflicts, they spread to all of society and instigated the process of retrograde involution.

The first turning point in the Yugoslav crisis was the suspension of the 14th Emergency SKJ Congress. When the federal Party collapsed it initiated the final disintegration of SFR Yugoslavia. The breakup of the communists' summit was the last confirmation of their inability to reach a compromise. Key leaders judged that the right time had come to establish their own power on the state and national level. Since the amount of power available in the center was limited, any gain by one person meant a loss for another. Since no one was ready to renounce their share of projected or already secured power, there began a crucial inter-communist battle for power. As soon as the nationalists joined the fray, the compromise needed to retain the common state of Yugoslavia took on utopian qualities.

The political situation in the previous phase had been created by the irreconcilable contradictions of Party socialism. Malformations inherited from the common Yugoslav state were added to them in the second phase. This is why a refashioned past, tailored to the daily needs of those involved, was introduced into the political conflicts. Everything that had seemed highly unlikely and the worst alternative in the initial phase started to take place in 1990.

Disagreements regarding the nature and appearance of the future Yugoslavia continued to be at the center of political conflicts. Soon the question of whether, when and how its members would break up received the same status. It was increasingly certain, particularly after governments were changed in the elections, that the western republics no longer wanted any kind of Yugoslavia; or rather, they might accept it but only as a confederation[2] or tariff union.[3] Even the policies of the Serbian leadership were open to new alternatives. The variation of an independent Serbian state was making the rounds, but the question of its borders was left open.[4]

The institution of 'divorce' proceedings intensified the problem of how to break up. The moment the nationalism-aroused masses were pushed into the political arena, the chances for a peaceful split radically decreased. In addition, intensifying conflicts among the republics had drastically reduced the number of modalities for the dissolution. The increasing number of armed incidents portended an internal war. This phase of the crisis can thus be denoted as a period in which the last chances were missed for a peaceful restructuring of state and ethnic relations in Yugoslavia. This was also a period in which ideological, political, state, military, propaganda and psychological preparations were initiated for inter-republic warfare.

Impending signs of internal warfare returned the JNA to the center of interest. Everyone was weighing and awaiting the Army's reactions, each side counting on the Army for its own reasons. Most of the population hoped that the JNA would prevent any warfare, but key actors expected the Army to help them achieve their goals, or at least not hinder them. The military commanders, however, turned out to have made their own calculations. The defense of socialism and Yugoslavia continued to be their political priority, but the top generals had to take a stand with regard to the changed political environment, and the new actors.

During 1990, the communists lost the elections[5] in four out of the six republics and left the government. As soon as they were elected into power and given legitimacy, potential separatists became public proponents of secession. After electoral changes in Macedonia and Bosnia-Herzegovina, there was a drop in the number who supported[6] a strong federation. During that time the modern federalists became even more entrenched in their federalism, but also prepared a contingent plan for themselves.

The polarization of republican actors narrowed the military commanders' maneuvering space and diminished their support. This forced them to seek more dependable political allies. They were closest to ideologically like-minded thinkers with whom they shared similar interests. Joining ranks with them, the military commanders necessarily came into conflict with the other actors in the crisis, particularly since they had adopted the discretionary role of the ideological arbiter in negotiations about Yugoslavia.

2.1 The Political Disintegration of Yugoslavia

The political configuration of Yugoslavia changed radically during 1990. After the opposition won at the elections in Slovenia and Croatia, there were no longer any dilemmas regarding these republics' intention to leave Yugoslavia. From that moment on the fate of Yugoslavia and its inhabitants depended directly on the political will of the new and/or old republican power-holders.

Previous clashes between communistic 'democrats' and 'Bolsheviks' regarding socialism immediately swelled into a direct clash between the political and national (ethnic) elite in Serbia, Croatia and Slovenia. During the course of the conflict differences disappeared between the national and communistic approach to Yugoslavia. In the western republics the communists had adopted the main goals of their opposition before elections, but this had not saved them from defeat. Unlike them, after Slobodan Milošević took hold of power and the Serbian national program gained a monopoly, the communists in Serbia and Montenegro succeeded in consolidating their power at the elections.[7]

Blocking the federal center of the communists' distribution of power opened up two possibilities in principle. It seemed realistic to expect that power would finally be returned to the political system's institutions, although they had atrophied.[8] There were even greater chances, however, that the new and old power-holders would do everything they could to hold onto their monopoly of power.[9] This was quickly confirmed by new constitutions in Croatia and Slovenia that endorsed the power of republican leaders, making them immutable, so to speak.[10]

Since the battle for power determined political trends in 1990, all important events and participants revolved around it. The constitutional (re)organization of Yugoslavia was in the center of the battlefield, with the redistribution of power proceeding in parallel on the federal and republican level. In spite of their rivalry, republican power-holders and their local opposition worked in unison with respect to Yugoslavia. The policies of double standards[11] and fait accompli prevailed; in principle, all the republics operated outside the system and against the Yugoslav constitution. In further changes to the SFRY constitution, all the republics except Montenegro had unconstitutional starting positions. Contrary to this, republican power-holders kept strictly to constitutional procedures in their republics. Whenever necessary, they introduced new procedures.[12]

The political disintegration of Yugoslavia resulted from two connected, but opposing approaches to its reorganization: first, from the attempt to use legal procedures to constitutionally reorganize and reconstitute the federal state; and second, from unilateral and illegal changes to the constitutions of the key republics – Slovenia, Croatia and Serbia.

During 1990, four basic variations of Yugoslavia's reorganization were in play. The first, supported by the SFRY Presidency, aimed at revitalizing the Constitution through optimization of the federation. The substance of this concept changed during the year, and the number of its adherents declined. Slovenia and Croatia rejected it from the outset. This variation intertwined and collided with the second: SIV (the federal government) offered to constitutionally reform and transform Yugoslavia patterned after a modern society. Under the united attack of the central republics the number supporting reforms quickly dropped, and in the end only the initiator of this variation – SIV – stood by it.

The western republics presented their own (third) variation against the previous two. They proposed the conclusion of a confederal contract between the republics (nations). The proposal rested on a radical change in the essence of the Yugoslav state.[13] A fourth variation appeared in reaction to this – amputation. The Serbian side countered the confederal proposal with the variation of a reduced, rump Yugoslavia. They asked for the republics' secession to be regulated by law,[14] which Slovenia and Croatia refused. Although arising on the political margins and as a historical reflection of earlier conflicts among the 'three tribes' comprising the Southern Slav people, upon the outbreak of war the amputation of Slovenia and part of Croatia grew into a strategic goal of the Serbo-Montenegrin and military policy.

The initial mainstays of the constitutional transformation of Yugoslavia were the Presidency of SFRY and SIV. Their position, however, was extremely delicate. Both federal centers were already without power and thus did not have enough constitutional strength and active means to prevent the political disintegration of Yugoslavia. Growing conceptual differences between the SFRY Presidency and the federal government also greatly contributed to the reform variation's lack of success. While members of the Presidency, as advocates of their republics, constantly revolved around the federal-confederal axis, Ante Marković's government represented the view that importance lay not in the name of the new state, but in the fact that it resulted from reforms.[15]

The government built its optimism on the first successes of the economic policy and on the support of most of the population.[16] The SFRY Presidency tried to find a compromise between the republics and start comprehensive 'top-down reforms'. Unlike the Presidency, the government counted on minimal constitutional changes that would allow the reorganization of the economy and produce autonomous reasons for the democratic reintegration of Yugoslavia. The federal government's desire to remove political obstacles to reform[17] as soon as possible was immediately opposed by the governments of the central republics.[18]

Since a solution that was acceptable to everyone could not be found within the system, the SFRY Presidency, in conjunction with the republics, went outside the constitution. They offered the Federal Assembly a program of measures to solve the constitutional crisis whereby the citizens would first vote at a referendum on Yugoslavia and then a special decree would organize the state. The program proposed the following solutions:

- Passage of a new constitution to regulate relations between the ethnic groups in a new way.
- Transformation into a federation based on a special agreement.
- An asymmetric federation with some confederal republics.
- The secession of some republics.

Depending on referendum results, the plan was for the Federal Assembly to sanction the new situation and define it constitutionally as a federation – unchanged or smaller should any republic secede – or else state that SFR Yugoslavia no longer existed and legally set the borders between its former members. Since this did not produce the desired results either, on the eve of the Slovenian plebiscite the Constitutional Committee of the SFRY Assembly tried to obtain a moratorium on unilateral constitutional changes until the final agreement on the future organization of the country.

The republics reacted differently to the proposed changes to the federal constitution and SIV reforms. Although they ultimately boiled down to the same thing, different methods and excuses were used to obstruct reforms.

During 1990, Slovenia's leaders rushed doggedly towards an independent state. They justified their intentions as 'disjoining based on the right to self-determination'. In order to avoid negative international and legal consequences, the Slovenian leadership explicitly denied that Slovenia was seceding. They responded to new proposals for constitutional changes by using tactics and arguments from the previous period, thus buying needed time to effectuate their own independence and sovereignty.[19]

After elections, Slovenia's new government (DEMOS – the Democratic Opposition of Slovenia) continued towards the same goal on previously prepared ground. The offensive tactics[20] of the Slovenian leadership surprised their other Yugoslav partners once again and deprived them of the initiative. In addition, Slovenian representatives pretended to be cooperative in the federal bodies, although they ignored all their decisions. They even accepted the proposal for a referendum on Yugoslavia, but under the condition that it be held separately in each republic. They held their December plebiscite on this basis, and then declared Slovenia an independent state.[21]

Although the Slovenian policy was a skillful combination of ethnic egoism, desire for an independent state and ideological-political mimicry, its creators were the most adroit and successful in this phase of the crisis. Slovenia achieved all its short-term and long-term goals with the least expense. They were certainly aided by their favorable geostrategic position, ethnic and territorial homogeneity, and particularly by the other rivals' behavior. The facts indicate that in this phase of the crisis the Slovenian leadership alone found an optimal political model to reach their supreme goal quickly – a sovereign and independent national (ethnic) state. Owing to their rational policy, the state and national interests of Slovenia always had supremacy over all ideologies. And vice versa: every ideology was acceptable that led to the final goal. Thus the Slovenian leaders were quickly able to gain their public's approval for separation. They found an additional argument for Slovenia's urgent departure from Yugoslavia by naming Serbia and the Serbs the main opponents of democracy.[22] The policies of Slobodan Milošević provided abundant arguments for this.

The use of Serbophobia, which had become a synonym for anti-Yugoslav feelings, did not result in any great political harm to the Slovenian leaders. Their geographical distance from Serbia, and the absence of a Serbian community in Slovenia, enabled the Slovenian leaders to count on Milošević's readiness to accept Slovenia's departure from Yugoslavia sooner or later. But Croatia's use of a similar model immediately had adverse results.

After the HDZ election results, Croatia headed irrevocably out of Yugoslavia. For numerous reasons, however, Croatia's path to sovereignty was volatile.

The first reasons were caused by Croatia's 'phased delay' after Slovenia in its preparations towards a national (ethnic) state. The next reasons were owing to the existence of a large community of Serbs in Croatia. Thus the new Croatian government avoided a referendum on an independent Croatia and transferred the decision on future secession to the authority of the republican Assembly.[23] A referendum was also avoided so that it could not be used to give legitimacy to the plebiscite that had already been held by the Serbs in Croatia.[24] These reasons also include the HDZ fear that a referendum would give the federalists an opportunity to increase pressure, and even use the Army. At the same time, the HDZ government was afraid of missing the chance to finally create a Croatian state. This increased their impatience and aggressiveness even more. They therefore used every opportunity to strengthen the Croatian people's xenophobia and encourage collective paranoia.[25] The induction of fear facilitated the new government's job of ethnically cleansing the police and state apparatus, and creating the core of a Croatian army.[26]

The central group of obstacles blocking the Croatian state from easily gaining independence came from several sources. With the announcement of its unilateral withdrawal from Yugoslavia, the new Croatian government caused a conflict of interests with modern federalists, and with Serbia in particular. The aggressive use of Ustasha symbols in the HDZ pre-election campaign renewed and expanded the Serbo-Croatian national and state dispute. With the inclusion of Croats from the diaspora, particularly those with Ustasha views, the HDZ government stirred political and inter-ethnic revanchism.

Defining Croatia as a 'national state of the Croatian people and a state with members of other peoples and minorities', the HDZ discontinued the Serbian people's constitutive position and denied them the status of a people (ethnic group).[27] After refusing to acknowledge the Serbs' right to self-determination in Croatia, the HDZ clashed with their political representatives. When push came to shove, this legitimized the Serbs' use of force in their resistance.

The intention of Franjo Tudjman's government to withdraw from Yugoslavia at once was accompanied by the territorial and political withdrawal of Serbian communities from Croatia.[28] At the Slovenian-Croatian proposal of a confederation, the leaders of the Serbs in Croatia responded with a plan to join the Bosnian and Serbian Krajina areas into an independent Serbian state. The HDZ's ambitions to create a state did not stop at Croatia's border; they included open aspirations towards Bosnia-Herzegovina.

Although the conflict between the Serbs and the new Croatian government cannot be understood outside the general context[29] and without an analysis of the influence of Milošević's policies, there were several other reasons behind it. Even though the DHZ's vehement campaign against the Serbs might have endangered the Croats' ultimate goal, Tudjman made political use of this conflict during the phase of stabilizing and totalizing his power. The conflict helped him to homogenize the Croat population, and gave additional legitimacy to his rule within Croatia. The protection of Croatia's sovereignty allowed him to install an authoritarian regime, thus enabling the political domination of extreme forces in Croatia. Vice versa, this gave additional encouragement to the growing nationalism and extremism in ruling Serbian circles and those around them.

The desire to create their own national state without delay, at any price, and within historical borders, made the Croatian government's policies inconsistent; they were constantly in the breach between the rational and irrational, desire and possibility, means used and declared goals. The government's collision with 'the disruptive Serbian factor' made the chances of Croatia's peaceful realization of its 'thousand-year dream' more and more difficult. Owing to the joint effects of Tudjman's messianism and inflamed ethnic animosities, these policies were unable to provide Croatia with immediate, positive results.[30]

The attitude of the Serbian government towards the reorganization of Yugoslavia in 1990 was inconsistent and contradictory.[31] On the declarative level, the Serbian policy was opposed to the policies of Slovenia and Croatia. However, in the practical realm it was complementary to them.[32] Thus it necessarily led to the same extreme result – the accelerated corrosion of Yugoslavia. Although the key representatives of a modern federalism, Serbian leaders consistently opposed any expansion of the federation's economic authority. Their reasons were based on the claim that SIV was pursuing a policy that was harmful to the interests of the Serbs.

After the constitutional revocation of the autonomy of Serbia's provinces, work accelerated on the constitutional organization of Serbia's sovereignty. At that time the possibility of future secession was put into the Constitution. Since the new Constitution gave the Serbian Assembly the right to decide on whether or not to bring the republican constitution in line with the federal constitution, Milošević had reached the position of a separatist with regard to Yugoslavia.[33]

Serbia's political position at the time was unfavorable for many reasons. The secession of Slovenia and Croatia had led to the discontinuation of the only state that gathered together all the Serbs with the status of a constitutive and equal people. The confederal model did not have sufficient guarantees for the protection of the collective and individual rights of the Serbs outside Serbia. In addition, Serbia's policies were torn between those advocating secession from Yugoslavia and those advocating Kosovo's secession[34] from Serbia, since Yugoslavia's integrity was being threatened at the same time as Serbia's as a home state.

The fundamental handicap of Serbia's policy was its ambivalence towards Yugoslavia. This is testified by the authorities' instrumental attitude towards Serbia's role in the creation of (the first) Yugoslavia. Serbia's new ideologists twisted and window-dressed the fact that Serbia had been the key internal factor in the formation of Yugoslavia. They particularly avoided admitting that the country had been tailor-made to fit Serbian interests at the time. The omission of this fact allowed Milošević to orchestrate the explanation of the Serbs' dissatisfaction with Yugoslavia as being an outside conspiracy and/or betrayal within Serbian ranks. The Serbian government received double benefit from these proceedings. The hypothesis of a conspiracy redirected the Serbs' dissatisfaction towards the outside and towards others; the manipulated public immediately targeted all Yugo-rivals and alleged enemies of the Serbs, and their foreign mentors. With the hypothesis of betrayal, Milošević's communist predecessors were blamed for Serbia's troubles, along with all insufficiently good or wrongly good Serbs, i.e. opponents of his regime.

Milošević resorted to this maneuver because the only way he could consolidate his power in Serbia, after the collapse of socialism and the pluralization of Yugoslavia, was on a national (ethnic) basis. Even more exacting nationalism was the only way he could be victorious against the opposition, which had already started their campaign for power on a national and anticommunist platform. This brought Milošević the support of the leaders of the Serbs outside of Serbia. The argument of the threat to the Serbs in Kosovo was then quickly expanded to the position of the Serbs in Yugoslavia, and particularly in Croatia. Thus the pace of rising Croatian secessionism was met by a rise in the misuse of the Serbs across the Drina River in the policies of the Serbian regime.

Serbia's position was additionally weakened by the fact that it was easier for Slovenia and Croatia to bring down a state that was already in decay than it was for Serbia to save it, particularly because Milošević did it in a manner that systematically removed all chances of the survival of any Yugoslavia whatsoever. Owing to their arrogance, and miscalculations, Serbia's leaders were clearly not qualified to deal with the situation. They were the last to get rid of Bolshevism, at least declaratively. They resisted the introduction of a multiparty system, thus strengthening sectarianism in

Serbia's political and national space. Judging by the results, and bearing their goal in mind, they also miscalculated the JNA's power to preserve Yugoslavia, just as they miscalculated the scope and meaning of international support for the country's integrity.

2.2 The Army's Ideological Arbitration

In spite of changes in their milieu, during 1990 the generals were explicitly against any non-socialist,[35] and particularly anti-socialist reforms. They were thus all the more convinced that the JNA had the obligation to intervene politically in the crisis. The JNA's involvement in politics was facilitated by the fact that the SFRY Presidency and SIV had no effective control over the Army.

The military commanders had concluded at the beginning of the year that the disappearance of the League of Communists of Yugoslavia (SKJ) or its evolution towards a modern leftist party would lead to the certain collapse of Yugoslavia. So they publicly and internally refused to acknowledge the disintegration of the SKJ. Maintaining that the SKJ was the sole integrative factor of society, and it alone could save Yugoslavia, the generals did all they could to resuscitate the clinically dead Party. The JNA leaders therefore took upon themselves the role of the SKJ's renovator and savior,[36] in the process trying to cause a split in the republican communist parties. After the proposal that the membership should vote at a referendum on the further fate of the SKJ, the military commanders called upon 'sound forces' in the SK Slovenia to distance themselves from their leadership.[37]

The generals' role as mediator became possible because the SKJ leaders had avoided a clear definition of the future status of the military's Party before the SKJ's final Congress. The western republics, however, were no longer alone in their request to discontinue the League of Communists in the JNA.[38] In spite of this, the military commanders held onto their Party organization until the formation of the SK-PJ (Savez komunista – Pokret za Jugoslaviju – League of Communists – Movement for Yugoslavia) and the JNA's collective membership in it.[39] The generals not only took part in its foundation, but their presence at the promotion of the SK-PJ[40] clearly confirmed their political platform. That platform, in fact, was spelled out in General Kadijević's interview in December 1990.[41]

During this year the military commanders did not keep solely within the Party circle using strictly ideological means. In accordance with the JNA's proclaimed goals, they tried various ways to influence current events within the course of daily politics.

The generals continued to contest the constitutional basis of political party pluralization. They insisted on the view that a predominantly ethnic pluralization would necessarily lead to ethnic conflicts and the disintegration of Yugoslavia.[42] For this reason the military commanders decided to use all the means at their disposal to influence the course and outcome of elections in the republics. Political meetings with republican leaders were initiated for this purpose; it was no accident that the first meeting was held between delegations from the JNA and Serbia. Their communiqué in favor of the federation was taken as an ultimatum in Slovenia.[43]

The generals were determined above all to prevent the increasingly certain change of power-holders in Slovenia and Croatia if they could. With this view in mind, they brought charges against Janez Pučnik, the DEMOS leader, during the pre-election campaign in Slovenia. Then on the eve of elections General Kadijević visited the 5th military region that included Slovenia and Croatia. Not even the joint communiqué of the outgoing Croatian leadership and SSNO (Ministry of Defense)[44] could remove suspicions about the motives of the JNA's leaders, which became evident after the military commanders judged that changes in the governments in Slovenia and Croatia would lead to fratricidal war.[45]

The Army tried to influence public opinion and the voters' views in Slovenia and Croatia through their newspaper 'Narodna armija' ('People's Army'). The propaganda targeted the DEMOS in Slovenia and the HDZ in Croatia, the pretext being their demand to create republican armies. The cutting edge of the Army's political attacks was directed at the principal opposition leaders in all central republics.[46] The Army's newspaper used a modified pattern of '1941' (division into fascists/antifascists) for this, resting on the dichotomies 'communist-anticommunist' and 'Partizan-Ustasha/Chetnik'.

The military commanders' campaign against those with nationalist and anticommunist ideas in Slovenia and Croatia was counterproductive. Furthermore, it made them part of their opponents' propaganda scheme, supporting the thesis about a 'Yugo-communist' and 'Serbo-communist' conspiracy against democracy in Slovenia and Croatia. This is why the Army leaders' attempt to beat their opponents using ideological means on their (national) terrain was destined to failure from the outset. Furthermore, the ideological activities of the Army leaders directly refuted the 'Yugoslav and people's' character of the JNA.

To make matters worse, loud 'anti-Army' propaganda continued under the new governments in Slovenia and Croatia. Various methods were used to change the JNA's systemic position, military and political power and its influence. During 1990 the two republics worked synchronously in several key directions against the JNA and the system of defense.

The first was based on the twofold systemic undermining of the JNA's power:

- With the unilateral completion of their state sovereignty these republics radically restricted the authority of the JNA and the SFRY Presidency as the Supreme Commander of the Armed Forces.[47]
- They joined forces to block all JNA attempts, supported by Serbia, Montenegro and analogous parts of the SFRY Presidency, to prevent the derogation of their authority and assure their functional systemic position.[48]

The leaderships in Slovenia and Croatia gradually removed the systemic sources for filling and supplying the JNA. With rejection of the budget and the stoppage of all payments, they prevented stable financing of the JNA. Reducing the recruits from their republics, they destroyed the system of filling the JNA with a periodic turnover of new soldiers.[49]

The political implications of these measures were directly visible. The 'recruit blow' additionally contested the 'Yugoslav and people's' character of the JNA. Keeping recruits in their home republics gave further fuel to the orchestrated national odium towards the JNA. The recruit problem was at the same time a trial run whereby Slovenia's and Croatia's leaders tested the resistance of the military commanders and the defense system to unilateral changes.

Slovenia and Croatia acted in a second direction by constantly increasing political pressure on the federal leaders and the JNA. First they kept calling for the depoliticization of the JNA. Then in the name of the principle of parliamentary democracy they demanded the discontinuation of the Party branch in the Army. And in particular, they sought the exclusion of JNA (leaders) from political negotiations on the future organization of state and national relations in Yugoslavia. Thus they denied the military commanders any right to participate in the ongoing resolution of the crisis, or its further complication.[50]

Valid in principle, these demands were certainly not motivated solely by democratic considerations on the part of the Slovenian and Croatian governments, who wanted to minimize the JNA's military-political impact on their future prospects. Their constant pressure was an attempt to prevent the military commanders from the potential use of force at the moment of their separation. Political pressure in Slovenia and Croatia was simultaneously used to mobilize their publics for (future) resistance against Yugoslavia and the Serbs.

The third direction against the JNA took the form of fierce and comprehensive propaganda. The main goal was to denigrate the JNA and denounce it nationally and ideologically within its own environment and abroad.[51] For this reason the topic of a military putsch was constantly bandied about in Slovenia and Croatia. The spirit of the 'conspiracy theory' was used in their republics to generate fear of the 'Serbo-communist' and 'Yugo-unitarist' JNA. This propaganda reached a high point with General Kadijević's interview in December 1990.[52]

A crucial blow against the position and power of the JNA came from a fourth direction with the creation of republican armies. Slovenia and Croatia started direct preparations to clash with the JNA when they formed national armies consisting of militarized and ethnically cleansed police, took over home guard units and illegally imported arms.[53]

The military commanders' response was that they would not allow the creation of republican armies; should they be formed they would be disarmed. Previous attempts to thwart the formation of such armies had been made with the support of state bodies. At the initiative of the military commanders, the SFRY Presidency adopted Guidelines to prevent the advent of irregular circumstances and eliminate them. This resulted in the JNA taking over control of the arsenals and arms of the Territorial Defense in Croatia and partially in Slovenia. Slovenia protested at once, thus preventing the military commanders from taking complete control of their Territorial Defense.[54]

The conflict with the western republics was only one dimension of the military commanders' overall position. Differences with regard to key elements of the crisis made this relationship clear, and there was no room for any dilemma. The Army leaders' relations with the SFRY Presidency and the government, however, were not transparent. Even greater controversies were caused by the military commanders' relationship with Serbia.

Viewed externally, the military commanders' relations with the Presidency and federal government remained inviolable for a long time. Behind the scenes, though, the divisions, disagreements and conflicts had already started. They were caused by different evaluations of the causes for the country's worsening security, thus no agreement could be reached on measures that should be undertaken. The address[55] before the SFRY Assembly by Janez Drnovšek, representative from Slovenia and president of the Presidency, was the starting point of the conflict and breakup between part of the Presidency and the military commanders. Since the federal government refused to accept the military's evaluation of the situation, their relations with the JNA leaders cooled. After this, suspicions about the political motives of SIV and Ante Marković (from Croatia) started to circle through military corridors. The first address by Borislav Jović from Serbia as president of the SFRY Presidency, however, not only met with the military commanders' approval, it was greatly based on the Army's analyses.[56] From that moment onward, Jović used every opportunity while in that position to publicly support the military commanders and their activities.

The real relationship between the federal government and the military commanders at that time can only be judged indirectly, 'between the lines'. Although smoldering outside the public eye, it was already possible at that time to establish the basic reasons for the political rupture and conflicts between the military commanders and SIV.[57]

The first reason was owing to conceptual differences in the appearance of the future state of Yugoslavia and how it would be reconstituted. Remaining within the framework of the 'federation-confederation' antimony, the military commanders had opted explicitly for a modern federation with genuine subjectivity. Contrary to this, the prime minister was striving to overcome this antimony through reforms. The second reason came from different evaluations of the 'political-security' situation in the country. With its proposal to change the command in the border region,[58] the federal government had somewhat obliged the military commanders. But this law was not passed owing to Slovenia's opposition.

In spite of the military commanders' public determination and often their arrogance, they still did not dare do anything independently without the permission of the Presidency and federal government. This led to a constant rise in the discrepancy between the military's evaluation of the situation, guarantees that were given to the public, and the repertoire of measures that were undertaken. This, along with the rest, indicated that the military commanders did not have the courage and/or power to publicly break the law, particularly since they were constantly making reference to it. The military commanders' behavior during 1990 was greatly determined by their political proximity to Serbia's leadership. This was shown by the Army's earlier support of Milošević at the 8th CK SK Serbia meeting, delivered by former Minister of Defense General Nikola Ljubičić.[59] The military commanders' activities in this period certainly cannot be properly understood outside the developing Serbian-military affiliation. However, this alone cannot be used to explain the political involvement of leading JNA generals at that time.

In this phase of the crisis there were no public indications that the military commanders were nationally biased or had teamed up with any of the participants, not even with the Serbs. The high political agreement between the Army's and Serbia's leaderships in this period rested on numerous overlapping interests and was directly confirmed by their identical attitude towards Slovenia and Croatia's confederal proposal.

Although bewildered, the military commanders noted quite accurately the emerging sides of the state and social crisis. They even surmised the possibility of its tragic denouement, and constantly warned, appealed, guaranteed, and even threatened. In the whirlwind that ensued, they were no able to build a relatively independent and neutral, effective political approach to the crisis. The official views of the JNA regarding the crisis indicated that the central corps of generals was a slave to their ideological beliefs. The claim that there could be no Yugoslavia without socialism clearly revealed the intellectual and analytical limits of the military commanders with regard to understanding reality. Furthermore, the generals did not even show any internal desire to learn the real reasons for the state and social crisis. During this period the political powerlessness of the military's ideology was laid bare, leading to the ultimate consequences. This was soon shown to be only the flip side of its military powerlessness.

2.3 Illusory Monolith

Owing to the discontinuation of the SKJ, the ideological legitimacy of the military commanders soon faded within the internal Army context. Influenced by its surroundings, the JNA's resistance to political and ethnic divisions in society rapidly declined. Convinced that the OSK JNA was a key factor of internal integration, the military commanders refused to remove the Party organization from the Army. They hoped this would prevent ideological, political and ethnic divisions among the officers.[60] The military commanders' loyalty to ideological methods indicated that they were not capable of finding effective mechanisms to preserve the cohesion and functional discipline of JNA in the new conditions.

The conflict-ridden finalization of the crisis forced the Army leaders to publicly admit its negative influence on the JNA's unity and battle readiness. In spite of this, they continued to claim that the JNA was capable of executing all the tasks assigned to it. The generals used what was already standard procedure to locate the negative influences outside the Army, not allowing any public or internal doubts to be cast on the validity of their policies or how they commanded the JNA. Reality nonetheless forced the generals to try to decrease the negative impact of the crisis on the JNA. They undertook a variety of measures with different classifications and scopes in order to protect the military organization and its members. For methodological reasons we will classify them here into two basic, interconnected and contingent groups.

The first set of measures was preventive. The goal was to prevent, neutralize or at least mitigate the negative impact of the political disintegration of Yugoslavia on the JNA. Parallel work was done on strengthening the ideological-political and moral-political unity of the JNA. Attention was centered on the officer corps.

The military commanders immediately undertook the ideological-political and informative treatment of the officer corps. The highest officers were involved in this, with the exception of the Minister of Defense. With the authority of their rank and function, it was considered that they would have an easier time forming the desired political views among the officer corps. This procedure was also supposed to ensure the authentic transfer and interpretation of the military commanders' views about the crisis. The internal deportment of the key generals was marked by the 'special war' approach to current proceedings and events. In conjunction with the 'conspiracy theory' they persistently enumerated the external and internal enemies of socialism and Yugoslavia. The leaders of Slovenia and Croatia were continually targeted for their anti-socialism. The generals alarmed the officers with foreign and internal enemies' plan to bring capitalism back to Yugoslavia, the main illustration being the collapse of socialism in Eastern Europe. The SIV reform project was soon used as cardinal evidence of this. The military commanders' Manichaean approach encouraged a 'black-and-white' view of reality among the officers depicted in the paired concepts: 'revolution/counterrevolution', 'socialism/anti-socialism.'

The key handicap in the JNA's internal information system was its regular lagging behind events. This inevitably resulted from the cumbersome military organization and complex internal information system. The delay was due primarily to the procedure of the military commanders giving shape to the controlled information. Every piece of information went through a multiple editing process consisting of several levels before being sent out. The negative effects of chronic delay became visible when information from military sources came face to face with information from civilian sources. Just at the moment when information from Army Headquarters or the Political Administration was to have the desired impact, a large number of JNA members already had different information about the event in question.

In the internal information system during 1990, the military commanders increasingly stressed reasons of state along with ideological reasons. They insisted on the JNA's obligation to preserve socialism and Yugoslavia, but also to help solve the crisis. In this regard, the generals insisted on and held to the illusion that the officers were a solid monolith in terms of their views. This was facilitated by the stereotypical reactions of the officers, which rested on their ideological (prior) knowledge of the solution, aimed at the JNA's violent intervention in the crisis. For this reason the military commanders often had to calm the officers' growing dissatisfaction with the political situation in Yugoslavia.

This created the impression that the JNA's ideological and political discipline had become lax. The room for critical and opposing views was temporarily broadened. Although security officers and commissars regularly noted such remarks, the commanders primarily did not react to them. At that time only nationalistic remarks were subjected to ideological and disciplinary accountability. The loosening of ideological discipline in the JNA was also aided by the removal of taboos regarding the discussion of certain subjects. Since the crisis had caused mental and emotional confusion among the officers, the military commanders were forced, albeit unwillingly, to reduce the list of (un)desirable political views.

In spite of this, the leading generals increased political pressure on the officers. On the eve of elections, JNA members in Slovenia and Croatia were sent instructions that obliged them to vote for the left. The weekly 'Narodna armija' soon took over the role of a political daily. Military topics were sidelined, and current political events became the center of attention. This newspaper was even assigned the role of the organ of patriotic – Yugoslav and socialist – forces and the promoter of their congregation around the JNA.[61]

The high point of internal pressure was reached in this phase with the formation of the SK-PJ. The officers had been informed that joining the SK-PJ was their patriotic duty and that refusal would be treated as opposition to the military commanders' policies.[62] Anyone who hesitated was recommended to leave the JNA by himself, since he no longer had a place there.

The military commanders used another set of measures to partially examine the validity of the system and concept of ONO (Total National

Defense). Gradual changes were made in order to adjust the JNA and the SFRY Armed Forces to the new conditions.

First discussions were opened on developing and strengthening the JNA's moral and political unity.[63] The topic was imposed by the crisis, but the intentions of the Political Administration were set in advance. All they wanted was to find an effective solution to what was not even internally acknowledged: dysfunctional elements in the Army's production of the desired morale among the soldiers and officers.[64] The internal effects of treating MPS professionally were certainly minor. The military commanders did not react to the difficulties that were noted in producing desired JNA morale based on the ideological postulates of the SKJ. Instead, they declared the creation of ideological-political unity among the officers and the military commanders a primary task. Thus agreement with the generals' policies became a standard of the battle readiness of the units and all of the JNA. The military commanders intention was to force the officers to give them carte blanche for the political (mis)use of the Army.

Changes in the environment nonetheless forced the generals to formal, and often fictive changes in the JNA's organization and operations. There was a series of renaming institutions and adjusting internal norms. The Political Administration of the Ministry of Defense was renamed the Administration for Moral Guidance, but its sphere of work remained essentially the same. Then the Law on Total National Defense and the Armed Force Regulations were freed of ideological trappings. Decorative changes were also made to the goals and contents of the IPO and PO programs.

Everything was removed from the Regulations that directly pointed to the ideological involvement or political obligations of those in the Armed Forces. All provisions were erased that referred to the SKJ. The attitude towards religion also changed and servicemen were allowed to visit places of worship and attend religious rites outside their working hours. It was allowed to keep religious press and literature in military facilities, but it was forbidden to propagandize religion.[65]

Partial changes were made to the goals and contents of the ideological-political education of the officers and soldiers. Political education was replaced by a program of moral guidance. Ideological references were removed from the goals and the focus was shifted to defending SFRY and developing patriotism in order to achieve the desired moral state in the individuals and military collective.[66]

The course of the nominal depoliticization of the JNA drew attention to the fact that the generals had started to make gradual adjustments out of necessity. Since they could no longer justify the existence of the OSKJ in the JNA, they resolved to remove political parties from the Army. By order of General Kadijević dated October 8, 1990, all political party activities and organizing were forbidden in the JNA under threat of sanctions.[67] This, however, was just a momentary concession to public demand as shown by the fact that the order was issued in October, and the OSKJ in the JNA was not discontinued until December at which time everyone collectively joined the SK-PJ.

The real readiness of the JNA commanders for (self) change is shown by discussions at the Meeting on optimizing the concept and system of ONO.[68] The very fact that the military commanders were 'optimizing' in the sphere of defense without the order of the state leaders and/or Federal Assembly shed suspicion on this undertaking. Every thought of radical change to the Concept and System was removed by the name, which reduced the critical examination just to optimizing ONO. This approach rested on the premise that the theoretical and practical validity of the postulates and performance of KONO had been proven, and was thus unquestionable. This was actually the military commanders' attempt to establish just how much social changes had influenced the Concept and System of ONO, and thereby the JNA.

All hopes of change were removed with the final evaluation of the Chief of the General Staff, Blagoje Adžić, that KONO had proven its validity and exemplarity.[69] Even so, he demanded that the ONO concept, doctrine and system establish a unity that would reestablish unity among the Armed Forces. This was actually the military commanders' desire to prevent the already initiated republicanization of the territorial components of the system. General Adžić had even ordered the reexamination of 'some basic philosophical and ideological-political principles and sources of our concept'. He stated that this had to do with 'two categories – the armed people and the socialization of defense'.[70] Thus the elaboration of a new doctrinal solution for emergency situations was ordered along with a new strategy for armed conflict. It was also requested that the territorial components of ONO be brought within a realistic framework.

Discussions could not avoid a set of problems connected to the current political situation and the JNA's attitude towards it. The warning went unheeded that taking ideological-political sides and the military's daily involvement could be counterproductive to defense. The opinion prevailed that a neutral status for the JNA was unacceptable, and particular attention was drawn to the need for the JNA's and the military commanders' daily political involvement.[71]

At the consultative Meeting, the military commanders avoided making any explicit disclosure of the critical points of the concept and system of defense. The situation required them to rigorously examine the military-political sustainability of KONO and its ability to adjust to changes in the social environment. The generals also failed to establish how and to what extent changes in society and the external environment had jeopardized ONO and the Armed Forces, and analogous to this, whether, how much and how current political changes had jeopardized Yugoslavia's internal security. This was the only foundation that made it possible to establish the scope, depth and order of changes in the sphere of defense.

Had they undertaken necessary changes in the ONO System and Concept, the military commanders could have mitigated their ideological dysfunction, and this was the General Staff's urgent and primary task with regard to the situation in Yugoslavia. At the Meeting, however, the generals completely disregarded the key element of every defense – the human factor.[72]

The military commanders were not able to go beyond the daily, short-term view. They approached changes from the aspect of evaluating the scope of their control over individual elements of the defense system. A situation occurred similar to the subsequent repudiation of the constitutional foundation of the ONO Committees. They had not been discontinued until it was realized that there were no guarantees that the Committees would act in accordance with the military commanders' orders, but were more likely to follow the orders of the republican leaderships. Now it was the turn for the Territorial Defense (TO). First there were organizational and formational changes to the peacetime structure of the JNA: instead of Army regions that primarily coincided with the territories of the republics, military regions were created.[73]

Not until it was discovered, too late, that republican TO headquarters and units might be (were) nucleuses of republican armies, and that in the event of internal war would operate under the orders of republican power-holders, did the military commanders admit that the territorial component of the defense system was excessive and inefficient.[74]

The Army's concealment of the weaknesses of the ONO Concept and System and its political maneuvering with the status of the TO were soon interrupted by an interview with General Kadijević, Minister of Defense. He maintained that 'territorial defense, such as it was created at the end of the 1960s and beginning of the 1970s, is objectively a great deceit (...) This confirms without any doubt that Territorial Defense was built from the very beginning not as an expression of socialist self-management but as a base and framework for republican armies'.[75] The military commanders had thus made a radical about-face in less than seven months: in May 1990 the Chief of the General Staff ascertained the validity of KONO, and thereby its territorial components – in December that same year the Minister of Defense qualified the creation of territorial defense, as part of the ONO Concept and System, a contrived deceit.

This statement was the first public sign of the military commanders' mental chaos and insecurity. With the insinuation of conspiracy and deceit, their loud assurances that the Armed Forces (JNA+TO) were capable of preserving peace in Yugoslavia turned out to be pure propaganda. This was indirect admission that the generals had no control (command) over the entire Armed Forces, and that in the event of internal war the JNA and TO might clash with each other. Kadijević's statement, inter alia, was a sign that the military commanders were entering the final circle of progressive 'political paranoia'. With the announcement of a thirty-year-old internal conspiracy that they had discovered by themselves, the military commanders initiated the game of public self-deception and self-justification that lasted until the JNA disappeared in the war.

Notes

1   For more information, see: Sekelj, Laslo, *Jugoslavija, struktura raspadanja* (*Yugoslavia, Structure of the Country's Disintegration*), Rad, Belgrade, 1990, especially pages 263-267.
2   At the new Federal Assembly's first meeting, F. Tudjman announced, 'We hold that the sovereignty of Croatia as a state, in a community with other peoples of today's SFRY, can only be assured on a confederal basis, as a contractual union of sovereign states.' (Borba, 31.05.1990, 3).
3   Lojze Peterle, new president of the Slovenian government, explained that 'Slovenia would advocate a soft federation along the lines of an economic community with a tariff union, national (republican) armies but with a common defense strategy, in principal separated from foreign policy' (Borba, 16-17.06.1991, 10).
4   Slobodan Milošević, president of the SR Serbia Presidency warned of this: 'Should there be any change in the form of Yugoslavia's organization, i.e. into a confederalization, all constitutional issues would remain open. A confederation is not a state but a union of independent states, therefore (...) should a federal Yugoslavia be rejected, the question of Serbia's borders would be an open political question.' (Borba, 26.06.1990, 2).

5 DEMOS won in Slovenia in the second round (Borba, 17.04.1990, 1), while the HDZ won in the first round in Croatia (Borba, 23 and 25.04.1990, 1); at elections in Macedonia many votes, but not an absolute majority, were given to VMRO-DPMNE and the Albanians' Party of Democratic Prosperity; in B-H there was a so-called ethnic census, i.e. SDA, SDS and HDZ received for the most part all the votes of their ethnic communities (Borba, 22.11.1990, 1).

6 At the end of the year, they primarily supported Yugoslavia as a community of sovereign (republic) states; compare: Executive Council of the SR Macedonia Assembly, Basic Principles for the Organization and State-Legal Status of Yugoslavia, initial elements, items 1-3 (Borba, 17.10,1990, 4) and the new proposal of a federal constitution adopted by the B-H Presidency (Borba, 25.10.1990, 1).

7 For a comparative analysis of the essence of these processes see: Zoran Obrenović, *Srbija i novi poredak* (*Serbia and the New Order*), in the chapter 'National parties, national oppositions, the people', Gradina, Niš, 1992, 19-79.

8 Ante Marković, president of SIV, said, 'Finally, regardless of whether the SKJ is one or several organizations – the state must function and it will function.' (Borba, 24.01.1990, 5).

9 'It is time that the Croatian people extract all the facts from history, bring the words of Ante Starčević and Stjepan Radić to life, and start to use guns and their wallets,' interview with F. Tudjman, RTZ (Borba, 9.4.1990, 4).

10 This is shown by Articles 94-106 of the Constitution of the Republic of Croatia (Narodne novine no. 54, Zagreb, December 22, 1990) and Articles 83-89 of the Constitution of the Republic of Serbia (NIP 'Službeni list SFRJ', Belgrade, 1990) that give the presidents of these republics almost unlimited constitutional authority.

11 This is also illustrated by the views of Zagreb professor Smiljko Sokol: 'If someone advocates the founding of autonomous provinces (Serbian – M.H.) in Croatia based on a people's referendum, then (…) the decision about that cannot be made by the will of the people in that part of SR Croatia, but the will of the people in the entire republic (…) and such proposals in the broadest sense run counter to the current constitutional order, and in this context jeopardize and destroy the territorial integrity of SR Croatia.' Interview in 'Slobodna Dalmacija' (Borba, 28.02.1990, 7); this did not prevent Sokol and like-minded thinkers from having a completely opposite attitude towards the sovereignty of Yugoslavia.

12 For the first multiparty elections, Milošević made the Assembly announce a referendum about which should be first, passing a new constitution or holding elections (Borba, 26.06.1990, 1).

13 The text 'Model of a Confederation in Yugoslavia' elaborated jointly by the republican presidencies in Slovenia and Croatia. See: Borba, 08.10.1990, 4.

14 This was explicitly demanded by S. Milošević, President of the SR Serbia Presidency in his letter to the SFRY Presidency regarding the August events in Knin. Among other things, he asked for protection of the constitutional order, the adoption of a new SFRY constitution and a law on secession (Borba, 20.08.1990, 1).

15 'It is not a question of whether Yugoslavia will be a federation or a confederation, but whether Yugoslavia will have a market economy or not, whether it will be a state based on law (...). Those are questions that both the federalists and confederalists are conveniently avoiding' and so 'they have foisted a false dilemma on the Yugoslav peoples just like a cuckoo's egg, whether they are for a federation or a confederation,' SIV Communiqué (Borba, 01.11.1990, 1).

16 'Borba's barometer' in May showed that almost three-fourths of the Yugoslavs considered A. Marković the most progressive individual at that time (Borba, 21.05.1990, 7).

17 Presenting five conditions for reform in his report, A. Marković said it was 'particularly important to adopt all amendments that relate to changes in the political system so that, based on them, multiparty elections could be held throughout the country.' (Borba, 16.11.1990, 1 and 3).

18 One of the means used by the republics was to block the federal budget: in September-October Slovenia owed the budget 162 million dinars, Serbia owed 2.166 billion and Vojvodina 250 million (Borba, 14.11.1990, 12); with passage of the Law on Republican Debt to the National Bank of Serbia and the Decision on Approving Loans for Bank Liquidity (SL Serbia – special issue no. 14/28.12.1990) Serbia issued 18 billion dinars without authorization and thereby invaded the monetary system. In response to SIV's communiqué, RIV Serbia said, inter alia, that 'it is not correct to raise this question regarding measures n Serbia alone' since others were doing it, too (Borba, 08.01.1991, 1-2).

19 Thus in March the Slovenia Assembly adopted the 'Declaration on settling relations that are of general importance to the Republic of Slovenia' that announced the supremacy of the Republic's constitution over the federal Constitution and the elaboration of a Proposal for a confederation (Borba, 09.03.1990, 3).

20 At the beginning of July Slovenia's Assembly adopted the 'Declaration on the sovereignty of the Republic of Slovenia'. Article 2 states: 'The SFRY Constitution, federal laws and other federal provisions are in effect on the territory of the Republic of Slovenia if they are not contrary to the Constitution and laws of the Republic of Slovenia', and Article 3 says: 'Pursuant to the principle of state sovereignty and the principle of the supremacy of the Constitution and laws of the Republic of Slovenia, republican bodies and organizations must make sure that all federal bodies

and organizations on the territory of the Republic of Slovenia operate in accordance with the current legal order in the Republic of Slovenia' (Borba, 03.07.1990, 3).

21 DEMOS announced a plebiscite, new constitution and Slovenia's independence (Borba, 15.11.1990, 4); the Slovenian Assembly adopted the Law on the Plebiscite and scheduled it for December 23, and the question read: 'Should the Republic of Slovenia become an independent and self-ruling state?' (Borba, 07.12.1990, 1). The SFRY Presidency maintained that the Law on the Plebiscite was unconstitutional, but this did not hinder the plebiscite from being held (Borba, 19.12.1990, 1).

22 For example, regarding what happened in Knin, the Slovenian Presidency judged that 'this is a policy that used the thesis that the Serbian people area jeopardized to break up Yugoslavia, a country built on the principles of benevolence and equal footing, and now it is aimed at the sovereign, legitimate and legal governments in Slovenia and Croatia, elected in democratic elections' (Borba, 20.08.1990, 3).

23 Article 135, paragraph 5 of the new Croatian Constitution states that in emergency situations the Croatian Assembly may, without a referendum, 'pass decisions on dissociating (seceding) in order to protect the sovereignty of the Republic of Croatia by a two-thirds majority vote of the delegates present.' The first paragraph of Article 140 announces that Croatia will remain in SFRY until a new agreement is reached with the possibility of leaving the joint state unilaterally. Paragraph 2 of the same Article gives republican bodies the right to make 'needed decisions in order to protect the sovereignty and interests of the Republic of Croatia' should 'a decree or procedure by a federal body or the body of another republic or provincial member of the federation disturb the territorial integrity of the Republic of Croatia or if it is put in an unequal position in the federation or if its interests are jeopardized'; op. cit.

24 Based on the 'plebiscite of the Serbian people within Croatia and outside of it', the Serbian National Council declared autonomy 'on the ethnic and historical territories in which the Serbian people live, and are within the current borders of Croatia' (Borba, 02.10.1990, 1); a decision by the Constitutional Court of Croatia suspended the execution of the Statutes of the Serbian Autonomous Region of Krajina (Borba, 03.01.1999, 1).

25 Using the methods of a 'special war', the new government, through F. Tudjman, constantly warned of conspiracy, setups, etc. On the eve of the referendum in Knin, Tudjman warned that the 'new government is confronted with a well-organized setup, a far-reaching plot to destabilize Croatia' by 'bringing the Serbian population to its feet' because of their alleged jeopardy, which is only a mask to bring down the 'democratically elected government in Croatia' (Borba, 15.08.1990, 1).

26 F. Tudjman's address to those passing the first MUP Croatia course was an indirect announcement of the formation of the Croatian militia – the nucleus of a future army (Borba, 10.08.1990, 3); soon afterward volunteer detachments were formed in Split and Zagreb (Borba, 16.08.1990, 3).

27 Compare: Constitution of the Republic of Croatia, Fundamental Principles, paragraph 3, op. cit.

28 In the pre-election campaign, SDS leader J. Rašković clearly indicated the high correlation between Croatia's attitude towards Yugoslavia and the Serbs' attitude towards Croatia (compare: SDS promotion in Zagreb, Borba, 09.03.1990, 14); at Croatia's announcement of its secession from Yugoslavia came the announcement of the Serbs' referendum on autonomy (Borba, 09.07.1990, 4), then at the First Serbian Assembly in Srb the 'Declaration on the sovereignty and autonomy of the Serbian people in Croatia' was adopted which, inter alia, established that 'the Serbian people in SR Croatia have the full right, together with the Croatian people or independently, to choose a federal or confederal state order during the establishment of new relations in Yugoslavia (...) Based on their sovereignty, the Serbian people in Croatia have the right to autonomy. The contents of that autonomy will depend on the federal or confederal organization of Yugoslavia.' (Borba, 26.07.1990, 3).

29 Some, for example Prof. Josip Županov, judged the August events around Knin as a rehearsal for the rapidly arriving civil war; for more information see: J. Županov's interview in Borba, 22.08.1990, 4).

30 This is shown by a later statement by Darko Bekić, Tudjman's former adviser: 'We had the chance and opportunity to build the state structure and the defense system and all the institutions of public control needed to successfully lead the state, and even transform the economic system, all at a slower tempo, but we became the victims of our own historical frustration and impatience.' (Borba, 14.12.1992, 7).

31 This category could also include the trouble Serbia's policies had with the principle of self-determination; according to the 1974 Constitution it only covered major ethnic groups, but parts of some of them in Serbia (the Muslims in Sandžak), and minorities, in particular the Albanians, had announced they would use this principle, too; in this regard, Alija Izetbegović said at the SDA promotional meeting in Sandžak: 'we will write down word for word what Rašković asks of Tudjman, and where the word Serbian people is written we will put Muslim, and should Serbia and Montenegro join together, we will ask for Sandžak's political autonomy.' (Borba, 01.08.1990, 2).

32 A typical example of this was Serbia's and Slovenia's refusal to adopt the Law on Yugoslav political parties (Borba, 06.06.1990, 4), which in the case of Serbia caused confusion owing to their persistent support for the electoral principle of 'one man – one vote' on the federal level.

33 The second paragraph of Article 135 of the Constitution of the Republic of Serbia says: 'When the acts of federal bodies or the acts of the bodies of other republics, contrary to the rights and obligations they have pursuant to the SFRY Constitution, disturb the equal footing of the Republic of Serbia or jeopardize its interests in any way, and no compensation has been provided, republican bodies are to pass acts in order to protect the interests of the Republic of Serbia'; Constitution of the Republic of Serbia, op. cit., 59.

34 After repeated demonstrations, the justified sentencing of A. Vlasi, and the intervention of the federal militia and Army (Borba, 25.01.1990, 3), Serbia's RSUP (republican police) took over all the work of public and state security, and the state of emergency in Kosovo was lifted (Borba, 18 and 19.04.1990, 1); after the Kosovo Assembly (VUR) rejected the decision by the republican Assembly regarding a referendum (Borba, 28.06.1990,1) and proclaimed in the street the 'Constitutional declaration of Kosovo' as a republic, Serbia's Assembly passed the Law on the discontinuation of the work of the Assembly and Executive Council of SAP Kosovo (Borba, 06.07.1990, 1 and 3); in September the so-called Kačanički constitution of Kosovo was illegally passed (Borba, 12.09.1990, 4 – the text of the constitution in Borba of 14.09.1990).

35 Admiral Petar Šimić, the Party leader of the JNA, said at the People's Assembly on Grmeč, 'The working people believe in the foundations that have been achieved, in their own possibilities and the goals that have been set of the social progress of socialist relations in society. They are not for turning back to any kind of state centralism or civic parliamentary law.' (Borba, 08.01.1990, 1).

36 For this purpose the Army party elaborated 'Basic plan of continuing the 14th Emergency Congress of the SKJ'; VPI 6/90, 11-13.

37 Compare: the report by P. Šimić, president of the OSK in the JNA (Borba, 15.02.1990, 1 and 5).

38 The Central Committee of the Democratic Party of Montenegro had sent a request to the CK SKJ and the CK SK CG to discontinue their organizations in 'the Yugoslav Army and all Yugoslav police services and the secret police of the federal units' (Borba, 12.01.1990, 7).

39 The Decision from the 10th Conference of the OSK in the JNA says: 'The SK Organization in the JNA, following the commitments and will of the great majority of their members, joins the League of Communists – Movement for Yugoslavia. This does not alter the right of the individual not to join the League of Communists – Movement for Yugoslavia, should he so desire'; VPI 2/91, 19.

40 The formal promotion of the SK-PJ was held in Sava Center and was attended by 'quite a few men in JNA uniforms', with particular note of the federal

Minister of Defense, the Commander of the General Stall and other military leaders (Borba, 20.11.1990, 4).

41 Reactions to the ideological-party involvement of the military commanders were diametrically opposed; Franjo Tudjman said, 'Kadijević has set himself in front of the supreme command, the SFRY Presidency and the government of which he is minister, which is worrisome and not seen previously in our history (...) an example never recorded before of a minister of defense trying to influence social and political trends'; Momir Bulatović, president of the Montenegro Presidency said: 'The Army's resolve can be felt, wanting to be an active participant in defending constitutionality and legality in Yugoslavia, and no serious or well-founded reproach can be made to that'; Janez Janša said: 'This is an attempt to pressure public opinion in Serbia to benefit Milošević's party, and to cause the greatest abstinence in Slovenia when voting on an independent Slovenia' (Borba, 04.12.1990, 4).

42 This was also maintained in a speech on Petrova Gora by Dušan Pekić, retired general, who at the time was very active in the Bosanska and Kninska Krajina area: 'The main participants in these horrible and tragic policies are the remains of Ustashe, Chetnik, White Guard and Albanian, as well as new national-socialist separatist forces who are waging a great, hysterical anticommunist and anti-Yugoslav campaign'; the Presidency of the CK SKH judged this speech a 'pamphlet with the most glaring lies and insults for the Serbian people' since the Serbs were never nationalists (Borba, 05.03.1990, 1).

43 The alleged 'categorical demand expressed in the communiqué from the meeting to adopt a new Constitution that would establish legal and political subjectivitiy of the federation (...) on the eve of elections (in Slovenia – M.H.) sounds like an ultimatum' as interpreted by the Presidency of the RK SSRN Slovenia (Borba, 27.03.1990, 5).

44 'The joint appraisal is that this is malicious misinformation on the so-called broader activities of the JNA and TO planned for the days of the upcoming elections in SR Croatia' (Borba, 05.04.1990, 4).

45 'The worst seems to be that passions have started to prevail over reason, the irrational over awareness. In the name of democracy and party pluralism, people with dangerous intentions and very imprudent dealings are taking or have already taken key position in society. Playing on the card of ethnic emotions, they, unfortunately have won the people's trust. They are blindly walking into the past, into changing borders and fratricidal war', General Simeon Bunčić, Deputy Minister of Defense for political and legal affairs, VIP 6/90, 8.

46 Similar treatment was given to the opposition leaders in Serbia – Vuk Drašković (Narodna armija, 15.3.1990, 5) and Vojislav Šešelj (Narodna armija, 27.9.1990.

47 With amendments 96, 97 and 98 of the Slovenian Constitution, the republic took over full authority in the field of defense, while federal bodies were left to command the Armed Forces only in the case of impending war and during war (Borba, 29-30.09.1990, 12); with amendments to the Law on TO, the Croatian Assembly also took over all peacetime authority; on that occasion Vladimir Šeks, one of the leaders of the HDZ, announced the creation of a Croatian army (Borba, 20.11.1990).

48 With this goal in mind, SSNO proposed to the SFRY Assembly a package of military laws that planned for: (1) the introduction of a special sales tax on goods and services to finance the JNA, at the time in effect as a provisional measure, (2) changes in the military court and prosecutor's office, particularly connected to the language used and the choice of defense counsel, and (3) regulation of the exports of arms and equipment (Borba, 22.05.1990, 1).

49 Political and systemic pressures from Slovenia, and soon afterwards from Croatia, on the recruiting system lasted the whole year: first the Presidency of SSRN Slovenia demanded that 50% of the Slovene recruits serve in their own republic, that more Slovenian officers be assigned to Slovenia in the first distribution, that one of the (technical) academies be moved to Slovenia (Borba, 30.01.1990, 5); this was followed by a request from the Slovenian Assembly to change the Law on ONO and for Slovene recruits not to go to Kosovo (Borba, 09.03.1990, 3); the Slovenian Assembly sent a request to the Presidency of SFRY through SNNO for Slovene recruits to serve only in the 5th VO (Vojni oblast – Military Region) and of that 50% in Slovenia, otherwise Slovenia would not send its September class of recruits (Borba, 25.07.1990, 14); soon after the republican secretariat for NO Slovenia announced that it would send only 50% of the recruits and send them only to the 5th VO and elsewhere only for those special assignments for which there was no one in the field (Borba, 10.08.1990, 12).

50 In response to the opinion of the Croatian Presidency that 'the JNA must not be a separate factor in the country's political life' (Borba, 14.07.1990, 2), the SSNO spokesman said at a press conference that 'the JNA is under obligation to protect the order established in the SFRY Constitution, not changes in society that are not legally based.' (Borba, 12.07.1990, 3).

51 'The military establishment is still faithful to Tito's program and federalism. They are totally communists and mostly Serbs. And, of course, they are opposed to democratic changes in Croatia and Slovenia because they are (…) communists and Serbs. Officially, the Army did not take a position against democratization and does not want to stop the process (…). In future the Army will have to bow to democratic changes and political reality', F. Tudjman, interview 'Le Monde' (Borba, 03.10.1990, 6).

52 The government of Croatia has asked that the minister of defense be replaced (Borba, 06.12.1990, 4) and the Croatian Assembly has asked for V.

Kadijević's responsibility to be determined and whether he should remain in that position (Borba, 07.12.1990, 1); the Presidency of the Republic of Slovenia sent a written protest to the SFRY Presidency with regard to the politicization of the JNA and V. Kadijević's statement (Borba, 07.12.1990, 3).

53 This is shown by the instruction sent out by the Republic of Croatia Center for Intelligence and Early Warning to all municipal bodies: 'Assure the constant observation of garrisons and all important facilities in your municipality. Prepare and be ready to act towards garrisons and facilities in accordance with assignments. Do not allow them to provoke you and by no means be the first to act'; the general guideline was accompanied by specific assignments for every municipality (Borba, 21.12.1990, 12).

54 The SFRY Presidency transferred to the Command of the 5th VO the command of the Republic of Slovenia's TO, and put SSNO and JNA units and institutions in charge of carrying out this decision (Borba, 03.10.1990, 1); the Slovenian leadership refused to carry out this order (Borba, 04.10.1990, 3), and when the JNA started to carry out the order it could only take over the empty command building in Ljubljana (Borba, 06-07.10.1990, 11).

55 See: (Borba, 08.02.1990, 1-3.)

56 When taking on his duties B. Jović emphasized that the Presidency would have to show the SFRY Assembly and the public that 'analyses by authorized bodies (SSNO – M.H.) warn of the great seriousness of our country's security situation, arising from the systematic and persistent disruption of its constitutional order.' (Borba, 16.05.1990, 1).

57 This is illustrated by A. Marković's reaction to Kadijević's interview: 'The JNA has a clear role in our society and the authority of the government and the authority of the SFRY Presidency as supreme commander are quite clear. Otherwise, the JNA is not required to give its opinion about reforms in the federal government or its support for them.' (Borba, 05.12.1990, 1).

58 The SIV had proposed that 'the region of authority of border military units be expanded to one kilometer from the border zone (otherwise 100 meters wide – M.H.) where the army would be able to check the identification of, search and detain individuals suspected of crossing the SFRY border without authorization' (Borba, 20.02.1990, 14).

59 Stipe Sikavica, feuilleton 'Godine raspleta' (Borba, 02-04.02.1993, 12).

60 'I would also like to present the opinion of the military leadership on the place and role of the SKJ in the Army (...) In this situation we should not be recommending the dissolution of the SK Organization in the JNA. Not because some people will tell us that we are conservative, but for the very reason that if the SK leaves the Army that would mean automatically linking our officers, who are 95-96% its members, to republican organizations of the League of Communists or some other party. That would lead to further

divisions in the League of Communists, radically dividing officers in their views regarding the policies of their republics, etc. Furthermore, that would mean breaking up the Army, or its unity (...) We will not allow the breakup of the SKJ Organization in the JNA which has remained, unfortunately, the only real communist organization. In the current situation that is our opinion and choice, and I would ask for that to be accepted as a political opinion.' General B. Adžić, ('Vojno delo', special edition, Belgrade, August 1990, 29.)

61 This is illustrated by a series of articles after V. Kadijević's interview wanting to show that the negative reactions were primarily the result of Kadijević's claim that the JNA would defend Yugoslavia; on that occasion, the reactions of Tudjman and Dračković were lumped together; compare: ('Narodna armija', 13.12.1990, 5-7.)

62 This is the tone and style used by Admiral Brovet, deputy minister, when addressing the members of the Center of High Military Academies in Belgrade in January 1991.

63 On 22.05.1990 the Political-Legal Section of SSNO organized a scientific-expert meeting on the topic 'Theoretical-Methodological Grounds for Monitoring and Evaluating MPS in the OS'.

64 The highly specific nature of the meeting is illustrated by the definition of its goal: 'A critical analysis of existing guidelines and a scientific-expert problematization of the method, means, technique and indicators to monitor and evaluate MPS in the OS, so as to provide the scientific-methodological foundation upon which to elaborate uniform guidelines for monitoring and evaluating MPS in the OS.'

65 Amendments to the Rules of Service (SSNO, Belgrade, 1985) went into effect on 22.01.1991 (Belgrade, SSNO, 1991); compare pages 5-10.

66 The provisional program of moral guidance to the JNA soldiers-sailors went into effect 20.06.1990; compare: (Provisional Program, SSNO, Belgrade, 1990, 5 and after.)

67 Citing amendments to the Law on Total National Defense and its Articles 64, paragraph 2 and 110, paragraph 1, 'every form of political-party activity in the commands, headquarters, units and institutions of the Armed forces' was strictly forbidden (item 1), and 'strict disciplinary and other legally prescribed measures will be taken against the JNA members who transmit, carry out or in any way actively operate from the position of political parties or associations in the commands, units and institutions of the JNA.' (item 2).

68 The meeting was held in May 1990; materials were prepared and published in two publications: a shortened version for the public came out in 'Vojno delo' 3-4/90 and almost all the papers were published in a special edition for internal use.

69 'When discussing the need to optimize the concepts of Total National Defense and Social Self-Protection, I feel it goes without saying that in the

many years since the war our concept of total national defense has passed its exam with flying colors.' B. Adžić, 'Vojno delo', special edition, op. cit., 24.

70 'I do not think it is wrong, on the contrary, but in these cases we did not have the right measure. For example, territorial defense had grown to almost a million and a half people (...) Of course, we must continue to opt for an armed people, but to a reasonable degree, according to objective possibilities. Thus, socialization yes, but not in excess. Because excessive socialization devaluated the military's calling and profession, and now ignoramuses are taking care of military strategy (...) Nonetheless, it cannot be said that our armed people and the socialization of defense was a failed concept, but we made a mistake in the dimensions it was given', B. Adžić, op. cit., 25.

71 Compare: the already cited speeches by B. Adžić, S. Brovet and the text by P. Škrbić, op. cit., 294-311.

72 He thereby betrayed his own strategic principle: 'in armed battle people have the main and deciding role.'; compare: *Strategija oružane borbe* (*Strategy of Armed Battle*), SSNO, Belgrade, 1983, 67.

73 Instead of five army regions (the first and second in Serbia, the third in Macedonia, the fifth in Croatia, the seventh in B-H, the ninth in Slovenia, an independent corps in Montenegro), three military regions were created (the first covered most of Serbia, parts of B-H and Croatia, the third covered southern Serbia, Montenegro and Macedonia, and the fifth covered Slovenia and most of Croatia).

74 Regarding the status of TO, certain negative tendencies were pointed out, among others that 'there is an increasingly rising tendency for Territorial Defense to turn into a republican, provincial, and even municipal army, not only with regard to the Constitutional and legally regulated authority of these socio-political communities in the development and equipping of Territorial Defense, but also with regard to its use, whereby it is often denoted as an attribute of statehood and sovereignty.' Ninković, J. 'Vojno delo', op. cit. 345.

75 Op. cit. 9.

Chapter 3

The Army's Destruction of Reality

Events that developed at the end of 1990 portended the end of SFR Yugoslavia in the flames of war. The political dissolution of the state was completed in the first half of 1991, and arms took over at the end of June. After first doing away with all the reasons for Yugoslavia's survival, local leaders started to break up the country in armed conflict. This state of severe and protracted conflict required radical solutions and also made them possible. This is period in which local leaders started to beat their war drums.

Yugoslavia's political end culminated in warfare that directly resulted from the use of force to put mutually exclusive plans into effect on the setting of national (ethnic) and state borders. This could only be done with the creation of new states in the same place as the former republics, and in order to do this Yugoslavia's international status and state borders had to be changed first. This procedure inevitably led to conflicts regarding the validity of internal borders between the republics. When several leaders aspired to the same territory, the use of arms was directly heralded.

So events in 1991-1992 and their direction were determined first by the political and then by the armed struggle to take over and/or preserve state and national (ethnic) territory. Territorial conquests in order to create (one) nation-states were inevitably preceded or followed by ethnic cleansing. The incompatibility of plans for a Greater Croatia and a Greater Serbia clearly indicated the central area of warfare and the conflicting sides. It was also clear that the territory and population of Bosnia-Herzegovina (B-H) would be included in their campaigns sooner or later. This portended the revival of all earlier ethnic and territorial conflicts in SFR Yugoslavia.

In the first months of 1991 it still seemed that the crisis could be solved by political means. This was because the republican leaders, after finalizing their state projects, had lined up precisely with regard to each other and all controversial points had been clearly defined. Although they had opposing interests and goals, they first tried to achieve them through negotiations. This, however, did not stop them from making preparations to fight for these goals. There was thus an increasingly visible discrepancy between republican leaders' public and secret activities, what they proclaimed and what was really going on.

The development of events in the final phase of the crisis forced the JNA out into the open. Although the military commanders temporarily withdrew from the public scene after the failure of their attempt to legally declare a military state of emergency in March 1991, republican leaders' preparations for war returned the JNA to the very center of events.

3.1 The Political Dissolution of Yugoslavia

In the first half of 1991, the final destiny of the second Yugoslavia and its population was determined on two interconnected but mutually exclusive levels of political decision making. An ostensible search for a compromise solution to the culminating crisis was made on the first level. A series of negotiations by republican leaders created the impression that they wanted to solve inter-republic and inter-ethnic conflicts in a peaceful manner. On the second level, which turned out to be crucial, these same negotiators were making comprehensive preparations on their own turf for internal war.

Regardless of the warfare finale, even with hindsight it is difficult to discover the real reasons for the negotiating 'marathon' by republican leaders.[1] The question remains unanswered as to whether these negotiations were only tactical maneuvers of the peace-loving warmongers. If the republican leaders were negotiating under false pretenses, then the internal preparations for war were understandable. But if they were truly interested in a peaceful solution to the crisis as they claimed, why weren't the necessary prerequisites to peace created? War could only have been avoided in Yugoslavia with universal pacification, with the JNA commanders under joint control. Instead of this, accelerated militarization was going on in every republic, while the JNA commanders had wrested themselves completely out of the control of the SFRY Presidency and the SIV.

In principle, the assumption is sustainable that none of the negotiators was a priori for war. They all hoped to achieve their goals by political means. But since none of them had rejected the alternative of war, they were all prepared for it. Thus their negotiations at the time left both solutions open – war and peace.

The initiation of negotiations did not slow down the decomposition of Yugoslavia in the least. On the contrary, even during negotiations all those involved acted along the lines of their maximal state and national (ethnic) programs. Slovenia and Croatia used this interregnum to legalize their withdrawal from Yugoslavia internally,[2] but in spite of this their leaders strove to give the impression that they were ready to reach a peaceful and democratic agreement. In principle, the federalists were also for an agreement, but at the same time they demanded respect for the constitutional procedure with the legal regulation of secession. In the process, they strongly emphasized their readiness to use all means to defend the federation. A new component in the negotiations was offering the option of a smaller federation comprised of only those peoples that wanted to remain.[3]

At the beginning of the year the previously marginalized republics – Macedonia and Bosnia-Herzegovina – completed their own plans to separate. Their representatives sent the clear message that they were not interested in remaining in a smaller Yugoslavia.[4] Although they defined their republics as sovereign and independent states, they were in principle prepared to accept a changed Yugoslavia, but only with all six of its members. At that time B-H was also considering the idea of dividing up into cantons by ethnic keys.[5] The Serbian side, however, was resolute in its position that should Yugoslavia disintegrate, the Serbs in B-H would not remain in a sovereign B-H.[6] This expressed the political will of the leaders of the western Serb communities to take their territories out of Croatia and B-H, which was actually only a local rejoinder to the Greater Serbia plans and ambitions of the Serbian political center in Belgrade. In conjunction with this, preparations were renewed for the previously announced joining of SAO (Serbian Autonomous Region) Krajina with Bosanska Krajina, although SAO Krajina had already decided to annex itself to Serbia.[7]

In spite of everything, there were sufficient assumptions for constructive negotiations since the key republics had clearly detailed their views of resolving the country's crisis. Serbia and Montenegro had completed their model of a 'democratic and federal' state. Slovenia had confirmed that 'in accordance with the decision passed at the plebiscite, it would separate into an independent, sovereign state'. In addition, Croatia had announced that on June 30, 1991 it would start to withdraw from the state if no acceptable solution were reached by then. Then Kiro Gligorov and Alija Izetbegović, leaders of Macedonia and B-H, intending to overcome the exclusiveness of the first two options, offered their 'Platform on the future Yugoslav community'.[8] The clear-cut starting positions offered the negotiators in principle the possibility of finding an acceptable solution for everyone through mutual concessions.

The series of negotiations, however, only confirmed and deepened the ethnic leaders' disagreements about the key elements of the state crisis:

- Were the peoples (ethnic groups) or the republics the mainstays of sovereignty and decision making on the right to self-determination resulting in secession.
- If Yugoslavia were to disintegrate, were the internal borders administrative and thus changeable, or were they state borders and thus unchangeable.[9]
- According to which procedure could relations be altered between the republics and between the ethnic communities, i.e. was dissociation (secession) a sovereign and unilateral right or was it only possible with the agreement of the other members of Yugoslavia.

Owing to the lack of compromise, negotiations necessarily ended up being one more in a series of tactical maneuvers by republican/ethnic leaders. Determined to achieve their goals unilaterally (by force), they used the negotiations in order to reached the best starting (war) position in the eyes of their own and the foreign public. The negotiators not only failed to create a political climate to peacefully solve the crisis, they used every opportunity to demonstrate that negotiations were not even possible.

With the failure of negotiations, these leaders missed the last chance to achieve their goals in the least expensive way – without war. Not everyone was able to achieve all their goals, so they did not all leave the negotiations with the same political capital. The seceding leaders managed to find additional legitimacy for their maximalist positions 'at home' and abroad. Putting conditions before the Serbian side that it did not want and/or could not accept, they gained new propaganda arguments for their claim that further state and national life together in Yugoslavia was impossible. At the same time, in order to obtain greater international support they presented themselves as innocent, democracy-loving victims of Serbian Bolshevism and hegemony.

At the beginning of 1991, along with everything else going on, the general search continued for external support and allies,[10] particularly since verbal support to an undivided Yugoslavia was no guarantee that foreign parties would not take sides. On the contrary, in the final lap of disintegration, an international race began around the redistribution of interests and influence in the central Balkans. The international 'marauders' had a particularly easy time with Slovenia and Croatia[11] who were guided by the principle that in order to gain a sovereign state it was worthwhile being subordinated to those promoting their interests in the world.

Apart from the federalists' opposition, there was a constant rise in the influence of external factors on attempts to solve the Yugoslav crisis. Results indicate that the secessionists were far more successful at playing the international card. Unlike them, the leaders of Serbia and the JNA miscalculated international factors. Furthermore, they stubbornly ignored the new topography of power in the international community. The strategic and tactical weaknesses of Serbia's policies were shown in their emphatic rejection of any nonfederal Yugoslavia. Refusing to even talk about a confederal and/or asymmetrical (2+2+2)[12] variation, Serbia deprived itself of the last chance to positively internationalize the Serbian national question. Had it entered into negotiations, Serbia would have been able to give foreign participants ample warning of the negative consequences the Serbs would suffer with the unilateral dissolution of Yugoslavia. Instead, Milošević with his arrogant behavior, based on the illusion that Serbia and the JNA had enough power to impose their solution, clashed with the European Union and the USA. This directly benefited the leaders of Slovenia and Croatia and provided additional confirmation of the unwillingness and inability of Serbia's leaders to consider and realistically calculate the influence of key international factors.

To make matters worse for Serbia, its leaders were not even able to find or create allies within the Yugoslav framework, unlike Slovenia and Croatia. Furthermore, at the very end of the crisis Serbia's leaders were at odds with the leaders of all the other ethnic groups.

Although increasingly harsh in expressing their dissatisfaction with Yugoslavia,[13] Serbia's leaders still had not publicly abandoned the federal model. But the demand to create an independent (pan) Serbian state was growing among Serbia's public. This variation in the given constellation, however, was not acceptable to Milošević. He had already decided to rely on the western Serbian communities and the JNA's strength to make at least a 'second-and-a-half' Yugoslavia. His offer was extended to Macedonia and B-H (the Muslims). In the process, Milošević was certainly guided by the political benefit that he and Serbia might have from such a creation. With the creation of a smaller Yugoslavia, the survival of all the Serbs would be provided in one territorially compact state. This would preserve the international-legal continuity of Yugoslavia, and prove the secessionism of Slovenia and Croatia. Furthermore, this would preserve (form) in Balkan proportions a respective state under Serbian domination.

This half-move, however, only postponed Serbia's radical severance with Yugoslavia and increased the incoherence of Serbia's policies. The Serbian position was also weakened by the fact that its leaders did not have clearly defined short-term and long-term goals. The fact that the Serbs' national interests had never been regularly – fundamentally, modernly, suitably and democratically – defined previously allowed Milošević to manipulate them using the support of key national institutions and the media. The only benefit from the six negotiations held by republican leaders was that the names of the true decision makers on war and peace in Yugoslavia finally became public knowledge. Since negotiations were being conducted outside the federal system, the fact was reconfirmed that no solution could be found within its framework. In spite of this, republican/ethnic leaders periodically returned the topic of 'Yugoslavia' to federal institutions, with different reasons behind such maneuvers. The leaders of Slovenia and Croatia wanted to show their own public and the foreign public that the federal system was dysfunctional, thus Yugoslavia was untenable. Milošević, however, thought this would show the need to re-federalize Yugoslavia. Each leader used what was left of the system to prevent decision making in federal bodies that would harm his strategic interests.

A parallel channel for the production of peacemaking illusions was provided by activities within the framework of federal institutions. Countless meetings were held with different convocations – from expanded meetings of the SFRY Presidency to the six negotiations and bilateral and trilateral meetings of republican leaders. Finding a modus for survival until a final agreement was reached on the fate of Yugoslavia and the future state position of its peoples was the job of all the system's institutions – from the SFRY Assembly to the federal government and republican bodies. An entire range of projects, although counter to each other, was finalized to solve the crisis, without a single one being realized. Countless orders were issued to prevent armed inter-ethnic conflicts, which did nothing to lessen the chances of warfare.

During this period the SFRY Presidency had been in actual fact released from its role as collective leader of the joint state, and became one more of the places where the final political battle was fought. The western republics did not leave the Presidency until they no longer received any benefit from it. The federalists kept it in its truncated form even after the outbreak of war, and it was only discontinued when they were forced to form the Federal Republic of Yugoslavia (FRY). Comprehensive maneuvering resulted in consensual but not productive compromises in the Presidency.

Conflicting goals and interests were the order of the day and the general disposition was given by the personal and ideological intolerance of the members from the most powerful republics.

The republican representatives in the SFRY Presidency waged a crucial battle around the role of the JNA, since preventing its internal use was a strategic prerequisite for secession. The representatives from Slovenia and Croatia tried a combination of pressure and concessions to prevent at least the premature use of the Army.

Serbia's leaders, however, wanted the SFRY Presidency to provide advanced legalization of using the JNA allegedly to preserve the constitutional order and integrity of Yugoslavia. For this purpose, Milošević introduced new members from Montenegro and Kosovo into the Presidency. This gave him the power to prevent every decision by the Presidency that did not suit him. In addition, counting on the Serb Borislav Jović, who was president of the Presidency until May 1991, and with the full support of the military commanders, Milošević seemed to have political initiative.

During this time the military-Serbian coalition was cemented, still nominally along the federal line. Bolstering each other, both sides were lulled by the illusion that they had the 'control packet of power' to preserve Yugoslavia by force if necessary. The mutual benefit they gained from working together could not hide the unequal positions of the coalition partners. The Serbs always had a way out by forming their own state, while the JNA had no such possibility in reserve. That fact made the military commanders dependent on the political will of the Serbian leaders. Thus Milošević had an easy time putting the JNA in the front line of the battle for the Serbs' ethnic and state interests and goals, although they were quite changeable and elastic.

In particular, the military commanders' final, but still hidden, pro-Serb shift took place during this period. The shift, of course, resulted from the combined effects of two nationally and politically opposing, and ultimately complementary platforms: Slovenia's and Croatia's secession from Yugoslavia, on the one hand, and Yugoslavia's defense by the Serbs and the Army, on the other. This had limited the military commanders' choices, but it would soon be shown that the dilemma of choosing between the state's survival and their own was resolved to their benefit.

During this time combined activities by the republican leaders led to the complete corrosion of SFRY's economic and political system. It was no longer possible to make a single decision within the federal framework that would help end the crisis by peaceful means. In order to finish the job completely, the SIV had to be eliminated, so the key republics headed for a final showdown with the federal government. Their intention was to do away with what little remained of any chances for pro-democratic reforms with a Yugoslav orientation. In the end, the SIV was used by the federalists to legalize the JNA's 'Slovenian expedition', and then was blamed for its failure.[14]

There has been no serious examination and analysis of the SIV's role during this period except for speculations in retrospect.[15] The government tried to take the initiative and give shape to an offensive antiwar alignment. An agreement was therefore proposed on the minimal operations of the federation until the final resolution of the crisis, i.e. a new agreement on Yugoslavia's appearance.[16] The federal government hoped to get the republics at least to agree to the continuation of partial reforms on items that had a consensus. For this reason, it requested the suspension of all unconstitutional laws and provisions, which the Constitutional Court had already declared invalid. The government tried on several occasions to return negotiations on Yugoslavia to the Federal Assembly. It reactivated, although unsuccessfully, the proposal on federal multiparty elections. Hoping to stop Slovenia and Croatia from breaking away, at the last moment the SIV proposed the principles and contents of a new common state.[17]

In spite of everything, it is not easy to determine the driving force behind the SIV's operations at the time. Setting aside suspicions surrounding the 'conspiracy theory', the answer seems to lie in its misjudgment of the internal and external participants in the crisis. The federal government expected, albeit without grounds, and incorrectly understood foreign support for Yugoslavia and its reforms. Trusting in common sense, rationality and the citizens' fear of war, they disregarded the destructive power of the nationalistic forces that had been released.

Until the 'traitorous' intentions of the federal government and Ante Marković are proven, accusations against them must answer the following dilemmas: first, if the SIV was simply at the service of secessionist policies as claimed by Serbian propaganda, why did Marković issue an order legalizing the JNA campaign against Slovenia?;[18] second, if the federalist coalition knew of the SIV's 'Trojan horse' role, why didn't they prevent its destructive impact earlier?; and third, how can the secessionists' zealous criticism and obstruction of the SIV be explained?[19]

The political dissolution of Yugoslavia was not possible, of course, without the public or tacit agreement of its inhabitants who were already opposed along ethnic lines. Republican/ethnic leaders' first war victories were actually against their own ethnic groups. Afterwards, the defeated ethnic groups merely had to be convinced that the only way to their own victory over the others was using arms. In order to rule out any thought of hesitation, republican leaders activated propaganda and repressive mechanisms directed towards preparing the people for war. The orchestration of interethnic conflicts,[20] creatively mediated by local power-holders, initiated the hyper-production of proof on the inevitability of separating along ethnic and state lines.

Increasing tensions in interethnic relations up to and beyond the incident level quickly revived the past. Key conflicts went along the 'S-C-S' diagonal, and then soon concentrated in the Serbo-Croatian area. Accordingly, the unresolved Serbian national question, with all its political and territorial consequences, became the central axis of current and approaching events. Kosovo was temporarily pushed into the background and marginalized,[21] and only served as a political argument used differently in the inter-republic conflicts – Serbia to attack the SIV, and Slovenia and Croatia to attack Serbia.

The intermezzo in negotiations was used to finalize state, political, international, ideological (propaganda) and military preparations for war. The seceding republics worked through several channels. They quickly took over the military sphere and authority of the JNA/OS of SFRY.[22] They legalized the creation of national (republican) armies. The smuggling of arms and auxiliary equipment intensified.[23] At the same time, every type of pressure increased against the JNA and its members and every move by the military commanders was used for political purposes.[24] They wanted to show at all cost that the Army, i.e. its commanders, was the instrument of Serbia's policies.[25] There were increasing demands in Serbia for the formation of a Serbian army. Rejecting these demands, the Serbian leadership once again supported the military commanders and the JNA in the name of defending Yugoslavia, but also to protect the Serbs living in Croatia.[26]

3.2 The Army Abandons Yugoslavia

Since Yugoslavia's political fate had already been decided, all that remained was to see how it would break up. Slovenia and Croatia were vitally interested in providing the peaceful 'extinguishing' of the JNA within the framework of their disassociation, because they had judged that only the Army could interfere in the realization of their intentions. In order to avert this danger, they proposed the sectional discontinuation of the

JNA[27] and/or its confederal transformation into republican armies, which would then be connected to a united command. The leaders of Slovenia and Croatia increased parallel political, propaganda and physical pressure on the JNA units and members located in their republics.

In principle, the JNA could not have escaped the fate of Yugoslavia – dissolution of the state had to lead to the dissolution of its army. But since there was little likelihood of an agreement being reached on the breakup, the manner in which Yugoslavia disappeared depended directly on the military commanders' behavior. In other words, the course and form of the common state's dissolution greatly depended on how the JNA was used.

Powerless, and over time less and less willing to prevent the use of force to change the country's composition, the military commanders actually determined the JNA's fate before the outbreak of war. Viewed historically, it might be said that the fate of the Party's Army was decided the moment the Party disappeared, so in 1991 its inevitable end had arrived. The disintegration of JNA in the war could be interpreted as tallying up the final score of the ideologically retarded Army.

In the given circumstances, however, the fate of the Army and thereby of the state crucially depended on the republican/ethnic leaders' tactics and the military commanders' reactions to them. The military and political collapse of the JNA resulted directly from the actions of the central triad of generals. Key decisions on the use of the JNA were made within a very small circle – General Veljko Kadijević, Minister of Defense, in conjunction with General Blagoje Adžić, Chief of the General Staff, and Stane Brovet, Kadijević's deputy, had the final say in everything.[28] Events would show that none of them was equal to the role that had been assigned them by the Party.

The political dissolution of Yugoslavia was accompanied, but also made possible, by the hidden entropy of the Army system, which was an expectable result of the collapse of the central – economic and political – system. The problem, however, was that the triad of generals avoided facing this fact. In their public appearances they kept persuading themselves and the population that the Army was ready and willing to prevent Yugoslavia's disintegration by means of warfare.

The political demise of Yugoslavia had reduced the military commanders' numerous dilemmas to several crucial questions whose answers they had to find by themselves:

- Should Yugoslavia be defended at any price using all available means, including armed force?
- Could Yugoslavia be defended by force, and if it could, how should this be carried out?
- What was the probability of success, and what was the price of forcefully defending a country that had been abandoned by everyone?
- In the event of such an undertaking, would the Army have reliable internal allies and who were they?
- How would relevant international factors react to the eventual use of military force?
- What should the Army do with the country if it defended it successfully, i.e. could it be the spiritus movens of the reintegration and functioning of the ruined common state?
- If the defense of SFRY failed, were there any alternative solutions for the JNA and the military commanders, and if so what were they?

In operational terms, at the beginning of 1991 the military commanders did not have a single precisely defined element allowing the use of the Army. First of all, they could not reliably establish whom the Army might have to be used against.[29] The generals still fostered the hope that the bond between the nationalistic elite and the masses was not firm. They counted on the immediate threat of war to bring the misled people to their senses and reduce military intervention to removing the power-holders.[30] Their misjudgments necessarily gave rise to miscalculated tasks and unattainable goals.

These were all signs that after two years of intensive ideological activism, the military commanders were rapidly losing the strategic initiative. Unable to define a single sufficient goal for the use of the JNA, they had condemned the Army to waiting, while letting their future opponents choose the time, place, form and goals of attack. Finding themselves in a reactive position, the military commanders were continually forced to redefine and reduce the list of the JNA's current and future goals and tasks.

This is best shown by constant changes in the strategic goal of the JNA's military and political activities. During the political finale of the crisis, the military commanders went within a short period of time from defending socialist, federal Yugoslavia and protecting its external and internal borders, to preserving peace until a final political solution was reached and preventing interethnic armed conflict, i.e. keeping the opposing sides apart, to finally declaring the protection of military units as the primary task of the JNA.[31]

To make matters even worse for the Army, the generals had failed to undertake sufficient measures to protect their units. Having left them in barracks, after the outbreak of war they were exposed to uninterrupted blockades. At the same time, the secrecy of the JNA's command had been breached and the leadership and public in Slovenia and Croatia had advanced knowledge of every one of the military commanders' important moves. To top it all off, the leading generals did not even manage to take an inventory of the JNA's immediate tasks and choose adequate forms, means and methods to use their units. The pressure of events and their misjudgments constantly forced them to define JNA tasks ad hoc.

There was even greater irony in the fact that no one had even asked the military commanders to defend the state. Furthermore, all the republican leaders made contradictory demands of the Army, each one assigning it a different role depending on their needs. They all called upon constitutional, legal, political and democratic principles which they themselves willfully violated.

Under the guise of depoliticization, Slovenia and Croatia demanded that the Army renounce in advance its constitutional right and obligation to defend the federal state. This could only have been done by the military commanders under the assumption that the republican leaders had already reached an agreement on the peaceful recombination or dissolution of SFRY. In spite of the fact that no agreement had been reached, the leaders of Slovenia and Croatia declared every announced intention by the JNA to carry out its constitutional role an attack on the still nonexistent sovereignty of their states. They gave no consideration whatsoever to the fact that it was their unilateral actions that had started the invalidation of the federal state's sovereignty much earlier.

Under Milošević's leadership, the federalists asked the JNA to act strictly according to the Constitution. They were not disturbed, of course, by the fact that Serbia had already left constitutional proceedings and excluded itself from the federal system. Furthermore, they demanded that the sole remaining federal institution operate in worthy fashion, as though they themselves had not systematically undermined the authority of the federation and worn away its last vestiges of power. The Serbian leaders asked the JNA commanders especially to protect the Serbs outside of Serbia. This meant that the Army would enter directly into conflict with other peoples in SFRY independent of its constitutional role and mixed ethnic composition. With this in mind, the Serbian leaders tried to present the rebellion of Serbian communities in Croatia and B-H as the autonomous response of the local Serbs to the revival of fascism and/or revanchism in these areas. Their main goal was to hide all links between these rebellions and the Greater Serbia plans of Milošević and the regime in Serbia.

In the first half of 1991, the military commanders used rhetorical aggressiveness and numerous initiatives to hide their fundamental hesitation and confusion.[32] The war orientation of the crisis dictated that the generals make a realistic appraisal of the JNA's war capacities and prepare to defend SFRY, but even then they were still not sure whether they should defend the country. Regardless of that fact, in the first months of 1991 the generals undertook feverish political activities along the lines of defending SFRY.

The JNA's military-political position was extremely unfavorable at that moment. The Constitution obliged the Army to defend SFRY's integrity, but its battle readiness had been considerably weakened by the changed relations in political forces. In addition, the military commanders' previous political and police activities had met with failure after failure, and every day brought new paramilitary competition to the JNA. There were even frequent requests in Serbia to form a republican army. The atmosphere had also radically changed in the JNA's social environment. The Army was quickly losing the support and confidence of more and more of the population and was the increasing target of attacks.[33] Assailed by the opposition's criticism of the regime in Serbia, the danger even threatened of JNA losing its last stronghold – Serbia.[34]

The top three generals' activities made the Army's position particularly difficult. They could not, and made no efforts to hide the discrepancy between their alleged legalism and neutralism, and their ideological interests and partiality. In addition, the generals persistently intensified military-propaganda activities modeled after '1941'. It should also be noted that the military's propaganda at the time treated the secession of Slovenia differently from that of Croatia. Until war broke out, the JNA never used the (anti)fascist argument against Slovenia. The military commanders even abandoned their earlier claim that there was a counterrevolution going on in Slovenia. This was owing to the fact that after the Serbo-Croatian conflict took center stage, the Army's interest in Slovenia rapidly declined. From that moment on the military commanders concentrated all their means on proving that fascism and the Ustasha were at work in Croatia.

There were ample reasons for such accusations against Tudjman's regime, particularly from Croats in the diaspora and those after revenge. In the same vein, the JNA's one-sided propaganda can be somewhat explained by the antifascist origin and socialist ideology of its members. The key reason, of course, lay in the fact that the HDZ's policies revived the Serbs' tragic experience with the Ustasha government during World War II. But it was the systematic anti-Croatian propaganda in Serbia that had a crucial impact on the military commanders' opinions. Thus the JNA and its members found themselves caught in the crossfire of extreme Serbian and extreme Croatian nationalism. Much as the fear of neo-Ustashas and renewed genocide caused by Tjuman's regime had driven the Serbs across the Drina River into a compact monolith and made them dependent on Milošević, the Serbs' and the military's propaganda, in conjunction with HDZ maneuvering, had hastened the majority of the Croats to Tudjman's side.[35]

In spite of everything, the military commanders regularly announced they would prevent the crisis from ending in war and the violent breakup of Yugoslavia. The moves they made towards this goal in the first half of 1991 directly testify to the fact that they had no clear plan or coherent strategy; they persistently substituted their lack of knowledge with the JNA's activities within the trite ideological framework.

Kadijević's triumvirate reached its ideological culmination on the eve of war with activity along the SK-PJ line. Although denying any connection with this party, the military commanders could not hide their high ideological and political agreement.[36] This is shown by internal information from the Political Department of SSNO, which was immediately leaked to the public: at the end of January 1991 the generals sent their last call to the servicemen to defend socialist Yugoslavia.[37] They had assigned the SK-PJ and the JNA key roles in this undertaking.

Although the military commanders had not renounced socialist and federal Yugoslavia, they nonetheless had to face the inevitability of its dissolution. The generals thus oriented most of their activity towards the SFRY Presidency, the federal government and the Federal Assembly, frequently submitting their evaluations regarding the military-political and security situation in the country. The measures and activities they proposed to remove the danger were a component part of these evaluations, whose deficiencies stemmed from the fact that the generals measured the pro-war direction of the growing crisis in accordance with their conspiracy theory. Although warning of the danger of civil war, they never seriously looked into its roots and generators. It was easier for the generals to blame external factors for the eventual breakup of Yugoslavia and civil war, particularly since their support for a 'peaceful and democratic' solution to the crisis[38] was objectively rhetorical. This also was true of the generals' belated insistence on legality, in whose name they asked the republican leaders to respect the Constitution, which had long since been rejected and excessively breached.

Although their evaluations of the real possibility of internal warfare were basically correct, results show that the generals did not deduce all the consequences. Above all, they did not undertake necessary military measures that might possibly have prevented an internal war.[39] In addition, the military commanders stubbornly neglected the fact that the collapse of the system had restricted their possibility to operate within the law. The military commanders' insistence on legality went counter to the JNA's proclaimed intentions and goals to use all available means to prevent war, particularly since it was clear that the Army would not receive the support of Slovenia and Croatia in federal institutions in order to save Yugoslavia or prevent war using forceful means. So the Army could only act preventively by breaking the law and the Constitution. By suddenly insisting on legalism, the military commanders excluded from the very outset any possibility of the JNA's independent operations. Waiting to receive permission to act in accordance with the Constitution and laws that no one was respecting anymore, they were actually hiding their indecision.

At the heart of the military's hesitation[40] was prolonged confusion and enigmas with no answer. The commanders were constantly at variance with their desire to have a political impact – take part in solving the fate of a Yugoslavia tailored after federalist concepts – and their inability to clearly define the JNA's role and play it effectively to the end. Thus the generals' search for legal forms for the JNA's activities can be understood as their flight from real problems, as well as a maneuver to obtain an alibi for doing nothing.

The proportions of the generals' confusion at the time is best evidenced by the deficiencies and inconsistencies with which the JNA's greatly touted antiwar actions were carried out. Before undertaking any actions, the generals renamed SSNO and the JNA's General Staff into the Supreme Command Headquarters.[41] This was to emphasize the seriousness of the situation and the need for a radical solution. In addition, acting from the position of Supreme Command, the generals wanted to put more pressure on the SFRY Presidency, republican leaders and the public. In spite of this, the military commanders' influence on the course of events was constantly diminishing. Furthermore, they did not have suitable answers to the quickly changing situation. Halfway measures had become a key characteristic of the generals' actions: not a single task that they themselves prescribed for the JNA was formulated properly or completely carried out.

This is shown by the fate of the SFRY Presidency's Order on the disarming of all paramilitary formations. In addition to reflecting the current relationship of political forces in SFRY, the Order revealed the tactical ideas of the powers in play.[42] At the same time, it depicted the marginal political position of the military commanders and the scope of their (in)ability. The Order specifically revealed the key military-political incompetence of the top JNA generals.

Since SSNO prepared the Order and proposed it to the Presidency, the generals were certain they could carry it out,[43] but the very text of the Order warned that their calculations were wrong and unrealistic. The indication that all formations were to be disarmed 'except those regulated by law and outside SUP (the police)' was broad and imprecise enough.[44] The generals seemed to be suggesting that Slovenia and Croatia should legalize their paramilitary formations as soon as possible, making them part of the republican TO and/or MUP.[45] Both republics, of course, took advantage of this to acquire even more arms and train the core of their future armies.

After the SFRY Presidency adopted the Order, it was still not clear who it actually referred to. Since Slovenia and Croatia had legalized the arming of their paramilitary formations according to local procedures, only illegal groups and individuals were left. With such premises, all Kadijević could do was order the Army to start making raids and house-to-house searches. Had that been the intention of the order writer (SSNO), the use of the Army in a police function could only have followed after a military coup and the immediate immobilization of TO and MUP republican units.

The next questionable moment came when ten days were given to execute the Order. The short deadline drew public attention and amazement at first. The generals wanted to give the impression that the JNA had a clear plan and sufficient strength to carry out the task within that deadline. In such conditions the 48-hour postponement of the deadline at the request of the representative from Croatia seemed like a generous gesture from the side having the upper hand.[46]

However, issuing the Order with a strategic goal that could not be carried out, the military commanders came face to face with the JNA's deficiencies.[47] To make matters worse, by issuing the imprecise and unfeasible Order, the trio of generals played right into Kučan's and Tudjman's hands; they used this opportunity to reinforce the psychosis of collective fear of an approaching military putsch.[48] This in return gave them new justification before the local and foreign public to continue arming and expanding their republican armies.

This Order was just the first of a series of orders and proceedings by the military commanders and the pro-Serb part of the SFRY Presidency that would never be carried out, something which was highly evident the moment of their announcement. The subsequent course of events regarding illegal arms imports is reminiscent of this. It is quite hard to grasp what the military commanders wanted to achieve at the time when they showed a documentary film on TV on illegal arms imports[49] and brought charges against Martin Špegelj,[50] the Croatian minister of defense.

Watching the film, even laymen wondered: if that's what happened why didn't the Army put an immediate stop to arms imports? The generals hid unconvincingly behind the constitutional and legal division of authority between the JNA and SUP. The 'film-up-their-sleeve' would only have made sense had the primary suspect, Špegelj, been arrested along with the group from Osijek. In that case the film could have been used as a media tool to prepare the public for the JNA's radical settlement of accounts with Croatian leaders rebelling against the constitutional order. Under the circumstances, the Army could only act radically if it intended to establish marshal law in the country.

It was clear that the military commanders intended to use the film as an excuse to arrest and try Špegelj and the Osijek group, hoping this would finally destabilize and compromise Tudjman's regime. But neither was Špegelj arrested nor was the Croatian regime undermined. Furthermore, Tudjman was given yet another opportunity to publicly expand the thesis about a conspiracy against Croatia.[51]

Špegelj's trial brought the generals another fiasco,[52] since they had played into the opposition's political-propaganda hands again.[53] The trial would only have made sense under two assumptions: first, if all the accused were arrested, and second, if the JNA had a plan and forces for limited intervention in Croatia in order to depose Tudjman's regime. So the sequence 'Order-film-trial' could only have been effective under the assumption that Kadijević was prepared to execute a military coup. In such a scenario, the military's omnibus could have been part of the public presentation of evidence in favor of the JNA leaders' need to suspend the system and the seceding power-holders.

The military commanders' initial mistakes in both cases clearly indicated their inability to respond properly to the challenges looming ahead. A true picture of the top generals was shown at the March session of the SFRY Presidency in which they proposed the introduction of a state of emergency.[54]

The seemingly autonomous appearance of Supreme Command Headquarters[55] at the session was a watershed in the key generals' prewar attitude towards solving the crisis. With their proposal to introduce a state of emergency, they had resorted to the last move left in the JNA's political arsenal. Asking the SFRY Presidency to adopt their proposal, the military commanders were actually trying to extract permission to use the JNA for an internal war. By linking the JNA's further actions to the Presidency's decision, the generals were simultaneously shifting their responsibility for the Army's previous (in)activity to the Supreme Command.

Events that took place in February and March 1991 gave the military commanders grounds for this move. They had understood foreign support for a united Yugoslavia as tacit agreement to the internal use of the JNA,[56] completely overlooking the fact that the emphasis of the central international power-holders had been on support for a democratic Yugoslavia. The generals found additional reasons in the unsuccessful disarmament in Slovenia and Croatia, and in Špegelj's failed trial. They thus concluded that partial interventions by the JNA could not stop the dissolution of Yugoslavia.

The generals' direct, constitutional justification for a state of emergency was the SFRY Presidency's majority decision in which all acts on disjoining were declared invalid. In addition, the military commanders were short of time, since Slovenia and Croatia were already finishing the formation of the core of their republican armies – the JNA's future enemies in battle. The armed incident in Pakrac clearly indicated the substance and proportions of the future Serbo-Croatian war. When tanks hit the streets of Belgrade on March 9, 1991, it was a crucial moment for the military commanders, since all previous, deeper reasons could have been used earlier as a reason to demand that a state of emergency be declared, or introduce it themselves.

Although the appearance of JNA tanks in the streets of Belgrade was covered by a request from the Serbian leadership and a decision by the SFRY Presidency,[57] there were multiple meanings behind that move. Responding at the critical moment, the military commanders stabilized the Serbian regime.[58] This also sent a signal to both Slovenia and Croatia that force would be used in other republics to protect the constitutional order. In addition, by intervening in Serbia, the generals wanted to show the JNA's national (ethnic) neutrality. But they couldn't hide their ideological and political bias;[59] with the preservation of Slobodan Milošević's regime, the military commanders wanted to keep a key prerequisite and crucial force to defend Yugoslavia and socialism within it, in accordance with their views of the crisis, and the JNA's needs. The generals' 'success' with the Belgrade intervention also encouraged them to use the same model throughout the country.

The generals' use of tanks had in fact bucked up their courage, giving them the needed self-confidence for radical action. But even though they had the direct support of Serbia's representative at the Presidency[60] session, the generals were unable to play out their hand properly.

This is eloquently shown by the subsequently published[61] list of measures proposed by General Veljko Kadijević in the name of the Armed Forces and Supreme Command Headquarters. An analysis of the measures clearly confirms the conceptual confusion and operational understatement of Headquarters at the time. The generals first demanded the introduction of 'a state of emergency throughout all of SFRY and the suspension of all acts contrary to the SFRY Constitution and federal laws'. This was a strike against the consequences and not the causes and mainstays of the problem. The generals failed to demand the suspension of the systems and all federal and republican power-holders who had passed these unconstitutional acts.

The generals' logical inconsistency is directly confirmed by the contents of the fourth and fifth items. In the fourth, the generals demanded that after the introduction of a state of emergency, political discussions be urgently continued 'on the future organization of Yugoslavia, while in the republics whose leadership are in favor of secession, a referendum should be organized at which every people (ethnic group) would be offered the possibility to directly and freely express their views, without any dictates and outvoting'. The Supreme Command's proposal did not indicate who would represent the republics in the continuation of negotiations. The generals had completely overlooked the fact that a state of emergency would not be necessary were the current leaders capable of reaching an agreement. Therefore, the military commanders should have demanded the suspension of all national-republican leaders, having previously worked out who would choose (determine) the new and legitimate negotiators from the republics and peoples, and how. In the same vein, the proposal to hold a new referendum in the republics required the generals to invalidate those that had already been held, in which the two republics joining forces to break up Yugoslavia had already received plebiscitary support.

Convinced of the validity of their plan, the generals then (item five) planned that 'following the will of the people shown at the referendum'... 'a new Constitution of the Yugoslav state should be adopted, multiparty elections should be organized and new government bodies constituted as soon as possible, and no later than six months'. The military commanders' initial wrong assumption was that right after a state of emergency was declared, the people would want to return to Yugoslavia, and all that was needed was a new constitution. The generals avoided facing the fact that most people, guided by their leaders, had already reached the point of rejecting Yugoslavia; it was thus more realistic that they would forcibly resist the JNA's attempts to renew the common state by means of a state of emergency.

The degree of ineptitude contained in the scenario, technology and scope of the state of emergency is shown by the other two items on the generals' proposal. They were intended to raise the 'battle readiness of the Armed Forces, including the mobilization of part of the units to a level which, in the Supreme Command's judgment, guarantees the prevention of civil war' (item 2) and 'to urgently return the disturbed system of the country's defense within the constitutional framework', along with disarming illegally armed formations, etc. (item 3). Anyone with an ounce of elementary logic must have wondered how the Army could introduce a state of emergency if it counted on reaching needed battle readiness only after the introduction of such a state. It turned out that the Supreme Command was asking for a state of emergency in order to stabilize the JNA, which meant that it did not have military and police capacities ready and able to carry out the proposed tasks.

This is probably a unique case in recent political history in which military commanders asked for authorization to introduce a state of emergency from a state body which, by the logic of a putsch, would have to first descend from power. Or, that an army abandoned the idea of internal intervention because political support was lacking from the leaders of the country. It was understandable for the generals to want their coup to be politically legal and legitimate. But it was incomprehensible for them to abandon it when they were denied support, particularly since they should have counted on this in advance – the balance of power in the Presidency clearly indicated that the generals' proposal would be turned down.

If the generals had counted on the vote of Bogić Bogičević, the Serbian representative of B-H in the Presidency, as the deciding fifth, they should not have tied their whole plan to him, particularly since they had concluded that it was the last minute to prevent the internal war looming overhead. Along with all the rest, the infantilism of the generals' attempt certainly indicated their insecurity. They didn't seem to know how to calculate the feasibility of their plan, and their fear of failure and unpredictable consequences stopped them at the last moment.

This is shown by the fact that during a break in the session, on March 13, General Kadijević flew to Moscow to see if he could get political and military support. This move clearly indicated the ideological blinders and limitations of the key generals at the time. Going to the wrong 'church' showed that the generals had both miscalculated and failed to acknowledge the new configuration of power in the international community. To top it all off, the JNA leaders had lost sight of the fact that the USSR and the Red Army were too preoccupied with their own problems at the time; even had they wanted, they could not satisfy Kadijević's request. Therefore, the generals' later explanation for giving up on the coup, because they did not have a 'strong foreign power behind them', neglected the notorious fact that they had sought support from the wrong side. It is a matter of speculation as to whether they would have received support from the West at the time, but it seems they did not even ask for it.

After the SFRY Presidency turned them down, the generals took it upon themselves to release the JNA from further responsibility for the fate of the country and its inhabitants. In accordance with this, they wrote a letter to the Presidency in which they dissociated themselves from the further course of the crisis and the multiplication of paramilitary formations. From that moment on, the JNA commanders became visibly disengaged and turned into observers of current events. Although JNA units took part in separating the conflicting Serbs and Croats during their preparatory stage for war, all in all the JNA's sphere of activity had been reduced to local and partial intervention. The generals reacted with derision[62] to the accelerated development of Slovenian and Croatian armies. Not even that was enough to warn them that they could no longer count on the complete peacetime composition, let alone wartime, of the JNA.[63]

After a series of Croatio-Serbian conflicts and increasing pressure on the JNA, in May 1991 the military commanders renewed their request to the Presidency to introduce a state of emergency. The text of the request and proposed measures clearly indicated lack of enthusiasm among the top generals, giving the impression they were doing it against their will. It seemed to be one more attempt by the JNA commanders to cover and excuse the failure of their policies. Therefore, the Presidency's measures to resolve interethnic conflicts in the Republic of Croatia,[64] that committed the Army, were left dead letters.

Right then, the generals seemed to be solving their internal dilemma about whether to defend Yugoslavia, and if so then how much. Of course, they did not officially deny for a moment their readiness to use the JNA for this purpose. However, the later course of events confirms that during this interval the generals came to a crucial decision for Yugoslavia and the JNA – they internally abandoned defending the state at any price.[65] Announcing that they would accept any solution reached by the republican leaders, the generals objectively gave up their federalist and constitutional position. This might have been interpreted as an expression of the generals' political realism and their agreement to a passive role for the JNA. But since there were no prospects of the republican leaders reaching a compromise, the military commanders were compelled to have an alternative solution to such a situation. And all the alternatives at that moment could be reduced to one single one – preventing internal war.

Notes

1 Tudjman's and Kučan's initiative was accepted by Gligorov and Izetbegović; at an expanded meeting of the SFRY Presidency, with the agreement of Milošević and Bulatović, the dynamics of negotiations was established – six meetings, one in each of the republics (Borba, 22.03.1991, 2).

2 In February, with adoption of amendment 99 to the republican constitution and the Resolution on the agreement to dissociate from SFRY, the Slovenian Assembly confirmed their decision to create an independent state. The Croatian Assembly immediately joined them with passage of the Resolution on protecting the constitutional order and the Resolution on dissociation (Borba, 22.02.1991, 1, 3, 15).

3 'As far as we are concerned, peoples (major ethnic groups) that want to leave Yugoslavia can do so, but in a legal manner and without violence (…) The question of the survival or dissolution of Yugoslavia as a joint state is the essence of all disagreements in discussions to date. All the disagreements can be reduced to that question (…) I feel the preservation of Yugoslavia is in our vital interest and that Serbia should use all means available to help all those throughout Yugoslavia who want to preserve it, to actualize that interest.' S. Milošević, address before the Serbian Assembly (Borba, 31.05.1991, 5),

4 'It is in Macedonia's interests to preserve Yugoslavia as a whole with the equal status of all its republics, providing equal conditions for a life together. It is not acceptable for Macedonia, however, to live in a reduced federation, because Yugoslavia's equality of interests and relations were established over a long period of time.' Kiro Gligorov.(Borba, 15.02.1991, 5).

5 The separation of 27 Serbian municipalities was the first step towards this, which the B-H government tried to annul with its Decision; more details: (Borba, 14.05.1991, 13.)

6   The attempt to adopt the 'Declaration on the sovereignty of the state and indivisibility of the Republic of B-H' led to conflict between SDA and SDS in the B-H Assembly; SDS rejected the Declaration in the name of protecting the Serbs' equal footing with regard to the Muslim-Croat majority, and because it opposed the Serbs' desire to live in a federal Yugoslavia (Borba, 15.02.1991, 6).

7   The Serbian Assembly refused to support the decision of SAO Krajina to unite with Serbia until the final outcome of negotiations on the federation (Borba, 23.04.1991, 9).

8   The Platform gave genuine subjectivity to the republics, and the Community was to be an international-legal subject; the Community would have uniform monetary, banking, foreign exchange, trade, customs and foreign credit relations, and joint defense (Borba, 04.06.1991, 10).

9   The government and the opposition in all the republics had the same opinion with regard to this dilemma; this is illustrated by a statement by Vuk Drašković, the leader of SPO: 'Should Croatia and Slovenia secede, the plan is clear: We will occupy our western borders and create a sovereign Serbian state. Whether or not there is a Yugoslavia – there will be a Serbia, democratic and very strong.' (Borba, 21.06.1991, 11).

10 The leaders of Slovenia and Croatia excelled at this; F. Tudjman made frequent visits to friendly countries (Austria, Germany) and sent a letter to George Bush, president of the US, in which he asked for intervention (Borba, 01.02.1991, 7), which led the federal prosecutor to undertake criminal proceedings against him (Borba, 02-03.03.1991, 12).

11 Thus Western Germany, in spite of a document from the Bundestag and repeated support for an integral Yugoslavia, although in a form that favored its disintegration (compare: Draft resolution by the Bundestag on the crisis in Yugoslavia, Borba, 18.06.1991, 15), heartily – politically, diplomatically, propaganda-wise and materially – helped Slovenia and Croatia achieve sovereignty; In the same tone, after Tudjman visited Vienna, 'Austria's determination to help Croatia in the democratic resolution of the political crisis in Yugoslavia' was emphasized. (Borba, 31.01.1991, 3).

12 This was a proposal by Alija Izetbegović presented at a meeting of the SFRY Presidency in Sarajevo on an asymmetrical federation (Borba, 23.02.1991, 1).

13 This was explicitly said in a Communiqué from the representatives of Serbian opposition parties, associations and independent intellectuals.: 'The Serbian people has been faced with a dilemma for decades: YUGOSLAV national feelings, for which it has sacrificed all its battles and all its victories, accompanied by human cataclysms, or UNITED SERBIAN national feelings.' (Borba, 31.01.1991, 4).

14 See: the statement by General Marko Negovanović, Deputy Minister of Defense (Narodna Armija, 06.07.1991, 9).

15 The first attempt of this type was made by P. Tošić, former SIV spokesman, in his book 'Kako sam branio Antu Marrkovića' (How I Defended Ante Marković), published as a feuilleton in 'Borba' with the same name during October 1993.
16 The SIV proposal with 11 items (Borba, 16.01.1991, 1 and 3); for this purpose the government proposed the adoption of 15 laws and proposals to supplement the laws; for details: (Narodna armija, 21.02.1991, 17.)
17 'The SIV considers that the construction of a new economic, state and political system provides an opportunity to establish the nature and substance of relations in the Yugoslav community on new democratic grounds. It is in the interest of all the citizens, major and minor ethnic groups and republics for Yugoslavia to be defined as a community of sovereign republics as states, organized in accordance with modern and democratic achievements in Europe and the world.' (Borba, 22-23.06.1991, 3-4).
18 On June 26/27 the SIV passed a Decision in which it allowed, in conjunction with SUP and SSNO, the commitment of 'border JNA units to defend the state borders'. The view that 'the manner in which the cooperation from paragraph 1 of this item is carried out will be established by mutual agreement between the minister of internal affairs and the minister of defense', allowed them to choose the form and means for operations. At the same time, SIV's Order (item 1) prohibited the 'establishment of so-called border crossings within the SFRY territory', and ordered SSUP and SSNO to take care of it; compare: SIV Decision, VPI, special edition, August 1991, 90-91.
19 Thus DEMOS leader J. Pučnik judged that the greatest danger to Slovenia's goals came from the SIV and A. Marković (Borba, 09.04.1991, 8); Tudjman even ascribed Yugoslav integralism to the government, but he supported the economic reform program for political reasons, even though Croatia suffered economic damage for that reason; speech at a formal meeting of the Croatian Assembly (Borba, 31.05.1991, 6-7).
20 The incident in Pakrac (Borba, 04.03.1991) was an introduction to conflicts in Plitvice (01.04.1991) which were followed by the prelude to war in Borovo Selo (03.05.1991).
21 This did not hinder the Albanians' political leaders from politically rounding out their program; with formation of the Democratic Council of Kosovo they legitimized their demands for Kosovo as an (independent) republic; details: (Borba, 06.05.1991, 2.)
22 In March the government of Slovenia sent the Draft Law on defense and protection into the adoption procedure, which defined TO as an exclusively republican armed force in which its citizens would serve their military service under oath to Slovenia (Borba, 01.03.1991, 3); immediately afterwards a

constitutional Law was passed that introduced a moratorium on Slovene recruits serving in the JNA (Borba, 07.03.1991, 1).

23 Tudjman admitted this at a rally in Zagreb, announcing: 'We have not prepared an armed uprising against the JNA, but have armed ourselves in order to defend the constitutional order (in Croatia – M.H.)' (Borba, 25.03.1991, 8).

24 The blockade of barracks in Osijek, Gospić, Maribor and other places reached a peak with demonstrations in front of the VPO Command in Split at which time a soldier was killed (Borba, 07.05.1991, 3); Tudjman indirectly gave the initiative for this in Trogir, asking of the population: 'Why haven't you gone to demonstrate before the VPO Command, so the world can see that this is not just a battle among the leaders, but of the entire people.' (Borba, 06.07.1991, 5).

25 The JNA intervention in Borovo Selo was judged the beginning of 'open warfare against the Republic of Croatia (...) We have been faced by engineered events that began the first days after the democratic government was established in Croatia; through dogmatic, communistic elements in the Army itself and around it and through the mobilization of Greater Serbia imperialistic circles, it is endeavoring to knock down the democratic government in Croatia and establish a Serboslavia or Greater Serbia.' F. Tudjman (Borba, 04-05.05, 1991, 2).

26 Furthermore, the Declaration of the National Assembly of Serbia asked the SFRY Presidency and Supreme Command Headquarters to 'not allow interethnic armed conflicts and civil war in Yugoslavia (item 3)' and 'commit the Yugoslav National Army, in accordance with its constitutional function, in SAO Krajina, Slavonja, Baranja, Western Srem and all the places where Serbs live, until a political agreement is reached to solve the situation that has arisen.' (item 9) (Borba, 03.04.1991, 5); The Croatian Assembly replied with a Declaration of its own (Borba, 17.04.1991, 2).

27 With a proposal on the principle to settle the rights and obligations between the Republic of Slovenia and the federation (item B., paragraph 1), Slovenia offered to take over the JNA facilities and equipment gradually to the end of 1993. In addition (item D., paragraph 2)., Slovenia took on the obligation of paying a contribution for the federal bodies and the JNA to the extent to which they undertook operations for its needs (Borba, 13.05.1991, 12).

28 'When making most main military-political strategic decisions, not even the general corps took part directly, rather just the very top with a few people, in particular the Staff of the Minister of Defense or even just the top of that body.' Djordje Stanić, retired general: Istine i zablude o ulozi Armije u jugoslovenskom gradjanskom ratu, Vojno delo no. 6/92, 7.

29 Strategic documents did not help at all, since they were based on two erroneous premises: first, that the great majority of the population would

defend the constitutional order (socialist self-management), and second, that the internal forces of the special war were marginal, and even with the help of foreign centers could not seriously endanger the security of Yugoslavia and the socialist regime; compare: Strategija ONO i DSZ SFRY, SSNO, Belgrade, 1987, 30, and Strategija oružane borbe, SSNO, Belgrade, 1983, 24, 74, etc.

30 At the meeting of the Federal Assembly's National Defense Council Admiral Brovet announced 'if the situation and development of events get out of control, the JNA will not go against the people, but against those who are preparing, organizing and provoking conflicts and are leading the Yugoslav people into civil war and bloodshed.' (Narodna armija, 16.05.1991, 13).

31 In a message dated May 7, 1991, General Kadijević warned the SFRY Presidency that since civil war had already started and the way JNA units had been used to date had not been effective, that 'Supreme Command Headquarters will not allow for the extremist behavior of the conflicting sides to refract through the JNA' and 'the Army will respond to every attack on its members, units and facilities (...) according to the rules of battle, which means using fire'; compare: Views of Supreme Command Headquarters, VPI 6/91, 14.

32 An interesting analysis of the contradictory position of the JNA at the time was made by Zoran Djindjić in the text 'Igra staklenih mišića' (The dance/game of glass muscles) (Borba, 16-17.02.1991, 2).

33 This is confirmed by the blockade of motorized JNA units near Lištica (May 7) that was only removed after a helicopter landing (May 9); details: (Narodna armija, 16.05.1991, 12.)

34 An illustration is the statement by V. Drašković that 'our people have not had a Serbian army for seven decades, since 1918 (...) This army now (the JNA – M.H.) is not a Serbian army' (Borba, 06.03.1991).

35 This is shown by Ivica Račan, leader of the former communists after the Croatian MUP attacked Borovo Selo and intervention by the JNA, or local resistance that he considered terrorism 'that is at work in Croatia. As far as we in Croatia are concerned, we resolutely express the view that we are using all democratic and political means to oppose aggression against Croatia and its territorial integrity, including, if nothing else works, organized armed resistance.' (Borba, 04-05.1991, 7).

36 The executive board of SK-PJ felt that 'Yugoslavia was not created at the negotiating table and it will not be torn apart at that table either', actually just repeating the earlier claim (threat) by the Army's commanders (Borba, 26.02.1991, 5).

37 The accuracy of the information, published by HINA (Croatian News Agency) and carried by Borba (31.01.1991, 4) was never disputed. Owing to sharp reactions from Slovenia and Croatia, the SFRY Presidency 'concluded

that this is information from one of the SSNO bodies, and not a command decision that would have the strength of an order for its members', thereby indirectly confirming the authenticity of the text (Borba, 07.02.1991, 1).

38 'Starting from the fact that any act that negates the existence of Yugoslavia and questions its borders is unacceptable for the JNA, the Army, acting in accordance with its views has undertaken numerous measures in order to protect the integrity of SFRY, prevent interethnic armed conflict and civil war and assure the conditions for a peaceful and democratic agreement on the future organization of the country.(' SSNO communiqué, 28.04.1991, in: VPI 6/91, 7.)

39 Indeed, at some moments (when the Order on Disarmament was issued during conflicts in Pakrac, Plitvice and Borovo Selo, after the attack on the RM Command in Split) the Army or its parts were put in a state of heightened battle alert that was always rescinded after political guarantees were given by Croatian or federal authorities; the movements of JNA units were registered in the public and always served the Slovenian and Croatian authorities as opportunities to accuse the Army; compare: Protest by the Croatian Government to SSNO owing to unannounced activities by military units (Borba, 06-07.04.1991, 3).

40 The top generals later justified their indecision by the fact that the state had abandoned them, while the second level generals found the reasons in V. Kadijević's indecisiveness; both one and the other claim that the JNA was capable of executing all assignments; an interview with General Aleksandar Vasiljević also shows this, (NIN, 19.06.1992, 65.)

41 Owing to numerous disputes, colonels M. Starčević ('Interpretation with premeditation') and B. Todorović ('Trying to contest the uncontestable') tried to prove the legal basis for turning SSNO into the Supreme Command Headquarters; see: ('Narodna armija', 28.03.1991, 6-8.)

42 The Croatian side interpreted the Order from the beginning in a manner that suited its needs, so the Council for National Defense and Protection judged that 'an order that gives such authority to the JNA and turns the army into a police force could be misused to suspend and even disturb the legally established institutions of a democratic government (...) The Council underscores that there are no illegally armed groups in the Republic of Croatia except in the Knin area (and) resolutely warns that the Republic of Croatia will use all available means to oppose every attempt by the Army to interfere in the operations of the constitutional-legal authority of MUP Croatia.' (Borba, 11.01.1991, 2).

43 Admiral Brovet persistently claimed even after the JNA's complete failure to disarm them: 'The Order from the SFRY Presidency is in force and we will carry it out, since we are obliged to because no one has made it inoperative.' (Narodna armija, 21.02.1991, 5).

44 Thus Janez Janša judged that after the deadline for disarmament expired 'nothing will happen since neither the Presidency nor the JNA can define which are the paramilitary forces', while M. Brezak, deputy minister in the Croatian government, maintained that 'except for active and reserve forces in MUP RH and except for armed JNA forces, there are no other armed forces in the Republic. The only illegally formed armed groups and individuals in Croatia are in Knin and all other places where the police stations of this ministry were robbed.' (Borba, 19-20.01.1991, 15).

45 SSNO claimed that rapid transformation of illegally armed HDZ members into MUP reserves in just the 48-hour extension to carrying out the Order had increased the number of reserve militia from 13,371 to 31,229 members, making the total number in MUP 50,000 men; according to: (VPI 4/91, 21.)

46 At the request of the Croats, the SFRY Presidency extended the deadline for executing the Order by 48 hours, until 24:00 on January 21 (Borba, 21.01.1991, 1).

47 Therefore SNNO merely informed the Presidency that the Order had only been partially carried out, and that 'the chance had been missed to disarm illegally armed groups with the application of abolition, i.e. without directly involving judicial bodies, based on the law.' (Borba, 23.01.1991, 1).

48 Thus HINA and 'Vjesnik' published the scenario of an alleged military coup, which led to a campaign to collect signatures for an 'Appeal for Peace', which was then sent to the Presidency and V. Kadijević (Borba, 21.01.1991, 5).

49 The film was shown on 25.01.1991, only on the JRT network; for the broader context and SSNO's data on arms imports, see: Supplemental information on the unauthorized formation of armed groups in SFRY, (VPI, 3/91, 19-24.)

50 The text of the indictment is in (VPI 4/91, 16-25.)

51 Commenting on SSNO's security evaluation of the situation after the disarmament failure, Tudjman maintained that this was proof that the JNA had been turned into 'a strictly anti-Croat military power' (Borba, 26-27.01.1991, 11).

52 The Croatian Assembly urgently passed the Law on Immunity that covered members of the government, so Špegelj, from the viewpoint of Croatian legislation, was outside the legal arm of federal bodies and the JNA (Borba, 21.02.1991, 5).

53 Huge demonstrations in front of the courthouse in Zagreb prevented the trial from taking place (Borba, 08.04.1991, 2) then it was continued without the presence of the main defendant (Borba, 19.04.1991, 8).

54 For basic data on the session and the reaction of some participants, see: (Borba, 14.03.1991, 16-17.)

55 This is also shown by B. Jović's statement that the Presidency session, which was to be held immediately, was called 'at the request of the Minister of

Defense'; compare: statement by B. Jović to Tanjug, 12.03. at 13:30, ('Narodna armija', 14.03.1991, 11.)

56 The military commanders had overlooked the fact that the West's support of Yugoslavia had always emphasized a democratic solution to the crisis which, owing to their indecision, was used by the separatists as routine cover for unilateral acts; but, for example, the statement by J. Delors on the US-EC summit ('It is in our interests to help Yugoslavia preserve its unity, but the form of that unity is exclusively the responsibility of Yugoslavia'; according to: Borba, 13-14.04.1991, 9), might also be interpreted as tacit support for the violent resolution of the problem in the name of the state's unity.

57 Compare: (Borba, 11-03.03.1991, 1.)

58 In the spirit of the 'conspiracy theory', at the SIV session Admiral Brovet justified the Army's intervention as preventing the application of the 'Chilean model' in Serbia and Yugoslavia (Borba, 16.03.1991, 7).

59 This is shown by V. Kadijević's subsequently published key argument against the military coup: 'Intimations spread by various semi-intelligence channels that the West, under certain circumstances, would support JNA intervention in order to save Yugoslavia, was always primarily intended to bring down the Serbian leadership with Milošević at the head', in: ('Moje vidjenje raspada' My View of the Disintegration, Politika, 1993, 88-89.)

60 The session was to last only one day (March 12) but the lack of agreement spurred Kadijević to go to Moscow on March 13 in conjunction with the Serbian side; after asking 'the Supreme Command Headquarters of the SFRY Armed Forces to consider the situation during the next day and establish what they feel should be proposed, or undertaken in the arising situation', Jović scheduled 'a new session of the Supreme Command of the Armed Forces for Thursday, the 14th of this month'; according to: ('Narodna armija', 14.03.1991, 11.)

61 For the complete measures proposed, see: (Narodna armija, 05.10.1991, 5;) all the citations of the Measures are from this source.

62 With adoption of the Law on Internal Affairs, the Croatian Assembly formed within MUP an Assembly of the National Guard that was a 'professional, uniformed, armed formation with a military structure', whose command was under the authority of the republican minister of defense (Borba, 19.04.1991, 5), then in June the Law on Defense established the Croatian Armed Forces, consisting of the Croatian Army and the Assembly of the National Guard, under the supreme command of the President of the Republic (Borba, 22-23.06.1991, 7).

63 F. Tudjman warned of this through the Viennese 'Courier', noting that 'on the first day of any possible conflict between the regular army and TO in the northern republics, 90% of the Slovene and Croat soldiers will desert.' (Borba, 24.01.1991, 5).

64 For a list of the measures from May 8, see: (VPI 6/91, 15-16.)
65 All of this had to have an impact on the general corps, so SNNO made a special communiqué denying the rumors of alleged disunity among the military commanders, i.e. showed their monolithic status; compare: (SSNO Communiqué dated May 6, 1991, VPI 6/91, 11.)

Chapter 4

The Destruction of Yugoslavia by Common Consent

The armed settlement of various accounts – from historical to individual – began at the end of June 1991. In terms of the participants' intentions, it was meant to be final. This gave the Yugoslav war a different structure from the outset; republics and peoples belonging to the same federal state were at war with each other. The Army wandered destructively about the battlefields, searching for a worthy goal and justification. It fought against some (Slovenia and Croatia) for the benefit of others (the federation and Serbia), who did not even officially enter the war, which was undeclared in any case. The generals justified their use of the JNA in the war by their alleged intention to save Yugoslavia and preserve peace until the 'democratic resolution' of the country's fate.

In June 1991, all those who believed[1] in the patriotic-liberation mission of their national (ethnic) leaders set out against each other. Those who had nowhere to escape to and nothing to take with them could not avoid the war, either. Using cannons to prove the exigency of interethnic war, the necessary belligerence was quickly produced, since one had to kill in order to survive. This is why former neighbors and relatives became mortal enemies: the war was a family affair, a backyard quarrel and neighborhood skirmish. Moreover, only then could it grow into an all-out war, for there are no ties that cannot be broken by bombs.

The participants had an unequal share in preparing for war, thus their war accounts were also unequal. What they had in common was that war brought the harvest of the fruits of their previous (in)activity. The destructive consequences of their previous actions caught up with them, literally and metaphorically. Although we already know the preliminary estimates of the war, the final balance still cannot be drawn up even ten years later.

The degree of (self)destructiveness shown on all levels of decision making about the war, and warfare itself, exceeded the darkest forecasts.

The second Yugoslavia and its citizens had been (self)destructing thoroughly and systematically for years with the full participation of the JNA and/or its republican offshoots. So we must continue searching for answers to the questions as to how and why this happened and whether it really had to happen.

The scope of our knowledge continues to be restricted by the insufficient reliability of available facts about the phased end of the war. The only thing that can be established today without any greater error is the chronological sequence of the main events. Their causal links, short-term and long-term consequences, etc., are still outside the grasp of any serious inspection. The lack of reliable facts hinders an analysis of the wartime activities of individual participants, and thereby the reconstruction of their military-political tactics and particularly their strategies, since sufficient proof still does not exist that a single one of the local participants had previously elaborated a comprehensive strategy.

The direct inclusion of the European-Atlantic community into the Southern Slav war[2] brought a multitude of new – individual and collective – entities into the game. Their reasons for intervening could not be discerned at once or fully understood. In spite of this, what resulted was the tendency for a rise in external interference to bring a drop in ultimate (territorial) results depending on the actions of local warlords.[3] There was a commensurate rise in the chances that representatives of the international community, owing to the ineffectiveness of their confused strategy, would nonetheless recognize positions reached during warfare.[4] This is clearly what the ethnic leaders counted on, and so in June 1991 they all bet on their war cards.

Since an examination and interpretation of the numerous dimensions of the Yugoslav wars exceed the scope of this analysis, our attention will be directed to the course of the JNA's war operations. A brief review of the strategies of the other participants will indicate the context in which the destruction of the common state was carried out by common consent.

On the eve of war, the 'Slovenian-Croatian' and 'military-Serbian' coalitions received their final profiles. Then they started fighting each other to redistribute the territory, power, resources and national souls of their subjects. During that time a radical change took place in the military-Serbian alliance, crumbling the JNA, and the generals became irrevocably subservient to the Serbian political center.[5] This was followed by a behind-the-scenes battle among the generals for the internal redistribution of power in the Army, the results of which were only visible at the beginning of 1992.[6]

In June 1991 the conflicting parties started to fight each other from unequal strategic and operational positions. A cursory evaluation of who had the best chance of winning did not favor the coalition of the northern republics. The JNA and the Serbian federalists nominally had weapons of better quality and quantity, greater numbers and better trained soldiers. At that time their victory seemed only a matter of technically carrying it out. What the Serbian-military coalition had overlooked, however, was the fact that Slovenia and Croatia had gained the advantage owing to a combination of internal and international circumstances, and their own skill:

- They both had a precise and announced military-political goal – attaining state and national sovereignty – and were able to concentrate all their forces and capacities on carrying it out.
- Previous consolidation of the masses into a monolithic, fanatic whole had brought them to the point where they were ready to sacrifice in the name of state goals and a (one) nation future.
- Both had already acquired strong international allies who only needed to be given convincing arguments in order to publicly come out on their side.[7] The only way Kučan and Tudjman could get these arguments was by 'drawing' the JNA and its Serbian mentors into war.
- The leaders of both republics had thoroughly studied their adversary – the JNA – and kept it under constant surveillance.[8] Then they chose the proper war tactic. Carrying out a variety of operations, they constantly exhausted the JNA psychologically and militarily. During that time Kučan and Tudjman, with the mediation of external meddlers, drew the military commanders into truces and negotiations, and thus kept them in a state of prolonged, severe provocation. This did away with the commanders' last bit of rationality and they constantly got caught by their opponents' stratagems, under the illusion that the Army was dictating the tempo.
- Slovenia and Croatia had made a far better evaluation of their position with regard to the national and political constellation in Yugoslavia. They made the maximum use of the military commanders' real fear of an early opening of the central (B-H) and southern (Kosovo-Macedonia) fronts. With the timely blockade of Army units, they prevented the JNA from regrouping operationally and tactically. Their successful defense also encouraged and facilitated B-H and Macedonia's departure from Yugoslavia. The political leadership of the Albanians took advantage of the changed relations and Serbia's preoccupation elsewhere to define

the concept of a sovereign Kosovo and establish parallel political institutions.[9]

The dynamics of warfare and its results indicated that the generals and Serbian leaders had not done a proper job of parrying the secessionists' strategy. Convinced of their military superiority, they underestimated Slovenia's and Croatia's battle potential, and did not even try to figure out the enemy's plans in advance. On top of everything, Serbia's leadership had alternative state and territorial goals,[10] and no price seemed too high to pay for them; they internally calculated on this being paid by the JNA members and the Serbs west of the Drina River, who were already prepared for war.

In spite of all this, it is not easy to establish how and why the JNA entered the war, or whether, as its generals constantly claimed, it had been drawn into war against its will.[11] We must first confirm whether the military commanders could have and wanted to stay out of the war. Only then can we deal with the question as to why the JNA allowed itself to be drawn into war, in a manner that least suited it.[12]

Available data partially support the generals' claim that the JNA was drawn into war. There are serious indications that Slovenia and Croatia, with external assistance, had judged that drawing the JNA into war would create all the necessary conditions to finally do away with Yugoslavia.[13] The only thing they could do, however, was induce the Army to fight on their territories, since they did not have sufficient forces at the time to transfer the war to Serbia. Then all they could do, with the help of the military-Serbian coalition, was to shift the war to B-H. This means that Kučan and Tudjman's strategy to attain independent states by means of war had consciously counted on human and material sacrifices. The main gain they expected was to receive international recognition of Slovenia's and Croatia's statehood. They expected additional gain from the international sanctions against the war-provocateur activities of the JNA and its Serbian patrons.

It is therefore instructive to follow the main course of Yugoslavia's destruction in the flames of war. The war's initial point was Slovenia's decision to leave Yugoslavia.[14] Croatia followed directly in its footsteps, as had been announced.[15] Then by decision of the federal government, the JNA and the federal police were authorized to reestablish order on Yugoslavia's western borders, i.e. to preserve its territorial integrity.

The differences in their duration, forces used, destructive effects and results necessitate relatively separate analyses of the Slovenian 'prelude to war' and the Croato-Serbian war.

4.1 War by Arrangement

The week-long exchange of fire in Slovenia clearly indicated that the JNA and Yugoslavia were destined to go to war. Both sides presented a simulation model of the successful end to an unsuccessful state and a loser Army.[16]

The Slovenian war lacked the emotions and fury needed to justify the epithet of being 'Balkan'. The Slovenian side did indeed have the necessary dose of national-liberation euphoria, but they were missing the Yugoslav (Serbian) companion piece. There was also no historical-traumatic grounds for a bloody substrate. The Serbs' disappointment in the Slovenes' egoism during the political conclusion of the crisis was not enough to generate the needed belligerent and/or avenging spirit among the Serbs. Thus, after leaving Slovenia, only the top JNA generals were outraged and surprised at the behavior of the Slovenian units and fighters.[17]

The armed part of the Slovenian story ended in just about seven days. Pressured by a trio of ministers from the European Community, a truce was called immediately and Slovenia's independence was suspended for three months.[18] The Brioni Declaration returned control of the border crossings to the authority of the Slovenian police.[19] It took less than one month to end Slovenia's seventy years in Yugoslavia. At the proposal of the Supreme Command, the SFRY Presidency passed a decision to withdraw the JNA from Slovenia.[20] This was an acknowledgement of the current state of affairs and Slovenia was allowed to leave Yugoslavia.

By offering armed resistance to the 'customs expedition', Slovenia had taken a great risk, exposing itself to the potentially destructive forces of the JNA and its military commanders.[21] This was not, however, simply bravery on the part of the Slovenian leadership; they chose the right moment to achieve the central goal of forming their own state.

The decision to take the risk was facilitated by hidden external guarantees that should the JNA and/or the federal state used any 'aggression', Slovenia would receive full political support.[22] The risk was likewise decreased by the simultaneous inclusion of Croatia in the war.[23] Above all, Slovenia's leadership could count on the readiness of its population to offer all-out armed resistance to the Army. In addition, without much margin for error, their tactics could count on the JNA's evident military-political weakness.

Slovenia's 'war' tactics were quite simple, but well elaborated and prepared in detail. At the first sign of movement by the JNA columns, a synchronous and universal blockade of the territory was initiated. All the roads and barracks were immediately blocked, and servicemen's families were blocked in their residences. The columns were exposed to fire and the blockaded units and families to psycho-physical torture.

The key effects of Slovenia's offensive defense were nonetheless achieved with total and skillful propaganda.[24] All means with a propaganda-psychological impact were used against the JNA. At the same time, a general international campaign was initiated against the JNA and Serbia with the support of the Austrian and German media.

To add insult to injury, Slovenia won the 'war' by relying on the concept of ONO, while the JNA lost relying on the same concept. Cynics might say that this was the first successful verification of KONO in vivo. Slovenia's resistance paradoxically showed both the negative and the positive sides to the ONO Concept and System. The system did not hold up under internal rebellion, since it necessarily led to conflict among its republican/ethnic constituents. But it confirmed the belief that with a well organized population motivated by clear goals, it was possible to defend oneself successfully from a much stronger attacker.

Nonetheless, all of this is not sufficient reason to coherently explain the JNA's disaster in Slovenia. Regardless of how militarily inept it was, the Army had sufficient strength to completely destroy Slovenia. Alleged and real betrayals and desertions cited by the generals at the time could not have completely immobilized the JNA in the initial phase. The 'compassionate argument' should probably be taken into consideration whereby it was not easy to order the widespread killing of yesterday's 'brothers' and the destruction of part of the homeland.[25]

So the answers to the JNA's waterloo in Slovenia should be sought elsewhere. Since we are unable to inspect the documentation, what remains are assumptions. Let's call them amputation assumptions.

First let's consider the official Army explanation of its role in Slovenia.[26] The generals claimed that the JNA had been ordered by state bodies to undertake the minimum measures necessary to prevent the republic's secession and changing of the constitutional order; thus to preserve the territorial integrity of the country. The top generals showed the limited scope of the intervention by the small number of units sent and their passive fighting.

The military commanders owe an answer, however, as to why they did not prevent Slovenia's violent secession in accordance with the JNA's constitutional obligation. The generals' claim is unconvincing that the JNA (temporarily) left Slovenia so as not to accept the role of occupying force in its own country. Clearly, in Slovenia the top generals were not capable of executing their official – Yugoslav role, and the armed resistance did not allow them to. The further development of events indicates that the generals did not even try to play this role. Thus the amputation assumptions become quite valid.

The first assumption reads: at the end of June 1991 the JNA only feigned intervention in Slovenia. The fighting was intended to cover the previous arrangement reached by the Serbia-Slovenia-generals triangle on Slovenia's leaving Yugoslavia. Thus the exchange of fire in Slovenia resembled a war by arrangement more than a real war. Two arguments are in favor of this: first, Serbia's leaders had no territorial pretensions in Slovenia,[27] and second, they wanted to save the JNA for the fight with Croatia. Serbia and the military had, of course, renounced the second Yugoslavia previous to this. In order to back out 'cheaply', Slovenia had to free a passage for JNA movements.[28] The Slovenian leadership might also have had to commit themselves to remaining militarily passive during the war in Croatia.

The second assumption reads: Serbian and Army leaders decided independently to amputate Slovenia, which enabled the republic's leaders to win the false war.[29] In this variation, by withdrawing from Slovenia the federalists removed the risk of possible international intervention. They also avoided expending their military forces too early, and could therefore completely concentrate on the approaching Croatio-Serbian war.

In both variations Slovenia's amputation could have been a tactical ruse by Milošević in order to gain time. If the Croatian rebellion was successfully crushed, the JNA could return to Slovenia later. This is shown by the generals' attempts to prove that the JNA's leaving Slovenia and Slovenia leaving Yugoslavia did not dissolve the federal state, and its fate would have to be solved later.[30] The scope and nature of the Army's intervention in Slovenia also shows that it was a hidden amputation.

The Supreme Command's decision to send two motorized columns with 1,990 lightly armed soldiers to the 'customs' assignment can be interpreted in a variety of ways, as it already has. It can be used to prove all theses – from those about traitors in the state and the Army, to those about the incapable and arrogant generals, to the favorite Slovenian thesis about their great victory. All of these theses collapse before the following two facts.

The first is Kadijević's unconstitutional decision to abandon the mobilization system.[31] Although it only acknowledged the actual state of events, it had far-reaching consequences. It had been clear even before the war that there would be no soldiers and reserves from Slovenia and Croatia. The Minister of Defense's decision did away with them in advance.

Issuing this order, Kadijević himself nullified what remained of the JNA's legality and legitimacy. He thus repudiated the Yugoslav (state-defensive) goal of the Army's warfare. At the same time, he disclosed the Army's most sensitive issue too early and without any real need. The reaction was not long in coming: requests by the B-H and Macedonian leaderships to exclude their recruits and reserves from the JNA.[32] Shifting to the system of filling the Army with volunteers, Kadijević made the JNA dependent on numerous factors. Above all, this act revealed the pro-Serb orientation of the military commanders, since the JNA could only expect a greater response to the battle cry from among the Serbs.[33]

The second crucial fact favoring the amputation assumptions was the JNA's withdrawal from Slovenia. This decision is the first material step towards the revocation of Yugoslavia. All later Army attempts to provide arguments justifying this decision have been unsuccessful. Croatia must have been the first to understand this as the acknowledgement of Slovenia's secession, and one more reason for its own departure from Yugoslavia.[34]

The military commanders' move provided key international factors with even more proof that Yugoslavia was unsustainable, since the JNA had given up defending the federal state. The Yugoslav peoples started to demonstrate this on their own with arms. So foreign actors decided to help the country split up in accordance with their own views and interests.

From that moment on, how the conflicting ethnic groups would divide up the territory became the central issue of the Yugoslav wars. Even before the war the Yugoslav participants had shown that unwillingness to compromise about conflicting interests stood in the way of any peaceful breakup. Guided by the right of a people to self-determination, but within current internal borders, foreign meddlers created an antinomy that cannot be resolved to this very day. Their model of separating the Yugoslav peoples was and remained fundamentally contradictory, thus inevitably unsuccessful. Recognizing the statehood of Slovenia and Croatia and later B-H and Macedonia, the international community aided in the violent dissolution of Yugoslavia. They tried to avoid and then remove by force the consequences of the territorial and ethnic recomposition of the area. Independent of their intentions and 'good services', they directly encouraged the outbreak of war and endorsed the strategies of the ethnic leaders.

4.2 War in Doses

While the JNA was stumbling about Slovenia, the Croatian government activated its plan to gain its own sovereignty. The Army, its members, their family members and all the other Serbian inhabitants immediately became the primary target of Croatian attacks. In the same vein, the JNA started extensive armed operations on Croatian territory in accordance with the Serbian leaders' plan that gradually saw the light.[35]

Immediately after leaving Slovenia, the Army commanders reduced the JNA's tasks to protecting the Serbs in Croatia and lifting the blockade against its units. Pressed by events and the new relationship of power, the generals abandoned their position of ethnic and political neutrality. Their decision to protect only the Serbs[36] crucially determined the proportions and initial results of the Serbo-Croatian war. Oriented towards protecting the territorial independence of Serbian communities in Croatia, the JNA commanders objectively became the mere executors of the Serbs' political will.[37]

However, the role of the JNA cannot be properly understood without answering the fundamental questions: could the Army's top generals have stayed outside the Serbo-Croatian war at the time, did they want to, and should they have withdrawn from Croatia? Any analogy with Slovenia is difficult to maintain for several reasons.

In the given circumstance, the Serbo-Croatian war was unavoidable,[38] one might say. Historical, territorial, constitutional, national/ethnic, religious and situational reasons all favored war. The die was cast, however, when the political leaders decided to realize their national and state goals by means of war. For this purpose, both sides began the wartime production of proof showing the necessity of a final and complete separation of the Croats and Serbs. This is best illustrated by the key arguments of both sides. The Serbs' principal proof of the need to have borders firmly set with Croatia and the Croats was their fear of repeated genocide.[39] The Croats' main argument stemmed from statehood and the right acquired on this basis to establish and protect their sovereignty by force,[40] thereby permanently removing the disruptive (Serbian) factor.

The Croats' argument lost its legal foothold owing to the fact that the HDZ (Hrvatska demokratska zajednica – Croatian Democratic Union) government had already violated that same principle with regard to

Yugoslavia, at the time the only internationally recognized state entity. But discussions of principle had already been exchanged for armed separation.

Just as it was not possible at the time, it is still not possible today to establish the validity and real degree of fear of (renewed) genocide[41] among the Serbs in Croatia. Regardless of how instrumental it was, that fear became quite real with the arrival of HDZ and Tudjman in power. Determined to quell the 'balvan revolution' by force, the new Croatian government gave the Serbs the justification to use force to protect themselves. Demonizing the Serbs with propaganda in the Ustasha style, Tudjman's government encouraged both Croatian revanchism and chauvinism. Then the emigrants' anti-communism, primarily of Ustasha origin, was easily transformed into Serbophobia. Along the way, Tudjman's government had managed to abandon antifascism and even revive anti-Semitism.[42]

None of this could pass by the Serbs unobserved, or be taken lying down. Historical memories were revived of the Ustasha genocide of 1941-1945. Those memories brought acute fear of a repetition of their tragic experiences with the Croatian government.[43] Rapidly gaining ethnic and nationalistic (self)awareness, the Serbs in Croatia cast off the 'error of brotherhood and unity'. With help from Belgrade,[44] they reduced their political program to definitive territorial separation from Croatia.

In the arising situation, the top generals in principle had several alternatives to choose from. The first was to remain neutral and try to separate the conflicting parties. The second solution would have been to act quickly and disarm or immobilize the conflicting parties and force them to compromise. The third alternative was for the JNA to immediately stand on the Serbian side and resolve the conflict in their favor. The first two alternatives were not realistic, since the generals had passed over opportunities to use them even before the war. Thus the third solution was compelling the only one.[45]

With the outbreak of war in Croatia, the military commanders were clearly shown that the Croats had no intention of stopping their attacks on JNA units. At the same time, there was no proof that Tudjman would renounce the use of force in solving the Serbian question in Croatia.[46] The military forces available to HDZ at that time were sufficient to put the remaining Serbs in Croatia in a difficult situation. Even had they wanted, the Army commanders did not dare remain on the outside. In addition, there were several deeper reasons that would not let the military commanders stand aside in the Serbo-Croatian conflict.

Croatia's separatism directly jeopardized the fundamental interests of the JNA and the generals. The ideological positions of the military and Croatian leadership were diametrically opposed.[47] The HDZ nationalism-chauvinism with Ustasha components was countered by the generals' socialistic Yugoslav national feelings and internally revived Serbian national feelings. For this reason, even in the prewar period both sides exerted all their efforts to destroy each other.

Therefore, irreconcilable enemies were set against each other in June 1991. The JNA was Tudjman's key stumbling block to the creation of the Croatian state, but at the same time the main instrument for its international recognition. Armed Croatian separatism had tied the hands of the military commanders and jeopardized the JNA's survival. The generals' only political and social support was in Serbia, and Croatia, with its repression of the Serbs, was Serbia's direct opponent. On top of everything, newly arising situational factors encouraged the conflict.

Attacking Army units and barracks, Tudjman's regime in actual fact started the war with the JNA.[48] The Croatian forces' terrorism against the Serbs and attacks on their territory had made new genocide very probable, if not certain. With this the generals received their long awaited chance and justification to settle accounts with their odious opponent. Qualifying Tudjman's regime as Ustasha-fascist,[49] they first tried to stand between the regime and the Croatian people. The generals wanted this argument to motivate soldiers from other ethnic groups to take part on the JNA's side in the war.[50] But above all, standing by Milošević, the generals justified the expectations of the majority Serb composition in the JNA, and of Serbia's public.[51] Of course, and not exactly by accident, in the process the generals had found themselves an existential refuge.

Information about the nature of the agreement between Tudjman and Milošević in Karadjordjevo[52] is missing for a serious analysis of the strategic plans of the Serbo-Croatian warlords. Second-hand interpretations only allow a hypothetical reconstruction.

It stands to reason that the negotiators were aware of the fact that solving Croatio-Serbian relations was the key to dividing up Yugoslavia. It was probably not hard for them to agree on the division of B-H. Both of them wanted to annex the Muslims ('the flower of the Croatian nation' – 'Serbs forced to convert to Islam') and their territories. It is understandable that the two of them could not agree at all on the status of the Serbs and their territories in Croatia. Following the logic of the previous course of events, their demands had to run counter to each other. But it is just as reasonable to assume that they had foreseen the possibility of territorial compensation to each other at the expense of B-H. In this respect, the bloody six-month Serbo-Croatian conflict can be qualified as a war in doses, which was managed all the while by Milošević and Tudjman, either tacitly or by arrangement.

It was indisputably clear to both of them that the feasibility of the arrangement directly depended on the JNA's behavior. Milošević could dissociate himself from the Supreme Command's actions by his constitutional lack of authority, but Tudjman knew the truth. Therefore, Milošević constantly tried to give at least the illusion of legal Army involvement tailored after his own interests and goals.[53] The only Army Tudjman wanted to see was a scattered one, so he concentrated on its total destruction.

The strategic-operational situation in Croatia was radically different from that in Slovenia. The JNA had many larger units in Croatia.[54] Most of the navy was distributed along the Croatian part of the Adriatic coast. Air space was controlled by the RV i PVO (Ratno vazduhoplovstvo i protivvazdušna odbrana - the Airforce). Elite motorized-mechanized units of corps and brigade status were located in the republic of Croatia.

In addition, Croatia's integrity had already been destroyed by the creation of the SAO (Srpska autonomna oblast – Serbian Autonomous District) of Krajina, Baranja, Western Srem and Eastern Slavonia. In accordance with this, the JNA had arranged its units in seven operational groups: Eastern Slavonia, Western Slavonia, Knin, Mostar, Herzegovina and the RV and PVO, and RM (Ratna mornarnica - Navy) groups.[55] The JNA also had mobilized backup in Serbian enclaves. If needed, the military commanders could include units located in B-H into war operations.

The beginning of battle operations, however, disclosed all of the JNA's defects. For unexplained reasons, the military commanders dismissed the September class of soldiers[56] and thereby weakened their already thinned units. Volunteers and subsequent forced mobilization had little impact.[57] In October 1991 the rump SFRY Presidency declared a state of war alert that legalized forced mobilization, but the results were no better. The JNA's additional problem was the undefined status of the volunteer and paramilitary formations. Their presence on the battlefields increased the confusion in leadership and command, and led in particular to criminalization of the war. It was not until the end of 1991 that Supreme Command thought of regulating their status and putting them nominally under the JNA command and jurisdiction.[58]

In spite of this, the Croatian side was in a far less favorable situation. They could only parry the Army with the number and motivation of their forces.[59] The arms they had illegally imported or taken away from the JNA had small firing power all together. But they had nothing to parry the Army on the water or in the air. Croatia's war commanders could only base their strategy on optimizing advantages that were not subject to quantification.[60]

Croatia's strategy rested on two central points. The first was crucial and hearty support from Austria and Germany, and through them most of the Western countries. For this reason, Croatia made intensive use of the argument of 'Serbo-communist' and 'Chetnik' aggression against their independence.[61] Owing to this they were successful in presenting the JNA and the Serbs to the world as the exclusive agents of aggression, while completely hiding their own war provocateur output.

The HDZ's other support was from the Croat population. This was simply the successful manifestation of targeted and profiled collective dissatisfaction with their centuries of stateless status.[62] As soon as war broke out, the Croats' overall frustration at being deprived of a state of their own for so long was immediately directed against the Serbs and the JNA.

Croatia's strategic strongholds (potential advantages) were strengthened by armed operations and all-inclusive psychological-propaganda operations. Propaganda went in three directions: towards the international public, towards their local population and towards what remained of the JNA.

The Croatian leadership gleaned suitable propaganda material from the JNA commanders' general confusion. Delivering daily proof of 'Serbo-Chetnik' bestiality, they easily assured the support of the population whose views were molded by the war, and received the favor of world opinion. The JNA commanders provided abundant material to be used as propaganda. When they ordered the siege and bombing of towns, Dubrovnik and Vukovar in particular, which was inexplicable from the military viewpoint, they directly assisted Croatian propaganda.[63]

Collective and individual fear caused by the propaganda incited the Croats to uncontrolled aggression against the Serbs. The revival of collective traumas linked to the Serbs strengthened the Croatian population's view that a final showdown that would separate the people along ethnic lines was inevitable.

Although the behavior of those fighting on both sides was conditioned by situational factors, the apparent chaos proved to have a system. The 'scorched earth' tactic used by both armies led to ethnic cleansing according to a preplanned strategy. Wherever the Serbs or Croats were in a minority they were forced to flee to territorially compact ethnic areas.

Naturally, the warring parties will never agree as to who was the first to start, i.e. whose initial aggression started the ball rolling.

This is where the propaganda power of misusing historical traumas was shown. Both the Serbs and Croats found their motivation in the '1941' pattern, except with opposite meanings. The Serbian side linked 1941 and 1991 for the sake of showing the continuity of the Croats' Ustasha, genocidal and fascist leanings. Croatia, however, with reference to the Independent State of Croatia, extracted the desire for revenge against the 'Serbo-communists' who had destroyed their first and only state in recent times. Propagandists were facilitated by the fact that most members of both peoples quickly became bogged down in the ethno-religious war. The soldiers no longer needed special motivation – every participant had already found his own reasons to fight.

On the operational-tactical level, the Croats saw their chance in preventing the JNA's deployment, thus they immediately activated plans to block all Army units. The blockade, of course, could only be effective where JNA units were located in a Croatian environment.

The goal was clear: simultaneous attacks on the barracks were to prevent the JNA from being deployed, carrying out maneuvers and regrouping. Using the 'Slovenian' model, the Croatian leaders had a disastrous impact on the JNA. Afterwards the Army was unable to carry out a single goal properly, not even the alleged protection of the Serbian people.

Croatia's success also rested on maximum utilization of the Army's open disintegration. Croatian officers and soldiers immediately left the JNA en masse. The Navy and Airforce also lost personnel; the percentage of Slovenes and Croats among the officers was up to 50%.[64] At the same time, Croat 'moles' and highly placed deserters[65] took extremely confidential military documents with them. This resulted in rising paranoia among the JNA ranks and widespread suspicion, particularly towards the non-Serb officers. During warfare in Croatia the military commanders had the additional task of making security checks of both the General Staff and the entire officer corps.

When the rump Presidency subsequently assigned the JNA the task of quelling the 'armed insurrection in Croatia against Yugoslavia'[66] the fact that the generals had sided with the Serbs could no longer be hidden. This revelation was intended for international use, since Belgrade only made it on the eve of negotiations in The Hague to settle the Yugoslav crisis. Confirming the existence of armed insurrection, the rump SFRY

Presidency was trying to find a constitutional basis to declare a war alert and force the mobilization of reserves in Serbia and Montenegro.

The military commanders' troubles at that time involved more than just defining the political goals with which to use the JNA. How the Army units were used indicates that the generals did not know how to determine operational-tactical goals properly, either. Their command constantly tacked between the maximum and minimum Yugoslav, or Serbian, goals.

Under the slogan 'the Army will go where the people want it', the military commanders had a relatively easy time taking possession of Eastern Slavonia and Baranja. The JNA very quickly took over Lika, Banija and Kordun, while it already had control of Knin. Then the Army occupied the hinterland above Dubrovnik, but for reasons that are still incomprehensible, Western Slavonia was easily let go and the Serbs who had lived there for ages started their exodus.[67]

The military commanders' problems arose when they had to determine the line of halt. Since Serbian warmongers aspired to all 'Serbian lands' (graves), the JNA's 'liberation' operations included many towns: Zadar, Šibenik, Split, Karlovac, Osijek, Vinkovci and Dubrovnik. The JNA 'liberated' the Slavonic Serbs' future capital city of Vukovar by razing it to the ground. No one, it seems, in the Serbs' decision making center could and/or wanted to determine exactly where and when what remained of the JNA would stop. This command confusion from the top of the JNA left enough space for lower and local warmongers to make a creative contribution to expanding the Serbo-Croatian war.

Indirect proof from command points supports the evaluation that Milošević and Tudjman were dosing the Croatio-Serbian war all the while, so that the final score could be made in Bosnia and Herzegovina. This did nothing to decrease the violence of limited armed conflict, but the results primarily stayed within the agreed upon framework. Milošević, with the help of the JNA, easily took over territories where the Serbs had a majority, and thus set up a para-Serbian state in Croatia.[68] At the beginning of the conflict Tudjman did not have enough armed forces to prevent this. But every step made by the JNA towards Croatian areas brought a multiple rise in the battle power of Croatia's armed forces, with a proportional drop in the desire by the Serbs fighting in the JNA to do battle outside their domicile territories. In accordance with this, regardless of the military commanders' desire to defeat Tudjman, they could not offer valid reasons to what was left of the JNA to fight all over Croatia. It is therefore no wonder that most of the units from Slovenia were moved to B-H and not Croatia. The generals were thereby preparing to extract a third Serbian army[69] from the JNA and finish up the ethno-territorial division of Bosnia-Herzegovina.

Pressured by the international community, the conflicting sides signed a total of 14 cease-fires, none of which was respected, until a relatively long-lasting peace was concluded and UN peacekeeping units arrived. The reasons for this should be sought in the fact that the international community (the EC and UN) could not implement any cease-fire and/or did not want for a single cease-fire to materialize in spite of the abundant guarantees they gave. In addition, the warring parties understood the cease-fires only as pauses and halfway stations on the way to achieving their goals.

This continued until a stalemate was established on the battlefields. Croatia had organized a more serious army in the meantime, equipped with sufficient arms, and the JNA could no longer beat it. At the same time, what remained of the JNA had stabilized after being cleaned out ethnically and in terms of fighting ability, and the Croatian army could not crowd it out of the Serbian territories which it had occupied. In such circumstances, and with pressure from the international community, the Vance plan was put into effect.

After the international recognition of Croatia (and Slovenia), the situation drastically changed to the detriment of the JNA and Serbia. Although Croatia had to accept the UNPA (UN Protected Area) zones, which postponed indefinitely the reintegration of the Serbian regions outside Serbia, its sovereignty was recognized within the borders defined at the end of World War Two. Therefore, any further presence of JNA units in that area could be considered aggression. The fundamental contradictions in Serbia's policies sharpened once again. The JNA was not renamed the Serbian Army, since Milošević wanted to wage war on someone else's territory, fought by someone else and under false appearances. That is also why he never officially declared a pan-Serbian state; he wanted to reach it through a rump Yugoslavia. Expecting to benefit from continuity with the SFRY state, he did not pull Serbia out of former Yugoslavia, rather made Montenegro part of a new two-member federation that retained the name of Yugoslavia.

4.3 Introduction to a Bestial War

At the beginning of 1992 the military-political situation in B-H and its surroundings was additionally complicated, but at the same time simplified. The independence of Slovenia and Croatia, and the announcement of a new

Yugoslavia, shifted the war mis-en-scene to B-H. During the war in Croatia, the ethnic-territorial breakup of Yugoslavia had been detained at the borders of this republic. Establishment of the UNPA (UN Protected Zone) had stabilized the situation in Croatia. After that, Milošević and Tudjman turned towards B-H. Their relocated war now included the Muslim (Bosniak) factor along with the Serbian and Croatian.

On the eve of the increasingly certain outbreak of war, the only unknown was whether, with whom, for how long and at what price the Bosniak side, initially the weakest, would have to enter into an alliance. Of course, no one was able to reliably foresee any possible reaction from members of the international community, the USA above all.

At the beginning of 1992, the territorial aspirations of the Serbian and Croatian intruders from their respective republics had become almost palpable. Although it was a bit harder to evaluate the Muslims' true capabilities of preserving a united B-H., there were enough reasons to doubt the future democratic and secular nature of their announced state.

In the meantime, all preparations had already been completed in B-H for the final division and setting of mutual boundaries. The broad spectrum of reasons for war was now added an argument by analogy: since the multinational and multi-confessional Yugoslavia had collapsed, a B-H along the same lines became impossible. This is why everything that was denoted as a terrifying possibility in the war in Croatia was taken to its bestial extreme in B-H. Widespread ethnic cleansing (genocide) became the basic method of forcibly creating separate national/ethnic (para) states.

The Croatian-Muslim coalition arose after the failed attempt to conclude a historic agreement between the Serbs and Muslims. It was nominally established on the platform of a sovereign B-H, while it actually functioned as a war pact against the Republic of Serbia and its army.

With the creation of Herceg-Bosna, the Croats had prepared the ground to achieve their strategic goal. The maximal variation included joining this part of Herzegovina to Croatia, and the minimal variation was intended to obtain (para) state independence for the Croatian community within B-H. By taking over key state functions, the Muslims believed they had instruments that could be used to legally preserve, or enforce, a united Bosnia and Herzegovina. This is why local the HDZ and SDS immediately applied the previously confirmed scenario of blocking the local JNA units. They felt that immobilization of the JNA would create the key precondition to materializing their intentions of statehood.

Before the beginning of war in B-H, four groups of participants with unequal power and opposing strategic goals had already been clearly formed. Later periodic and temporary changes in relations in the Serbian-Croatian-Muslim triangle changed nothing in fact. They were always interim moves by one of the participants, guided by the principle of momentarily extracting greater benefit or lessening injury.

The Serbian group came out publicly in the name of the right of the Serbs in B-H to national self-determination, which in the given context necessarily meant territorial self-determination. To support this, SDS showed that in any case the Serbs had greater land rights in the land registry in B-H. An additional argument for separation was the need for the Serbian community to protect itself politically from the Croatian-Muslim majority. The SDS initial, minimal goal of separation was to establish independent statehood of the Serbian entity, which would have the sovereign right to decide on remaining in some form of Yugoslavia or joining the motherland (Serbia) at some future date.

Postponing the topic of national (pan-Serbian) unification in SDS was dictated by the fact that the political leaders in Serbia still had not renounced a second-and-a-half Yugoslavia. Through their exponents – the rump Presidency and General Staff of the remaining JNA – they tried all means available to keep B-H within the new/old state. This is why Milošević publicly insisted on a peaceful and negotiated resolution to the status of B-H and its constitutive peoples, while together with SDS he was making direct preparations for the armed realization of their (the Serbs') goals.

The Serbs' interest in preserving at least some kind of Yugoslavia stemmed from several strategic reasons. The Badinter commission's findings concluded that the second Yugoslavia had disintegrated, and interested republics were directed to the EU's counter for recognition of their statehood. The Serbian government figured that the preservation of some kind of Yugoslavia would provide a valid argument proving that the northwestern republics had seceded by force. In this variation the blame for the internal war would be ascribed to the secessionists, and Slovenia and Croatia would be deprived of the right to their share of the SFRY legacy and/or war reparations. The Serbian leaders also hoped that through B-H they would entice Macedonia to stay and/or join the new state. The ultimate goal of the Serbian leadership was to use the second-and-a-half Yugoslavia to assure the territorial compactness of the Serbian communities. This would make the territorial reduction of Croatia easier, and the creation of RSK had already provided the first prerequisite in this regard.

With the creation of Herceg-Bosnia, the two-member Croatian group – RH and western Herzegovina – had created the prerequisite to territorially and militarily-politically expand the Republic of Croatia, the ultimate goal being a Greater Croatia. This required the inclusion of the Muslim parts of B-H in the unified state. In negotiations between Milošević and Tudjman, a future agreement was expected on exchanging the Knin Krajina for parts of eastern Bosnia.

Contrary to these competitors, the Muslim group, led by a nominally legal state leadership, aspired to preserve the integrity and sovereignty of the Republic of Bosnia-Herzegovina. However, the alleged civic vision of a future B-H was denied on a daily basis by the fact that SDA monopolized state insignias. In addition, there was rapid de-secularization, i.e. Islamization, of the political space.

The fourth – international – group turned out to be crucial for the course of the war in B-H and the attainability of the key participants' goals. After the USA took over management of the crisis (war), the emphasis was put on the use of external force. Consequently, peace was imposed after three years of war. The limited scope of the results, however, became clear immediately after the Dayton Agreement was signed; the external meddlers had focused all their actions on stopping (subduing) the war and not on removing its causes. Any other intention would have required the radical intervention of a democratic orientation throughout the Yugoslav region for which the European-American mediators had insufficient patience, motivation and money, both then and now.

In three of the four groups the political will of the center (Serbia, Croatia and the USA) determined the behavior of subordinated participants and their war/peace capacities. In return, the center's domination produced tension within each group. In the case of Serbia, this tension resulted in periodic open conflicts, since the dictum of the Serbian regime was countered by power-holding groups from Pale watching out for their own interests.

In general, two circles of cooperation and conflict were established among the active participants, with changing components and of uncertain duration. The first, which we will call internal, functioned according to the principles of a 'free-for-all war' and an 'alliance of two against the third', although Serbo-Croatian conflicts and cooperation ultimately never left the framework of dividing up B-H as agreed between Milošević and Tudjman.

In the second circle, local and external participants were involved in the same job, whose final result was determined by the political will of the USA. Using the principle of 'excluding the third', American politics had put the Croatian and Muslim sides under their protection and used them as an instrument to achieve their numerous peacemaking plans. This is why the USA concentrated on training the Croatian and Muslim armies, each individually and both together within the Muslim-Croatian Federation, to fight independently against the Army of the Republic of Serbia. American wanted to use combined means – arming the army of the B-H federation and putting military pressure on the army of the Republic of Serbia – to establish a military balance between the warring sides. Thus they only cooperated with the Serbian ('excluded') side and nominal aggressor to the necessary extent to get them to consent to their dictum.

The positions and military-political relationships of the forces of the future war opponents in B-H greatly depended on the behavior of what remained of the JNA. The relocation of most of the units withdrawn from Slovenia and Croatia in B-H could be understood in two ways. The high concentration of army compositions in principle increased the chances of preventing a three-nation war in B-H. However, since the war in Croatia had removed any illusions about the political neutrality and independent command of the Army leaders, it was clear that should conflicts arise the Serbian side would have a great military advantage.

Announcing the creation (preservation) of Yugoslavia was accompanied by securing what remained of the JNA for its future needs. Since the number of members and territorial scope of this creation did not depend solely on the Serbs' volition, Serbian and military leaders deliberated over a broader and narrower variation of what remained of Yugoslavia. The broader variation was based on RSK joining a four-member federation, whereby all Serbian lands would remain in a common state. The narrower variation was based on the creation of western Serbian states and their later joining with Serbia or what remained of Yugoslavia.

The primary task in both variations was conferred on the remaining JNA which was either to threaten the use of force or actually use it to coerce the political consent of the other participants, i.e. to occupy the desired territory within that framework. Thus the actual moves by JNA leaders should always be considered from the viewpoint of both variations. The twofold commitment necessarily produced confusion in the JNA and hindered the achievement of the ultimate goal. The Army, together with the rump Presidency of SFRY, was to preserve the allusion of a consistent battle to maintain some kind of Yugoslavia. The military leaders thus had to postpone the renaming (ethnic transformation) of the JNA until the Serbs' military advantage had been assured in B-H.[70] In addition, the generals had to provide additional guarantees to the non-Serb population in B-H that the JNA would be neutral and would prevent war.

By grouping the northwestern remains of the JNA in B-H, the Serbian leaders tried to pressure the Muslim side into accepting the option of a second-and-a-half Yugoslavia. For this purpose, military leaders emphasized that the JNA was directly interested in B-H remaining in a third Yugoslavia owing to the existing arms industry, airports, warehouses and other resources. The top generals even allowed the possibility of the JNA withdrawing from B-H, but only after 5-7 years. Thus at the end of 1991 and the beginning of 1992 the military leaders acted declaratively along the lines of a second-and-a-half Yugoslavia, but in the process consolidated reserve positions for its pan-Serbian compression. It can therefore be said that the primary task of what remained of the JNA was to create the military prerequisites to carry out the Serbs' political, territorial and state goals.

This is supported by the fact that most of the dislocated units from Croatia and Slovenia were positioned in RS. In addition, the top generals did not hesitate to publicly announce that the JNA would be used to protect the Serbian people in B-H and their sovereign will to (state) self-determination. With early occupation of the western parts of RS, the Army had provided strategic backing for the Serbian enclave (the Republic of Serbian Krajina) in Croatia. By occupying Eastern Bosnia, the JNA simultaneously provided Republika Srpska strategic and operational-tactical support from Serbia (FR Yugoslavia).

The military leaders' intentions are also shown by the fact that at the beginning of December 1991 the length of the military service of those in the JNA's conscript and reserve compositions was extended another four months. This order did not cover mobilized compositions and individuals from the warring areas (B-H) whose service time was extended until the end of warfare.[71] At the same time, in parts of the JNA positioned in Serbia it was ordered, and achieved with considerable effort, for Serbian officers originating from the other side of the Drina River to be transferred to units located in B-H. Plans were also prepared to evacuate and destroy military facilities and military-industrial installations in B-H should the variation of a reduced Yugoslavia fail to succeed.

In spite of this, until April 1992 military and state leaders did not change their political-propaganda cliché. They joined efforts to prove that SFRY was a victim of the forced secession of Slovenia and Croatia, and that in spite of this the JNA had preserved its Yugoslav character and peacekeeping role. For this purpose, in December 1991 numerous non-Serb generals, in addition to the Vukovar 'victors', were promoted to a higher rank. At the same time the military leaders unstintingly used the thesis of internal betrayal, which, in spite of the defeats, helped the professional and Yu-patriotic purging of the JNA. There also began ethnic cleansing, hidden at first, of the professional composition in the Army ranks tailored to the expected war in B-H.

From the viewpoint of our topic, the key question is could what remained of the JNA have stayed out of the conflicts in B-H, or reacted to them differently. The real question is whether the military's and Serbia's leaders truly thought they could keep B-H within a Serbian Yugoslavia by concentrating the armed forces and demonstrating their power. After all, Macedonia had already publicly withdrawn from any Yugoslavia and the rapid consent given to the peaceful dislocation of JNA units allows the assumption that Serbia's leaders counted on the use of economic and political means, in conjunction with Greece, to keep Macedonia in some sort of state association. It should be noted that the emerging Macedonian state was completely disarmed during the withdrawal of JNA units.

Operations by what remained of the JNA in B-H did not change essentially from that which already took place in Croatia. Only some of the dimensions of warfare were taken to the extreme – the siege and destruction of towns (Sarajevo) and ethnic cleansing according to land registries.

The only difference was that when the Federal Republic of Yugoslavia was declared, along with its Army, what remained of the former JNA was renamed the Army of Republika Srpska, and all dilemmas disappeared regarding its nature and goals. To make the paradox even greater, this was the first and only army extracted from the JNA that had clear and declared goals (regardless of their nature and fairness).

Notes

1 'History is involved with people, although its creators like to say that people are the reason for its involvement', B. Pekić, *Sentimentalna povest britanskog carstva* (*Sentimental History of the British Empire*), BIGZ, Belgrade, 1992, 110.
2 For basic data on the tempo and essence of the international community's involvement, see: Facts on the crisis in former Yugoslavia, Medjunarodna politika, special issue, 1014, 1.03.1993, especially 13-30.
3 The fact that the international community, i.e. its most powerful members, bears its own interests in mind with regard to the Yugoslav war is shown in the Declaration on the criteria for recognizing new states in Eastern Europe

and the USSR, and the Declaration by the Ministers of the EC Council on Yugoslavia in which it is explicitly said that 'the EC, in light of its own criteria (...), will recognize the independence of all those Yugoslav republics that fulfill the (explicitly detailed – M.H.) conditions.' (Borba, 18.12.1991, 2).

4   This is confirmed by the Dayton Agreement's verification of the two-entity B-H which, while insisting on the return of those exiled, indirectly legalized the results of ethnic cleansing; compare: Dayton Agreement, Naša Borba, 1966, in particular Annex 2 and Annex 4.

5   This is also testified by the Conclusions of the Serbian Assembly that asked for 'the presence and operations of the JNA in SAO Krajina, Slavonia, Western Srem and Baranja in order to prevent the escalation of interethnic conflicts', and the establishment of responsibility for the 'difficult state in the JNA, the betrayal of individual officers, the death and wounding of soldiers', and for the 'massive dislocation and genocide of the Serbs in Croatia'. The RS government was asked to 'undertake measures so that TO Serbia is completely prepared' to defend Serbia and the Serbian people (Borba, 9.07.1991, 9).

6   General Kadijević resigned for reasons of health on January 8, 1992 (VPI 2/92, 182) and his service ended February 25, together with that of 29 other generals, including his deputy Admiral Brovet (VPI 3/92, 261; Headquarters commander Adžić resigned on May 8, 1992, at which time 38 other high military leaders also retired (VPI 6/92, 159-160).

7   Regime writers Dušan Vilić and Boško Todorović tried to use the 'conspiracy theory' and 'special-war' understanding of the European and world environment to convince the Serbian public that Yugoslavia had been broken up by the global strategy of the USA (p. 34), and carried out by the Vatican and Germany (pp. 6-7) and DEMOS and HDZ (pp. 131-134); compare: *Razbijanje Jugoslavije 1990-1992* (*Breaking Up Yugoslavia 1990-1992*), DIK Književne novine – Enciklopedija, Belgrade, 1995.

8   This is also shown by the Army's analysis of the operations of Slovenia's intelligence service; compare: Milan Mijalkovski, JNA na nišanu (JNA on Target), VPI 7-8, 1991, 70-83.

9   At a referendum on September 30, 1991, the Albanians voted for a 'sovereign and independent Kosovo'; Hronologija, 44.

10 The goals of Serbia's policies were adjusted to the course of developments, and were necessarily conditional and capable of being withdrawn, and reached the public subsequently; so academician Mihajlo Marković, vice president of SPS at the time, announced that the JNA would not leave the territory of Croatia within its current borders, i.e. would withdraw to new borders between Serbia and Croatia (Borba, 10.10.1991, 13).

11 'We did not head off to war, and no one in the JNA behaved like that. Armed formations in Slovenia acted and continue to act towards the JNA as an occupying army and imposed on the JNA what is essentially a totally dirty war.', Major General Marko Negovanović (Narodna armija, 06.07.1991, 5).
12 'The Army's intervention in Slovenia, to put it bluntly, is one of the stupidest things that I have ever see in all the time I have followed political events. It was so counterproductive that not a single reason can be found to justify that scandalously stupid move.' Žarko Puhovski, interview (Nedeljna Borba, 14-15.09.1991, X-XI).
13 Compare: T. W. Carr, German and US Involvement n the Balkans: A Careful Coincidence of National Policies; www.emperorsclothes.com/articles/carr/carr2.htm.
14 The Slovenian Assembly passed a constitutional law (Article 1) declaring that 'the Republic of Slovenia is an independent and self-ruling state. The SFRY Constitution ceases to be valid for the Republic of Slovenia.' (Borba, 26.06.1991, 6).
15 The Croatian Assembly adopted the 'Declaration on the establishment of a sovereign and independent Republic of Croatia' and passed the 'Constitutional decision on the sovereignty and independence of the Republic of Croatia', whereby (Art. 1) 'the Republic of Croatia is declared to be a sovereign and independent state,' and (Art. 2) at the same time 'initiates the proceedings to dissociate from other republics and SFRY', and 'receives international recognition.' The 'Charter on the rights of the Serbs and other nationalities in the Republic of Croatia' was passed at the same time in which the Serbs were guaranteed the general rights belonging to minorities and all citizens (Borba, 26.06.1991, 6).
16 For a chronology of key events from June 25 to July 1, 1991, see: Borba, 02.07.1991, 16.
17 'No one in the Army could understand that they were fighting against those who hated Yugoslavia and the JNA from the bottom of their hearts. Instructed for decades in the spirit of Yugoslav national feelings, we couldn't believe that so much evil and hatred could collect in one place, and in such forms. They were deceitful and unmindful, acting in the most brutal manner. They spared no one, not even underage children, women and their former neighbors.' Blagoje Adžić, Chief of the JNA General Staff, statement to the public on the war in Slovenia (Narodna armija, 06.07.1991, 2).
18 Compare: Communiqué from the SFRY Presidency (Borba, 02.07.1991, 2); on that occasion Stipe Mesić (Croatia) was nonetheless elected president of the Presidency; at the same time the commander of the 5th army region, General Konrad Kolišek, was replaced.
19 Compare: Declaration, Annex 1, item. 1, VPI August 1991, special issue, 114.

20 'JNA commands, units and institutions will cease to be stationed on the territory of the Republic of Slovenia until a definitive agreement has been reached about the future of Yugoslavia (...) Transfers will be completed within three months of the passage of this decision.' Decision by the SFRY Presidency dated 18.07.1991; according to: VPI August 1991, special issue, 128-129.

21 For more on the Slovenian leadership's fears of more widespread use of RV and PVO, see: Vilić, D., Todorović, B., Razbijanje Jugoslavije 1990-1992, op. cit. 268-269.

22 This is also shown by the support that Hans Deitrich Gencher, German foreign minister, offered to the Slovenian leadership, then crowned with a visit to Ljubljana; details: *The Death of Yugoslavia*, L. Silber and A. Little, Radio B92, Belgrade 1996, 173-189.

23 As indicated by an increase in the number of armed incidents and attacks on the JNA units and members in Croatia from the moment Slovenia declared independence; compare: Review of Armed Incidents in Croatia from June 25 to July 2, Borba. 03.07.1991, 27.

24 For the Army's evaluation of Slovenia's propaganda, see: Slavoljub Randjelović, Smišljeno obmanjivanje javnosti, VPI, special issue, August 1991, 54-61.

25 'Even though the leadership and armed formations of the Republic of Slovenia acted towards the JNA as towards an occupying army, we simply could not have the same attitude towards the Slovenian people. This is why the main JNA forces, aviation, rockets, artillery, armored divisions and other units were never properly activated.' V. Kadijević, public statement (Narodna armija, 10.07.1991, 4).

26 For the Army's interpretation of the constitutional aspects of intervention in Slovenia, see: Miodrag Starević, Nasilje u službi razbijačke politike, VPI, August 1993, 22-23.

27 'The agreement by Serbian and Slovenian delegations (Milošević-Kučan), January 24, 1991, spoke indisputably about Serbia's agreement for Slovenia to secede from Yugoslavia whenever it wanted, unhindered and in a regular way.' Vilić, Todorović, op. cit., 231; the authors, however, do not cite any source for this claim.

28 The final agreement between the Slovenian government and the JNA on withdrawal was only signed four months later (Borba, 19-20.10.1991, 3); in this regard, Slovenia used the JNA's preoccupation with fighting in Croatia to hinder withdrawal in all possible ways and held onto a good deal of the military's equipment and arms.

29 Compare: Borisav Jović, The Last Days of SFRY – excerpts from his diary, Kompanija Politika, 1995, 344.

30 'The decision does not prejudice the future organization of relations in Yugoslavia nor does it question its territorial integrity (...) Transferring JNA units from the territory of the Republic of Slovenia to the interior of the country provides better conditions for the political structures of Yugoslavia to reach an agreement in a democratic and peaceful manner on the future of the common Yugoslav state', Rear Admiral Milosav Simić (Narodna armija, 27.07.1991, 5).

31 The key sentence reads: 'Cease with classical mobilization and shift to mobilization on a volunteer principle.', Order by the Minister of Defense (Borba, according to HTV, 11.07.1991, 9).

32 Kadijević's response to this was that 'solving the questions of recruits and replenishing the JNA in the manner you propose, the Yugoslav People's Army will cease to exist as one of the last joint Yugoslav institutions', and that would be the end of Yugoslavia. He added that replenishing the JNA would be carried out strictly in accordance with federal laws and other provisions (Borba, 17-18.07.1991, 3).

33 This is also shown by the conclusions of the Serbian Assembly that demanded 'that recruits from the Republic of Serbia be sent to serve their military service only in the JNA units on territories where peoples live who have chosen to live in Yugoslavia.' (Borba, 09.07.1991, 9).

34 Tudjman immediately maintained 'that the latest decision by the SFRY Presidency creates the conditions for Croatia to carry out its decision to become independent', and announced the request for the JNA to withdraw from Croatia (Borba, 20-21.07.1991, 2).

35 'The fact that the JNA assignments highly coincide with the interests of the citizens of Serbia is a historical combination of events within the context of Slovenia's and Croatia's behavior towards our social reality' and so there was no need to support 'some Serbian army' since 'what the JNA is doing coincides with the interests of the citizens of Serbia and the Serbian population wherever they live', General Tomislav Simović, Serbian Minister of Defense (Borba, 7.10.1991, 10-11).

36 'The secessionist goal of the Croatian government cannot be achieved without the complete pacification of the Serbian people in that republic, and pacification in these conditions practically means the physical destruction of the Serbs', General Radovan Radinović (Intervju, 03.08.1991, 57).

37 Pavle Obradović, vice president of the Serbian Assembly at the time, advocated that the JNA be 'wherever the people accept it as their own.' Within this context he elaborated the solutions that were available to the Serbian people (leaders): 'The first is life in one state without Slovenia and Croatia on so-called Croatian soil. The second is a state without Slovenia, Croatia within its Croatian part, without parts in Bosnia and Herzegovina and without part of Macedonia. The third is the creation an integral Serbian state

that will occupy the territory with a majority Serbian population.' (Intervju, 03.08.1991, 56).

38 'Whether the (Serbo-Croatian conflict – M.H.) can be stopped, I don't know. The conflict broke out independent of the Army)...) From what I know about the conflicts in Croatia, I don't see that there would have been fewer dead if the Army had not taken part.' Ž. Puhovski, op. cit.; Milovan Djilas had the opposite opinion: 'I think that the Army is primarily to blame for that (change in the nature of the war – M.H.), since the center of the crisis was nonetheless inside it. It could not resolve the Yugoslav crisis since it did not have state and political leadership. It could not stop the war machine, rather got involved in it. The Army was drawn into war by its wrong picture of the situation in Croatia and Europe, and its ambition to play the great historical role of the first to fight against the revival of fascism' (Borba, 21-22.12.1991, X-XI).

39 This is shown by the 'Lipanje Charter' by the Hrvatska stranka prava (Croatian Party for Law) dated 17.06.1991, which demanded the renewal and establishment of the Independent State of Croatia on its complete historical and ethnic area with the eastern borders: Subotica – Zemun – Drina – Sandžak – Bay of Kotor, according to: Hronologija, 39.

40 After the session of the SFRY Presidency in Ohrid, Tudman sent an appeal to the population of Croatia 'not to let themselves be provoked into war but to be prepared, in the near future, for an all-out war to defend Croatia.' (Borba, 23.07.1991, 3).

41 This fear was used by the Presidency of rump Yugoslavia to refuse the EC demand to withdraw the JNA from Croatia, in particular from the territory with a Serbian population (Borba, 12-13.10.1991, 5).

42 Tudjman later retracted his anti-Semitic statements from his book 'Bespuća historijske zbilje' and publicly apologized to the Jewish organizations in the US (Borba, 16.02.1994, 8).

43 The military leaders also used an argument of fear to justify the use of the JNA that coincided with the Serbian view: 'Unfortunately, the specter of fascism is knocking at our doors. Today it is hard to admit that fascism has a chance of reviving in this country, which was among the first to stand up against it', S. Milošević, speech on the occasion of five decades of the Serbian people's rise against fascism (Borba, 11.12.1991, 7).

44 'This is not a conflict between the Republic of Serbia and the Republic of Croatia. This is a conflict between the Croatian government and the Serbian people, this is some kind of state terror over the Serbian population in Croatia,' S. Milošević, interview Sky News (Borba, 08.08.1991, 2).

45 At the proposal of General Kadijević, the rump Presidency maintained that 'a clear definition should be made of all those who are in favor of preserving the Yugoslav state and practical measures should be undertaken to implement

these views by the peoples who want it and their legitimate representatives. At the same time, the JNA should be transformed into the armed forces of the Yugoslavia that will survive.' (Borba, 23.10.1991, 1).

46   'In the circumstances we face in which Serbia, with the protection of the Yugoslav Army, is striving to take all those regions with which it thinks to create a Greater Serbia, our view is to persevere in defending the territorial integrity of the Republic of Croatia, and with this in mind we have already passed a decision on the mobilization of both the reserve militia and the Assembly of the National Guard', F. Tudjman, speech at an emergency session of the Croatian Assembly (Borba, 02.08.1991, 4).

47   'Neo-nazism is at work in the Republic of Croatia. At this moment it is the greatest threat to the Serbian people in Croatia, but neo-nazism is directly opposed to the vital interests of the Croatian people and every other people in the territory of Yugoslavia.' V. Kadijević, statement after the introduction of a war alert (Borba, 4.10.1991, 6).

48   Therefore, the Supreme Command threatened the Republic of Croatia's leadership and armed formations with reprisals, since 'for every attacked JNA facility that is taken over, one facility of vital importance to the Republic of Croatia will be destroyed', and 'for every garrison that is attacked and taken over – a vital facility of the town in which the garrison is located will be destroyed' (Borba, 2.10.1991, 1).

49   The Army commanders have come out explicitly against the imposition of any ideological supervision and monopoly. Thus their being labeled communists by those who remain captives of ideological fascist single-mindedness of the worst kind, does not deserve any special comment.' SNNO information on the Conclusions of the Croatian Assembly (Borba, 9.8.1991, 6).

50   'At this moment the Army wants nothing more than to establish control in the crisis areas, protect the Serbian population from persecution and destruction and free the members of the JNA and their family members. In order to do this the Ustashe forces must be destroyed.' V. Kadijević, statement after the declaration of a war alert, op. cit.

51   'The direct goal of the Ustashe, fascist Croatian government is genocide over the Serbian people and the JNA soldiers who are doing their military service in Croatia. The government of the Republic of Serbia supports the citizens' patriotic attitude towards the JNA and its mission of peace and protection of the citizens' lives. Any other behavior in this critical situation would be equal to treason.' Communiqué from the session of the government of the Republic of Serbia (Borba, 21-22.09.1991, 7).

52   Among the first to point out the consequences of the secret agreement between Milošević and Tudjman was Ivan Zvonimir Čičak: compare: Borba, 29.12.1992, 17.

53 This viewpoint should be kept in mind when considering the Decision of the rump SFRY Presidency that the Army 'work and operate in the manner foreseen by the Constitution of SFRY, in conditions of war alert and in accordance with the decision of the Presidency of SFRY no. 36 dated November 21, 1984 which has not changed to date' (Borba, 4.10.1991, 1); this was immediately followed by the Order on partial mobilization (Borba, 5-6.10.1991, 1).
54 The territory of Croatia was part of the Northwestern (land) battlefield, and the entire Adriatic-Littoral area was covered by the Adriatic naval battlefield; according to: Radinović, R., Moć i nemoć vojske u raspadu Jugoslavije, Sociološki pregled, Vol. XXVII (1994) No. 2, 283-296.
55 Radinović, R., op. cit., 291.
56 Compare: Vilić, Todorović, op. cit., 233-234.
57 This is shown by the widespread refusal and avoidance of mobilization in Temerin, Šabac, Velika Plana, etc. (Borba, 21-22.09.1991, 7).
58 By order of the SFRY Presidency dated 10.12.1991, volunteers were 'in all respects equal to military personnel and those doing their military service' and thus 'volunteer formations that are currently operating outside the SFRY Armed Forces (…) are under obligation, within ten days of the date this order goes into effect, to bring their position in line with the SFRY Armed Forces the provisions of this order.' VPI, 1/92, 198-200.
59 For a long time the Croatian side justified the lack of general mobilization by a deficiency of arms and equipment to form new units; compare: Emergency Session of the Republic of Croatia Assembly (Borba, 2.08.1991, 4-5).
60 This is also shown by the analysis of the Chief of Staff, A. Tus: 'The main problem with the occupying army is the human factor. (…) If we calculate only military formations in the proportions of the forces, it is clear that the Yugoslav Army is more numerous and has in particular technical preponderance. If we include all of Croatia and the defense capabilities of its people, then that army does not have the advantage.' (Borba, 11.11.1991, 17).
61 For the Army's view of the Croatian (and Slovenian) propaganda, see: Stanko Živković, U vrtlogu laži (psihološko-propagando delovanje protiv JNA), VPI, 10/91, 22-31.
62 'The Croatian national identity, as purely Croatian, is primarily founded on the recollections and traditions of the medieval Croatian state. At the beginning of the 19th century, memories of that state started to fade. They were revived in the second half of the 19th century by national, often nationalistic Croatian historians and the Croatian Party of Law that strove to found the legitimacy of their program of Croatian independence on the documents and contracts that remained from the medieval Croatian state and assembly.' Aleksa Djilas, Osporovana zemlje (Contested Land), Književne novine, Belgrade, 1990, 47.

63   Thus it is no wonder that the (setup?) bombing of the Ban manor (F. Tudjman's residence) that coincided with the RH Assembly session when the Decision was passed whereby 'the Republic of Croatia as of October 8, 1991 rescinds state-legal connections upon which basis the current SFRY was created, together with the other republics and provinces,' and the Conclusions that 'the Republic of Serbia and the so-called the JNA committed aggression against the Republic of Croatia' and thus the 'so-called JNA is declared an aggressor and occupying army' (Borba, 9.10.1991, 3).

64   General Jurjević, commander of RV and PVO, stated the fact, although before the war began in B-H, that only about 10% of the officers had dropped out, but that in this form only 48% were Serbs, see: VPI 1/92, 164-168.

65   Among those with more important duties in the JNA were Admiral Grubešić, General Stipetić, colonels Agotić, Marček, etc. They were also joined by retired generals and admirals, such as Tus and Letica.

66   'The unilateral decisions by Slovenia and Croatia on seceding from Yugoslavia have glaringly breached the Constitution of SFRY (...) and Croatia has for several months been waging an undeclared war against Yugoslavia.' B. Kostić, vice president of the SFRY Presidency, statement after the declaration of a war alert (Borba, 05.10.1991, 5).

67   The government of SAO Western Slavonia announced that the 'people and fighters feel deceived more and more since support has not arrived, especially from the JNA', although 'at the beginning of November representatives of the government of Western Slavonia addressed once again the highest bodies in SFRY, Serbia and the JNA' (Borba, 19.12.1991, 10).

68   'The Supreme Command (...) has not place the military defeat of Croatia's para-army as the goal and task of the strategic plan of deploying the JNA, but the reduced and insufficiently precise task of protecting the majority Serbian population (...). The fact that the military commanders' strategic plan did not have the goal of the definitive military defeat of Croatian armed formations is shown by the suspension of all the JNA's widespread warfare after it crossed today's border of the Republic of Serbian Krajina.' Radinović, R. op. cit., 292.

69   'The JNA was the basis from which three armies were formed – the CRJ Army, the Army of Republika Srpska and the Army of the Republic of Srpska Krajina.' Veljko Kadijević, Moje vidjenje raspada, Politika, Belgrade, 1993, 16

70   'Postponing the beginning of the ethnic-religious and civil war in Bosnia and Herzegovina for more than seven months with respect to the beginning of the war in Croatia had a strategic importance for the JNA (...) particularly since Tudjman's Croatia and Germany under Kohl and Genscher were constantly pushing Alija Izetbegović to enter the fray as soon as possible', Vilić,

Todorović, op. cit., 234-235; of course, the authors do not corroborate this statement with any proof, either.
71 See: Communiqué from the Office of Information of SSNO dated 13 December 1991, VIP no. 1, 1992, 180.

PART II
THE JNA'S WARFARE BALANCE

Chapter 5

The Essence of the Yugoslav War

Today the inhabitants of former Yugoslavia are preoccupied with the problem of how to survive the consequences of ten years of war. Discussions about the causes, instigators and essence of the Yu-war lie outside their considerations. These consequences, however, have caught up with the war's main creators and protagonists. While they were sending others to fight the war was only a political topic for them, and often academic. They moved in the sphere of high principles of peace, or rather war for peace, democracy, state and national sovereignty, and national honor. Their offices protected them from death, but now the chances have risen that they might die after the war. Current and future criminal sanctions of the warmongers[1] will satisfy the appetite for justice and reveal part of the truth about the Yu-war. In the same vein, future historiographic research will gather information about the war that is inaccessible today.

In the Yu-war story, what is most difficult is to establish the true nature of the war. Even the mainstays of the antiwar movement have not succeeded in raising an across-the-board condemnation of the war in the name of humaneness and democracy.[2] Countless combinations of its different dimensions have been used to explain the nature of this war: national, religious, political, historical, territorial, sociological, socio-psychological and so on. The quality of the combinations and analytical results depend directly on the national and geographical origin of the author,[3] and the time of the explanation.[4]

The true nature of the Yu-war is hidden by the claims of all its participants that the war was forced upon them, and that they were thus drawn into it against their will. In the process, each of them called their participation by a different name, yet they all claimed to be merely defending their national and state rights that were endangered by others. These propaganda explanations covered up the true sources and essence of the war; as befits the nature of propaganda, the causes of the war were always external, and the other guy was always to blame. The former JNA alone was proclaimed the main culprit and aggressor in the initial episodes of the pan-Yugoslav war. It, too, claimed it had been attacked and drawn into the war when it was only carrying out its constitutional role – protecting the territorial integrity and borders of SFRY.

Additional confusion was created by the fact that none of the war commanders had clearly formulated their goals in advance. They spoke all the while about coercion and/or defense against attack. The true goals of the war only appeared gradually with time. Today it is impossible to establish reliably their minimum goals and their maximum goals. Even though the rattling of swords was heard as early as 1990, when war broke out it was uncontrolled – war happened to everyone and most of them didn't know what to do with it. In the beginning not a single one of the protagonists had a real notion of the combat potentials of their future opponents in war.

The presented genesis, however, confirms the well-known fact that various deciding factors of the Yu-war were animated and took on a life of their own by means of politics; opposing programs and goals with a potential for war had been formed even before the war, resting on mutually exclusive national-state interests. These programs were based on political and national grouping, or rather separation. Each political program then found itself a war leader, just as many leaders found themselves a program. In accordance with this, the value content of goods on the Yu-political market radically changed. There was a constant rise in demand for nationalistic, religious and mythical political values. A new political supply was formed to satisfy this demand.[5] As they materialized, the emerging factors of war then had a return effect on politics. and began their relatively independent life when the Yu-crisis turned into war. Politics was less and less able to control them and became increasingly under their dictate. The return effect of politics was then necessarily transformed into daily justification and legalization of the impact of the factors of war that had begun a life of their own.

Independent of the fact that the Yu-war changed form under the combined influence of numerous factors, knowledge at hand is sufficient to establish who actually waged war, against whom and for which reasons. Changes in form then changed the substance and nature of the war. In the same vein, as the war drew out the register of its causes also changed. In addition, immediate causes blurred the primary causes and goals of the war. Then with the logic inherent in war, the causes grew into new reasons to continue fighting, and the Yu-war changed its structure and took on numerous meanings. Understanding the real nature of the Yu-war thus requires an analysis of its key determinants and the dominant forms of its existence.

5.1 The Trill of Striking Motives

The assertion that the war in Yugoslavia was interethnic is true for many reasons. It was even classified by its creators as a battle for national survival, which quickly became a cruel reality for the opposing nations/ethnic groups. Individual and massive war crimes were committed under national symbols. Territories were ethnically cleansed for the sake of setting final national and state borders. Repressed national animosities and atavisms rose to the surface. The boundaries were erased for good between what was national, nationalistic and chauvinistic. With the passage of time the nationalistic radius of the spiraling war became wider as its angle grew steeper. All of life was subordinated to and measured by the national reason, which was interpreted using the chauvinistic key. New national heroes and traitors were produced en masse for the sake of the war.

Nationalism was the driving force behind the Yu-war and the nervous center of the opposing military machineries, particularly because it was not just a one-shot and/or propaganda product of new 'war economies'. The Yu-war revealed a devastating fact about living together in Yugoslav: after 70 seventy years in one state, the peoples gathered there had not succeeded in finding a sustainable model of multinational tolerance and cooperation. During the First and Second World Wars the Yugoslav people shed blood among themselves and within themselves. Since they had never made peace within their own nations, they were even less able to make peace with others. The permanent lack of catharsis facilitated the renewed (pre)war misuse of individual and collective traumas deposited in the national memory. This is why the warfare finale in 1991 destroyed all the previous – real and/or pseudo – mechanisms to preserve the multinational state community.

This was eased by the fact that the ideologies of repression and repressive ideologies in both Yugoslavias had prevented the creation of middle class prerequisites that would have democratically positioned the national dimension of the individual and collective identity. This is why the nation (ethnic group), although repressed and weighed down, cyclically broke through to the surface, but each time with even greater destructive power.[6] When the fundamental crisis of Yugoslavia's state community brought favorable conditions once again, the nation intruded as the lord of war and peace. The Yu-war was indisputably nationally determined and delimited.

There is, however, sufficient proof to contest the primordial status of the Yu-war's national factor. For example, in spite of all the warmongers' desires for nationalistic homogenization, it was not achieved in any nation. Resistance to the war within every Yu-nation, although of limited scope, never ceased. The great number of emancipated young people who fled abroad showed that they did not consider nationalistic goals sufficient reason to go to war. The extensive internal – political and spiritual – refugees, and widespread desertion clearly revealed the limits of the national production of war. What was even more indicative was the flight of able-bodied men from the war-torn areas. Although they were fleeing the crimes of their opponents in order to save their lives, few of them returned to their homeland to take part in the war. In addition, for a variety of reasons many of those belonging to the warring nations stayed in their new states. Furthermore, in the initial phase of the war all the armies had multinational units.

Thus a proper understanding the Yu-war drama cannot be found using the national reason alone; but an analysis of the national role as mediator is clearly required in order to understand the reasons for the bestiality of this war; particularly because the national factor never appeared alone. Condensed in the national reason were the basic differences between the opposing ethnicities, which were then multiplied with its assistance. For this reason, each of the differences only became a reason and motive for war when coupled with nationalism. This means that the outbreak of war reduced the numerous reasons for conflict in Yugoslavia to the national reason, which chauvinistic acceleration then turned it into a destructive form.

In former Yugoslavia, national was permanently linked to religious.[7] And vice versa. The historical connection between nation and religion was not broken in spite of forcing the people to atheism, as practiced in the second Yugoslavia. Quite the contrary: under pressure this link became deformed, and the rigidity of the communists favored the nationalistic misuse of the church (religion) and the church's (religious) misuse of the nation. The decline in the ideological values of socialism saw a concomitant rise in the frequency of religion's political manipulation. Then the negative impact of the economic crisis gave local churches the chance to renew and expand their social and spiritual stronghold.[8] The rise in the number of new faithful and converts allowed first the Serbian Orthodox Church and Catholic Church and then the Islamic religious community to grow stronger and return to the social and political scene of second Yugoslavia.

Owing to the collapse of Party socialism, and political pluralization on a national basis, churches became part of everyday politics.[9] Since they were anticommunist and thereby anti-regime, at the end of the 1980s they strongly supported the nationally declared opposition in their circle. The electoral victory of the opposition in Slovenia and Croatia in 1990 was, among other things, facilitated by public support from the leaders of the Catholic church there.[10] Unlike this, the Serbian Orthodox Church supported the political program of Slobodan Milošević,[11] which resulted in its being permanently torn between the communist government and the nationalist opposition. Even when it periodically distanced itself from the communist implementers of nationalistic policies, the Serbian Orthodox Church never renounced their goals.[12] Crisis developments in Yugoslav society thus enabled key churches to impose themselves in their nations as strong centers of non-institutionalized political power.

This is why the politically reactivated churches could not and did not want to be left out of the preparations for war. They added their own work to the unsettled accounts from the previous war, which were brought out in the phase of the political disintegration of Yugoslavia. As they counted and dedicated pits and victims from the Second World War, belated and with a fixed purpose, they heartily took part in the orchestrated production of new and vengeful reasons to continue the old wars. The activities of the churches reduced bygone national and religious schisms to daily politics, and then the power-holders used them for the wartime misuse of religion and nation.

In the case of Yugoslavia it was shown once again that nations and their religions could only become the handmaid of politics. Thus the Yu-war was also constituted as a religious conflict. Places of worship and believers suffered great casualties, and ethnic cleansing was accompanied by religious persecution. This is supported, of course, by the coinciding national and religious membership of the warring sides. Thus it is impossible to remove the national dimension of the Yu-war from the religious dimension.

All the above is still not enough to qualify the Yu-war as being religious. The fact, however, is not contested that numerous individuals and groups justified their participation in the war on religious grounds, or that the war was used to promote and install the interests of the churches and that an alliance was formed between parts of the clergy and the war elite. Furthermore, the linking of religious and national components in the war encouraged the (re)production of interethnic and inter-confessional hatred, which then gave a hard core of driving power to a large number of fighters. Turning them into fanatics, religion made it easier for them to fight and also compensated for the lack of political goals. In addition, the religious-national reason helped them rationalize the irrational essence of the war. The mortars that renewed old and produced new emotional-awareness grounds intensified and multiplied religious-ethnic prejudice to an extreme. Nevertheless, all of this is not sufficient reason to declare the Yu-war a religious one. This is supported by the argument that religious wars and/or religious reasons for war are archaic. In any case, even in times when such wars were waged, banners of faith covered quite mundane reasons and interests.

Under the influence of national-religious reasons, the Yu-war immediately established itself as a war for territory and changing borders. It formally began because of Slovenia's secession, which destroyed the territorial integrity of the former Yugoslavia. After that the Yu-war was waged in order to set new and/or reestablish old state and ethnic borders. This was emphasized by the Serbian leaders' announcement that any unilateral departure from Yugoslavia would lead towards changes in the republican borders.[13] At the same time, Tudjman and HDZ (Croatian Democratic Union – Croatian nationalist party) announced the renewal of Croatia within historical borders, which necessarily meant that Tudjman's and Milošević's paths to their desired borders had to cross and clash. The road from Zagreb to the Drina River and Zemun went across the line of Karlobag-Ogulin-Karlovac-Virovitica, which the cartographers from Belgrade intended to reach by forcing the Drina and Danube rivers. Both these routes went across Bosnia and Herzegovina, and so the war could not bypass it either. The territorial and ethnic demarcation of the Serbs and Croats first began in Croatia, and then continued within the Serbian-Croatian-Muslim triangle when it spilled over into B-H.

Although the conflict over future borders during the finale of the Yu-crisis accelerated the preparations for war, it triggered more than caused the war. Territorial disputes thus fall into the category of derived and secondary factors of the war. This does not deny the warring sides' desire to change their borders by force and regain the greatest territory possible. The moment the national elite legitimized the alteration of borders by force, conflicting territorial aspirations became sufficient reason for war. That is when territorial grounds necessarily merged with national-religious grounds, and then their joined forces had a crucial impact on the future contents and form of the war. Owing to this, the Yu-war was shown to be a continuation of interethnic annihilation from the time of the fascist occupation of the first Yugoslavia.

5.2 The Yu-War's Social Energy

The moment the national-religious-territorial trill of pernicious trump cards took control of the war, all its other causes and sources became ephemeral. For this reason it is difficult to prove that the Yu-war was directly caused by social reasons, as shown by the fact that not a single one of the war leaders used social arguments to produce war. Indeed, the need to create ethnically pure states was justified by the thesis that this was a precondition to the nation's future social prosperity. Thus, in the strict sense of the word, the Yu-war can be called civil only if by this we mean the internal armed conflict of the nationally and religiously opposed inhabitants of Yugoslavia.[14] The social sphere was simultaneously the most distant and yet closest to the Yu-war. In other words, social reasons were not the direct cause or trigger for war, but after its outbreak additional reasons to continue it were extracted from the social sphere.

The war's infusion with social elements stems from the well-known fact that it was waged in the existing social environment and the inhabitants of Yugoslavia were its social material. Thus it is much easier to establish the social effects than the social causes of the Yu-war. If we exclude those who were killed and wounded, the first and most serious consequence of the war was the forced – internal and external – migration of hundreds of thousands of people. At the same time, the war radically impoverished the broadest layer of society. Poverty was accompanied by the progressive collapse of the social fabric. On top of everything else, the forced change in the ethnic and demographic composition of the new states radically changed the sociological-graphical picture of former Yugoslavia. In addition, the war brought marginal social layers onto the scene. The incidental war criminal ended up as the basic criminalization of the emerging societies and states. At the same time, social changes started in the depths of these societies and their ultimate repercussions were not yet visible. This, along with the rest, accelerated the process of the disaggregation of society which was in any case insufficiently defined in social terms.

The war gave rise to a new and differently structured society. Complex social dynamics was. reduced to the whirlwind of nationalistic movements around the war and because of the war. A new configuration of social and particularly military-political and economic power was established. The content and number of those belonging to the governing classes changed;

the impoverished middle classes became a faceless part of the governed masses.[15] Propagators of the high goals of war were recruited from parts of the non-manufacturing classes. Owing to the destruction of the material basis of their own and social reproduction, the manufacturing classes lost their social identity. At the same time, their existence depended more and more on the newly arising power centers. Since they had been brought below the existential minimum, they became the driving force behind the Yu-war.

What kept the social sphere greatly distant from the Yu-war was the fact that the social reasons for war, or rather against war, were constantly wrapped in national packaging. The impoverished and lagging state of their nations (republics) was explained by the poor system and privileged position of other nations in Yugoslavia. Furthermore, everyone claimed that they were being exploited by others.[16] Owing to this, the population's rising social dissatisfaction at the end of the 1980s was transferred to national-religious reasons for war. Mechanisms already installed in the social system to mediate and manipulate the population's social needs were used for the transfer.

Since the structure and dynamics of Yugoslav society were determined by totalizing politics,[17] social conflicts were also mediated by politics. The instances, mechanisms and mainstays of mediating the social sources and causes of war were located in the sphere of politics. This was additionally facilitated by the fact that social conflicts in Yugoslav society always had an ideological dimension, but were also camouflaged.[18] Sooner or later, however, national and nationalistic considerations always penetrated through the ideology; since national considerations belonged to the sphere of ideology in the second Yugoslavia, national status was determined by ideological instruments.[19] So nationalism in the second Yugoslavia used self-management (ideological) phraseology and the accompanying system to create a permanent political and social stronghold for itself. At the same time, as the ruling ideology lost its persuasiveness, it used nationalism to prolong its existence.

On the eve of war when the socialistic collectivity was replaced by the national, new space was freed for the unlimited demonstration of individual and group frustrations. Then dissatisfaction induced by the position of one's own nation was used for the political promotion of nationalistic elites. At the same time, all the reasons for group and individual dissatisfaction were sublimated to national frustrations[20] and compensated for by them. The transfer of social conflicts into national conflicts concealed, above all, their economic and political sources. By bringing national arguments into the conflict, social energy was redirected to members of other ethnic groups. This left the key sources and causes of social handicaps once again outside the reach of the dissatisfied. Chopping up the social space nationally prevented interest-based linking and political organization of the handicapped layers and groups on the level of the Yugoslav society as a whole.

The precedence of ideology as a mediator was founded on the manner in which the Yugoslav society at the time was socially structured and differentiated. Since it was ideologically determined from above,[21] the production of surplus power was its basic raison d'etre.[22] The economy's subordination to ideology put an end to the autonomy of the individual and caused deformations in the social structure of society.[23] First, the revolutionary intervention of 1945 changed the social structure of society, which was not sufficiently ramified as it was. Then, based on changes in the nature of property, old classes and layers were done away with by force and new ones were created.[24] This simultaneously broke off economic incentives for social (interest) differentiation and links between members of society. This was followed by the accelerated and artificial creation of new social layers and groups. Industrialization based on the Soviet model was achieved with a combination of economic and repressive measures. Then came the sudden and massive migration from rural areas towards the towns with no economic justification.[25] There was a parallel petrifaction of the revolutionary structures of society based on the monopoly of collective property and power.[26] Consequently, a closed society arose with clearly defined classes and layers having growing social distance between them and decreasing social mobility.[27]

Yugoslavia society was therefore formed under the coercion of politics and ideology.[28] The ideological monolith that resulted stopped the social diversification of society. Feigning political pluralism and the organization of interest groups prevented the articulation and legal competition of different interests.[29] The ultimate irony was that the order identifying with the working class actually prevented its social formation and class consciousness.

Furthermore, with the introduction of self-management society was only decentralized and atomized but not democratized. This new division additionally prevented integration of the population's economic interests, removing the danger of global social conflicts but multiplying the number of conflicts on lower social levels. Segmentation achieved a twofold effect: conflicts were placed in the local framework and occurred among members of the same class and layer. Thus the manufacturing classes spent their social energy on settling accounts with each other without any chance of getting at the heart of their disadvantageous position. Anesthetized by the illusion of self-management, they became suitable material to be ideologically shaped and used for daily political purposes. When the nation (ethnic group) finally took possession of the political arena, social conflicts were transformed into national, and social dissatisfaction changed its substance and direction.

The role played by individual classes and layers in producing the Yu-war's social energy was unequal, of course. Since Yugoslav society had crucially differentiated with respect to the accessibility of political power, management and production classes arose within it.[30] The genesis of the political preparations and course of the Yu-war clearly indicated that these two groups played essentially different roles in the war.

Although the management classes changed personally, and after multiparty elections ideologically, they had a crucial effect on the outbreak of war. Facts indicate that two parallel types of competing management classes existed during this period. The first type was created by the communist nomenclature, which prepared the war politically. When they lost the elections in Slovenia, Croatia, Bosnia-Herzegovina and Macedonia, they supported the war programs of the new-nationalist management classes. Where they remained in power after the elections (Serbia and Montenegro), these management groups put on a nationalist guise. The second type consisted of nationalist management classes that were recruited from different social sources. They included a variety of groups and individuals that were not infrequently incompatible. Thus former communists, communist dissidents, extreme political emigrants, militant parts of the clergy and neo-fascists found themselves on the same side. They were held together by radical dissatisfaction with the Yugoslav state framework and their readiness to destroy it regardless of the price.

The production classes, of course, were the social raw material of the Yu-war. The reasons for this stemmed from their previous social status. Owing to their systemic and systematic powerlessness, existential dependence and ideological treatment, they were only the object of politics. Their resistance to new ideological manipulation drastically dropped owing to their sudden impoverishment caused by the crisis in the 1980s. Furthermore, the crisis turned them directly over to new manipulators. The longstanding habit of looking for and/or accepting external and irrational reasons for their unfavorable position made them appropriate objects to be manipulated by the new national elites. To make matters worse, members of the production classes and other powerless layers went very quickly from being the objects of manipulation to active participants in the destruction of war.

The (pre)war corrosion of the social structure and disintegration of the political system made room for the work of political pressure groups[31] that had a direct influence on the development of events in Yugoslavia. Most of these groups were recruited from three social sources. The first group consisted of members (associates, allies and descendants) of forces defeated in the 1941-1945 civil war. Their political program rested on anticommunism and chauvinistic revanchism, and was directed towards achieving the earlier, failed imperial programs of their nations. The second group, ideologically related to the first, arose from the ranks of postwar political and economic emigration. It had a direct influence on political happenings in Yugoslavia in the phase of political pluralization and the first multiparty elections in all the former republics. This is why most of the local noncommunist pretenders to power had the economic, political and propaganda support of these emigrants. This is also why emigrants were immediately included in new governments in all the republics except Serbia and Montenegro. Owing to this, emigrants had a considerable influence on the (pro)war strategy and tactics of the local nationalistic elite. The third group consisted of disempowered and retired communist nomenclatures. Their informal power was based on their mentorship of the still-ruling communist clubs. Owing to them the group of old communists made a powerful contribution to the Yu-crisis ending in war. The lobby of retired generals[32] held the central place in this circle. The moment the former generals divided up by ethnic group and started to clash, they became the key promoters of the '1941' model. Working together with Milošević and Tudjman, they immediately returned the conflict in Croatia to the setting of the Second World War, thereby canceling any possibility of compromise between Serbia and Croatia. When the same model was transferred to B-H, the Yu-war basically became a repetition of the past.

Presented findings about the social environment at the end of the 1980s confirm that all necessary social preconditions for war had been extracted from the deep – economic and political – crisis in Yugoslav society. But these were not necessarily preconditions for war. The deep-seated crisis opened numerous possibilities for an alternative outcome and its social consequences created at least the same preconditions to radically reform and modernize Yugoslav society. Thus the social environment at the time was both the point of departure and the destination for factors that produced the Yu-war. Each group of factors derived its force and energy from the social being of Yugoslav society, and then in return shaped and used it for their own needs. The war was therefore the ultimate social derivative of Yugoslav society, but what remained of society quickly became a derivative of war.

5.3 Cumulative Effect of the Legacy

Constitutional and systemic deficiencies in the second Yugoslavia's socialist order directly facilitated the country's disintegration in warfare. The entire constitutional-systemic legacy had reached the (pre)war sphere through this order. Conflicts at the end of the 1980s were both a replica and a product of previous constitutional developments, particularly since the state of Yugoslavia constantly dealt with the same problems throughout its 70 years of existence. Its leaders were endlessly looking for the optimum form of state; the fact that Yugoslavia met its end in internal war indicates that they were unable to find the proper solution to any of the country's problems.

The reasons for the final dissolution of Yugoslavia thus stem from the country's basic problems during 70 years of existence. In spite of this, the dilemma remains unresolved: since it was never completed as a state,[33] was Yugoslavia only an interim situation or was it the historically justified and easily squandered chance for the Southern Slavs to live together. The fact that it disappeared might easily lead to a conclusion regarding its historical (im)possibility. At the same time, such a conclusion, which is easily reached from analyzing the contradictory being of the state of Yugoslavia, simultaneously postpones any confrontation with the important causes of its dissolution in warfare.

Discussing the (un)sustainability of Yugoslavia requires an understanding of its constants as a state, with the realization that it is easier to determine what it did not have as a state rather than what it did have. Before discussing everything that Yugoslavia could have been given the possibilities available upon its inception, it must first be established why Yugoslavia was not a lasting and modern state. This is particularly important since the deficient state system and chronic political conflicts constantly kept the possibility alive that Yugoslavia might dissolve, as shown by the dissolution of the first Yugoslavia in 1941.[34]

It is a well-known fact that Yugoslavia's statehood united dissimilar entities. In the beginning not even their constitutional position was the same. The people with 'three names' (Serbs, Croats, Slovenes) had the status of the constituent, while the other ethnic communities were denied this. They all brought their inherent differences into the state – economic, political, national, religious, cultural and linguistic. The unequal starting positions necessarily led to the joined entities' different political and state aspirations.

Owing to this, Yugoslavia was the scene of constant clashes between greater or lesser conflicts of interest. Changes occurred in relations among political forces, joint interests and the means of waging political battle, but without any positive results. Clashing interests were periodically repressed,[35] maintaining the illusion of their prospective, lasting reconciliation. When the Yu-crisis entered its final phase at the end of the 1980s, these repressed and irreconcilable differences emerged with all their force. What Yugoslavia had been was only a mechanical and not functional community of different entities, and necessarily an unsuccessful state.

Furthermore, Yugoslavia never let go of the reserves and particular calculations accepted by its own creators. The periods of euphoric Yugoslav national feelings[36] at the moment of its inception (1918) and renovation (1945) only hid Yugoslavia's temporary nature. This is why it was the subject of repeated negotiations among the national elite. The endless disputes about Yugoslavia's identity and sovereignty stemmed, among other things, from different understandings of a people's right to self-determination. The thesis of this right having been used up by joining Yugoslavia was intended to show and constitutionally found the country's sovereignty.[37] Contrary to this, the claim that the right to self-determination had not been used up and did not expire contested Yugoslavia's authentic sovereignty.[38] This reduced it to an arranged and therefore *ad hoc*, changeable state community. For this reason, Yugoslavia's viability directly depended on the momentary political and national constellation and (ill)will of internal and external political forces.[39] This is why the country suffered from the chronic lack of political legitimacy, and the legality of every one of its governments was contested. as shown by the failed attempt at the self-management legitimization of the socialist rule.[40] The temporary and conditional nature of Yugoslavia confirms that it was basically an unaccepted state.

Yugoslavia's history is marked by constant conflicts between monistic and pluralistic forces, concepts and goals. The endless battle between unitarianism and separatism, or centralism and federalism, took place on the same level.[41] In the first Yugoslavia, Slovenian and Croatian federalism opposed the centralized (unitary) state. At the time, the federalists were politically willing to stay in the common state, but on changed grounds. In the second Yugoslavia, however, the political substance and meaning of these state options changed.

In the final act of the second Yugoslavia, modern federalism, which was represented by the former unitarists, was rejected by the former federalists who had become confederalists, and then ended up as secessionists.[42] Experience from both Yugoslavias indicates that the ruling elite had the same political reaction to the same state challenges. Federal demands in the first Yugoslavia were opposed by the attitude: one people (with three names), one state, one king. In the second Yugoslavia, the formula against an official confederation read: one party, one leader, one revolution (one goal) and one state. Domination of the external factor of functionality indicates that Yugoslavia was a permanently unformed state community both constitutionally and systemically.

Ever since its origin the state of Yugoslavia had sought a worthy model for its constitution. There were six constitutions in 70 years, four of which arose during socialist Yugoslavia; all were immediately changed by numerous amendments.[43] In spite of this, political conflicts regarding the nature of the state never ended. Yugoslavia was thus in a permanent state of constitutional crisis. Owing to this, it lacked democratic political institutions and effective mechanisms to reconcile conflicting interests.[44]

Yugoslavia was an undemocratic, authoritarian state whose authoritarianism was fed by the conflict between centripetal and centrifugal forces. The federal state was constantly stretched between separatism and unitarianism. Opposing demands were actually only the external expression of the different starting positions of the country's constituents and their different expectations. The state's small democratic and integrative capacities prevented the reconciliation of these conflicting interests.

Owing to Yugoslavia's unfinished and politically temporary nature, the integration of its inhabitants into a stable and harmonized community was missing. This was the other side of the 'political seesaw' on which Yugoslavia and its population had been 'teetering' for 70 years. In return, social non-integration in conjunction with separate and/or unitary tendencies prevented Yugoslavia's state and political completion. The roots of this lay in the permanent domination of politics over the economy. The lack of economic integration made it impossible for Yugoslavia to become a politically stable and permanent state community. The 'work' of a market economy was politically hampered in the first Yugoslavia and broken off in the second. This shortened the duration of Yugoslavia and impeded its citizens' civic development; the nation (ethnic group) thus became their central focus of identity.[45] Consequently, Yugoslavia was a non-integrated state and social community.

The constitutional-systemic disorder in the relationship between power and government supports this statement.[46] In principle, a political system should legalize and legitimize the unequal distribution between social power and government.[47] It then redistributes them and corrects them with regard to joint interests of state. In addition, systemic mechanisms of government founded on separation should provide the effective control of power, providing the initial conditions for compromise solutions to social and political conflicts, which is a prerequisite for a permanent state and social community.[48] The Yugoslav system, however, never had enough power. It was always outside the reach of the system, and thus those holding power ruled the system. During its short history, Yugoslavia was a powerless (disempowered) state.

The 'control package' of power in the first Yugoslavia was held by the elite gathered around the king, and in the second by the leader of the communist party, Josip Broz Tito. The system only served to legalize and implement their power. The internal redistribution of power and authority was made informally. Thus the national elite were constantly disputing over the amount, substance, and scope of their acquired or desired power and authority. This is why the federal state was constantly targeted by national oligarchies intending to reduce the state's power for their own benefit. Since this was always a battle for centralization or decentralization and not for the democratic control of power/authority, numerous changes to the constitutions and system did not have positive results. The political history of Yugoslavia can thus be understood as a lengthy and unsuccessful resolution of unitarian-separatist squaring the circle.[49]

Owing to its powerlessness, Yugoslavia's political system was necessarily defective. Then the defective system renewed its state of powerlessness. Deprived of autonomous driving power, it did not have self-development, self-protection and self-correction mechanisms. Subjected to constant derogation and blockades inside and outside the system,[50] Yugoslavia's political system suffered from entropy. Yugoslavia survived its first disintegration (1941), which turned out to be just a postponement of the final dissolution. After 50 years of incubation, the dissolution virus took hold of the second Yugoslavia and finished it off.

The course of the second Yugoslavia's disintegration confirms general findings regarding its constitutional and systemic being. After the system's crisis intensified in the 1980s, it became clear that it was a contradictorily constituted system of crises.[51] In spite of this, the system was functional until the collapse of socialism; regardless of how much it cost, it kept the communist oligarchy in power. The top Party people[52] periodically managed to remove 'plugs' in the system and it functioned according to their needs until the next blockage, with the expense of enormous social energy. Nonetheless, its fundamental dysfunctional nature could not be hidden. The worst thing was that the system was unable to satisfy the social needs and interests of its subjects. Power-holders used different means of manipulation – from repression to social corruption – and succeeded in holding the widespread dissatisfaction in check for a long time. When the crisis corroded their power they directed this dissatisfaction to the federal-confederal sphere and gave it a national charge.

After the collapse of the Yugoslav League of Communists, the system was unable to acquire sufficient power to function independently. All attempts at reconstruction and revitalization were blocked by the Serbian-Croatian-Slovenian axis.[53] Derogation of the constitutional-systemic assumptions and mechanisms of Yugoslavia laid bare the powerlessness of the federal government. Since the system did not have the mechanisms to amortize and peacefully resolve internal conflicts, its dysfunctional nature ended up in self-destruction. The second Yugoslavia with its existing constitutional-systemic assumptions and in a radically changed constellation, could not save itself. It could neither prevent the preparations for war nor stop the war once it started.

Notes

1   Vladan Vasiljevi immediately warned of this possibility; compare: Na šta je spremna vojska? (What is the Army prepared to do?), Vreme, 07.10.1991, 6.
2   For more on this: Mihajlo Mihajlov, Govor ne zaustavlja juriš (Talk doesn't stop the onslaught), Borba, 17-18.08.1991.
3   This is shown by Miroslav Lazanski's bias in the article 'Ko je izvazvao rat' (Who provoked the war), Politika, 06.10.1991.
4   An illustration of this is the text by Ivan Torov: 'Naoružani arbitri – Armijski prodor u neizvjesnost' (Armed arbiters - the Army's breakthrough to uncertainty), Oslobodjenje, 29.09.1991, 5.
5   Compare: Vladimir Gligorov, Politička vrednovanja (Political Valuation), Partizanska Knjiga, Belgrade, 1985, 10-11, 85-115.
6   See one of the approaches in: Ljubomir Tadić, Da li je nacionalizam naša sudbina? (Is nationalism our destiny?), author's edition, Belgrade, 1986, 65-70.
7   'Religion has remained the watershed of nations, and that is a basic rule. It appears only to be true for the Serbo-Croatian linguistic area, but it is essentially connected to both the Slovenian and Macedonian where language

and culture in backward agrarian societies have not defined the historical border of the nation. It has always been religion. In terms of type, it is a sectarian, religious type of nationalism.' Milorad Ekmečić, Stvaranje Jugoslavije 1790-1918 (Creating Yugoslavia 1790-1918), Prosveta, Belgrade, 1989, Vol. 1, 15.

8   This is confirmed by research results in the Belgrade region in the mid-1980s. See: Dragomir Pantić, Klasična i svetovna religioznost (Classical and Secular Religiousness), IDN, Belgrade, 1988, 145-157.

9   For more on the pre-election relations between the Church and DEMOS in Slovenia, see: Borba, 01.04.1991, 6.

10 For more on the relationship between HDZ and the Church, see: Vjernici uzimaju riječ (The faithful take the floor), Borba, 01-02.01.1991.

11 This is shown by the SPS document Predlog srpskog crkvenonacionalog programa (Proposal of a Serbian Church-national program), compare: Borba, 22-23.07.1989, 11.

12 Compare: Memorandum of the Holy Bishop's Council of the Serbian Orthodox Church, Borba, 29.05.1992, 8-9.

13 'Should Yugoslavia collapse, something I would not like to happen, the borders of Serbia would not be cut with regard to any AVNOJ or Brioni or any other scissors (...) In my opinion, should Yugoslavia collapse the western borders of Serbia would have to be determined according to the principles of natural and historical rights, in accordance with the ethnic map that was in effect on 6 April 1941.' Vuk Drašković, interview in Start – no. 1/1989, 135.

14 'But civil (war – M.H.) is also deprived of the speculative justification that we picked up for external wars – rejecting all moral considerations, particularly when not waged around the ruling system, rather the same system under different tutors and different names, we might add', B. Pekić, op. cit. 121.

15 According to data from Dr. Mirosinka Dinkić from the Economic Institute in Belgrade, during the 1980s changes appeared in the middle classes in Serbia and Montenegro that indicate their impoverishment and depersonalization, in: Borba, 15-16.08.1992, IV.

16 For more on this see: Ljubomir Madžar, Ko koga eksploiteše (Who is exploiting whom) in: Serbian Side of the War, Neboša Popov (ed.), Republika, Belgrade, 1996.

17 'In socialist societies the market took on a second class role. Market operations do not allow conscious social regulations and it determines the property relations prices and rents, and the position of most social protagonists, and their class status. This role of the market in socialist countries has for the most part been replaced by the leading role of the communist party which has fused with the state. Social relations in the field of economics are regulated in advance, carefully planned and voluntarily, by

political activity through the process that is known as planning'. Tomc Goraze, Društvena stratifikacija i razvoj nacija u posleratnoj Jugoslaviji (Social stratification and the development of the nation in postwar Yugoslavia), Sociologija, no. 2-3/89, 502.

18 In Yugoslav society there are 'at least four levels on which opposing interests are formed and create the conditions for potential or open social conflicts: a) conflicts stemming from social differentiation that is institutionalized by social inequality (class conflicts are formed on this level); b) conflicts on a national basis; c) conflicts along the line of ideology in interpreting the desired organization of society (shown primarily in the sphere of culture as the conflict of ideology/politics and creativity); d) conflicts that arise from the lack of harmonizing the interests and needs of the individual and society/state.' Zagorka Golubović, Kriza identita savremenog jugoslovenskog društva (Modern Yugoslav society's identity crisis), Filip Višnjić, Belgrade, 1988, 326.

19 'The basic function (of the system of dogma disguised in substantive rationality – M. H.) is to totalize and supervise society... The doctrine expounded by the party is the mandatory credo for all members of society; all other values and interpretations are excluded; they cannot be openly investigated or at the least, in a sometimes very awkward way, must be in line with the last spoken words of the sovereign,', Feher Ferenc, Heler Agnuš, Markuš Djerdj, Diktatura nad potrebama (Dictatorship over needs), Rad, Belgrade, 1986, 279.

20 'Among the defensive reactions to frustration that are the most important to understanding social behavior are: (1) aggression, (2) regression, (3) withdrawal, (4) repression, (5) reaction formation, (6) rationalization, (7) projection, (8) autism, (9) identification', Kreč, Kračfild, Balaki, Belgrade 1972, 123.

21 'The basic principle of the Soviet type of domination that was the only one achieved in practice in all periods of Soviet history is the principle of the leading role of the party... Although the party decides about everything, it cannot rule without social institutions. So what is the basic function of the party? Simply this: in a one-party system the party is sovereign, it is the source of all power.' Feher Ferenc, Heler Agnuš, Markuš Djerdj, op. cit., 230-231.

22 'It is being shown how an essential characteristic of 'real socialism' is actually the reproduction of surplus power as the supporting, formative political and – considering the status of society in such denials – essential social relationship', Žarko Puhovski, Povijesnost socijalističke realizacije društva (History of the Socialist Realization of Society), Naše teme no. 12/84, 2950.

23 'Replacing the dominant figures (in 1945 – M.H.) was not simply replacing the political elite with different projections on the development of the social system, but replacing all dominant figures; the new dominant political figures took over dominant positions in the sphere of the economy, which means that they filled the empty positions of the mainstays of the process of modernization in the sphere of industrial technology and, generally speaking, the economy', Malden Pešec, Slom jugoslovenskih elita modernizacije (The collapse of Yugoslavia's modernization elite), Sociologija, no. 2-3/89, 456.

24 'There were two basic directions of change in the structure of society after 1945: the first in which there was a deep transformation of the basic social classes and their internal composition, so that they became the 'class remains', and the second in which, within the framework of state ownership, there was structuring of social groups that were not the basic classes in the true sense of the word.' Vlada Milić, Revolucija i socijalna struktura (Revolution and social structure), Mladost, Belgrade, 1978, 65-66.

25 'Great changes in the number of members of the classes and self-identification, which is the result of rapid industrialization, calls into question the existence of class 'cores' of collectivity that represent 'relatively stable and lasting' components among people with similar class positions. (...) Judging by the experience of other societies in the process of industrialization, several generations are needed in order to develop a new homogenous class core. And this supports the claim of class disintegration in Yugoslav society which has experienced an enormous outflow from the class of private farmers, a great influx into and outflow from the working class, and a powerful inflow into the middle and ruling class.' Tomc, Gorazd, op., cit. 506.

26 'The new class draws its power, privileges and habits from a special form of ownership – collective ownership, i.e. ownership that it manages and distributes in the 'name' of the nation, in the 'name' of society.' Milovan Djilas, Nova klasa (New Class), Narodna Knjiga, Belgrade, 1990. 48.

27 'The existing social structure is the result of an extremely tumultuous process of vertical mobility, natural for a post-revolutionary epoch that is simultaneously a period of essential structural transformation (from agrarian/rural to industrial/urban society). The stabilization of these provisional processes reveals the immanent form of mobility of socialist society. It cannot be unequivocally defined as either open or closed. The self-renewal of the group is the basic form of reproduction, which indicates the class nature of society.' Mladen Lazić, U susret zatvorenom društvu (Towards a closed society), Naprijed, Zagreb, 1987, 104-5.

28 'As far as socialist society is concerned, today the view is broadly accepted that the primary basis of stratification is the individual's position in the political social subsystem. This position takes on crucial meaning because the

predominance of political over economic logic is characteristic of socialism. Therefore the social proponents' distance from the center of political decision making becomes important for an understanding of daily life in such societies.' Tomc Gorazd, op. cit. 502.

29 For problems on the articulation, competition and legalization of interests in Yugoslav society, see: Silvano Bolčić, Interesna dimenzija razvoja (The interest dimension of development), CEKADE, Zagreb, 1987, in particular 23-74.

30 'The clearest class differences (and opposition) are along the lines: a) the approach to work roles, in particular the division into the unemployed and those who can get a job or have a job, and in the accessibility to those types of work that express the class division of labor, and b) the approach to political power (functions). In the first line, divisions are expressed in the form of employed-unemployed and manual-non-manual workers, and in the second in the form of the division into management and production classes (although in this plane confrontations with the management class expand to the non-production classes who are removed from the power centers owing to their social position)'. Z. Golubović, op. cit., 300.

31 Referring to the analysis by Morris Diverget (Introduction to Politics, Savremena administracija, Belgrade, 1966), we might say this was a combination of 'illegal groups' (p. 90) and 'pressure groups' (p. 99-103), whose arsenal of means and legal status changed with changes in the political constellations in the former republics.

32 Although there are no official data, it is estimated that by 1990 around 1,000 participants in the National Liberation War (WWII) and officers were promoted to the rank of general. Most of the Serbian war generals came from regions in Croatia and B-H where the Ustashe and various yataghan divisions committed massive war crimes against the Serbian population.

33 For more on this see: Zoran Djindjić, Jugoslavija kao nedovršena država (Yugoslavia as an incomplete state), KZ Novi Sad, 1988, 19-38.

34 For more on this see: Istorija Jugoslavije (History of Yugoslavia), group of authors, Prosveta, Belgrade, 1972, 457-471.

35 Such attempts include the January 6 dictatorship of King Alexander and Tito's party showdown with nationalist leaders in the 1970s; compare: The Proclamation of King Alexander (January 6, 1929) and a document linked to the 'Road Affair', the massive movement in Croatia and liberalism in Serbia;' compare: Branko Petranović, Momčilo Zečević, Jugoslavija 1918/1988 (Yugoslavia 1918/1988) – thematic collection of documents, Rad, Belgrade, 1988, 313 and 1147-1171.

36 This is illustrated by the Declaration (Zagreb, June 5, 1917) and the Resolution (Zagreb, June 5, 1918) of Starčević's Party in which mention is

also made of the people with 'three names'; compare: Jugoslavia 1918/1988, op. cit. 84-85 and 89-90.

37 Compare: Borba, views of CK SK Serbia, 14.07.1989, 1 and 3, Presidency of SR Serbia, 26.07.1989, 6.

38 Compare: 'Basic document of Slovenia 89', Borba, 24-25.06.1989, 11 and the Thesis of the Presidency of CK SK Slovenia on interethnic relations, in which the proposal of an asymmetrical federation is made; Borba, 30.06.1989 and 2.07.1989, 7.

39 'In the same vein, this book represents the principle that the unification of Yugoslavia was not only their (the peoples') consideration. This is one of the legacies of mankind's history... Had the unification of Yugoslavia in 1918 depended only on the Yugoslavs, they would not have united.' Milorad Ekmečić, op. cit. 16.

40 'Within this model (of an integral state) the basic process takes place in the form of destroying and colonizing civic society by all-powerful actions of the state and politics. What is important about this type of relationship is that within it the functional precedence of the political system (and state) is reproduced with respect to culture and the economy, and a relationship is established between 'systemic imperatives of survival' with the precedence of reproducing the imperative of political administration with respect to the imperative of economic rationality and political legitimacy', Milan Podunavac, Politički legitimitet (Political legitimacy), Belgrade, 1988, 254.

41 This is shown by political disputes about the nature of the state as set out in the draft Vidovdan Constitution. Autonomist statements by Slovenian cultural workers (February 1921), the opinions of Etbin Kristan and Jovan Djonović, national delegates, and the Separate Opinion of the Yugoslav Club on the draft Constitution (April 6, 1921) illustrate the federalists' demands. Contrary to this, there was centralistic-unitarian criticism of the Constitution, for example from Matko Laginja. Compare: Jugoslavia 1918/1988, op. cit., 178-198, together with the comments of the collection compiler.

42 For more see: Vojislav Stanovčić, Federalism/Confederalism, Univerzitetska riječ, Titograd, 1986, in particular 7-27 and 77-105.

43 For more see: Ustavni razvoj socialističke Jugoslavije (The constitutional development of socialist Yugoslavia), a collection of works by a group of authors and documents, Eksportpres, Belgrade, 1988.

44 For more on the procedural side of the problem see: Lidija R. Basta, Ustav i demokratija – šema tri interpretacije (Constitution and democracy – outline of three interpretations) in the collection Two Centuries of Modern Constitutionality, Belgrade, Serbian Academy of Science and Arts, 1990, 283-298.

45 See: Žarko Puhovski, Mijena i povijesnost (Changes and Historicity) in Prijepori oko političkog sistema)Disputes about the political system=, Zagreb, 1985, 103-110.
46 See: Žarko Puhovski, Moć i program (Power and the program), Naše teme, no. 7-8/86, 1158-1165.
47 For more see: Nojman Franc, Demokratska i autoritarna država (Democratic and authoritarian state), Naprijed, Zagreb, 1974, 69-85, and Ljubomir Tadić, Nauka o politici (The Science of politics), Rad, Belgrade, 1988, 79-100.
48 See: Jovan Mirić, Manjina, većina, konsenzus (Minority, majority, consensus), Naše teme no. 11/89, 2762-2772; for the same thing but in a different way: Zvonko Lerotić, Još jedanput: od nacionalne individualnosti do načela konsezusa (Once again: from national individuality to the principle of consensus), Naše teme, no. 7-8/86, 958-978, in particular 971 onward.
49 This is shown by the discussion between Dušan Pirjavec and Dobrica Ćosić at the beginning of the 1960s on Slavic national feelings, Yugoslav national feelings and socialism, i.e. the nation, integration and socialism; compare: Dobrica Ćosić, Akcija (Actions), Prosveta, Belgrade, 1964, 203-267.
50 See: Zoran Djindjić, op. cit., 128-145.
51 See: JovanMirić, Sistem i kriza (System and crisis), CEKADE, Zagreb, 1985; Vojislav Stanovčić, Kriza sistema i system krize (Crisis of the system and system of crises), op., cit., 195-218.
52 See: Vladimir Goati, SKJ, kriza, demokratija (Yugoslav League of Communists, crisis, democracy), CEKADE, Zagreb, 1986, in particular 7-72.
53 On the ideological-theoretical justification of different concepts of organizing the federation, see: Slobodan Samardžić, Pred-federalna Jugoslavija: različite zamisli jugoslovenskog federalizma (Pre-federal Yugoslavia: different ideas about Yugoslav federalism), THEORIA, 2/1989, Belgrade, 53-67.

Chapter 6

The Powerlessness of the Military's Might

All understandings of the disintegration of Yugoslavia, regardless of their differences, have one thing in common: emphasizing the JNA's role in the disastrous outcome of the crisis. The evaluation has been forwarded that the JNA might have been able to prevent the outbreak of war if its operations had been more effective.[1] These unfulfilled expectations are primarily based on the allegedly great, and unutilized, political power of the top generals stemming from the Army's military power – its monopoly over the armed forces.

The insufficient amount of research on the JNA's military and political role in Yugoslavia's disintegration can be explained by analytical oversight. In addition, the Army's social and military essence was unknown and/or not given enough consideration. The JNA had been shielded for decades from parliamentary and public control, and been buttressed by ideological glorification, easily giving rise to unfounded expectations. Thus, an understanding of the JNA's destructive role as well as its collapse requires knowledge of its military and social nature. It is only from these premises that we can evaluate whether the JNA could have acted otherwise; and if it could have, then why it failed to do so. Reliable results are only to be found within the context of an analysis of the developments, causes and essence of the disintegration of the state of SFR Yugoslavia. This is because estimations of the scope of the Army's power(lessness) easily skate over the complex and quickly changing social, political, national, ideological, state and international context.

A better understanding of the JNA's role in the second Yugoslavia's disintegration in the flames of war requires the reconstruction of critical and potential turning points (crossroads)[2] of the crisis which, had the top generals acted otherwise, might have elicited better results. The JNA's great political independence at the end of the 1980s allowed its leaders to choose, in principle, between arising alternatives and even create new ones.

The results, however, indicate that the top JNA generals were unable to develop, let alone carry out, a single effective alternative to prevent the dissolution of the state and the internal war. This brings us back to our initial, key question: Could the JNA and the military leaders have acted differently in the crisis?

Our intended reconstruction might be called speculation, its authenticity contested by the fact that when the crisis crossroads were crystallizing the top generals had very little room in which to choose. In spite of this, such a reconstruction has investigative grounds.

Identifying the critical points of the crisis increases our chances of finding the internal logic behind Yugoslavia's political erosion and wartime destruction, and whether or not it was inevitable. This also makes it easier to evaluate the prospects at the time of finding compromise and/or nonviolent alternatives. Such findings enable a re-assessment of the activities of each of the domestic actors and shed light on their basic motives for choosing the alternative of war. Then, within this context, we will be able to verify whether there were reasons to expect the JNA to act differently. Only then can we establish whether the reasons for the Army's powerlessness were of a political or military origin, that is, whether the political incompetence of the top generals made the Army professionally powerless or whether, during the (pre)war situation, all of the JNA's military deficiencies rose to the surface and were then simply multiplied by the military leaders' policies.

Modeling the military leaders' choices, their optimum choice at the first crossroads increased their chances of making the same choice at the second crossroads. Their wrong choice at the first crossroads made it more likely that they would make the wrong choice at the second, third and every subsequent crossroads. Making a good choice required the existence of sufficient and interconnected prerequisites, with all the consequences of making such a choice having been deduced or calculated.

Without fulfilling and/or creating sufficient prerequisites, the top generals could not make the optimal choice at a single crossroads. The lack of sufficient prerequisites at the first crossroads made it hard for needed prerequisites to arise that would result in a good choice at the second crossroads. In the same vein, by not suffering all the consequences of their first choice, the unfavorable and then accumulated and multiplied consequences of every subsequent choice were implicitly denied. Denying such consequences can partially explain the ideological being of the Army and the key generals' arrogance. However, not calculating all the ultimate consequences of the JNA's further activities indicates that the military leaders did not respect the basic procedures of their own profession.

The generals' wrong choice at the first crossroads decreased their chances of making the optimal choice at the second, which made any turnabout at the third quite unlikely. Specifically, since the generals continued their ideological orientation at the first crossroads (the dissolution of the League of Communists of Yugoslavia - SKJ), it is hard to expect subsequent choices to be any different or better. In addition, any later change in their choice and the direction of their activities drastically decreased the feasibility of the new options. Thus we must establish whether and to what extent the top generals really were able to choose in the given circumstances. This requires isolating the impact of the military leaders on the JNA's behavior from the influence of other actors, which is not at all easy.

For this purpose we will reconstruct the JNA's various possible (pre)war interventions in the crisis in order to measure the political scope of its military power as the crisis reached a head. Our points of departure are that the JNA's power to intervene was ultimately thwarted by factors outside the Army that were primarily uncontrollable, immeasurable and incalculable; but also that the JNA's failure was the ultimate product of its immanent military-political deficiencies. It is only by crossing these two groups of factors and analyzing their interactions that we can discover the reasons for the Army's powerlessness and collapse.

The modalities of the JNA's reactions to the Yugoslav crisis were certainly limited by the constellation of political forces in play and the rapidly changing situation. In spite of this, the top generals had several variations to choose from, although interconnected and difficult to distinguish, in the individual phases of the second Yugoslavia's social and state crisis.

Several reasons hinder the use of analytical models. It is quite difficult, for example, to determine the time limit of each alternative. Then there is the problem of how to measure the impact of numerous dependent and independent variables, and the external and internal risk of any potential choice by the top generals. This is particularly true when measuring the impact of the multiethnic and multi-confessional structure of society and the Army on the JNA leaders' choices. It is even harder, particularly after the fact, to judge the feasibility of different options at the time, and to calculate the amount of Army power and force needed for their implementation.

The key problem is in reliably determining the reasons why the Army leaders chose or rejected one or another alternative. Another problem is how to establish whether and to what extent their choice was conditioned or rationalized by someone's interests, and if so, whose. It is also difficult to measure the influence of the personal composition of the Supreme Command Staff (SNNO and the JNA General Staff) on the quality of the choice that was made. This is particularly true when measuring the influence of the top generals' ethnic affiliation on their choice.

In the same vein, it is hard to establish the exact proportions of the top generals' political independence when choosing among the options for the JNA's operations. For example, political neutrality was an essential prerequisite for most alternatives. Bearing in mind the JNA's profile, this requires answering the question as to whether the military leaders were at all capable of being nationally, ideologically and politically neutral. In other words, was it possible to expect the top generals to remain neutral in their personal values and interests when the JNA had lost its systemic, political and social support (security); the top generals had yet to reach that neutral position, although they were supposed to, and willingly, amid the worsening crisis and contrary to their ideological origins.

The genesis of the JNA's involution in the crisis nonetheless allows the construction of several ideal-typical variations. As they are outlined, we will bear in mind the previously presented situational framework within which the top generals were solely able to operate, and focus on the nominal possibilities available to the top generals and the JNA.

Owing to their relationship towards the forces in play and their level of independence, by the beginning of the war the JNA and the top generals could have, wanted to, or had to play one of the following roles:

6.1 Irrevocable Submission to State Control after the Dissolution of SKJ

This is the most effortless and only normal social and systemic position for every army. Submission to the state and democratically elected civil authorities releases the army, among other things, from political responsibility for the fate of the current rulers. However, as already shown, after the JNA leaders' unsuccessful and persistent defense of socialism, they even tried to release themselves from responsibility for the fate of the country.

Returning to the state after the collapse of SKJ meant in principle a passive-executor role for the military leaders. This required the establishment of an equidistant political and ideological position with respect to the forces in play and their programs. As events were to show, the top generals could not and did not want to accept this for several reasons.

Sufficient state and political prerequisites did not exist in 1990 for the Army to be under the control of civil authorities. The Congress that dissolved SKJ was the beginning of the end of the second Yugoslavia. The accelerating disintegration of the state and society was taken to extreme nationalistic-chauvinistic consequences. It was no longer possible to establish a political consensus around any of the variations to (re)organize Yugoslavia. Federal centers of power and authority were powerless and blocked by the republics. At the same time, basic differences existed between the SFRY Presidency and SIV – the Army's nominal commanders – regarding the country's organization. So when the Party disappeared, there was no authority with sufficient power to command the Army. In addition, the commanders that did exist had neither sufficient power, nor interest, to define relevant state goals and impose them on the top generals as being of supreme importance.

At the end of the 1980s, the top generals had gained great political independence owing to the constitutional-systemic interregnum. For the first time they were in a position to choose almost independently between current political alternatives. Their understanding of this unexpected independence, however, was the freedom to choose, regardless of the specific circumstances. This was the root of their first great strategic oversight: the illusion that socialism and Yugoslavia in its existing form could be saved independent of the will of the republican and national power-holders, and even contrary to it.

Consequently, the Army leaders did not want to renounce their previous role as the political and ideological guardians of socialism and 'Tito's Yugoslavia'. They proved unable to separate the problem of the survival of socialism from the problem of the survival of the state of Yugoslavia, and to give them individual treatment. The generals did not want to accept the fact that 'safeguarding and building socialism' was not within the JNA's jurisdiction. The Army's attachment to socialism was greater than any reason and interest of state. This led to a far-reaching twisting of the argument: state interests – safeguarding the territorial integrity and wholeness of Yugoslavia – were reduced to safeguarding socialism in Yugoslavia at any price. Thus the military leaders continued to pursue their (own) Party policies instead of the state's policies.

The top generals' partial interests were actually hidden behind the ideological reasons for defending socialism. With the disappearance of SKJ, the generals lost their primary means to take part in the distribution of social and state power. Even more important, SKJ's self-dissolution had resulted in the JNA leaders losing the central part of their social identity; they no longer had any pretense for their daily involvement in politics. The parallel blockade of the economic and political system directly jeopardized the foundations of the JNA. The very survival of the Army and its members was threatened.

Owing to the military leaders' ideological hibernation, during 1990 they lost their chance to play the role of repressive mediator exacting political compromise from the national/ethnic elite. Had they become duly subordinate to the state and renounced the defense of socialism, the top generals could have preserved sufficient legitimacy to put linear military-political pressure on all the actors, which might have forced a peaceful agreement on the fate of Yugoslavia. When the top generals finally tried to play this role at the SFRY Presidency meeting in March 1991, the situation in the country had radically changed.

Additional reasons behind the military leaders' unsuitability for this as well as all other roles stemmed from the fact that the JNA could not transform its own self. In order for the JNA to become an efficient instrument of the state after the collapse of SKJ, it would have had to undergo a radical transformation, something it was not capable of doing. Along with their ideological blinders, the military leaders were pressured by the inertia of a great, closed system that needed initiatives for change from the outside. And there was no one on the outside anymore to initiate such change, since the national-republican leaders were busy tearing the country apart. In addition, radical changes to the JNA's being and the system of defense would have destroyed the inter-army mechanisms of the distribution of power, and jeopardized the individual and group interests that had been established. In particular, changes would have deprived the central group of generals of the political power they had acquired with respect to society and the Army. Putting themselves under the command of the state, the military leaders would have ceased to be an independent (daily) political factor. Furthermore, they would have lost their unrestricted freedom to fashion the Army as they saw fit and their, practically speaking, unrestrained grip on the state budget.

6.2 Alliance of Reform with the Federal Government

The Army leaders' relationship towards the Federal Government (SIV) and the reform program was their second potential crossroads (turning point). It seems that if the Army leaders had given hearty support to reforms and the Government this might have tipped the scales towards a positive resolution of the crisis. In order to play this role, however, the generals would have had to renounce their ideological ambitions first and become subordinate to the state as personified in the Government; after the SKJ fell apart, the military-political involvement of the top generals could only be justified by reasons of state, and by constitutional and international law. And this would only happen with the approval or at the order of SIV and the SFRY Presidency.

At the beginning of 1990, had the military leaders stood publicly and irrevocably alongside of reforms and, in cooperation with Ante Marković's Government, shown its readiness to use force if necessary to assure peace until a final agreement about Yugoslavia was reached, they might have prevented the crisis from developing into war. But the JNA's political support of the Government without the threat of force probably would not have meant very much. Thus, in this variation the top generals had to send a clear signal regarding their readiness to carry out a coup for the sake of reforms and/or compromise about the fate of Yugoslavia. This also required that the key generals accept the reform program and subordination to the Government. The last moment for this was the announcement of the second package of governmental reform measures in July 1990. Two reasons supported this: first, SIV still enjoyed the support of the broader public,[3] and second, the JNA had not yet started to erode internally along national/ethnic lines, thus their effective alliance was possible on the Yugoslav state platform.

The prospects of this variation lay in the fact view that during SIV's evolution from 'new socialism' to the (pro)civic reconstruction of Yugoslavia it had managed to define a valid program that was in principle capable of resolving the crisis. Judged from the viewpoint of the program's goal – the radical resolution of the crisis within the Yugoslav scope – it was necessary and suitable enough. But owing to changes in the Yugoslav political constellation, and that within the republics, this program was clearly unfeasible.

One of the reasons for the Government's failure was the lack of capital for reform purposes. Promised international financial support was missing,[4] and internal accumulation had been spent long ago. Thus the Government was critically handicapped, both economically and politically. It could not provide financial support to restructure the economy, nor could it use economic means to parry political obstructions to reform. It seems that the only way the Government could have brought the top generals to its side at the time would have been to buy their loyalty. Had Ante Marković received the money he needed from the West, his financing of the Army's development programs (for example, building a supersonic jet) and the social needs of the JNA's members might have been enough to bribe the top generals, and at least neutralize them ideologically if not bring them over completely to the Government's side.

Indeed, until the beginning of the war the top generals did not officially contest the Government's reform program, although they distanced themselves from it objectively. They intuitively suspected that it was dangerous for their own political and economic position. A market economy and political system tailored to it would sooner or later impose radical changes on the JNA's being and position. Thus the military leaders were increasingly suspicious of the Government's reform program. They saw it as the intentional restoration of capitalism in conjunction with the so-called world anti-socialist conspiracy and its (Yugoslav) hirelings.[5] The military leaders also had reserves towards SIV owing to the Government's approach to Yugoslavia; its attempt to supercede the confederal-federal dichotomy did not correspond in the slightest to the top general's unambiguous preference for a (socialist) federation. If this had yet to make SIV a political opponent, it certainly was not an ally of the military leaders and the other federalists. Another reason was that the Government had not accepted the military's evaluation of the country's 'political-security' situation or its arsenal of proposed measures.

A limiting factor to any hypothetical cooperation between the Government and the JNA can also be found in the fact that both were very quickly left without broad social and political support. The nationalistic elite took over all the population's energy for reform and redirected it destructively for their own benefit.

We would note one other (sub)variation of cooperation between the Army and the Government, although it was not very likely. The campaign against Slovenia was the JNA's last moment to carry out a coup in favor of SIV. There are no indications that any initiatives in this regard existed, but such a combination might have had some prospects. By analogy to South Korea, the top generals and the Government might have been able to preserve minimum state (pre)conditions for market economy reforms. This would probably have increased the chances of stopping the spiraling war at the first turn.

6.3 Independent Putsch

The variation of a military putsch which would suspend the Constitution, the system and its subjects until a new agreement was reached on Yugoslavia had been around for a long time and was publicly known during the political part of the crisis. All the participants exploited it for their own reasons. The military leaders publicly denied such a possibility on several occasions and were distinctly in favor of legal moves. It is interesting to note that the generals' subsequent writings reject this possibility since it was allegedly a 'great, but nonetheless very illusory deception'.[6]

A military coup was feasible in principle throughout the political part of the crisis. However, as time passed and the crisis heightened, its chances dropped as its 'price' rose. It seems as though a military coup could only have succeeded had it been carried out within the communist coordinates of the system. The coup did not necessarily have to have a communist substance, but the framework and mechanisms of what remained of the system could have been used to carry it out. Furthermore, an anticommunist or neo-socialist platform for the coup might even have succeeded more easily than the rigid Bolshevistic platform represented by the top generals.

The last propitious moment for a coup was on the eve of the first multiparty elections, since it was clear that nationalist-separatist forces would win at the elections in Slovenia and Croatia. After the electoral legalization of separatism, the multiethnic makeup of the state and the JNA became an insurmountable obstacle to a military coup. Thus the putsch could only have been carried our properly and without any great (armed) resistance before the radical and final nationalistic reorientation of most of the population. Before the elections, the military leaders could have gained public support for a military coup by acting from the Yugoslav state position,[7] and by criticizing the extant state of socialism and announcing a reform-minded pro-civic option.

The top generals, however, were not capable of independently articulating a political strategy that would be acceptable to both the internal and international public. Since they remained within the ideology of socialism until the last possible moment, the military leaders were unable to provide broader public support for a coup. Moreover, even if the generals had taken over power with a coup they did not have a clear, new vision of Yugoslavia. In other words, they could not formulate an attainable and acceptable goal that would justify their actions. Therefore, they were unable to calculate with any assurance whether they had enough internal and external political support for a military coup.

In addition, the military leaders could not objectively establish whether they would have any internal allies for a coup. The ease with which they had marked their ideological and state opponents turned the tables on them in their search for allies. The modern federalists were an unsatisfactory ally since they shared the generals' common illusion that their power was enough to prevent Yugoslavia's unilateral breakup. Furthermore, the modern federalists had already prepared a reserve state variation for themselves in which there was no place for the JNA as it was.

The generals' mental confusion is also shown by their attempt to obtain the SFRY Presidency's approval for a hidden military coup in March 1991. From the strategic point of view, however, the military leaders had chosen the worst moment for their intention, since the Slovenian and Croatian public were already ideologically and organizationally prepared for all-out armed resistance to the JNA.

In spite of this, at the end of 1989 and beginning of 1990 most of the professional soldiers in the JNA were inclined towards a radical resolution to the state crisis. Therefore, undertaking proper actions, the military leaders would have been able to assure at least the Army's full support of a coup. However, there were insurmountable obstacles once again, this time in the form of the JNA's system of organization and the leading generals' inability to prepare a coup and carry it out. The key generals' lack of personal and group courage for such a risky undertaking should also not be excluded.[8]

In order to take over the state government and/or protect the constitutional order, the top generals had to have elaborated war plans and units at the ready with distinct goals.[9] The military leaders clearly saw a coup as an equation with too many unknowns in which they did not know how to and/or did not even want to calculate the JNA's combat possibilities. Thus all that remained was to justify the JNA's hesitation with legalistic phrases, which did not in the lease prevent them later from amputating Slovenia and abandoning the call-up system at the beginning of the war.

But even if the JNA had carried out a coup there were no guarantees as to whether the top generals would take the role of mediator in negotiations about Yugoslavia's future or would end up as dictators. There was even less likelihood that they would have exacted a South Korean or similar solution. This is because the top generals were incapable of defining clear tactical and strategic goals of a coup even for the JNA, let alone anyone else. The Army's internal intervention might have prevented and/or postponed war, but it could not have resolved a single one of Yugoslavia's fundamental problems as a state and social community. This is because, inter alia, the seceding republics would have greeted a coup as a move to favor the modern federalists, i.e. Serbia, and an internal war would once again have been highly probable. Since an independent coup would have meant removing the Serbian political center from power, such a variation would have necessarily brought the JNA into conflict with Serbia, something the top generals were not prepared to do.

6.4 Accepting and Supporting the Recomposition of Yugoslavia

In the home stretch of the political crisis two opposing concepts of Yugoslavia's constitutional makeup had crystallized – confederal and federal. In simple terms, the first followed the 1974 Constitution, tending towards independence of the republics and a fundamental change in the hybrid state structure. Contrary to this, the federalist variation undertook a revision of the '1974 model' and the redistribution of power and authority from the republics towards the federal center. What they had in common was an unequivocal change in the status quo, and based on this a crucial polarization of political and national forces. The JNA and its supreme commanders could not remain outside these processes. Regardless of the fact that the top generals had already come out clearly in favor of a 'modern federation', let us examine whether they could have assisted in the peaceful recomposition or decomposition of Yugoslavia.

6.4.a Support for turning Yugoslavia into a confederation

Even without any special analysis, the reasons why the JNA was incompatible with the confederal model are easy to understand. When this model became official (October 1990) the crisis had already spread to the national (ethnic) fiber of society. Political conflicts had been transformed into national and nationalistic conflicts, and everyone found refuge in their ethnic group. The political erosion of the joint state had already entered the final phase. Immediate and comprehensive preparations were being made for an all-out war against each other.

Unwilling and unable to discover the true reasons for the collapse of 'real self-management', the top generals declared anti-communism and national-separatism to be the main causes of the crisis. They therefore used the '1941' blueprint in the Manichaean manner to classify people into allies and opponents. Burdened by the Army's revolutionary pedigree, the top generals were unable to extricate themselves from the ideological cliche for a long time, and thus lumped all demands for change together under the counterrevolutionary title. When the generals realized that reasons of state lay behind everything, it was already too late – national-separatism had already been legalized and established itself.

The military leaders explained their resistance to the confederal recomposition of Yugoslavia using constitutional-systemic and defense-security reasons. Regardless of how formally valid they were, these reasons were just one more rationalization by the generals. It is true that the SFRY Constitution gave the JNA its dimensions in accordance with the federal organization of the country, but it was also true that based on this the Army had almost unlimited sovereignty in the military organization of society. The federal variation not only rescinded the federal foundation of the Army as it was, but directly endangered the top generals' autonomous power. Rejecting this variation, in the name of carrying out the JNA's constitutional role, the top generals publicly refused to change their systemic position and renounce part of their power.

Another reason to reject the confederation was the fact that the JNA top generals and officer corps were unprepared to accept the risks involved in searching for existential refuge in the newly arising states. The JNA members' ideological, psychological and value-system connection was with Yugoslavia and worked against the idea of a confederation. This was particularly true of the majority Serbian members who understood the transparent agreement between the military's and Serbia's support for a federal Yugoslavia as protection of their national as well as existential interests.

But the main reason the JNA was not able to support a confederal Yugoslavia was the growing alliance between Serbia's leaders and the top generals based on common interests and ideology as well as on their national/ethnic affiliation. Their high political agreement in this period was based on numerous overlapping interests, existential above all. Owing to the Army's systemic-conceptual characteristics and needs, only a federal Yugoslavia could guarantee its survival, and thus it was directly interested in such a Yugoslavia. Serbia's interests at that time were also designed and articulated with respect to a federal Yugoslavia. This is why the JNA was a key instrument of Serbia's policies since the Army protected its state, national and political interests. The emotional and value-based (?) substance of the military-Serbian alliance provided ideological closeness. Similar ideological-political views on all key problems of the crisis made them natural allies. In addition, in the prewar phase Serbia's leaders had a powerful tool at their disposal to discipline the top generals and the JNA. Using the model of the 'anti-bureaucratic' revolution, Milošević could have easily incited chaos in the JNA or replacement of the commanding officers, and in the redistribution of military power installed and rewarded officers loyal to him.

It is therefore no wonder that the top generals refused even to discuss the confederal variation. But this brought them into a new circle of inconsistencies, both political and principled, from which they could no longer extricate themselves. Along the way, they and Serbia's political leaders made a big tactical error: within the framework of discussing this model there had been a chance to internationalize all dimensions of Yugoslavia's confederalization, particularly its repercussions on the position of the Serbian people in the future states. This, of course, required that they first renounce every idea of solving the problem by force. In this variation, the military-Serbian coalition could have removed the negative effects of the Slovenian-Croatian instrumentalization of democracy among the international public. This also offered a chance to find external allies powerful enough to help protect the Serbs' national and state interests in the process of SFRY's decomposition.

The top generals' constant insistence on the JNA's constitutional obligation to ensure a peaceful and democratic resolution to the crisis also supports their acceptance of discussions on the confederal model; particularly since a democratic resolution to the crisis meant, in principle, the equal footing of all alternatives, respect for constitutional or agreed upon procedures and voluntary acceptance of the solution by all parties. Towards this goal, the military leaders should have excluded the JNA from ongoing ideological and political conflicts, and then, standing equidistant from all conflicting sides, the Army should have been an additional guarantee that the final solution would be reached by peaceful means.

Whether or not the confederal variation was truly feasible and/or acceptable to the individual actors is unimportant for our further discussion. However, having classified themselves ideologically with socialism and politically with a modern federation, the top generals lost their legitimacy as the guarantor of a peaceful outcome. They had thereby removed the Army's last chance to carry out its constitutional role by political means.

Standing unambiguously alongside one of the alternatives, the military leaders had become an opponent of the other alternatives, and not only ideologically. They had disqualified themselves from the role of neutral mediator and shock absorber in inter-republic and interethnic disputes. After that, the JNA could no longer be even the repressive mediator of a political agreement on Yugoslavia's fate, without facing resistance. The Army's preventive demonstrations of power and separating the conflicting sides thus had no effect. On the contrary, they were always interpreted in terms of the conflicting parties, to the detriment of the role (allegedly desired) of the JNA.

It turned out, however, that the top generals were not even capable of playing the role of alleged protector of the federation and socialism, and then of Serbia's state and national interests. Since they had already consciously come into conflict with the secessionist republics, the top generals had to calculate and foresee all the consequences of their decisions, and prepare a plan to use the JNA. To this end, they should have carried out a coup or amputated Slovenia at the best possible moment. In the process, they should have counted on armed and passive resistance from most of the population and on erosion along national lines among the Army officers. They should have formed special units for this purpose capable of making quick, surprise attacks and establishing control over republican power centers. They should have taken the JNA units outside the war theater, thus preventing them from being blockaded in their barracks. In the same vein, owing to information leaks, they should have prepared alternative (real and false) plans for operations, commanders and executors. And so on and so forth.

Even assuming that the generals' desire to keep their power intact ultimately determined how they used the JNA, it can still be shown that they behaved irrationally. Yugoslavia's systemic erosion was doing away with the generals' sources of real power and the scope within which to use it. It was highly likely that the top generals, along with what remained of the federal state, would lose all their power and authority with respect to the western republics. So the only way the generals could have reestablished their power was by force. Since they did not have sufficient ability, knowledge and military force to do this, the military leaders could have found a way out for themselves by bringing the JNA to the confederalists' side.

In principle, the confederal variation offered the generals the chance to preserve some power, although transformed and redistributed. By adjusting the JNA to the confederation model in which it would maintain some joint functions and joint supreme command in the case of external danger, the military elite had the chance to resolve their personal status according to national-republican quota. Indeed, breaking up by republics would weaken the central military power, but the Army would still remain an essential all-Yugoslav factor. Conflicts might arise among the new/old military elite regarding the share and redistribution of power, but cooperation was also quite possible since their interests were very similar. Within the confederal model, the republican military elite and their delegates in the federal military center would continue to wield considerable political power. Of course, this was only possible under the assumption that the top generals were aware of the fact that a federal Yugoslavia could not survive in its existing form. The generals were required to defend any Yugoslavia that could be reached by political compromise. This was the only variation that would give the JNA the legitimacy it needed to prevent war at any price, and exact and/or impose peace.[10]

6.4.b Support for the creation of a new 'Pan-Serbian' state

Although the top generals' preference for only one variation seriously raised doubts about their readiness to defend any Yugoslav state, regardless of its organization, we will consider one other alternative. Hypothetically placing the military leaders in a confederal or some other Yugoslavia would have brought them into direct conflict with the Serbian factor. This conflict could have been avoided if the top generals sided at the proper time with the policies of Serbia's leaders. This would also have required them to make a pro-Serbian transformation of the JNA.

This is exactly what the propaganda said against the JNA and its top generals. The secessionists' main argument against the JNA was its alleged 'Serbo-communism', while the Serbs' propagandists were bothered by the Army's belated pro-Serbian orientation. Both one and the other considered the JNA's pro-Serbian orientation as being immanent. But the Army's path to 'Serbian national feelings' was nonetheless more complicated than it seemed.

Pursuant to the principle of a people's right to self-determination, if we accept without further examination that Serbia was justified in insisting that all the Serbs live in one state, then a questions arises regarding the JNA's role in such a state. We must check once again whether the Army could have contributed to the creation or protection of such a state, but first we must evaluate the realistic basis for Serbia's goal at the time, and then the validity of the strategic-tactical operations for its realization. From this viewpoint, the JNA and later its Serbian remains objectively had the task of creating the initial territorial and military prerequisites for Serbia's goal. But it should be emphasized that this only happened at the speed of the forced and unilateral decomposition of Yugoslavia. By protecting SFRY, the Army was in actual fact protecting the only state of all the Serbs. It was not until such a Yugoslavia was destroyed that the Army was forced to become the open protector and instrument of Serbia's political interests and goals. The fact that the Army was soon to be without a state and territory had a direct influence in this regard.

We wonder in the end whether the top generals could have and wanted to be subjugated to Serbia's policy towards Yugoslavia any earlier. Had there been a 'Serbian lobby' in the JNA from the beginning, and had the initial goal of Serbia's and the military's leaders been a third Yugoslavia, the finale would have been understandable. All that would be left to ask is whether such a result could have been achieved without war or with considerably less destruction. Theoretically, the JNA with Serbia's support could have staged a sudden coup and established a military dictatorship leading to a division of the territory tailored after a 'Serboslavia'. This would, at least initially, have preserved the basic interests of the military elite and part of the Army's members.

If all or part of the top generals had secretly glided towards the Serbian viewpoint (goal) at the time, they still did not dare turn it into the JNA's official policy, primarily owing to the multiethnic composition of the Army. Had they done that publicly before June 1991, the JNA would have put itself out of action even before the war or else the war might have started first in the Army. This by no means belies the fact that the military leaders misused the Army, but it is just as true that the first official indications of the JNA's pro-Serb alignment date from the war in Croatia.[11]

The JNA's further pro-Serb transformation followed the logic of war and coercion. This is shown by the collapse of the call-up system, the top generals' need to prove themselves additionally and subsequently, the inauspicious situation on the battlefield, the all-Croatian armed resistance, pressure from the international community, etc. What is most important, however, is that when the internal war ignited the top generals were no longer able to define and carry out a single Yugoslav goal. Furthermore, no one asked or expected this anymore. The moment the Serbs, in conjunction with the Slovenes and Croats, started the forced division of Yugoslavia, the top generals no longer had a choice.

The Army leaders certainly calculated on the Serbian political and national factor and coinciding interests regarding Yugoslavia. It is not to be excluded that the top generals hoped they could use the Serbian factor to preserve the JNA's position. The course of events at the end of the crisis indicates that Serbia's government intended to use the JNA for its own purposes. Taking refuge behind the rump Presidency of SFRY and the top generals, Milošević had nominally kept Serbia out of the war. However, using the JNA with Kadijević's full cooperation, he succeeded in fulfilling all his initial goals. This, among other things, allowed him to shift responsibility for the military defeat in Slovenia and Croatia to the top generals and the JNA, thus creating a scapegoat for internal and external use.

Consequently, the JNA could not have preserved Yugoslavia since others had already started to tear it apart. The Army certainly could not have defended Yugoslavia against the will of the Serbian factor. Had the military leaders even tried to be neutral at the time, the JNA would have been in the same situation, only with a different opponent. Had the top generals moved to defend any Yugoslavia at all, they would have necessarily come into conflict with Milošević and the agitated Serbs. Then the Army would have experienced the same fate: it would have been treated as an aggressor and/or occupying force in Serbia and would have split internally along the Serbian national line.

The moment they entered the war, the military leaders did away with any possibility of using the JNA otherwise. Becoming subservient to Milošević, the top generals' only impact was in accordance with his orders and for his goals. From that moment on, all the political oversights of Kadijević's triumvirate started leading towards their ultimate, destructive consequences.

Notes

1   D. Nikoliš distinctly represents this viewpoint, whereby 'in order to play this role (preventing disintegration through war – M.H.), within that short, lightning-quick, fateful historical time – from the end of 1989 to January 1991 at the latest (or even spring that same year), the JNA had to: (1) take the state government of SFRY into its hands, along with all republican and federal state functions, including revocation of the SFRY Presidency; (2) remove all republican, Party and political leaders and their main people on the political scene; (3) suspend all political parties; (4) prevent any possible arming of the population outside of the JNA's control and block the illegal import of arms into Yugoslavia; (5) open up the process of the peaceful,

political, democratic resolution of the state's organization and the form of life that the Yugoslav peoples would have, and resolve the national (Serbo-Croatian) question within Yugoslavia'. Compare: Dušan Nikoliš, Državna i politička uloga JNA u procesu raspada SFRJ 1989-1992. O ulozi koju JNA nije odigrala a mogla je i morala da odigra; in: Novi svetski poredak i politika odbrane Savezne republike Jugoslavije, Federal Ministry of Defense, Belgrade, 1993, 518.

2   In the prewar phase, in our opinion, the following events (processes) can be included in this category: the dissolution of SKJ, the SIV reform program, the federal-confederal polarization of the forces in play and the SFRY Presidency Order on disarming paramilitary formations; in the war phase these were: the 'customs expedition' to Slovenia, the war in Croatia and getting entangled in warfare in Bosnia and Herzegovina.

3   'Borba's barometer' in May 1990 indicated that almost three-fourths of the Yugoslav population considered Ante Marković the most progressive individual at the time (Borba, 21.05.1990, 7).

4   The only chance SIV had to succeed was with a strong injection of money from the West; economic results alone might have been able to buffer and stop, or maintain within the systems and institutions, the national divisions imposed by the republican leaders. However, material support from the West (USA) could not be seriously expected for at least three reasons: strategic (finally taking over the monopoly of world power), economic (without guarantees to secure the capital and its profitability) and ideological (anti-communism spiced with revanchism or triumphalism).

5   This is shown by V. Kadijević's views, although presented subsequently, in the brochure 'Moje vidjenje raspada', op. cit. 108-110.

6   This is what V. Kadijević claimed afterwards: 'The reports that have appeared through various semi-intelligence channels that the West, under certain circumstance, would support the JNA's intervention in order to save Yugoslavia, always had in mind, above all, bringing down Serbia's leadership with Milošević at the head'; compare: op. cit. 88-89.

7   An indirect indication of this is 'Borba's barometer' from the end of 1989 whereby as much as 84% of the Yugoslav population was prepared to defend the borders of their country from any outside attack (Borba, 30.10.1989, 6).

8   This is supported by some evaluations of Kadijević, although after the fact, made by General Aleksandar Vasiljević in an interview in the weekly NIN; compare: NIN, Belgrade, 17.07.1992, 56-59.

9   They were in any case obliged to do this by the Constitution and the official document on strategy; compare: The Strategy of Total National Defense and Social Self-Protection, Ministry of Defense, Belgrade, 1987, 152.

10 For arguments on peace in favor of a confederation, see: Slobodan Antonić, Za i protiv konfederalizma, (For and Against Confederalism) Gledište, no.3-4/91, 43-64, in particular page 59.
11 Compare: interview with General Radinović, Intervju, Belgrade, 03.08.1991, 57-59.

Chapter 7

Foundations of the Army's Powerlessness

The key reasons for the JNA's powerlessness and thus its failure lie in how the Army was constituted; the wartime outcome ultimately resulted from its political and social nature. The deeper roots of this military organization can be found in the civil-military heritage of the Serbian and Yugoslav society. Although the communist system physically destroyed the political heritage of the states that preceded it, the army it created never grew beyond this prior framework.

The Serbian heritage[1] that was inserted into the first Yugoslavia[2] and then passed on to the second Yugoslavia[3] can be condensed into several points:

- The general lack of democratic traditions and institutions facilitated the undeviating domination of authoritarian models of government in which the army was the ruler's key support.
- Frequent Serbian and Yugoslav wars (for liberation, unification, disassociation) constantly increased the army's social and political power. This slowed down the country's transition from a state of war to a state of peace and prevented democracy from taking root. All of this favored society's militarizing tendencies.
- Serbia's and Yugoslavia's constant lack of instruments and procedures that would put democratic control over the armed forces led to the army's systematic exclusion from accountability before parliament and the public. This resulted in the prevailing model of a client and politicized (Party) army.
- The fact that the army was protected from democratic controls, along with its inherent group mentality, encouraged the military leaders' frequent interference in social processes (crises). The army's political activity was based on the personal loyalty of the (noncommissioned) officer corps to the ruler. This necessarily led to the army's ideological

self-identification, the misuse of patriotism and the servicemen's diminished notion of combat (professional) morale.
- Since special scientific disciplines were undeveloped, the public did not have sufficient knowledge about civil-military relations and civil society did not establish competent control institutions. This led to a predominantly ideological approach to civil-military relations and there was a decrease in the rationality behind the army's organization and society's defense.
- The lack of a free and critical public combined with the secrecy that surrounded military-defense matters facilitated the army's becoming a taboo subject. Insufficient awareness of the need for democratic controls encouraged an idolatrous attitude towards the army by the public and the media.

Placed in the center of social and political life, the mythologized army in Serbia and then in the Yugoslav state received the status of an ontological entity. The army's right to its own will and power stemmed from the contribution it made to creating (renewing) states and preserving the existing order. Based on this, the army was attributed with having previous knowledge about history and thus knew the fundamental interests of the state and nation. This line of thinking allowed the military elite to presume the obligation and acquire the right to intervene in social reality both politically and, if needed, with force.

7.1 The JNA's Systemic Protection from the People

The JNA's position and field of activity were nominally defined by the Constitution. The Army's task of defending the constitutional order opened up the possibility of its internal use.

Article 134 of the FNRJ (Federal People's Republic of Yugoslavia) Constitution from 1946 states that the Yugoslav Army, inter alia, 'serves to maintain peace and security'.[4] A constitutional law from 1953 gives the Federation, and thereby its army, the duty of defending the country and 'protecting the social and political order'.[5] In Article 114 of the SFRY Constitution from 1963 this order is called a 'socialist social and political system',[6] so the JNA's obligation to protect the constitutional order had to do with its socialist nature.[7] Item 3 of Amendment XLI to the 1971 Constitution assigns the Armed Forces of SFRY, consisting of JNA and TO, the task of defending the constitutional order.[8] Article 240 of the 1974

Constitution confirms the Armed Forces' obligation to protect 'the social system of SFRY established by this Constitution'.[9]

The creators of these constitutions, of course, failed to define just what was to be protected in the 'constitutional order'. They also avoided any details on how this order might be jeopardized and the procedures and means which the Army should and/or dared undertake to protect it. Holes in the constitutions left sufficient space for the discretionary use of the Army in internal conflicts.

The ideological essence of every constitution in the second Yugoslavia removed any doubts about the subject of protection: the socialist order, understood as the materialization of the unrestrained will of the Party and the Leader. The Army's primary obligation, therefore, was to use all available means to protect what these two called socialism. To this end, the Army had to guarantee the permanent political monopoly of the communists.

This is supported by the fact that changes in the concept of the second Yugoslavia's defense and the organization of the JNA directly depended on the state of relations between KPJ/SKJ and SKPb/KPSS, and FNRJ/SFRY with the USSR. During the 1941-1945 war political commissars were the Bolshevist determinant of the Partisan units. From 1945 to 1948 the Soviet model of organizing defense and the Army were adopted completely. During the conflict with the Inform biro (1948-1953), the JNA gradually returned to its Partisan model, while Yugoslavia reached the forecourt of NATO through its defense agreement with Greece and Turkey (1953). The renewal of Party and state relations with the USSR in 1955/1956 also encouraged military cooperation, but the JNA held onto its autonomy. The 1968 military intervention in Czechoslovakia by the USSR and the Warsaw Pact countries had a direct effect on establishing the concept and system of ONO and DSZ in Yugoslavia. However, independent of the conceptual about-faces and organizational changes in JNA, the regime never renounced the institutions of the political commissar and security officer. Through these two services, the Party leaders had full political control over the JNA and its members while Tito was alive.

The Army's political power surpassed the constitutional framework and depended on the momentary needs of the Party and Leader. Thus it acted as an isolated and protected component of the one-party state. The JNA's dual nature resulted from the fact that it was simultaneously (a) a subsystem functioning on Party principles, and (b) a relatively independent system functioning on internal and professional principles. Consequently, within the JNA there was constant permeation and collision between the Party's omnipotence and the internal self-will of the general corps.

The former JNA based its identity on its antifascist and communist origin, and was part of the Revolution fetish. As the new order took root, it grew into the avant-garde and then was promoted to the main guard of the purity of the idea of socialism and its legacy. The JNA's monopoly over the country's external defense was expanded to the internal defense of Party values and goals. The Army found additional self-identity through the principle of brotherhood and unity and its origin in the people.

In addition, the political power of the JNA and the generals was based on the fact that they were completely shielded from the public. For this purpose the Army was practically speaking moved outside the system, which was only a façade anyway. The Army's ties to the Leader and Party did away with the need for any feigned parliamentary control. Furthermore, normative possibilities for the institutional control over the JNA were reduced by transferring constitutional-legal authority to the decree level. In addition, the Army and its members, as well as the civilians working within its scope, were under the authority of the autonomous military judiciary. All of this favored the emanation of hierarchical arbitrariness in inter-Army relations.

The JNA's power grew additionally with the creeping militarization of society, which was carried out under the pretext of implementing the ONO and DSZ concept.[10] Assigning defense the category of 'social self-protection' brought the installation of the Orwellian mechanism of total control over society in which citizens were initiated into protecting their own and society's safety by publicly and secretly denouncing those who were not likeminded thinkers.

The Party's domination of the Army resulted in the ideological organization of the JNA and, through it, of the whole system of defense. The ONO and DSZ concept and system rested on a twofold ideological twist. First the Party's socialism project was declared real and then ideological reality became the source and demiurge of total national defense.[11]

This is why the Party was installed in the center of the system. It controlled all civilian[12] defense entities through the Committee for ONO and DSZ and all Army defense[13] entities through the SKJ Organization in the JNA. It was assigned the role[14] of guide and leader; Party parameters were used to define combat morale,[15] training and education, and the administration and command of the JNA and TO.[16] Ideological criteria were used to evaluate the ethnical-political state of the Armed Forces as a key element of their combat readiness.[17]

The servicemen's combat morale was produced from the 'revolutionary and people's character of the JNA'. The state of the Army was evaluated based on how its members valued 'the constitutional order, socialist self-management, brotherhood and unity, equality among the nations and nationalities of SFRY, the leading role of SKJ, SFRY's independent and non-aligned foreign policy, total national defense and social self-protection'.[18] Political activities in the units were an indicator of individual and collective loyalty to the state and the Party.[19] The entire MPS (moral-political state) approach was built on the conviction that self-management socialism produced a body of unchanging motivational goals and defense values about which there was a high level of agreement among the citizens and members of the Armed Forces (OS).[20]

The instruments used to evaluate MPS were intended to disclose and sanction the Party loyalty of JNA/OS members. For this purpose the entire Army was permeated with a network of Party organizations, and the military structure had its Party analogue. The officers' work and Party roles were combined,[21] so ideological reasoning superceded professional reasoning in the Army's operations.[22]

Since military and Party command were intertwined, the arsenal of means to discipline JNA members increased along the hierarchical vertical. The ultimate goal was to produce, and coerce if needed, the ideological unanimity of all the servicemen.[23]

Fighting against the 'special war'[24] was the underlying concept of JNA members' ideological preparation. On the trail of communistic sectarianism and exclusivity, people, ideas, movements, ethnic groups and states were classified in the Army as friends or enemies.[25] This put Yugoslavia, its regime and army in the center of a conspiratorial world that constantly used 'their weaknesses' in order to destroy them.[26]

In accordance with this, the JNA officers had the unremitting obligation to protect themselves and their units from hostile ideological influence.[27] This is why the entire system of defense and each individual in it was under the constant control of the military security service, although its field of activity was unknown to most of the JNA members.

The Army's ideological super-determinant necessarily led to its professional powerlessness. By the same token, the lack of democratic controls allowed the military leaders to arbitrarily evaluate the level of JNA/OS combat readiness. Even the Main Inspection of the People's Defense, which was supervised by the generals and consisted of officers, was subordinated to a general – the Minster of Defense. A false impression of the Army's true capacities and abilities was created in society and the Army by this self-evaluation according to ideological criteria.

7.2 Social Profile of the JNA

The JNA's structure and composition were nominally commensurate to the federal and multi-ethnic state. The officer corps depended on the JNA and the regime for their existence and status. And since the survival of the JNA depended on the political will of the Party favoring Yugoslavia as it was, the (noncommissioned) officers identified with the country's makeup at the time. Through systematic indoctrination they were also emotionally linked to Yugoslavia as a socialist state.

Accordingly, the Army could only exist under socialist premises and propositions. This is why the Army and its officer corps were the authentic – social, political, cultural, ethical, etc. – substrate of their society. Closed society gave rise to a closed military organization – exclusive and sectarian. Furthermore, the main characteristics and contradictions of society were crystallized in the JNA and taken to the extreme. As long as the Party state functioned, the basic deficiencies of the JNA had only latent potential. The moment this state disintegrated, the mechanism to preserve and/or coerce monolithic behavior stopped working, and the initial contradictions of the JNA came to light in a destructive form.

The JNA's singular political role was supported by the special social status of its members. The Army's wide-ranging exclusiveness gave rise to a military corporation under Party patronage. This was constantly supplemented by new areas of exclusiveness, with new attributes gradually added to the professional singularity of the servicemen. The system of vertically rising benefits gave those employed in the Army privileged status.

This led to autarchic tendencies as shown by the top generals' strivings to become functionally detached from society. The development of the military-industrial complex increased the JNA's technological and economic independence. The Army also acquired considerable foreign currency independence with its arms exports. Its logistical self-sufficiency increased with the creation of a system of military farming estates where the soldiers worked free of charge. In addition, the JNA had special subsystems for education, health care and social-pension insurance. A chain of military vacation centers and subsidized commissaries also arose.

The unique social and economic position of the officers favored the production of a group mentality within the Army. Awareness of their exceptionality brought awareness of the uniqueness of their material and political interests. This led to the conviction that they were justified in putting the JNA's interests above everything else. This conviction resulted in the (noncommissioned) officers' readiness to defend their status and appreciable privileges.

The Party-police profile of the Army stemmed necessarily from the broader social and systemic surroundings. The rigid official and interpersonal relations in the JNA were a replica of the authoritarian foundation of society. This is why the Army was a highly closed social organization.

In the JNA, the social composition of society was reduced twofold. The first reduction necessarily followed from the fact that young people had uneven and diminishing interest in a military career.[28] This is why the JNA was not equally represented by the main social layers and all the ethnic groups. In addition, the candidate's psycho-physical abilities were not enough to enter the Army. The social-class origin and Party-police correctness of the candidate's parents were crucial for his admission. Civilian and military security services were in charge of investigating their origin and suitability.

This diminished social foundation to fill the JNA was then reduced by the constant triage of the officer corps. An individual's professional promotion depended directly on whether he fulfilled ideological and security criteria. The principles of selection were arbitrary, to be sure, and depended on one's superior who could apply them discretionarily with respect to personal preference, town of origin, national/ethnic or self-interest reasons. This is why negative selection and careerism prevailed in the personnel policy. Over time rank lost its functional characteristics and increasingly took on social and corruptive features.[29]

Furthermore, over time the JNA became engulfed in the classical syndrome of a bureaucratic mammoth. The constant rise in the number of higher ranked officers and the decline in the number of lower ranked and troop officers gradually turned the pyramid of ranks upside down. Top military command and administration thus became increasingly unwieldy.[30] The tangled authority of the Ministry of Defense and the General Staff led to a duplication of departments and fictively employed officers.

At the beginning of the 1960s the JNA was caught by the 'green trench soldier' syndrome. In order to compensate for the poor turnout of young men in the military academies, the Party and military leaders opened secondary military schools.[31] This lowered the entrance age of future officers from 18 to 14 and greatly increased the JNA's prospects of modeling future officers according to the desired profile. Then the means opened up to rapidly promote noncommissioned officers into officers. The results of this undertaking became visible in the 1990-1992 period when generals of noncommissioned officer origin held important duties in the JNA. The principle of absolute obedience achieved by drills in the noncommissioned officers' schools was thus taken to perfection.

The social-psychological atmosphere in the JNA was characterized by the systematic de-individualization of its members resulting in the widespread production of unauthentic personalities. This is witnessed by the fact that at the end of the crisis and during the war, the JNA did not record a single case of professional and/or political resistance by the officers with regard to the top generals' (pro)war policy.

Training and education nurtured a strict, black-white model of behavior and opinions. The repressive core in relations in the JNA was outwardly softened by the broadly applied system of awards. Since the number of decorations and awards was carved up in advance by units, this undercut their purpose. The system shifted from singling out the best to filling quotas, and decorations and awards were earned as a matter of course, independent of real merit. When the JNA took over the Soviet model of incentives in the 1970s, there ensued an inflation of plaques, badges, decorations and awards.

After the decades of anti-intellectualism, at the end of the 1970s pseudo-intellectualism reigned in the JNA. After Tito was awarded an honorary doctorate, all active and retired generals were offered the title of PhD,[32] indicating that the JNA leaders wanted to decorate their power with other social status symbols. This led to the hyper production of military master's degrees and doctorates with its byproduct of ghost writers and plagiarists who were later promoted as a reward for their services.[33] At the same time, the military's publishing activities became the means by which great amounts of money ended up in private pockets.[34]

The JNA's social structure was determined by how it was organized and its formations. The place a serviceman held in the military division of labor determined the level he belonged to and his share in the internal distribution of power. This share then had the return effect of determining the individual's and/or group's socio-economic and political status. The layers were clearly divided: generals, higher officers (major-colonel), lower officers (second lieutenant to captain first class) and noncommissioned officers. The social map was supplemented by a conglomerate of 'civilians working in the JNA' who were also structured by education and job.

The general corps, of course, possessed unlimited central and internal power. Power was further divided within this elite according to rank and position. Although the general corps' power was based on the principle of seniority and the right to command, it was expanded by numerous legal and sub-act discretionary rights.[35] This power grew additionally owing to the lack of effective instruments to protect the JNA's constitutionality and lawfulness. The only way servicemen could protect their rights was within the military organization, according to a hierarchical procedure, thus their protection depended on their superiors. The privileged status of the generals was constantly increased by expanding the advantages that belonged to it, ranging from a special housing fund that was assigned by a secret rule book, to hunting grounds, special airplanes and vacation centers.

The distribution of power in the JNA primarily coursed outside of organizational and formation structures. Informal interest groups based on personal and often national ties were created vertically and horizontally. Outside of the Army there was also a strong lobby of retired generals who had direct influence on proceedings in the JNA. This was particularly true of generals dating from the National War of Liberation (World War Two).[36]

The JNA's social being was fundamentally determined by the multiethnic composition of the officer corps. The contingents of recruits were also multiethnic, of course, but during the peacetime phase this did not have any special impact on the Army's operations. The uniform training system and the single language of command (Serbo-Croatian), along with internal mechanisms for adjustment to the social and work environment, temporarily put all the recruits on equal footing. Potential discrimination was additionally curbed by political, moral and disciplinary sanctions for intolerance and/or nationalistic outbursts. If the strict regime could not do away with such behavior it at least suppressed and/or postponed it.

Indeed, any departures from such behavior correlated directly with the situation in society and the current policies of the SKJ leaders. Pressure put by military security and the commissars on individual categories of recruits always grew after settlements of account among the factions in the Communist Party or the Party's political conflicts with national (nationalistic) movements in one of the republics. For example, after the massive demonstrations in Priština in 1969, during the Albanians' military service most of them were under the constant surveillance of security officers and their associates.

The JNA's fundamental internal principle was the national equality of the officer corps, which was made possible after 1945 by the suppression of war traumas. Different procedures were used to first modify the trauma and make it relative. Then public scrutiny was removed and any discussion of the causes for the interethnic war was prevented. Redefining the circumstances of war concealed the original reasons for the trauma; oppressors and victims were depersonalized and the trauma was first emptied of concrete substance and then generalized, reducing it to the framework of the antifascist war. The final touch was given by the Party, which distributed the responsibility for both the good and bad effects among the Yu ethnic groups using the formula 'everyone is (a bit) to blame'.[37] This gave the illusion of bridging the interethnic gap, blazing the trail towards the ideology of brotherhood and unity.

This entire procedure rested on the Party's reinterpretation of the recent and distant past; viewed from increasing distance, knowledge of previous events became less and less reliable. In return, this required a new Party version of history.[38] The rest was a matter of course: the new truth was passed on to the end user through the all-inclusive system of indoctrination. For the JNA, the end users were soldiers and officers.

The Party and military leaders were constantly searching for a model that would provide the equal representation of all ethnic groups in the JNA's (noncommissioned) officer corps. The unequal numbers of the Yu-nations was an insurmountable obstacle; in spite of all attempts they were unable to assure an equal influx of candidates from all the ethnic groups and republics. Nonetheless, the officers' national composition primarily corresponded to each ethnic group's share of the total population.[39] The national balance was additionally strengthened by administrative measures. Combined national and republican quotas were introduced in enrollment in the military schools; if the national quota was not filled then the republican quota was used. For example, Muslims and Croats had enrollment priority from B-H and Croatia. Serbs from these republic could only enter the competition if the ethnic quota had not been filled. The same thing happened for Kosovo and Vojvodina. Then a 'national quota' was introduced to promote colonels and generals in order to guarantee checks and balances in the distribution and use of central military power. Units and their commanders were also formed and filled using the principle of mixing soldiers from different ethnic groups and stationing them outside their republics.

In order to produce 'brotherhood and unity' among the (noncommissioned) officers, the Army used all available means – from indoctrination through incentives to repression. Thus the JNA used the 'melting pot' model rather than assimilation. While Tito was alive these considerations were of secondary importance since he chose and appointed generals to his liking, independent of their national affiliation. To date there is no serious proof that he gave precedence to any one ethnic group.

After Tito's death the republics' influence rose with regard to the choice and distribution of generals, but the minister of defense had the final word. Until May 1991 the JNA personnel policy continued in principle according to the standard practice, nominally respecting parity representation of the ethnic groups in the general corps.[40] A discriminating factor, to be sure, was the individual's readiness to 'defend socialism and the modern federation'.

The JNA's social profile can be evoked by the portrait of an average (noncommissioned) officer. This portrait, however, does not take note of personal and collective self-awareness, the score of vices vs. virtues, or any serious deviations. The picture looks like this:

- *Social origin*: mostly from lower (poor) and marginal layers and groups.
- age upon entrance: 14 and/or 18.
- *General conditions upon entrance*: psychophysical health and indistinct school success.
- *Special conditions upon entering*: parents' Party-political suitability and expansive national-republican quotas.
- *Elementary military schooling*: 3-5 or 8 years (secondary school 'green trench soldiers' and platoon second lieutenants).
- *Education profile*: military specialist with a short course covering all ideological knowledge.
- *Philosophy of life*: unequivocal notion of reality and life conceived as a conspiracy from three features of dialectical materialism and four features of historical materialism,[41] easily changing ideology and values.
- *National identity*: initially repressed Yugoslav national feelings that could be renewed and used by national quotas upon entering the colonel-general zone.
- *Types of dependency*: the regime for his life, the Party/Leader for his religion and his superiors with discretionary power for his job.
- *Integrative mechanisms*: repressive military and Party discipline; the all-penetrating military security service; common interests; professional, peer and group solidarity; ideological homogeneity; permanent political differentiation; constant search for internal enemies; a cocktail of incentive-repressive measures.

- *Source of internal tension and social distance*: latent intolerance etween the Partisan officers and former officers, wartime and postwar officers, officers and noncommissioned officers, active servicemen and civilians, soldiers and troop commanders, commanding and administrative personnel, key and secondary generals. All of this was mediated by different statuses, by the hierarchical distribution of power and privileges, and within the context of growing national, political and ideological conflicts in society, the Party and state.
- *Group characteristics*: an illusory monolith crushed by hidden conflicts of interests on all levels; shielded from reality; social corruptibility; ideological servility; personalized loyalty; deficiency of rationality on the state level; lacking a moral and professional codex; self-evaluation based on self-control.
- *Professional path*: rapid promotion based on excessive ideological purity, irreproachable confidentiality and hierarchical submission, and depending on the power of one's patron.
- *Social transfer*: with their rising rank and intra-Army power, having little to do with knowledge and ability, the generals' usefulness grew in civil – Party, police and state – affairs.

The scope of socialist and Yugoslav patriotic feelings, and the military socialization of the JNA (OS SFRY) officers were destroyed during 1990. Owing to the progression of the crisis, the atmosphere changed radically in society and the Army;[42] its length generated a crisis in the JNA members' moral, ethical and ideological convictions, and in that of the entire Yugoslav population. Most people found a way out of the existential crisis by accepting to be converted, thus confirming the readiness of the population for new ideological molding.

This widespread conversion was a defensive reaction by the powerless population faced with the disintegration of the foundations of individual and collective life. Following the homeostatic principle, conversion facilitated adjustment to the changing situation, particularly since the social reasons for dissatisfaction were transferred into national reasons. It is therefore no wonder that the ideologically divided and conflicting inhabitants gave the new/old regimes widespread support, not wondering about their real substance. Uncritical identification with the nation (ethnic group) and leader was an attempt to decrease individual and group hardships. The population's negative energy was then easily transferred into dissatisfaction with the position of their own ethnic group. Finally, propaganda was used to elicit the conviction that attaining independence and a (single) nation state was a prerequisite to social progress.

Although in the final stretch of the crisis all the necessary social-psychological prerequisites had been created for war, they did not necessarily have to lead to war.[43] Their potential only turned into reality when the national-republican elite went into action.

The initial political seed found fertile ground in the JNA. The national awakening of the JNA officers took place at more or less the same pace as the rest of the population. However, the mental and emotional confusion of the officers was hidden under the shroud of the JNA monolith until June 1991. This latent nationalism was slow to emerge and had a delayed reaction. It was only with the beginning of the war that most officers had to make an irrevocable choice of sides. Existential reasons additionally concealed national reasons. Thus, when making their choice, all JNA officers ultimately behaved rationally.

Notes

1 Vuksanović-Anić, Draga, Stvaranje moderne srpske vojske (Creating a Modern Serbian Army, SKZ, VINC, Belgrade, 1993, 114-131.
2 Bjelajac, Mile, Vojska kraljevine SHS/Jugoslavije 1922-1935 (Army of the Kingdom of the Serbs, Croats and Slovenes), Institut za noviju istoriju Srbije, Belgrade, 1994, 1944; 44-54, 134-147 and 241-256.
3 Hadžić, Miroslav, Armijska upotreba trauma (The Army's Use of Trauma), in: Serbian Side of the War, (ed) Nebojša Popov, Republika, Belgrade, 1996, 562-568.
4 The Constitutional Development of Socialist Yugoslavia, 1988, 354.
5 Ibid., Article 9, 355-6.
6 Ibid., 397.
7 Ibid., Article 255, 421.
8 Ibid., 457-8.
9 Ibid., 515.
10 The system of defense included some 1.5 million people, while decision making about defense was made at 125,000 instances from the local community to the top of the federal state; compare: Dogradnja ONO u okviru promena u svetu i Jugoslaviji (Amendments to ONO within the framework of changes in the world and Yugoslavia), Vojno delo, special edition, August 1990, 25 and 353.
11 'The extent to which self-management processes prevail over and surpass the boundaries of the traditional sphere of life and human activities, founded in the old manner of social life, is the extent to which the sphere (area) of

defense and military thought in general becomes an area and component part of the direct revolutionary activity of man and that of his narrow and broader collectivity', Dr. Radivoje Jovadžić, Dijalektika odbrane (The Dialectics of Defense), VIX, Belgrade, 1983, 32.

12 'Committees for ONO and DSZ are coordinating and operational-tactical bodies in the organizational system (...). In their work of implementing the views and policies of SKJ in ONO and DSZ, the committees are responsible to the bodies that appoint them and to the SKJ organization.', Strategija oružane borbe (Strategy of Armed Warfare), SNNO, Belgrade, 1983, 59.

13 'The leading ideological-political role (of the SK – M.H.) in the armed forces is founded on the role of the SK in our society and its special responsibility to defend and protect socialist self-management Yugoslavia, as established in the SFRY Constitution.', ibid. 140.

14 'The League of Communists exercises its leading role in ONO and DSZ through activities within the political system of socialist self-management (...). The League of Communists has the special role and responsibility regarding the organization and work of the committees for Total National Defense and Social Self-Protection'; ibid, 49.

15 'Combat morale is founded primarily on the socialist self-management awareness, freedom-loving and revolutionary traditions, and the convictions of our working people and citizens in the justification of the goals for which they are fighting'; ibid., 67.

16 'The unity of leadership and command is based on the unity of the military-political goal, the ideological-political unity of the commands, the staffs, the units and officers'; ibid, 126.

17 Instructions on Monitoring and Evaluating MPS in JNA, SSNO, Belgrade, 1979, item. 2.

18 MPS Instructions for TO, op. cit, item 3.

19 TO members were evaluated on the 'development of (their) socialist self-management awareness', their 'acceptance and adoption (...) of the goals and paths of development', and on 'the development of (their) conviction regarding the success and prospects of our socialist self-management society', MPS Instructions for TO, op. cit., 7-8.

20 'The system of monitoring and evaluating MPS begins with certain prerequisites which are constants: within the general meaning of unity, the existence of the national and social interests of JNA members, the existence of a positive attitude among the vast majority of JNA members towards defending the country, the positive influence of the character of the JNA, as the army of a self-management socialist society'; MPS Instructions for the JNA, op. cit., 50.

21 'Those serving in the armed forces are under obligation to actively work on implementing the policies of the League of Communists of Yugoslavia in

their unit or institution, in socio-political and other organizations, and in the environment in which they live.' Regulations of the Armed Forces, SSNO, 1985, item 13, 20.

22 This is shown by the items in the Report from the 9th Conference: 'Ideological questions on modernization of the JNA', 'Current ideological questions regarding training and education', 'Building moral forces and political unity in the Army', 'Ideological questions regarding the personnel policy', 'Security and self-protection', op. cit., 8-24.

23 The military's Party 'must continue to appear as a decisive factor in strengthening awareness and moral-political unity, preserving and deepening the revolutionary-class, all-national and Yugoslav character of the JNA', Program of the ideological-political tasks of OSKJ in JNA, Document from the 9th Conference of OSKJ in JNA, op. cit., 69.

24 The '(1) political system of socialist self-management, (2) an independent and non-aligned foreign policy and (3) the importance of Yugoslavia's geo-strategic position' are 'the reasons why SFRY is often a prime target of attacks by the superpowers and their allies using the methods of a special war', Specijalni rat protiv SFRJ (Special War Against SFRY), GŠ JNA, Belgrade, 1981, 44.

25 'The special war has the involvement of (...) the remains of class-based enemies, nationalist, irredentist, unitarian, bureaucratic-state socialism, liberalistic, clerical and other counterrevolutionary and reactionary forces.', Strategy of Armed Warfare, op. cit., 31.

26 'Yugoslavia is being exposed to the activities of special war forces. Aggressive and other reactionary forces from the outside, working in conjunction with the internal enemy, are trying to destroy the stability of Yugoslavia's socialist self-management system, compromise its international reputation and non-aligned foreign policy, and weaken its defense and self-protection ability.' Ibid, 30.

27 'The overall system of ideological-political education and guidance in the OS (Armed Forces) is directed towards developing resistance among OS members towards harmful ideological influences and psychological-propaganda effects', Special War Against SFRY, op. cit., 117.

28 Compare: Secondary School Students' Incentive to Enroll in a Military Academy, Center for Adult Education, Psychological and Social Research, JNA, SSNO, 1974-75, volume 1-9.

29 The unwritten rules of advancing to lieutenant colonel were expressed in the motto 'the only thing that will stop him from getting the rank is if he's run over by a tramway'; every other rank required a patron in addition to fulfilling the conditions.

30 This was particularly true of command from the level of the corps to the army level (RV i PVO, RM) and for administration in the Ministry of Defense and GŠ JNA.
31 In 1961 an experimental preparatory secondary school was opened for the Air Force Academy in Mostar. After that military secondary schools were opened in Belgrade, Ljubljana and Zagreb and were supposed to fill the Military Academy for ground forces. The latter two were soon closed for lack of interest.
32 It is therefore no surprise that retired general Mihajlo Apostolski came to the JNA to get his doctorate, even though he was president of the Macedonian Academy of Arts and Sciences.
33 In the mid-1980s it was a public secret in military circles that colonels Radovan Radinović, Miraz Tapusković and Vuleta Vuletić had written books for Admiral Mamula. All three quickly received the rank of general and important places in the hierarchy.
34 The second edition of the book by Army General Lubičić was printed in 100,000 copies and translated in four world languages. Compare: Nikola Ljubičić, Opštenarodna odbrana – strategija mira (Total National Defense – Strategy for Peace), Vojnoizdavački zavod, Belgrade, 1977, 382.
35 The right to allot apartments, make special promotions and transfer servicemen.
36 Compare: Mamula Branko, Slučaj Jugoslavija, CID, Podgorica, 2000, 33-45.
37 Tito thoroughly explained the platform of imposing wartime symmetry among the Yugoslav ethnic groups at the Fifth Congress of KPJ; compare: Fifth Congress of KPJ, stenographic notes, Kultura, Belgrade, 1949, 9-118.
38 Thus the origin of the concept of ONO and DSZ was moved from 1968 further into the Party past: 'The social-historical inception of creating total national defense in Yugoslavia is linked to the period of the ideological and organizational stabilization of KPJ from the mid-1930s, particularly after Josip Broz Tito became the head of KPJ.' Borislav Sikimić, Odbrana u ustavnom sistemu SFRJ (Defense in the Constitutional System of SFRY), VIZ, Belgrade, 1985, 81.
39 For more see: Bjelajac Mile S, Jugoslovensko iskustvo sa multietničkom armijom 1918-1991 (Yugoslav Experience with a Multiethnic Army 1918-1991), Udruženje za društvenu istoriju, Begrade, 1999.
40 This is shown by the composition of the top JNA command: the commander of the First Army was General Spirkovski (Macedonian), the commander of the Fifth Army was General Kolsek (Slovene), the commander of the Air Force was General Tus (Croat) who succeeded General Jurjević (Croat), the commander of the Navy was General Grubjesić (Croat), the chief of the Center of Military Academies was General Radanović (Croat), the assistant to the Federal Secretary for Research was General Vrtar (Slovene), the SSNO

deputy was Admiral Brovet, the president of OSKJ in JNA was Admiral Šimić (Croat), chief of the People's Defense Main Inspection was General Ružinovski (Macedonian), chief of staff of the First Army was Silić (Croat), etc.

41 See: Istorija Svesavezne komunističke partije (boljševika), Kratki kurs (History of the All-Union Communist Party (Bolsheviks), A Short Course, Kultura, Belgrade, 1945, 121-153.
42 Compare: M. Popović, Pathological Forms of Social Stratification, Sociological Review, Vol. XXVI, No. 1-4, 1992, 49-56.
43 This is shown by the research results of Srećko Mihajlović. See: Nezadovoljstvo gradjana i socijalni protest (Citizens' Dissatisfaction and Social Protest), Sociological Review, op. cit., 109-120.

PART III
CHANGING WITHOUT CHANGE

Chapter 8

New Model of an Old Gun

Those involved in breaking up the second Yugoslavia were undeniably guided by a measurable quantity of special, mutually eliminating interests; the deadline for their execution was immediate and the price of no great concern. The value of the goods in demand –national states – set the price and turned those paying it (the inhabitants) into an item on the still unwritten bill of costs.

Second Yugoslavia's disintegration in war was symbolized by a battle for pocketbooks and wallets,[1] and for rifles and machine-guns. It went without saying that the national leaders knew what they would do with the money and troops when they got them. The inhabitants of their states expected tangible benefits as well. They were promised that their 'brother peoples' would no longer exploit them and they would bear arms in their own 'backyard' under the command of national military leaders.

In order to come into being and survive, the new states had to create their own armies. This is why the JNA was their most important common target; but it was not rescinded until it had achieved the current goals of the Serbian regime. At the same time, it gave rise to the cores of the emerging national armies.[2] Unlike countries in Eastern Europe in which old armies found themselves new (elected) political chiefs, in the former Yugoslavia old and new political chiefs, with the help of the war and JNA, found themselves attractive armies.

The initial stabilization of the new states raised the following question: what could these states and their citizens expect from their armies? The first answers can be found in a comparative analysis of the profile of these armies and the JNA, since the direction of their postwar differentiation can only be determined by measuring the new armies' distance from the JNA.

The war directly determined the profile of the regimes and armies in the new states. This made it difficult for the central Yu-states (FRY, RH, entities in B-H) to leave behind once and for all the socialist system of producing surplus power.[3] This even hastened the installation and stabilization of authoritarian regimes in them.[4]

The national-religious substance of the war, stemming from the battle of the national elite for territory,[5] was crowned by ethnic cleansing and the creation of states that were ethnically pure, so to speak. This was confirmed by constitutions in Croatia and the entity of Republika Srpska, while in others it was hidden behind the declared state community of all citizens.[6]

Although they arbitrated the results of the war, foreign meddlers did not even try to demilitarize the Yu-region, and so its pacification was missing.[7] The danger of renewed warfare in order to revise the imposed peace,[8] was only removed when NATO put the whole territory under its control and Tudjman and Milošević left power. This slowed down the new states' and armies' shift to a peacetime regime.

Based on their contribution to the attainment of statehood and/or parastatehood, or hiding the Serbian regime's participation in the war, the new armies became an important internal political factor. This prevented them from being brought in line with the position of armies in modern democratic states.[9]

The instability of the regimes and the autonomous-secessionist tendencies in the new states led to the constant danger that the armies would be used internally. In addition, the political and military elite had teamed up for the sake of joint interests and this slowed down the de-ideologization and professionalization of the new armies. This also increased their joint resistance to public and parliamentary control.

In order to more easily compare the armies that arose in what had been the former Yugoslavia, we will classify them into two groups.

The central line dividing them is drawn by how they were formed and their relations during the war. The first group contains national/ethnic armies that date from the end of the crisis and were then finalized and verified during the war: the Armed Forces of the Republic of Croatia (OSH), the Croatian Defense Council of Herceg-Bosnia (HVO), the Territorial Defense of the Republic of Slovenia (TOS) and the Muslim Army of Bosnia and Herzegovina (ABH). The Army of the Republic of Macedonia (VRM), which arose out of necessity and against its will, can be placed provisionally in this group. The opposite group includes armies that arose by renaming the Serbian remnants of the JNA: the Yugoslav Army (VJ) and the Army of Republika Srpska (VRS). The Army of the Republic of the Serbian Krajina (VRSK) belonged to it until it was dissolved by Croatia's 'Storm' attack.

The three-part Serbian army was the only one to fight all the other armies, except the Macedonian. Once the arranged war was over, the Slovenian army and state withdrew from events in the former Yugoslavia and had nothing to do with their direction. The Croatian army from the republic and the diaspora developed during clashes with the JNA, and soon fought against the Muslim Army of B-H. In the same vein, the ABH arose during war with the JNA and VRS, which did not prevent it from fighting Croatian armies as well.

The uneven results classified these armies into victors and defeated. The scattered JNA and the Serbian regime's crushing outcome were turned into the victories of other armies and their political leaders,[10] thus the new armies were evaluated in different ways in their own environment and their self-perceptions were not the same. Analogies from more recent history appear at once: in terms of their self-awareness as liberators and their privileged status, the armies of the new states are reminiscent of the JNA in 1945, while the overall degradation and frustration of the VJ and its officers resembles the 'former royal army' in the first years of communist Yugoslavia.

8.1 Hidden Traces of the Legacy

This elementary classification speaks little of the social nature of these armies. Additional information is provided by comparing the sustaining principles of their internal organization and the nature of their relations with the civilian authority holding power over them.

The lines of warfare clearly distinguished armies with official discontinuity with the JNA and those with hidden continuity. The armies from the emerging states went into war or came out of it with a new image and new ideologies: changes were made to all the symbols, the system of organization, the system and language of command, models of replenishing troops and logistical support.[11] What changed in particular was the basis of identification and the morale (combat) substrate of these armies. Their national-liberation convictions were given great support by the incoherent wandering of the disintegrating JNA on their territories.

Although the Serbian armies emerged during the war, their severance with the JNA was postponed. Changes in the symbols were symbolic. The Orthodox evolution of the VRS expressed above all the relationship among political forces in Pale; it was intended to provide the VRS's noncommunist combat morale and serve as the national-religious identity of the warring power-holders.[12] Contrary to this and in line with the Serbian regime's expected benefit from self-proclaimed continuity with SFRY, and the senior officers' emotional and self-interest attachment with the JNA, the VJ remained the guardian of its heritage.

Two older, principled reasons advise caution when evaluating the (dis)continuous scope of the new armies. Reason number one: the new armies could only be independent to the extent to which their home states had broken with the generators of authority resting in Yugoslavia.[13] Reason number two: since the wartime division of SFRY was made with the disproportionate transfer of its fundamental contradictions to the emerging states, the new armies bore visible traces of the JNA. In other words, by rescinding SFRY the new states did not do away with their common social and historical heritage and surroundings, nor did they acquire immunity from the 'JNA syndrome'.

A comparison of OSH and VJ with the JNA, showing their similarities, supports the above:

- These two armies, as paradoxical as it seems, are linked by their silence regarding the JNA. Proof of this is the evident lack of fundamental analyses of the military-political and social being of the JNA, and thus the essence and cause of its involvement in the war that ended in its collapse.[14]

It is easy to understand why all interest in their former army ceased. As the war moved around the republics and the JNA was driven out of one after the other, all interest in its fate faded. Since the JNA had been declared the aggressor, the new states considered it merely the object of armed attacks and propaganda-operative campaigns.

As the Serbian armies detached themselves from the JNA, those with authority over the Army archived it. The generals who were heir to the JNA's wartime misuse returned to it periodically;[15] granting amnesty to themselves and the Serbian regime, they held firmly to the official version of the JNA's role in the war. It is therefore no surprise that they strictly avoided key topics, such as: the Party's super-determination of the JNA, its group mentality, the course and results of Serbia's teamwork with the Army, manipulation of the combat and officer corps, the Army's participation in the emergence of paramilitary formations, war crimes, etc.

Nonetheless, other intentions are hidden behind the situational and manipulative reasons for remaining silent about the JNA. With their silence they wanted, among other things, to avoid the consequences of their common, Party-state past.

Everyone wanted not only to free their nation and power-holders from responsibility for the war, but also to deny at the same expense any links with the development and misuse of the JNA. Since, according to some,[16] Serbia's domination of the Army had always been tacit, the aggression of the 'Serbo-communist JNA' became 'self-explanatory'. As the creation of the Territorial Defense had been devised to introduce national armies, according to others,[17] the Serbs' use of the JNA was only a forced response to violent secession and the danger of repeated genocide of the Serbian people.

Additional reasons for the silence are found in the postwar reality of the Yu-states. Any scrutiny of the JNA's fundamental determinants necessarily imposed parallels with the new armies. Such undertakings might give rise to the warranted fear of repeated military-Party theatrics.[18]

Let us recall: for decades the sole, ultimate constant in the generals' use of the JNA was to serve their own interests. They agreed among themselves to substitute loyalty to the Leader and Party with their own absolute power in the Army. They used the death of the Leader to appear on the public scene. Finding their legitimacy in his cult, the generals took on the right to arbitrate ideologically and politically in state affairs. When their Yugo-socialist notions of loyalty to themselves crumbled, they turned their sympathies towards the Serbian side which was the only one to offer them a state in which to find refuge and justification.[19]

The new states' small remove from their former homeland thus cautioned of real danger that the generals of the new armies, should they have to choose between the regime and the citizens on one of the dividing lines of their states,[20] would once again choose the side of the regime, which was actually their own side.[21]

- On the eve of war, the JNA was rightfully denoted as the ideological bastion of communistic conservatism. Opposite them were the national democrats who promised the creation of modern armies without repressive indoctrination. The war disproved both one and the other: the Serbian generals in the JNA did not remain faithful to socialism and the Yugoslav idea nor were the new armies free of ideology.

The uneven (in)consistency of the national leaders and programs only changed the role of ideology in the armies during and after the war. Where national ideologies were in line with political and territorial goals, the new generals and armies had valid justification for war (TOS, OSH, ABH). It was thus not until the end of the wars that the Serbian armies and generals could have discovered, had they wanted, the shallowness of the regime's ideology: pan-Serbian national feelings was shown to be only an instrument to preserve Milošević's absolute power.[22]

The end of the war brought a rise in both differences and similarities. Confirming their national political correctness with victories, the generals of the new armies earned the right to take part in dividing up the power and authority that had been acquired. After the Dayton Agreement, Serbia's leader, however, forced his generals to accept defeat and acclaim his new ideology of pacifism. Then he pushed them under NATO bombs in Kosovo, thereby hiding his contribution to the Serbian-Albanian conflicts.[23] He finally stripped them of power, but did not stop using them for political purposes. This is where the differences disappear between Serbia's and the other armies: they had all been and still were ready to participate in the regimes' manipulations with war, peace, and power, in the name of patriotism or any other suitable reason.[24]

The ideological-political allegiance of these armies, based on their wartime loyalty to the national leaders and ideas, outlived the peace.[25] It is therefore no surprise that the leaders and generals were unprepared to abandon each other to the tribulations of parliamentary and public control. For the sake of preserving their Caesar-like emblems,[26] the leaders maintained their power over the ideologically dedicated and personally loyal armies. Only Tudjman could save the Croatian army from the consequences of democratic controls, just as Milošević alone, watching out for himself, could save the defeated Serbian generals from responsibility for the war and its disastrous results.

- Party-police suitability had been the guiding principle behind the JNA's personnel selection and was at the same time the main repressive instrument with which to turn the (noncommissioned) officers into a monolith. With the outbreak of war the ideological-supernational monolith split along ethnic lines. As of that moment, ethnic suitability became or remained the key discriminating feature among the servicemen in all Yu-armies; the rationality behind this fact is hard to contest owing to the type of war, and its prolongation to the postwar period even among like-minded thinkers is understandable.

Thus the former communistic differentiation quickly changed to national-patriotic in the new armies, and was carried out using the same arbitrary criteria. The real scope within which this principle was maintained soon became visible. After removing ethnically unsuitable personnel, all the armies, with the support of their masterminds, then searched for and found unreliable individuals among fellow ethnic members and/or comrades in arms.[27] Military and civilian security services had a key role in this work, covering all the new armies along the lines of the JNA model. These services, by the way, were the only ones to come out of the war untouched,[28] which facilitated their combined protection of their predecessors' heritage (UDB (State Security Administration) and KNOJ (Yugoslav People's Defense Corps).

The first to feel the brunt were the former JNA officers: as soon as their wartime utility expired, they were relieved of their duty, regardless of their national suitability. For example, Serbian officers from the JNA were constantly viewed with suspicion in the Rupublika Srpska and the Republic of Serbian Krajina owing to their communist past. They were additionally classified according to their readiness to participate in the war in Croatia and Bosnia-Herzegovina.[29] An eliminatory skirmish took place in Croatia's army between the emigrant officers (from the JNA), the immigrants (from the diaspora) and the autochthonous war commanders.[30] Not a single Yu-army was excluded from such happenings.[31]

If we disregard differences in form, we can easily recognize this differentiation as the special war method of eliminating the 'other guy' which was a well-known practice in the JNA. Even if we understand it as a form of inter-army tussle to acquire or distribute power, i.e. as an instrument used by the regimes to produce loyalty, this is not enough to remove the new armies significantly from the JNA model.

- The social identity of the JNA servicemen, and those in other communist armies[32] was produced by a combination of methods. Their systemic exclusiveness, unique status, social corruption, existential dependence and ideologically anaesthetized state resulted in the servicemen's group mentality and relatively autarchic armies.

Therein lie some of the reasons for the rapid national and systemic dissolution of the JNA and the readiness of the officers to take part in the ideological-political manipulations of the previous regimes as well as those that were newly arising. This also explains the lack of any professional rebellion in spite of the ample opportunities JNA generals were provided on the eve of and during the war. In any case, a political rebellion could no longer be expected since the JNA members and their compatriots were hastening to defend the nation.

The fact that these armies maintained systemic features that favored the creation (renewal) of a group mentality additionally justify their comparison with the JNA.[33] Furthermore, democratic deficiencies in most of these states heralded the existence of such a group mentality, since it alone, within a normal framework, can hold back the modernization of an army and democratic control over it.

- In the last decade of its existence, the JNA was confronted with a lack of valid – social, political and value system – sources to maintain the desired combat morale among its members and units.

At first glance, the victorious Yu-armies should not have had problems with the combat morale of their men. Arguments were within reach: they had attained their key war objectives, and all that was left was to guard their national states from external and internal danger. Before the NATO bombing, even the VJ had found a way to come out a winner: success lay in the fact that it had prevented the war from spreading to SR Yugoslavia and preserved the territorial integrity of the state. After withdrawing from Kosovo, Milošević and the military leaders declared victory over NATO.

However, the motivational strength of collectivistic ideologies faded as the war moved into the past. As long as mortars were being launched, houses were torched and people expelled, combat morale practically produced itself on a daily basis – destroying the 'Chetniks'/ 'Ustashe'/ 'Balija' (derogatory for Bosnian Muslim) and revenge were enough reason to wage war willingly. During the war great patriotic goals, supported by the ideological-propaganda drilling of the army and public, easily replaced and/or postponed the satisfaction of lower-level group-individual goals and interests.

With the arrival of peace, the convictions of these ideologies increasingly depended on the tempo and quality of projects for national and state prosperity. These were quite measurable and operational categories – each person could easily turn them into a sum of money in his pocket, a level of personal and family security and prosperity.

Therefore, when 'bread' reached the agenda, as it did in FRY, RH and B-H, the struggle for personal and family survival quickly demystified all the great goals and words. At that point the combat morale of the national armies could no longer be renewed using worn-out, misused values.

In spite of this, the regimes in FRY and Croatia used tried and true means from the JNA (SFRY) to maintain the national-patriotism of the citizens and the combat morale of their servicemen. Relying on the so-called theory of internal and external conspiracies they encouraged xenophobia and chauvinism in their armies and public opinion.[34] Based on this, citizens who believed these conspiracies turned into 'assault' patriots, while force was used to coerce the hesitant into 'repressive' patriotism.

The armies of the central Yu-states are additionally linked by the 'Hague transversal'. Owing to the reasonable suspicion that numerous war crimes were committed under their auspices, the international community has taken over their criminal prosecution. Although only partially personalized, these criminal liabilities directly disturb relations within the armies. The Hague's demands to turn over individual soldiers and/or officers can, over the short term and with the support of co-responsible political elite, strengthen internal solidarity based on having fought together in the war.

However, the situation will change if and when the international community uses sanctions against some states and armies for not handing over those under suspicion. Then the intimate and internal division into guilty and innocent will increase interpersonal tension, which might lead to hidden or open conflicts and schisms within the armies. And all of this necessarily has a negative influence on combat morale.

- From its origin almost to its disappearance, the JNA and its general corps built their extra-institutional power and public influence on the cult of Josip Broz Tito. However, just as they fell over themselves to show their loyalty to the Leader while he was alive, the republican leaders competed in fleeing Tito after his death, taking his place among their ethnic groups. Unlike them, until the war broke out the military leaders were unswerving guardians of the cult. But just like those following the Ketman survival strategy of disguising one's true feelings, with the outbreak of war the army leaders quickly renounced their former false god in order to more easily embrace the idol of Serbia. The newly awakened military turncoats began emulating their national leaders.

For this reason, OSH and VJ remained prisoners of the 'Tito syndrome'. Not only because the systems of authority were no different from the previous ones, but also because their leaders with their Caesar-like ambitions were worthy successors of their great teacher. Any external differences stemmed from the uneven success of Milošević and

Tudjman in commanding their armies and achieving their war objectives.

Franjo Tudjman took over the cliché: he had a variety of parade uniforms sewn up, moved into Tito's villa on Brioni Island and surrounded himself with a guard. As a nation-builder and liberator, he took over the role of the unlimited supreme commander. Just in case, he put the First Croatian Guard Corps under his direct command.[35]

Slobodan Milošević resisted the temptations of the commander's uniform all during his reign. But as president of Serbia he set up an internal army under the name of the police. Its militarization was completed with the introduction of the ranks of officer up to general. He had twofold benefit from this: among the policemen he developed new operating motives for career-minded men, thus additionally increasing their dependence on their personal efforts. By encouraging competition between the military and police generals he directed them together to fight for their political and budgetary inclinations.

Milošević did not receive the formal prerequisite to legally command the VJ until he was elected president of FRY. However, he had put the Army irrevocably under his control previously, using it through others. When Milošević arrived in the White Palace, he reactivated all the services and revived the symbols of his predecessor, thus it was only a matter of time before he would have reached for the uniform and the hero's decorations. First the VJ generals appointed him supreme commander against the FRY Constitution, and then after withdrawing from Kosovo they proposed he be awarded the decoration of national hero. The Leader, however, was heroically condemned on October 5, 2000 and history sent him to The Hague.

- One point that distinguished the VJ and OSH from the JNA lies in the fact that both were still operating without official concepts and doctrines.[36]

No one, not even those with authority, knew why and how these armies would be used. This raised a dilemma: was this due to the unfavorable concurrence of circumstances or the conceptual vacuum that was intentionally maintained.

Available information indicates the Milošević and Tudjman intentionally avoided defining the roles of their armies in political terms. The initial reason was their need to leave themselves room to use them arbitrarily – internally against their opponents and externally towards Bosnia and Herzegovina. At the same time, had they defined the goals and tasks of their armies in detail, they themselves would have been under obligation. This would in principle have allowed military leaders to legally refuse any eventual misuse of the army. Since this vacuum bothered neither the VJ nor the HV generals, they clearly accepted the irregular status of the armies under their command and all the consequences that followed.

In spite of the above comparison, there is reason to maintain that even if they had not arisen from the JNA, the armies of the new states would have had the same or similar basic principles. In other words, the profiles of these armies in their limited duration could only be marked but not determined by a return case of the JNA. The essence of these armies was directly determined by the nature of the ruling orders, which created them in their own likeness during the war.

Once they achieved independence, the new states were able to create armies that suited them. Similarities with the JNA could no longer be explained by their origin; the reasons for maintaining the model of Party armies thus lie in the civilian-military relations of each of the successor states. And these relations in fact only summarize the nature of their ruling orders.

Notes

1 For more, see: Madžar Ljubomir, Ko koga eksploatiše (Who is Exploiting Whom), in: Srpska strana rata (The Serbian Side of the War), (ed) Nebojša Popov, Republika, Belgrade, 1996, 171-200.
2 For more about this, see: an interview with Martin Špegelj, Croatia's former Minister of Defense; D. Hudelist, Interview: Martin Špegelj, Erasmus, Zagreb, No. 9/1994, 42-64.
3 Compare: Puhovski Žarko, Socijalistička konstrukcija zbilje (The Socialist Construction of Reality), u: Napuštanje socijalizma, (Abandoning Socialism) (eds) V. Gligorov, J. Teokarević, IMRP, Belgrade, 1990, 9-24.
4 For more, see: Antonić Slobodan, Vlada Slobodana Miloševića: pokušaj tipološkog određenja, (Slobodan Milošević's Rule: an Attempt at Typological Organization) Srpska politička misao, Belgrade, no. 1/95, 91-131.
5 Banac Ivo, Srbi u Hrvatskoj: povijest i perspective (The Serbs in Croatia: History and Prospects) in: Srbi u Hrvatskoj - jučer, danas, sutra (The Serbs in Croatia – Yesterday, Today, Tomorrow), Croatian Helsinki Council for Human Rights, Zagreb, 1998, 13-25.

6   Compare: Novi ustavi na tlu bivše Jugoslavije (New Constitutions in Former Yugoslavia), International Politics,, Faculty of Law, Faculty of Political Science, Belgrade, 1995.
7   Which would only be possible within the scope of a cathartic inquiry into the participation of their own governments, armies and individuals in crushing their former compatriots, in which case it would not be a bad idea to consult the experience of Germany's denazification; compare: Stobbe Heinz-Gunter, Denacifikacija u Nemačkoj (Denazification in Germany), in: Srpska strana rata (The Serbian Side of the War), Nebojša Popov (ed), Republika, Belgrade, 1996, 726-731.
8   See: Nedovršeni mir (Incomplete Peace), Report from the International Commission for the Balkans, Radio B92, Naša Borba, Belgrade, 1998. and Hadžić Miroslav, The Security profile of the Balkans, in: The Balkans in '97, Foreign policy papers, European Movement in Serbia, Forum for International Relations, Belgrade, 1998, p. 91-118
9   Compare: Žunec Ozren, Vojska i demokracija (The Army and Democracy), Erazmus, Zagreb, no. 3, 1993. 47-55.
10 According to: Žunec Ozren, Democracy in the 'Fog of War': Civil-Military Relations in Croatia, in: C. P. Danopoulos and D. Zirker (eds): Civil-Military Relations in the Soviet and Yugoslav Successor States, Westview Press, Boulder, 1995. 213-230.
11 Changes were made to uniforms, flags, oaths, ranks, insignias etc; compare: Bebler Anton, Civil-Military Relations in Slovenia, in: C. P. Danopoulos and D. Zirker (eds): Civil-Military Relations in the Soviet and Yugoslav Successor States, Westview Press, Boulder, 1995, 202.
12 Compare: Vojska nikla na ruševinama JNA (Armies arising from the ruins of the JNA), Revija 92, Belgrade, no. 198, 16.05.97, 15.
13 'Civil-military relations in Croatia mirror the development of democracy in the country.' Žunec Ozren, Democracy in 'The Fog of War': Civil-Military Relations in Croatia, op. cit., 219.
14 Government and professional circles kept silent, as shown by the small number of bibliography units dealing with the (pre)war role of the JNA; compare: Bojana Vukotić: Jugoslovenski autori o krizi i raspadu Jugoslavije (Yugoslav authors on the crisis and disintegration of Yugoslavia), Sociološki pregled no. 4/95, Belgrade, 565-581; Dobrila Stanković, Zlatan Maltarić, Svetska bibliografija o krizi u bivšoj Jugoslaviji (World bibliography on the crisis in former Yugoslavia), Medjunarodna politika with a group of publishers, Belgrade 1996.
15 With a twofold goal: justifying its siding with the Serbs and showing the transformation of the Yugoslav Army (VJ); see some of the interviews of former chiefs of the VJ General Staff: Života Panić (Vojska, 31.12.1992) and Momčilo Perišić (Vojska, 27.04.1995).

16 Compare: Bebler Anton, The Military and the Yugoslav Crisis, Sudosteuropa, No.3-4, 1991, pp.127-144.
17 Compare: Radovan Radinović, Moć i nemoć vojske u raspadu Jugoslavije (The power and powerlessness of the army in the disintegration of Yugoslavia), Sociološki pregled no. 2/94, Belgrade, 283-296.
18 This is shown by the attempt by Janez Janša, the Slovenian Minister of Defense, to use the Slovenian army in internal political battles; according to: Bebler Anton, op. cit., 206-210.
19 Remington Robin Alison, The Yugoslav Army: Trauma and Transition, in: C. P. Danopoulos and D. Zirker (eds): Civil-Military Relations in the Soviet and Yugoslav Successor States, Westview Press, Boulder, 1995, 165.
20 These include changes of governments through elections; political crises in the case of the biological or political death of a national leader, social unrest of broader proportions, etc.
21 This is shown by the VJ General Staff's attitude towards the 1996-1997 protests in Serbia; they very quickly abandoned their nominal neutrality in order to solve the problem 'within the framework of the system's institutions', which were run by the SPS (Socialist Party of Serbia) under Milošević's control; compare: Naša Borba, 7.01.97, 2.
22 Popov Nebojša, Srpski populizam - Od marginalne do dominatne pojave (Serbian populism. From marginal to mainstream), special supplement, Vreme no.. 135, Belgrade.
23 Hadžić Miroslav, Security Ranges of NATO Intervention in Kosovo, Working Papers 27, Copenhagen Peace Research Institute, 1999.
24 For example, during the pre-election silence General Stevanović, commander of the RV and PVO in the VJ, announced that not a single 'Serbian general, in prevailing conditions, would agree to be a minister in Panić's (Milan Panić – M.H.) government' (Večernje novosti, Belgrade no. 24.793, 2); the first chief of the General Staff of the Macedonian Army, General Asprovski, tried to shift control of the army from Parliament to the President of the Republic; uporedi: Isaković and Danopoulos, In Search of Identity: Civil-Military Relations and Nationhood in the Former Yugoslav Republic of Macedonia, in: C. P. Danopoulos and D. Zirker (eds): Civil-Military Relations in the Soviet and Yugoslav Successor States, Westview Press, Boulder, 1995, 182.
25 This is shown by the client status of OSH and its politicization tendencies (Žunec Ozren, Okučanski zaključci (Conclusions from Okučani), Erazmus, Zagreb, no. 12, 1995,7-20), and the quiet entropy of the VJ as a one-shot army (Hadžić Miroslav, Postsocijalistička transformacija vojske (Post-socialist transformation of the Army), Sociological Studies, Institute of Social Sciences, Belgrade, 1993, 91-118).
26 Podunavac Milan, Princip građanstva i priroda političkog režima u postkomunizmu: slučaj Srbija (The principle of the citizenry and the nature of

the political regime in post-communist societies: the case of Serbia) u: Potisnuto civilno društvo (Repressed Civil Society), (ed) Vukašin Pavlović, Eko centar, Belgrade, 1995,.230.
27 The last non-Bošnjak high officers were removed from the ABH through retirement: Jovan Divjak (a Serb) and Sjepan Šiber (a Croat); see: interview with Jovan Divjak (Naša Borba, 7-8.07.97).
28 Thus, for example, the 'Labrador' and 'Opera' affairs can be treated more as purges that settled accounts within the service than as an opening up towards the public; compare: Feuilleton on the 'Opera' affair, Pobjeda, 8-23.03.1998.
29 This also brought an internal (hidden) division in the VJ into Serbs from Serbia Proper and those from outside it.
30 The attempt by Andrija Hebrang, Gojko Šušak's successor as Minister of Defense in the Republic of Croatia, to curb the power of the so-called Herzegovian lobby by replacing 12 high general dignitaries, allegedly for their schooling, ended with his resignation.
31 For more details see the contributions by Yu-authors in the collection by C.P. Danapoulos and D. Zirker.
32 Jonse Ellen, Red Army and Society, A Sociology of the Soviet Military, Allen & Unwin, Boston, 1985, str. 92.
33 Compare: Žunec, 1993, 54 and the FRY Constitution, Article 139, op. cit.
34 Neumann Franz, Demokratska i autoritarna država (Democratic and Authoritarian State), Naprijed, Zagreb, 1974,246.
35 According to: Žunec Ozren, Democracy in 'The Fog of War': Civil-Military Relations in Croatia, op. cit., 220.
36 According to: Žunec Ozren, Okučanski zaključci, op. cit.; Hadžić Miroslav, Postsocijalistička transformacija vojske, op. cit., 231.

Chapter 9

Self-Transformation of the Yugoslav Army

Milošević gained considerable, lasting political benefit from the wars he waged, regardless of their setbacks. In this respect, Milošević is used here as a metaphor and personification of the entire regime that arose from the roots of communist Yugoslavia. Although Milošević shaped the regime he inherited to suit himself, it was the key support to his establishment of unlimited power. The old regime provided the new ruler with the complete instruments and related infrastructures to reproduce his personal power. Numerous social-interest groups ranging from local communities to the highest state levels were in the same boat; they had been dependent on the old regime and now were dependent on the new regime.

The first benefit was the preservation of political continuity; with a few modifications the communist order continued its life in the third Yugoslavia. The wars brought a straightforward change in Ideological identification as Serbian nationalism replaced socialism. But Milošević was bound by neither the previous ideology nor the new one. As he fled from trans-socialist reforms of the second Yugoslavia into war, Milošević destroyed the prerequisites for the democratic reconstitution of Serbia and Montenegro, renewing his power uninterruptedly until he had exhausted all of the state's social, national and economic resources.

Milošević's key benefit came from his control over the JNA and Serbia's police. Subordinating Kadijević's trio to himself, he took possession of the military's power and under the name of the JNA waged war in Slovenia, Croatia, and Bosnia-Herzegovina. Then he extracted a new formation from it called the Yugoslav Army (VJ). Even though he was forced into operating from a new state, his power did not decrease over the Serbian para-states. Milošević used the fact that the armies in the diaspora were dependent on the motherland and the VJ to discipline the Serbian leaders on the other side of the Drina River.

As soon as FR Yugoslavia was created, it was announced that the Army would undergo professional transformation in order bring it in line with new needs, yet not even the initial prerequisites for this were created during Milošević's reign.

9.1 Shortage of Prerequisites

FR Yugoslavia has remained an incomplete, under-accepted and unstable state. It is therefore a provisional state, in a transient and transitory phase. Since the reorganization of the second Yugoslavia by means of war is still ongoing,[1] the outcome remains to be seen. In this regard, crucial decisions about the fate of the states of the peoples of former Yugoslav are being made by the European-Atlantic alliance.

If this were not enough, the new Yugoslav state was created in an unconstitutional manner. In addition, the constitutions of Serbia and FRY are not in line with each other, and they are actually two colliding orders living together. This has led to multiple breaches of the FRY constitution without any punishment.[2] Then unconstitutional laws were passed that undermined the principles of the rule of law and division of power, and decreased the legal security of the citizens.[3]

Unitarization of the federal state falsified its (con)federal foundation. During 1998 Montenegro's legal government was banned from federal bodies. Then it unilaterally took over the functions of the federal state except for defense and air traffic control. In this respect FRY today is a fictitious community which is nominally held together by the Yugoslav Army.

When power moved out of the system, the parliamentary order and party pluralism lost all meaning. Instead of democratic procedures, political despotism and repression took over. Key decisions were made outside the system whose only purpose was to subsequently legalize them.[4] With creative reading of the Constitution, legal and electoral engineering, the prospects of legally changing the order and/or changing the government through elections became virtually impossible.[5]

This led authoritarianism to devolve into a dictatorship and there was widespread violation of human rights.[6] The regime's eagerness to hold onto power regardless of the cost hindered any compromises in resolving the crisis. The aggressive division of citizens into patriots and traitors antagonized society and during 2000 the crisis took on potentially violent proportions.

The FRY economy, which had been depleted by the war, was worsened by marauding privatization and government takeover.[7] Orchestrated assaults of inflation robbed the citizens and both accumulation and amortization were pumped dry.[8] The regime quickly spent the economic source of its power and prospects grew of society ending up in 'warring communism'. This deprived the state and its citizens of a modern strategy of social development, and its final departure from socialism was thus postponed.

FRY's exile from the international community and the regime's self-isolation deprived the state of a valid foreign policy and security strategy.[9] The combined effect of the regime and foreign meddlers put the third Yugoslavia in an unfavorable defense position.

The misuse of Serbian national feelings during the war[10] destroyed the individual and collective identity of the dominant ethnic group. Denying the identity of the Montenegrin nation blazed the trail for conflicts among the clans in Montenegro. The minority ethnic groups therefore evolved towards a potential isolationism of their own. In addition, the prevalence of collectivistic ideologies denied the civil constitution of Serbia and FRY (Article 8 of the FRY Constitution, 1992; Article 1 of the Constitution of the Republic of Serbia, 1990). NATO's taking over Kosovo from Serbia encouraged further decomposition of the federal state. The prospects grew that Montenegro would leave FRY and Vojvodina and Sandžak would separate in the future. This reduced the prospects of a democratic renewal of society and the willing preservation of the common state.

The war finalized the destruction of the cultural and spiritual achievements, and thus the basic moral values, of the Serbian and Yugoslav society. The constant misuse of ideologically reduced patriotism enabled the public domination of isolationism, provincialism and xenophobia.

Milošević's power over the VJ resulted additionally from gaps in the FRY Constitution, but also from the fact that the constitutions of Serbia and FRY contain colliding provisions on defense and the Army.[11] A comparative examination reveals the following:

- Defending the country – According to the federal Constitution FRY has jurisdiction over defense and security.[12] The federal Assembly 'decides on changes to the borders of FRY; decides on war and peace; declares states of war, imminent threat of war and martial law.'[13]
  According to Serbia's Constitution it 'sets up and safeguards' the 'sovereignty, independence and territorial integrity' of the state and the 'defense and security of the Republic of Serbia and its citizens'.[14] Its

National Assembly is authorized to 'make decisions about war and peace'.[15]

- Defense policy – The federal government[16] among other things 'establishes and pursues internal and foreign policies',[17] 'creates and terminates federal ministries',[18] 'directs and coordinates' their work[19] and 'orders general mobilization and organizes preparations for defense'.[20] When the Assembly cannot convene, after hearing the opinion of the President of the Republic and the President of the Federal Assembly Council, the federal government 'declares states of imminent threat of war; states of war or martial law'.[21] If the Assembly cannot convene when the country is in a state of exigency,[22] the federal government takes over its authority and 'acts passed during a state of war' may 'restrict individual rights and freedoms of the citizens, except those in Articles 20, 22, 25, 26, 27, 28, 29, 35 and 43 of this Constitution'.[23]
The government of the Republic of Serbia has no explicit jurisdiction in the defense policy. However, since according to Article 90 it 'pursues the policies of the Republic of Serbia', 'passes regulations, decisions and other acts to execute the law', 'directs and coordinates the work of the ministries' and 'supervises the work of the ministries', the defense policy is implicitly within its field of activity.

- Armed forces – The federal state has the Yugoslav Army 'that defends (the state's) sovereignty, territory, independence and constitutional order'.[24] The Law on Defense says that when the country is in a state of exigency the police 'may be used to carry out combat tasks, i.e. wage war or offer armed resistance.'[25] In this case they are 'under the control of Yugoslav Army officers who command the fighting.'
Serbia's Constitution does not name any republican armed forces, although it mentions them.[26] They could include the MUP (Ministry of the Interior) forces who safeguard the Republic's security and prevent any undermining or disturbance of the constitutional order,[27] particularly since internal affairs includes 'efforts by authorized republican organs to safeguard the Republic and its citizens'.[28]

- The supreme command – According to the FRY Constitution 'the President of the Republic commands the Yugoslav Army in war and peace, in accordance with the decisions of the Supreme Defense Council' consisting of 'the President of the Republic and presidents of the member republics,' while the President of the Republic is 'the President of the Supreme Defense Council'.[29]

The President of FRY is explicitly[30] the only one with the right to independently 'appoint, promote and dismiss officers of the Yugoslav Army as defined by federal law; he appoints and dismisses presidents, judges and judges of the jury of military courts and military prosecutors.' The President's obligation to command 'in accordance with the decisions of the Supreme Defense Council' appears verbatim in the Law on the Yugoslav Army.[31] Paragraph two of the same Article lists the tasks and authority of the President in commanding the Army.

The President of Serbia is also supreme commander,[32] but of unnamed armed forces. He 'governs the armed forces in peace and war and the national resistance in war; he orders general mobilization and partial mobilization; he organizes preparations for defense in accordance with the law'.[33] If the National Assembly is prevented from convening, after being given the opinion of the federal president, he 'determines the existence of an imminent threat of war or declares a state of war'.[34] When the country is in a state of exigency the President of Serbia may[35] also by himself or at the proposal of the federal government 'pass acts on matters within the authority of the National Assembly' that 'might restrict individual rights and freedoms of the citizens'.[36] At the same time, he has the right to 'declare a state of emergency and pass acts to undertake measures as required by such circumstances, in accordance with the Constitution and the law'.[37]

- Defending the constitutional order – The Yugoslav Army is explicitly ordered to defend the constitutional order of FRY.[38] The Armed Forces of Serbia, however, are not obliged to protect the constitutional order of the Republic. The police are charged with this task.[39]

- When the country is in a state of exigency – The federal Constitution recognizes three such states: state of war, state of imminent threat of war and state of emergency[40] that are declared by the Federal Assembly.[41] When it cannot convene, this right is taken by the federal government.[42] Sufficient reasons to declare these states are defined in the Law on Defense.[43] A state of imminent threat of war is declared 'if there is danger of attack or another form of external threat to the country'. A state of war is declared 'if an attack against the country is imminent or has already started'. A state of emergency is declared 'if there is internal unrest of larger proportions and its violence endangers the constitutional order of the country, or when there is a natural or other disaster which greatly threatens the lives of the citizens and their property and material goods.' According to the first paragraph of Article 5 of the same law, a state of exigency is 'declared for the entire country'. The second paragraph allows exceptionally that 'a state of emergency may be declared for part of the country'.

In all three cases the President of FRY 'in accordance with the decisions of the Supreme Defense Council, orders measures to prepare the Yugoslav Army, mobilize forces and use the Army, and other operations and measures undertaken by the Yugoslav Army in order to prevent and remove dangers threatening the country's defense and its security'.[44]

The Constitution of Serbia does not define states of exigency and does not even mention them among the authority of the National Assembly. The President of the Republic, however, is given the authority to declare them.

According to the FRY Constitution there are federal and republican armed forces, which are commanded by independent supreme commands. At the beginning of the VJ chain of command is the Supreme Defense Council (VSO) whose decisions are carried out by the President of FRY. His commanding authority is thus restricted by previous Council decisions and should derive its legality from the Council. The President of Serbia, however, in governing the armed forces is restricted solely by the republican constitution and laws. According to the letter of both constitutions, the internal use of force can be ordered separately by the Supreme Defense Council of FRY and by the President of Serbia.

This constitutional collision allowed Milošević from the function of President of FRY, which only had the magnitude of protocol, to put his informal power into practice. It was new proof of the system's façade function, since central power moved to Milošević. The moment the VJ was formally under his authority this constitutional collision lost any practical meaning.

Milošević also benefited by ambiguity in the FRY Constitution regarding the use of the Army to defend the constitutional order. The concept of 'constitutional order' cannot be understood from the Constitution, and how it can be threatened is also unclear. Nothing is said about how or what means the VJ should use to defend this order, although it can legally do so during a state of emergency.[45] And this is if there has previously been 'internal unrest of greater proportions whose violence endangers the constitutional order of the country'. By broadly qualifying the conditions under which the Army defends the constitutional order, the merits of the matter are left to the political will of the ruler.[46] The federal organs' authorization to restrict the rights and freedoms of the citizens in states of exigency stems from this provision.[47]

The next gap arose from unregulated procedures in the VJ supreme command. According to the FRY's federal structure, supreme command of the VJ is delegated to a collective body. By transferring part of their rights to the federal state, the republican members gained the right to co-command the Army through their representatives in the VSO.

For functional reasons, execution of the Council's decisions is delegated to the President of FRY. This satisfies the need for a single superior and for subordination in the military organization. This also avoids triple command at cross purposes. Lest the FRY President endanger the rights of the co-commanders, the Constitution requires him to abide by the Council's decisions when commanding the VJ. The importance of this principle is confirmed by its transmission into legal acts.

The framer of the Constitution, however, did not follow through with the concept of group command of the Army. Since the Constitution does not define the decision making procedure in the VSO, it is not clear whether decisions are made by consensus or overrule. In the same vein, there is no mention as to whether all members of the VSO must be present in order to make decisions or whether this is possible when it is incomplete. Whether or not this is resolved in the VSO Rules of Procedure cannot be confirmed since the public has no insight into it. If the concept of overrule is allowed in the VSO, then this changes the initial intention of the Constitution to guarantee equal footing among the republics. This would allow for a decision on the internal use of the VJ in one of the republics to be made without the presence and agreement of its member in the VSO.

The Constitution also does not provide the means to check whether the commands of the FRY President are in line with VSO decisions, i.e. whether, how and when the Council checks that the President is carrying out their joint decisions and that his actions have legal support in the VSO decisions. Also, it is even less clear as to how the Council can cancel or change such actions if they are counter to its decisions.

Gaps in the Constitutions include the lack of procedures to set up the command and political accountability of the VSO. Not only are there no means to sanction individual responsibility within the VSO, but it is not clear to whom the Council is collectively accountable. A broad interpretation of the Constitution might find the federal Assembly as a control, but it cannot be proved that it has the right to call the VSO to account for its actions.

Therefore, respect for the procedures and authority in the Army's supreme command depends on relations among the political powers. Since central power lies outside the reach of the institutions, the VJ can be used outside of the procedures,[48] and thus could be easily misused during moments of internal crisis.

9.2 The Yugoslav Army's Capacity for Transformation

The VJ's current appearance and status are determined by the joint actions of three factors: its military-political origin, the nature of the regime, and how it is used politically (during war). The enduring loyalty of the rulers of FRY (Serbia and Montenegro) to the communist model has kept the VJ in a client status. Thus it is necessarily heir to the basic properties of its predecessor – the JNA.

Ever since the VJ's creation, the top generals have claimed countless times that is has been transformed, and after the withdrawal from Kosovo its reconstruction was announced. On the eve of elections in 2000 the generals gave the military's doctrine to Milošević to sign, although its elaboration is the responsibility of Parliament and not the Army. In addition, this was done without previously defining FRY's defense policy and strategy.

Two facts are missing for a serious evaluation of the generals' achievements. First, what plan was used to reconstruct the Army, since neither the federal Assembly nor the government passed such a plan. And second, who checked and/or verified the alleged changes, using which procedure.

Obstacles to the VJ's transformation necessarily followed from basic deficits in the third Yugoslavia, which is why procedures for parliamentary control of the Army were not activated. Furthermore, the regime used the generals to settle ongoing political accounts and during pre-election campaigns. In addition, it smothered public scrutiny and prevented the controlling influence of the media and non-governmental organizations.

Keeping the Army outside the system and public scrutiny was motivated by political and war-related reasons. Until the Dayton Agreement the regime used the Army only as strategic backing and a logistical and personnel base for the western Serbian armies. The internal protection of the regime had already been transferred to Serbia's police. When peace was declared, the Army became superfluous to the regime, which had no money or time for it. The Army only returned to the public scene when Milošević became President of FRY.[49]

The Army was put to use by the regime in 1998 after the KLA (Kosovo Liberation Army) offensive and was somewhat rehabilitated during the NATO aggression, because for the first time it had a clear and justified state goal. In spite of this, it was only defending itself in Kosovo. But it gave Milošević an alibi for losing Kosovo, something which had been announced long before. To make matters worse, after withdrawing from Kosovo the top generals turned into SPS and JUL party storm troopers.[50]

The ease with which the regime used the Army had several other sources. First, the Army was operating all along without a defined defense policy for FRY. In addition, eight years later the federal Assembly still had not elaborated a strategy to defend FRY and a doctrine on the use of the VJ.[51] It even took 18 months after the state was established for laws to be passed on the Army and defense. For this reason the professional soldiers and citizens still do not know the goals for which the Army will be used, whom it will fight and how it will be used.[52]

Since it was deprived of points of reference determined by the state, the VJ could not be transformed properly. The entire affair was then reduced to adjusting the Army's organization and numbers to the new state.[53] Owing to the lack of a state plan, the resulting self-transformation suited the know-how and needs of the elite generals and Milošević.

Then the transformation turned into the patriotization of the Army. Relying on 19th century Serbian traditions, a new ideological and national identity was formed for the Army,[54] although a dilemma remained as to whether citizens/soldiers who were not Serbs would adopt these traditions as a source of combat morale. In spite of this, the regime formed the VJ as a national army and not as one of all the citizens. To this end personnel were purged according to patriotic criteria.[55]

The Yugoslav Army also bears all the JNA's wartime defeats, resulting in social-psychological and professional frustration in its ranks. In addition, during the war in Kosovo from 1998-1999 more than 20,000 men failed to answer the call-up. The Army also suffers from a refugee syndrome; as the JNA withdrew all the officers who did not want or could not stay in the new Yu-states poured into it. Most of the refugee (non) commissioned officers and their families are thus homeless.[56] At the same time there was a drastic impoverishment of the Army and its members since the economy was ruined during the war.

The sanctions against FRY, which included the ban on importing arms and military equipment, increased the VJ's technical lag. The circle was complete when NATO bombed the military industry, thus hindering revitalization of the Army from domestic sources.

The sum total of findings is that the Yugoslav Army still does not have a clear professional and socio-political identity, and its transformation potentials cannot be reliably measured.

9.3 The DOS Dividing Line

In October 2000, the Army generals subordinated themselves to the new rulers. They were forced to do this by public pressure and the fact that most of those in the VJ were not ready to use force to keep Milošević in power. DOS (Democratic Opposition of Serbia) did not acquire effective control of the Army, however, until it was elected into power in Serbia.

Before the elections, DOS announced the general outline of reforms in both civil-military relations and the VJ, highlighted by democratic control of the VJ. To date there is no proof that DOS is committed to this concept. Furthermore, it has not offered any program whatsoever to reform the Army and the defense sector.

Milošević's heritage along with situational circumstances have partially justified DOS, since all energy has had to be directed towards the survival of society and the state. In addition, this entire period has been characterized by a duality of government. DOS took over power but still does not have sufficient strength to overrule the system it inherited.

It seems that DOS has given up on its post-electoral acceleration of events out of fear of clashes, as though caught unawares by the speed with which the old regime collapsed. Pressured by Vojislav Koštunica, DOS has kept things legal, which is otherwise difficult owing to the contradictory Constitution and unconstitutional laws. This allowed the remains of the old regime to consolidate and obstruct changes before they had any effect.

An important reason for the extended duality of government lies in the fact that the new authorities were caught in a vise by the Montenegrins. The rulers in Montenegro didn't for a moment want to renounce the benefits from their unconstitutionally acquired sovereignty and help dismantle the old, defeated regime. At the same time, the Montenegrin epigone of Milošević (the Socialist People's Party) grabbed the chance on the federal level, through DOS, to compensate for its lack of legitimacy and power in its own republic. To the joy of the Montenegrins, the international vise that was built into UN Security Council Resolution 1244 opened up, shifting Kosovo from Serbia to Yugoslavia.

At the same time, the Serbia/FRY capacity for pro-Europe reforms hit rock bottom. The democratic reconstitution of FRY almost became impossible and/or redundant after it was rescinded in Montenegro and Kosovo. The new government stopped the KLA from pouring into southern Serbia only with the approval and support of the European-Atlantic community. DOS, however, cannot consent to this community's fulfillment of Resolution 1244 and the Kumanovo agreement. This hampers their prospects of influencing the future status of Kosovo.

DOS's tactical ambivalence made the formative phase last too long. It reflected the lack of an operational program to effectively transfer authority and power. Behind this lay the lack of a comprehensive strategy of reform, which was unable to materialize in an ad hoc coalition based on an anti-Milošević platform; particularly since time has revealed inherent limitations in DOS with regard to reforms and administration.

Although DOS has its origins in resistance to communism, most of the parties in DOS still do not have a political identity. Going along with Milošević's plan to unite all the Serbs by force, they became hostages to his shifting policies. The opposition and regime were joined for reasons of self-interest and became dependent on each other, and were a prerequisite to each other's survival. This is why Milošević was never endangered by autonomous pressure from the opposition; his problems came from losing the war and/or internal errors.

The sterility of the opposition parties in Serbia stems from their contradictory being. Even though they identify with the principles of freedom and democracy, most of them still have not overcome the contradiction between a collectivistic and individualistic approach to the state and national/ethnic problem in Serbia.

The opposition's powerlessness has been explained all along by the thesis of the leaders' clashing vanities, as a Serbian fate. This was only a screen for conflicts among the parties about the future division of power. It was therefore more important for the opposition leaders to prevent their competition from succeeding than to depose Milošević. What was actually hiding behind the scenes was advanced fear of the early loss of future and desired participation in the new government.

The inhibitions became clear after the opposition took over power. DOS members compensated for the lack of programs with disputes about the tempo and scope of changes. The central line of conflict and future breakup has been drawn from the differences in how they treat the wars and their results. Regrouping is taking place within DOS along this axis and will soon end with its dissolution. It is therefore no surprise that the key parties in DOS – the Democratic Party of Serbia and the Democratic Party – are more concerned with how to acquire as much power as possible as their future stake, than how to respond to the social and state crisis.

In such circumstances, as expected, DOS has delayed putting the VJ under democratic control. For this purpose, the constitutions of FRY and Serbia would first have to be amended or new ones passed, with full awareness that the federal one will not be recognized in Montenegro and could not be applied in Kosovo. If, however, Serbia's constitution is brought in line with the federal constitution, Serbia runs the risk of being left without any state attributes should Yugoslavia disappear. Above all, DOS should initiate the radical transformation of the Army, but there is not enough time and money for that now, nor a valid program. It should also not be excluded that DOS wants to avoid any conflicts with the top generals or part of the officer corps who are disinclined to change.

DOS is obviously avoiding a serious, public discussion of reforming the Army. The problem is thus reduced to personal changes in the military leaders. The President of FRY has explained the lack of changes by the need to preserve institutions. For reasons unknown to the public, he has conditioned the Army's activities with the survival of General Pavković and his staff. At the same time, by renaming the Federal Ministry of Defense the Ministry of the Yugoslav Army, the federal government has shown that it knows little about civil-military relations and defense, particularly the role of the Ministry in the democratic control of the Army. The federal Assembly has exhausted all its interest in the Army to date by adopting a restrictive military budget. In the same vein, the federal Assembly's Defense and Security boards are still not doing their jobs.

In spite of this, the VJ is at the bottom of the scale of reform risks, but it takes a strong first place on the scale of complexity and cost of making changes. However, on the scale of DOS and/or Koštunica's priorities, Army reforms are down at the bottom. This is shown by the fact that DOS has still not stepped outside its principled resolution to create a modern, professional and small army. In addition, there is no information regarding the plan, the funds that will be used and the cost DOS will pay to achieve these goals.

This is supported by the fact that the generals, appointed by Milošević, are handling the alleged transformation of the Army, once again independent of the Assembly and government and outside the public eye. This has provided them the opportunity to capitalize on their new loyalty. By emphasizing their loyalty to the new leaders they want to hide their pre-election pretorianism. They have thus resorted once again to publicly currying favor with DOS, and President Koštunica in particular. So the top generals have once again personalized their loyalty and joined ranks around the new president of FRY.

Even if they wanted to reform the VJ, the new authorities must first establish a starting point. In order to put the VJ under democratic control instruments and procedures must be prepared. This requires knowledge of what the state will look like so that the army will be commensurate to it. The structure and scope of the needed army will be determined in accordance with the size and authority of the state. It is only based on clear defense and security parameters that the state can begin to transform, reduce and modernize the army such as it is today. Since DOS is not alone in deciding on the fate and appearance of Yugoslavia, it is forced to arbitrate together with the army it inherited in order to reach final decisions. For this reason DOS has taken measures to assure its political control of the Army, and the scope of initial reforms has been defined using the criterion of lesser risk for itself. However, postponing fundamental reforms in Serbia's Army and police cautions of potential danger: should the internal crisis intensify, parts of these apparatuses would be able to support the restoration of the old regime.

It is therefore essential that the armed forces in Serbia and FRY – the para-police and paramilitary forces – be put urgently under democratic controls. This, of course, directly depends on the tempo of the country's socio-economic and political reforms. When reforming the Army it has inherited, the new government must consider the following facts:

- The professionalization and modernization of the VJ is a complex, lengthy and socio-economically expensive process that in the planning and implementation phase requires the involvement of all the state's potentials, particularly scientific.
- The transformation of the VJ is only possible within the scope of fundamental social changes based on modern strategies of social development.
- The VJ cannot change by itself, rather this process must be carried out according to a state plan, under the leadership and control of the Assembly, the government and the Supreme Defense Council, with the participation of the public.
- The Army's capacity for transformation is unknown, but social, political-ideological and professional resistance can be expected from part of the (noncommissioned) officer corps; the corps of generals or

key individuals within it will be the least to favor changes, since they would bring a decrease or loss in their current power and privileges.

- Creating a professional and modern army requires a radical – political, systemic, conceptual, organizational, value system and ideological – break with the JNA and SFRY.
- A new military organization cannot be properly founded without cutting loose the 'war baggage' of the JNA and VJ, and this requires professionally establishing the causes, essence and consequences of their involvement in the war, and then politically sanctioning, and if necessary legally prosecuting, those who gave the orders and carried them out.

What is thus to be expected is a transitional cohabitation of indeterminate length of the new system and the old Army that is undergoing transformation. For this reason, numerous short-term interventions must first be made in order to activate the existing systemic potentials that would subordinate the Army to the Assembly, and use its human and material resources to start the transformation.

Notes

1 This is confirmed by the war's moving to Macedonia.
2 See: Slobodan Samardžič, Ustavni problemi demokratske transformacije SR Jugoslavije (Consitutional problems of the democratic transformation of SR Yugoslavia), in: Lavirinti krize (Labyrinths of crisis), Slobodan Samardžić, Radmila Nakarada, Djuro Kovačević (eds), Institute for European Studies, Belgrade, 1998, 75-98.
3 See: Kriza i obnova prava, (Crisis and the renewal of power) Zoran Ivošević (ed), CUPS, Begrade, 1999.
4 See: Vucina Vasović, Organizacija vlasti i demokratija (The organization of power and democracy), in: Lavirinti krize, op. cit., 99-124.
5 Compare: Vladimir Goati, Izbori u SRJ od 1990. do 1998, Volja gradjana ili izborna manipulacija (Elections in FRY from 1990 to 1998, the will of the citizens or electoral manipulation), CESID, Belgrade, 1999, particularly 238-244.
6 See: Human Rights in Yugoslavia 1999, Belgrade Center for Human Rights, Belgrade 2000.
7 For more on this: Bozo Stojanović, Jugoslovenska privreda (The Yugoslav economy) in: Lavirinti krize, op. cit., 247-263.

8 The mechanisms with which the state robbed the citizens are documented in u: Mladjan Dinkić, Ekonomija destrukcije (The economy of destruction), second edition, VIV, Belgrade, 1995.
9 Compare: Dušan Lazić, Spoljna politika jugoslovenske države (Foreign politics of the Yugoslav state) in: Ustavna i pravna pitanja jugoslovenske drzave (Constitutional and legal matters of the Yugoslav state), Vesna Petrović (ed), Belgrade Human Rights Center, Belgrade, 1999, 35-57.
10 For more on this: Trivo Indjić, Nacionalizam – izmedju političke emancipacije i zloupotrebe (Nationalism – between political emancipation and abuse) in: Lavirinti krize, op. cit., 227-243.
11 This annulled Article 115 of the FRY Constitution whereby 'the constitutions of the republic members, federal laws, the laws of the republic members and all other provisions and general acts must be brought in line with the Constitution of the Federal Republic of Yugoslavia' (Laws, 1993).
12 See: Ustav Savezne Republike Jugoslavije (Constitution of the Federal Republic of Yugoslavia) in: Zakoni o Vojsci, odbrani, imovini i finansiranju (Laws on the Army, defense, property and financing), VINC, Belgrade, 1993, 15-55, Article 77, Item 7.
13 Ibid, Article 78, Item 3.
14 See: Constitution of the Republic of Serbia, Official Gazette, Belgrade, 1990, Article 72, Items 1 and 3.
15 Ibid, Article 73, Item 6.
16 Article 99.
17 Item 1.
18 Item 6.
19 Item 7.
20 Item 9.
21 Item 10.
22 Item 11.
23 The Constitution of FRY nominally rests on modern cultural achievements. In the federal state 'power belongs to the citizens' (Article 8) and the state, which is 'founded on the rule of law' (Article 9) 'recognizes and guarantees the freedoms and human rights of the citizens recognized by international law' (Article 10). The Constitution therefore strictly protects man's undisputed right to live (Article 21) and 'the inviolability of man's physical and psychological integrity, his privacy and personal rights' (Article 22). Then numerous articles of the Constitution (23-68) guarantee the citizens' right to personal freedom, freedom of their convictions, of conscience, thought and the freedom to publicly express their opinions. They are also guaranteed the right to ownership and inheritance. Thus 'the government of the Federal Republic of Yugoslavia is organized on the principle of division into legislative, executive and judicial powers' (Article 12). The principle of

political pluralism is declared as 'a prerequisite and guarantee of the democratic political order in the Federal Republic of Yugoslavia' (Article 12). This gave rise to a set of laws on political associations and actions, freedom of speech and public appearance, and publicly criticizing the work of state and other organs. In accordance with this, freedom of the press and other types of public informing are guaranteed.

24 Article 133, Paragraph 1.
25 Article 17.
26 Article 83, Item 5.
27 According to Budimir Babović, Ljudska prava i policija u Jugoslaviji (Human rights and the police in Yugoslavia), IGP Prometej, Belgrade, 1999, 81.
28 The law on internal affairs of Serbia, Article 1., cited according to: Budimir Babović, op. cit.
29 Article 135.
30 Article 136.
31 Law on the Yugoslav Army, in: Laws, op. cit, Article 4, Paragraph 1.
32 Article 83.
33 Item 5.
34 Item 6.
35 Item 7.
36 The framer of the republican constitution, unlike the federal, avoided enumerating what civil rights can and cannot be suspended in a state of exigency.
37 Item 8.
38 Article 133, Paragraph 1.
39 According to Budimir Babović, described source, 81.
40 With the adoption of 'Measures to prevent the emergence of a state of imminent threat of war' in October 1998, one more state was introduced which is unknown in existing constitutional laws.
41 Article 78, Item 3.
42 Article 99, Item 10.
43 Article 4.
44 Law on Defense, in: Laws, op. cit., Article 8.
45 Compare: Marijana Pajvančić, Ustavnost vanrednog stanja (The constitutionality of a state of emergency) in: Ustavnosti i vladavina prava (Constitutionality and the rule of law), Kosta Čavoski (ed), CUPS, Belgrade, 2000, 435-455.
46 During 1998, in spite of activities by the KLA, the regime did not declare a state of emergency even on part of the territory, although they claimed that terrorism and separatism was at work in Kosovo.
47 See: Kosta Čavoski, Ratne uredbe (War regulations), in: Ustavnost i vladavina prava, op. cit.. 457-479.

48 Thus there is no proof that Milošević used the VJ in Kosovo based on previous decisions by the VSO.
49 For more on this see: Miroslav Hadžić, Javne cutnje o vojsci Jugoslavije (Public hushing up of the Yugoslav Army), in: Ustavna i pravna pitanja jugoslovenske drzave, op. cit.,. 82-110.
50 For more on this see: Miroslav Hadžič, Civilian Control of the Yugoslav Army, in: Civilian Control of the Army and Police, Miroslav Hadžić (ed), Center for Civil-Military Relations, Media Center, Belgrade, 2000, pp. 33-87.
51 The introductory report said that the VJ should be used 'to assure the survival of the state of Yugoslavia and prevent its disintegration into two separate national states, since this is in accordance with the freely expressed will and interests of the Serbian and Montenegrin peoples to live in one state, and because this is a necessary condition for the fatherland's concern for the Serbian people living outside of Serbia' (Radinović, R., Chief of the Administration, op. cit., 20). Of the total five elements of the goal two more refer to the internal political use of the Army, while there is no word about defense from external aggression as a goal, i.e. it is located in the function of defense.
52 In February 1993 the Administration for Strategic Studies and Political Defense of the Federal Ministry of Defense organized the conference "New World Order and the Defense Policy of the Federal Republic of Yugoslavia". Proceedings from the conference were published under the same name (VIZ, Belgrade, 1993). Ideas circulating at the conference included an alliance of Orthodox peoples and states (p. 543), and linking Euro-Asian socialist areas (p. 567) as possible solutions to the unfavorable geopolitical and strategic position of FRY.
53 The figure of 75-80,000 members of the VJ was bandied about in public (Bojan Dimitrijević, Press Club). At the same time the information was given that the VJ had 105 generals, which speaks eloquently of how Milošević bought the loyalty of the military elite.
54 Compare: Negovanje i vrednovanje tradicija u Vojsci Jugoslavije (Fostering and Evaluating Traditions in the Yugoslav Army), VINC, Belgrade, 1993.
55 Proof of this is the list of negatively defined criteria for officer selection: for example, it is required that all 'patriotically unconfirmed' officers should not remain in the Army without saying who could establish the degree of their patriotic confirmation and how; compare: editorial comment 'Deep Cut in Personnel', Vojska, 14.10.1993, 5.
56 Before withdrawing from Kosovo and Metohija, the Army disclosed the figure of 28,000 military refugees (officers plus their families.).

Conclusions

I

'When the principles of evil become the principles of state power, evil liberates man's barbarian instincts so effectively that it can be compared to an epidemic. Caught up in this epidemic, everything that has previously been considered unnatural becomes natural. Infected by the virus of evil installed in the center of power, as long as the virus is inside them people are not aware of what they are doing. This is why evil as a principle is particularly dangerous when the state power itself is equated with the principles of evil.'

Agneš Heler[1]

Most of those analyzing the collapse of the JNA assert that Slobodan Milošević, as the personification of Serbia's political elite from the end of the 1980s to the end of the 1990s, is alone to blame for the disintegration of Yugoslavia. Since the JNA was and/or ended up at his service, then it is also principally to blame for the outbreak of war and its expansion. Consequently, the JNA necessarily shared the fate of the unwanted state and the mistaken policies of Serbia's power center. In spite of available evidence and the results produced by the war, this premise is disputable even on the logical level.

First of all, Milošević and all the other 'miloševićs' (Kučan and Tudjman, and then Izetbegović, Karadžić and the others) judged to be exponents of the local power elite, were products of the second Yugoslavia's social system. They were only possible in such a Yugoslavia, and were therefore its necessary consequence. Furthermore, had everyone else wanted to preserve Yugoslavia, Milošević would have had a hard time breaking it up. Thus Milošević was used by his partners, or rather rivals, as a good pretext to pull out of the country. Under the prevailing circumstances, however, unilateral withdrawal was only possible by means of violence. The universal use of force then led to internal, all-out war. This does not mean that Yugoslavia would have survived, but the fact that it disintegrated in war is the joint product of all the 'miloševićs'. The JNA's

'Slovenian expedition' sent by order of the still legal government, was only the trigger and not the cause of the Yu-wars.

The relatively independent actions of the top generals in the political home stretch of Yugoslavia's state crisis were thus the product of all the national-republican figures. Pacification and/or political neutralization of the JNA required the republican oligarchies' readiness for compromise, leading to a peaceful resolution of the crisis. The republics would also have had to renounce the creation of parallel armies and paramilitary formations. A prerequisite for this would have been putting the JNA under effective civilian control, something only possible under the assumption that there was a clear plan for its transformation and/or agreement to divide it up. Having such a plan would have potentially decreased the existential fear of JNA members with regard to the dissolution of the federal state. At the same time, this would have narrowed the space in which the generals manipulated the ideology of Yugoslav national feelings, and the Army as a collective body. Given the new/old government elites' resolve to establish national states by force, the lack of an effective plan to resolve the future status of a (changed) JNA forced the military leaders and (non-commissioned) officers to make a political choice and come out in favor of war.

The easiest thing is to say that the military leaders became Milošević's prisoner and then offer this as the key to understanding the second Yugoslavia's disintegration in war. This leaves out the question as to how it all came about. In the given situation and constellation, the outcome was obvious; everyone had a part in it, but the parts were as uneven as the prices they paid. Even so, everyone took part in tallying up the war bill. Owing to the power they acquired by war, the nationalist elite were able to present their bills to the local population, most of whom had willingly taken part in preparing and waging war. At the same time, using ideological criteria, rigid federalism, monism and operations based on the '1941' model, the military leaders directly facilitated and assisted the post-communist replacement of democracy by nationalist and authoritarian-totalitarian regimes.

In spite of everything, it is certain that the JNA leaders would not have been able to wage such lengthy, destructive, hopeless politics and war had there not been a previous constitutional and systemic disintegration of the central state power. In addition, the key generals initially had hearty support for their undertaking from conservative forces among top state, party and military officials, but also from broad layers of the population. Kadijević's willfulness, both political and with regard to the war, was additionally encouraged by the nationalist-separatist egoism and chauvinism of the new, anticommunist and revanchist governments in Slovenia and Croatia. The generals' main support, of course, came from the Serbian government and official Serbian public. The misuse of the JNA was also facilitated by the fact that its officer corps was existentially dependent and ideologically anaesthetized by the old regime. The ease with which the (non-commissioned) officers replaced communist ideology with nationalistic is therefore no surprise. To make matters worse, the repressive organization of the JNA directly favored the political and bellicose autocracy of the top generals.

This means that the situational behavior of the military leaders was determined by the basic – military-political and social-psychological – characteristics of the JNA, which is why the JNA and its commanders were unable to play a single one of the possible roles of pacifiers; nor were they any better at playing the combat role when the time came. Several basic reasons were influential in this regard:

First, every army is the substrate of its own society and system. The JNA was therefore only a specific condensation of Yugoslavia's society and system, whose characteristics had been taken to the extreme by the crisis and war. All the fundamental contradictions and failings of the Yugoslav state and society were built into the Army, but with delayed action. Owing to the Army's systemic protection and hierarchical (ideological and political) framework, it hid them for a long time and successfully amortized them. But the moment society and the system cracked, the JNA had to crack, too. All that was uncertain was when it would happen. It was illusory to expect the Army alone to remain viable in an irrational, undemocratic and ineffective society.

Second, regardless of its professional qualities, no army can maintain a failed regime and unwanted country by force. This is certainly impossible in conditions of internal – interethnic and religious – war. Not a single army, the JNA included, can calculate in advance and guarantee the positive outcome of waging war – combat is the only way to test an army's validity. On the whole, one and the same army cannot act with the same effectiveness in external and internal warfare. Internal war is the hardest for every army, and often an insurmountable task.

Third, a revolutionary army, such as the JNA considered itself to be, cannot be expected to come out from under the ideological 'helmet' by itself. Since the JNA was ideologically determined, the Army and the military leaders were necessarily involved in the political entanglements of the Yu-crisis. At that moment the interactive coalition of politics-Army was reversed. Owing to the dissolution of the SKJ and the federal state, the JNA became a direct and relatively autonomous political entity, but limited in two respects: it could not resolve political problems, and the top generals' verbalistic, arrogant and aggressive interference in politics handicapped them militarily, and they necessarily failed under their own (professional) premises and usage.

Fourth, the JNA could not save the ruined and eroded state by itself, a state that was already in national and ideological disrepute and had been rejected. Therefore, in principle, the Army could only have used its power to prevent or postpone war, i.e. assist the peaceful decomposition or recomposition of Yugoslavia. And this was impossible because of the readiness of opposing nationalistic elites to achieve their conflicting political and territorial pretensions regardless of the price. Whenever a national state becomes the primary goal there is no room for a multiethnic and super-national state. Thus, at the beginning of the war the JNA had to split along its national/ethnic seams.

In addition, during the Yugoslav crisis and the wars that ensued, the military leaders were not free to choose their behavior. The fact that they could not dictate the tempo and direction of the crisis' development left the Army in a constant reactive and passive position. In spite of their desires and aggressive participation in daily politics, the JNA and top generals could not independently forecast and plan a single advance move, and were forever in a strategically unfavorable position.

The secessionists, which included Milošević after passage of the Constitution of Serbia in 1990, had a far easier time breaking up the state than the military leaders who tried to preserve the ruined and rejected country. In the end it turned out that they had poorly judged both the interests of the people and their subordinates' ability to defend Yugoslavia. Furthermore, the top generals themselves were unable to resolve the dilemma as to whether to defend the country at all, and if so then how and why, with what means and for how long. Since the generals did not have viable answers to this dilemma before the war, the moment it broke out there was no way to find them anymore. What made this even more difficult was the fact that the military leaders had no choice, unlike Serbia, which had already opened an alternative way out; the Army could not save the country it belonged to and so in order to survive it had to lean towards the one that Milošević offered. And he was the only one making any offer.

There is no denying that Serbian-Army relations are the key to understanding Yugoslavia's disintegration in war. Although this relationship can be isolated for the purpose of analysis, it cannot be explained independent of the multiple interactive connections of all the Yu-participants. Thus it is difficult, without making serious mistakes, to single out only the Serbian-Army segment of the network of political-interest connections that the military leaders had with the other Yu-participants on the eve of war. Retroactively and unidirectionally 'reading' the inevitability of the Serbian-Army alliance conceals the numerous reasons for and contradictory course of its advent. Furthermore, its unquestionable extension into the past introduces new confusion into the otherwise tangled sequence of crisis-war causes and effects. This subsequently assigns the rank of necessity to a potential alliance that was indicated on the eve of war. It avoids or gives insufficient consideration of the fact that the alliance arose proportionate to and following the tempo of the (pro)war entanglement of the crisis. Thus an evaluation solely from the viewpoint of results simplifies the complex process of the rapprochement between the top military's and Serbian leaders' interests.

The transparency of the military-Serbian alliance on the eve of and during the war (wars) does not show all the reasons for their mutual attraction, complementariness and provisos. Whirling in this vortex were permanent and temporary, basic and situational, intentional and coerced, systemic and nonsystemic, ideological and national, existential and power-hungry, and other reasons. The only way to detail their effects reliably is by taking into consideration the manner in which they joined forces at the end of the 1980s and produced the prerequisites for the point of contact between the military's and Serbia's leaders. The findings that have been presented allow us to assert:

- Owing to the characteristics of Yugoslavia's society (state) and depth of the crisis, a military-political coalition between the leaders of Serbia and the Army was quite probable, if not inevitable.
- The military-Serbian coalition was particularly facilitated by the lack of civilian controls over the military leaders, and the two-thirds majority of Serbs among the professional and conscript composition of the JNA.
- In the political home stretch of the Yu-crisis, until war broke out, a relationship of twofold instrumentalization had been established between the military's and Serbia's leaders in which the question of who would (mis)use whom and for what purpose remained open, at least in principle.
- The military's and Serbia's leaders drew politically close in accordance with the extent of the crisis and how it intensified, and with the special separation-nationalistic reactions of the Slovenian and Croatian leaders

to it, as well as the Serbian government's revived imperialistic ambitions.
- The wartime symbiosis between Milošević and the top generals was one of the necessary consequences of the national-chauvinistic form and content of the uncontrolled disintegration of the central authoritarian system, and its cloning in the emerging states.
- The central (S-C-S) participants used the war to prove the validity of their reasons for national-state independence, while the JNA and Serbian leaders' arrogance and aggressiveness additionally legitimized their armed separatism and supported the installation of authoritarian-nationalistic regimes which, together with the others, brought to full circle the massive manipulation of the second Yugoslavia's population.

All of this, of course, does not release the Kadijević triumvirate from political and moral responsibility for misusing the JNA and its members. Those who are competent – domestic and/or international institutions – will judge their possible criminal accountability. Indeed, the following list of the traumatic effects of their arbitrary use of the JNA should be placed on the account of General Veljko Kadijević and his top associates:

- By guaranteeing the citizens a peaceful resolution to the Yugoslav crisis and preventing internal war, they immediately facilitated (accelerated) individual and group flirtation with nationalism and war.
- Their ideological, and ultimately selfish and particular treatment of the Yu-crisis facilitated the installation of authoritarian regimes in the former republics and accelerated their national legitimization.
- By agreeing to the alternative of war they, in conjunction with national-republican elite, left the citizens of Yugoslavia without a homeland and forced them into one-nation states.
- Misusing the JNA for the goals of the Serbian regime they traumatized, physically and psychically, all non-Serbian peoples in the second Yugoslavia.
- Turning the JNA into a pro-Serbian army they misused all their subordinates.
- Their false protection of the Serbian people helped bring them into the war and facilitated the misuse of the trauma from their historical memory, thus giving them a pseudo-catharsis with the war (settling historical accounts) and traumatized them once again.

II

The wars between the Southern Slav peoples confirmed the high motivational power of the ideology of 'blood and land'. They were also a reminder that the motivational domain for war is practically speaking unlimited. The Yu-participants' bellicose energy originated in the combined effects of motives with different sources and ranks; for years they had been intertwining to produce the modern and historical, national and religious, political and ideological, economic and social, individual and group, internal and external motives to fight each other.

With deepening of the Yu-crisis there was a rapid rise in the frequency with which national traumas from historical memory were put to effective use. They became the central lever of the mechanism for collective and individual rationalization of the war. Historical traumas were linked to and covered by the unbounded spectrum of situational war motives. By referring to them, collective and individual participants found 'forgiveness of their sins', in advance and/or subsequently, for all types of destruction and war crimes.

The lack of any catharsis after 1945 inevitably encouraged the 'gray production' of historical traumas. Living in a 'gray zone' of feelings, they gained strength and conviction, thereby growing in their potential motivational strength. The lack of catharsis suppressed, but also 'modernized' the traumas by opening them up to daily political 'reading'. But it was above all the lack of systemic instruments to curb and sanction barbarism that accelerated the objective political initiation of 'lower levels of consciousness'.

The (pre)war revival, production and misuse of trauma were an essential indicator of the Yu-peoples' relationship towards their own historical and spiritual heritage, showing the dominance of a reductionist, Manichaean and instrumental concept of their own history. The widespread internalization of the trauma also revealed the brainwashing side of the preceding political socialization. The widely adopted model of a 'special war' did not show its terrifying effectiveness until redirected to the collective 'internal enemy' – former brotherly peoples. Systemic depersonalization founded on systemic disempowerment, when joined with ignorance and ideological ideas, resulted in the Yugoslav population's great pliability to political manipulation, but also their need for it. Thus the 'blank spots' in more recent Yugoslav history grew into new historical (mis)understandings.

Ultimately, the fundamental lack of integration of the state/social community combined with its undemocratic makeup made the Yugoslav peoples and their elite eternal rivals instead of partners. Owing to this, a state of constant conflict was maintained in Yugoslavia which only changed in form, accent and intensity. The politically initiated and articulated national dissatisfaction with the joint state and others in it produced a constant feeling of historical and tangible deprivation.

At the end of the 1980s, power-hungry elite extracted collective aggression from national (ethnic) frustrations in conditions of intensifying crisis, and then turned it against other, different members of the same community. Thus the ideologically tailored narcissism of small and historically lagging peoples easily found the key reasons for the trouble in others, those closest to them.

The spreading Yu-wars led to the ultimate state and social settlement of Yugoslavia and the peoples assembled in it. The wars confirmed the shortage of sufficient reasons for the country's survival. The only thing that war confirmed, however, was the inability and then unwillingness of the national elite to preserve and revitalize the rational reasons for the country's continued existence. The outcome confirmed that not a single one of Yugoslavia's (national) creators was satisfied with the country, and that none of them had accomplished the goals that had led them to take part in its creation. These wars were the final answer to the unresolved initial problem of national and civic coexistence in a common state. The desire to achieve national states thus resulted in a bloody redefinition of interrelationships. Viewed in this light, the Yu-wars might be interpreted as the logical consequence of the fact that the country's former constituents had been prevented from satisfying their interests and goals within the framework of Yugoslavia. This consequence, however, stemmed from their endeavor to realize particular and egotistically conceived national interests regardless of the price and independent of the needs of others.

In spite of this, these wars were not the Yugoslav peoples' destiny, rather the product of their joint actions. All the reasons for war were generated in the sphere of politics – they were politically articulated, rationalized and mediated. The central point of these wars was a political showdown between the national elite using violent means. This birthplace of the Yu-war (wars) and its key generator then, through the inherent logic of war, extracted secondary factors of interethnic annihilation. The mise-en-scene was gradually prepared during the 1980s as the central authoritarian system was phased out. Instead of being replaced by democracy, the national elite preserved and strengthened authoritarian clones in their republics. This was the nationalistic modification and metamorphosis of communist authoritarianism. War only confirmed that two or more authoritarian beings cannot survive forever in the same social (state) space. Since every authoritarian regime seeks totalization, conflicts between such regimes were necessary during the redistribution of what still remained of central power. As the last link in the chain of central authoritarianism, the Army necessarily had to crack when the country disintegrated.

Yugoslavia's disintegration in warfare was only one of the possibilities with which to resolve the crisis and reorganize relations between the ethnic groups and the Republic at the end of the 1980s, particularly since there were real chances of positively overcoming the crisis at the time. It turned out, however, that the democratic political will arising on the wave of anticommunism was not enough for this to happen, i.e. the causes, agents and mainstays of the war option were too deeply rooted in the foundations of society. In other words, it turned out that the Yugoslav state community did not have sufficient social, political and institutional capacities at its disposal to democratically resolve the crisis. Results clearly show that the elite at the time were no match for the fundamental and structural crisis in Yugoslav society, although they made maximum use of one of the resulting possibilities with regard to their particular goals.

This is why the Yu-wars essentially turned into a short course of previously experienced history. The malformations of a sick society rose to the surface once again and were treated with the wrong medicine. To make matters worse, war was based on the 'principle of evil', i.e. evil was raised to the level of a principle. Since the history course was shortened it was necessarily intensified, but was nonetheless the requisite product of inadequate and aggressive reactions of the national elite to the unresolved and omitted tasks of their own history. These reactions were thus freed from and intensified by the destructive accumulation of previous Yugoslav history. The attempt to settle old accounts necessarily ended with them growing larger, while those submitting the bills went bankrupt. For the umpteenth time, history on Yu-territory had its way with those who wanted to mold it or change it after the fact. The price, of course, was paid by the peoples who believed in those who had corrected past history and were producing new history.[2] Finding themselves in condensed historical time and facing the challenges of yet-to-be-experienced democratic history, the citizens of Yugoslavia set war as their true civilizational and historical measure.

III

After the collapse of socialism, the USA and its allies took on the role of the primary (re)organizer of the world, and put the second Yugoslavia under their authority as early as 1991. Ten years later, the Euro-Atlantic community's intervention has only succeeded in confirming the country's bloody – state and ethnic – dissolution, with its support.

In order to evaluate the scope of the Euro-Atlantic Alliance's involvement in former Yugoslavia, considerable preliminary analytical work is needed. First, the determinants and course that gave rise to the strategy of the Alliance's approach should be accurately ascertained, as well as the criteria for the choice of goals and means. This requires a discussion of the real relations between the EU and USA. There should be a parallel examination of the configuration of power within the European Union and its influence on intervention undertakings in the Yu-war. Since the USA accepted the leading role, the European Union necessarily ended up as second. After initial, independent mediations (July 1991- April 1992), it lost the initiative during the war in Bosnia-Herzegovina. In spite of this, the EU and USA primarily operated within the framework of a joint policy in the Balkans, but the USA had primacy in formulating and implementing the policy. This, of course, could not remove the negative effects of their conflicts of interests regarding their joint approach to the Yu-crisis and war, particularly since their nominally united approach was not always accompanied by united action. Some of the Alliance members acted not only independently, but often did the opposite.[3]

An evaluation of Euro-Atlantic interventionism requires the elaboration of a reliable methodological procedure. Numerous problems immediately arise in this regard: an evaluation means there is reliable evidence on the results that were produced; and there is the problem of measuring the scope of individual and/or group participation in their achievement. In addition, a cost-effective analysis must be made of investments to date. Then a procedure must be established to evaluate the results; in this regard, how the results are judged depends directly on the time frame.

For example, Alliance results would certainly take on different values if we measure them against July 1991[4] as opposed to July 1995.[5] In the same vein, our perception of the scope of the Dayton Accord changes over time. In November 1995 this Accord was treated as a great achievement on the part of the Euro-Atlantic Alliance. Five years later it was shown that the imposition of peace had by no means removed the prospects of an ethnic division of Bosnia-Herzegovina. There is also the fact that findings indicate

NATO bombings of FRY in March 1999 and March 2000 had different aims in many respects. Thus any evaluation of the justification and scope of NATO's attacks against Serbia would be necessarily different, particularly since the KLA has started considerable return payments for all the negative consequences of the UN and NATO's poor administration of Kosovo.

Consequently, regardless of the time frame that is chosen, everything that the USA and EU can proclaim as their success is subject to rational investigation and questioning. In the same vein, of course, arguments can be found to justify every (recognized) failure. For example, if the Alliance credits the imposition of peace in former Yugoslavia as its success, the question immediately arises as to why peace was established in phases, or why war was not prevented in its inception. In other words, since it had taken over the right, or considered it had the obligation to manage the crisis in the Balkans, the problem remains as to how to explain why the Euro-Atlantic community allowed the Yu-war to continue for 10 years.

Throughout the Yu-crisis and particularly during its war finale, all foreign participants were constantly searching for a valid position, both individually and collectively. Results indicate that they have yet to find a productive approach to stopping the Yu-war and permanently resolving the state status of the members of former Yugoslavia. Some of the important reasons for this certainly lie in the unpredictable nature of the Yu-war spiral and the local warlords, but also in the external interveners' lack of a clear strategy.

It is easy to show that the Yu-participants had a hard time measuring and estimating external factors. The decisions of the Euro-Atlantic Alliance were most certainly outside their effective range, which doesn't mean the Yu-participants didn't want to influence the actions of the external interveners, and partially succeeded in this regard. There is a paradox in the fact that even though the Euro-Atlantic Alliance monopolized the management of the Yu-crisis, it did not succeed in properly evaluating the Yugoslav situation and putting the forces of war under its control. The Alliance's powerlessness had a twofold effect.

Owing to its poor judgment, the Euro-Atlantic Alliance was a captive of its initial understandings of the real nature and causes of Yu-warfare. It gradually lost contact with the reality of war and was less and less able to understand its internal logic and constantly renewing energy. Owing to its lack of will and/or ability to control the local participants, the Alliance was unable to stop the war. This prolonged failure then caused political frustrations within it which encouraged the easy use of external force. Since it had permanently adopted the initial division of Yu-participants into blameworthy and innocent victims, the Alliance increasingly contradicted its alleged principled nature and political consistency. Although it immediately condemned the Yu-war and refused to recognize any territorial results, the Alliance did not succeed in removing the autonomous reasons for the war's continuation and expansion. Consequently, in spite of all its efforts it was unable to stop the war for good. To make matters worse, by selectively sanctioning the confrontational output of the conflicting sides it facilitated, and ultimately encouraged, continuation of the Yu-war.

The lack of an effective strategy, additionally emphasized by the solo actions of individual Alliance members, enabled most Yu-participants to find a shortcut to attaining national states by means of arms. The success of this procedure rested on two premises: first, the arrogance and aggressiveness of the Serbian regime, the JNA and then VJ leaders, and second, the readiness of the Alliance to breach quite often and arbitrarily interpret its own principles. All that remained for the wartime creators of the new states was to make effective use of the Serbian regime's mistakes and the Euro-Atlantic Alliance's lack of strategy. Experience from Slovenia to Kosovo indicates that by relying on the Milošević regime's undersupply of intelligence and democracy and the USA's oversupply of will, power and impatience, the illegal status and unconstitutional armed uprisings of the YU-separatist movements became internationally legalized and legitimate.

Since the foreign interveners had already chosen sides in 1991, based on ideological criteria, it is not surprising that they used their favorites to continue managing the Yu-crisis. This is how crisis management turned into expanding the war and shifting it as needed by the local warlords. The USA thus based its management on the intent to put local warlords under its control, which likewise made it possible for Milošević to have the status of being primary to blame for the war, as well as a key factor in the future peace.

This led to the 'carrot and stick' principle and its inconsistent application. America's self-appropriation of the right to share the Yu-war profits and losses was applied in a manner that is irresistibly reminiscent of the Pope's long-gone trading in indulgences and anathemas. Slovenia's and Croatia's leaders were immediately forgiven their sins, regardless of their contributions to inciting warfare. For their verbal loyalty to democratic principles, America quickly handed them independent states, with hearty help from Milošević and General Kadijević. The Bosnian warlords were handed the same thing but only after three years of annihilation in the Serbian-Croatian-Muslim triangle. The Kosovo hotspot was ignored until it was judged that military intervention could bring considerable strategic gain. This brought the leaders of Albanian separatism to the 'holy see' and purified them of their sins. Only the Serbs/Serbia were permanently pinned down by anathema, as America removed or returned their leader in accordance with its current needs.

Unwilling to help truly remove the social and political causes of Yu-warfare, in the end America decided to repress and prohibit them by force, thereby condemning itself to permanently repairing the consequences. Crisis management was reduced to putting the new states under a NATO protectorate. After quickly renaming the local warlords peacemakers, it was not hard for America, with the threat of violence, to get them to agree to the (irreversible?) deployment of NATO forces around former Yugoslavia.

The principles of NATO interventionism that crystallized in former Yugoslavia give rise to reasonable doubts about the *pax-Americana*. We would also note that they have shed additional light on some of the secondary paths to acquiring global power. They have also brought within its proper scope the ideological part of America's story about the incentives behind its sacrifice for the prosperity and freedom of the peoples of the world. This is convincingly shown by the two USA (NATO) intervention principles that crystallized in former Yugoslavia:

The first principle: goals that are worthwhile for security purposes and are of indisputable value – peace, human rights, democracy – can be achieved (protected) using unsuitable means.

Consequently, the intervener has (appropriates) complete freedom in the choice of procedures to protect them. Owing to the nonexistence of (higher) authorities of control, he is released from the obligation to act in a timely, suitable, purposeful, just and consistent manner. Therefore, he arbitrarily decides where and how much the universal values of civilization are endangered. And whether their protection deserves the use of arms, political-economic sanctions or providing comprehensive assistance.

The rule seems to have been introduced whereby moving away from the West brings a tendentious decrease in the real values of human rights and democracy, with a rise in their instrumental value. This means that depending on their needs the (Euro-Atlantic) interveners can avoid, postpone, selectively practice and even misuse the international protection of human rights and democracy.

It is certain that the war (wars) in former Yugoslavia jeopardized both the universal and elementary rights of the population caught and confined there. In spite of the international legal prohibition of warfare, one state was destroyed by armed force and several states arose. Borders were redrawn. War crimes were committed. Populations were changed and thinned out by ethnic cleansing, etc. It is also certain that without external intervention the Yu-wars would have continued almost to mutual destruction, for they were directly conditioned by the local warlords' unwillingness to solve a single problem by means of compromise. It is therefore difficult to dispute the justification of political intervention.

It is all the more difficult to give a reasonable explanation for the antinomy of the Euro-Atlantic intervention in the Yu-crisis:

- Restraint in the phase when ethnic conflicts were being prepared and broke out.
- Quickly siding with individual protagonists.
- Stopping the war only after the participants had achieved their political and territorial goals.
- Tacitly and selectively allowing subsequent corrections to war results.
- Absence of any demilitarization and denazification for the sake of fundamental pacification.
- Biased distribution of war gains and losses.
- Renaming warlords peacemakers.
- Tacit support to the strengthening of authoritarian-nationalistic systems.
- Selective and restrained (calculating) persecution of those suspected of war crimes.

We allow that the USA and EU were guided in the Yu-crisis by their own interests. Strategic factors of economy forced them to achieve their security goals quickly with the least possible risk of their own losses, along with the rule that war damages should be paid by those who caused them. Since most of the Yu-population supported war and the ruling regimes, it is logical that they should bear the consequences. It is also possible to defend the West's basic decision to let the local citizens carry out democratic reforms in local societies and change the current regimes through elections.

What is disputable is the collective punishment of citizens, and specifically of Serbia, that thwarted this intention; of course, assuming that such an intention existed. The Alliance's expectation that the true causes of war would disappear simply by prohibiting war after it broke out, without any radical changes in the Yu-societies, therefore seems cynical. Another of the West's similarly ranked intentions was to achieve regional security without first disempowering the key Yu-proponents who were jeopardizing it.

Foreign interveners' current efforts to preserve a multiethnic, multicultural and multi-confessional B-H, Kosovo and Macedonia are particularly touching. This is being done after direct and indirect support for the disintegration of SFRY by war, a country that was all of that, at least nominally, or might have been after democratic reforms. Their powerful support for the return of all refugees, primarily in the form of resolutions, has a similar sound. These people were ethnically cleansed from their homelands without the foreign interveners doing anything serious to prevent or stop it at the time.

Foreign interveners have clearly used only their 'firefighting arsenal' to date in former Yugoslavia. In spite of its high cost, the armed imposition of peace seems to have been more cost-effective than extending long-term 'Marshall Plan' help to the Yu-states and peoples to get them out of war.

The roots of this lie, inter alia, in the strategic delay and/or reluctance of the USA to respond properly to the challenges that arose with the collapse of the world socialist system and the disintegration of the USSR. The influence of the American military-political establishment's triumphalistic and revanchist sentiments should also not be excluded. It is difficult to expect a great and final (bloc) victory to be accompanied by systematic help to the loser, in particular since he might quickly become a rival and competitor once again.

There is every prospect that the West was conceptually and operatively, and particularly economically, unprepared (reluctant) to suffer all the consequences of achieving its strategic goal – the elimination of socialism. This put it in a reactive position which, using the logic of global structures and its own inertia, stimulated the use of repressive economic, political and military methods. Most likely this was because bringing the post-socialist and newly arising countries militarily into NATO, allegedly as a guarantee of their social and economic reformation, held first place on the list of American priorities to (re)integrate into Europe.

Without excluding the assumption that this was ultimately intended to further strategically marginalize Russia, there is reason to doubt the scope of one-dimensional (military) integration of the Euro-Atlantic region, primarily because a higher degree of military, potentially repressive links among most European states is not a sufficient prerequisite for their comprehensive integration. That is to say, it does not necessarily lead to the market-democratic transformation of closed states, particularly those in which the generators of oligarchic power have yet to be dismantled. On the contrary, stressing military links leaves sufficient internal space for new/old government elite to feign a (pro)democratic transformation. Thus the concept of Euro-Atlantic security which, on the one hand, puts pressure – even 'corrupting' pressure – on Russia, but on the other hand 'builds the house from the roof down' – offering the candidate states first military and only then (not certain when and under which conditions) socioeconomic and other involvement – cannot have pretensions towards (completion) and longevity.

The second principle: stopping local and regional, and particularly internal (civil) wars is a worthy goal in itself. External military (NATO) intervention is only justified, however, it if simultaneously achieves strategically more important and far-reaching benefits.

Strategically modeled intervention should enable the intervener to squeeze out of every crisis (war) sufficient military-political benefit for himself, without greater risks.

Although the strategic importance of former Yugoslavia has temporarily diminished in the new constellation, the Euro-American alliance had already acquired considerable, lasting benefit through its successive involvement in the Yu-war, even before the bombing of FRY.

For example, the USA and EU found and created valid arguments on Yu-battlefields not only for NATO's survival but also for a rise in its global power. By taking over jurisdiction of the Yu-crisis they immobilized the UN and blocked its collective security mechanisms. Admittedly, the USA continues to drop by the Security Council, but primarily when its resolutions require legalization. The conflict in Kosovo has given it a new chance, within the Alliance and between strategic partners (rivals), to examine the level of tolerance towards any possible use of NATO without the approval of the UN Security Council.

On the territory of former Yugoslavia, the USA found new means to strengthen its military-political influence in Southeastern Europe. Before that, through the Security Council, it had promoted NATO to a UN intervention-peace force. Keeping the command and management of the peace forces (NATO units) within its jurisdiction, America has preserved full independence in the military-political extraction and maintenance of peace.

Although the central states of Yu-origin (B-H, FRY) have not yet been included in the Partnership for Peace, the USA has brought them within its zone of influence by means of peacekeeping operations, enabling the unhindered installation of NATO forces in hotspots in the area, for an extended period of time.

This brought the USA and NATO new privileges, both for the same price. Their direct, military-police control of the entire territory has strengthened their protectorate over B-H. The Dayton Accord has made all military and police entities their subordinates. The Yugoslav Army and the Croatian Army[6] have been put within their field of influence. Then, with the occupation of Kosovo, they became an internal military-political factor in FRY, with a chance to practice war crisis control and management procedures in real conditions. In all likelihood this has once again taken them away from the task of establishing a strategy to prevent local and regional war conflicts or stop them in an early phase.

Notes

1. In: Borba, 19-20.06.1993, X-XI.
2. 'But civil war is deprived of the speculative justification which we have somehow accumulated for external war – rejecting all moral considerations – particularly when it is not waged around the ruling system but for the same system under different tutors' and different names, we would add; Borisav Pekić, op, cit., 121.
3. For one of the views of Germany's role in the decomposition of the second Yugoslavia, see: T.W. Carr, German and US involvement in the Balkans: A careful coincidence of national policies? http//www.emperors-clothes.com/articles/carr/carr2.htm.
4. The arrival of the first EU triad to Yugoslavia and signing the Brioni Agreement on a three-month moratorium on actions by federal authorities, including the JNA, and Slovenia's separation.
5. When the Army of Republika Srpska attacked Srebrenica and, according to the reasonable suspicions of the Hague Tribunal, the war crime of genocide was committed against civilians; the commander of the Drina Corps, General Krstić, was sentenced by the Tribunal to 46 years in prison.
6. Phelan, Donna, The Agreement on Subregional Arms Control of the 'Dayton Agreement', Disarmament no . 2, UN, New York, 1996.

Bibliography of Cited Works

Aćimović, Ljubivoje (1990), KEBS u 1990-im godinama (OSCE in the 1990s), *Međunarodna politika*, Belgrade, No. 970.
Aćimović, Ljubivoje (1991), Politika SAD prema Jugoslaviji i Srbiji (The Policy of the USA towards Yugoslavia and Serbia), *Međunarodna politika*, Belgrade, No. 998-1000.
Adžić, Blagoje, Chief of the JNA General Staff (1990), Interview, *Vojnopolitički informator (VPI)*, PU SSNO, Belgrade, No.1.
Adžić, Blagoje (1990), Očuvanje jedinstva oružanih snaga – preduslov opstanka Jugoslavije (Preserving the unity of the armed forces – prerequisite for the preservation of Yugoslavia), *Vojno delo, special issue*, Belgrade, August.
Alternativna kretanja u Jugoslaviji (Alternative movements in Yugoslavia) (1988), *Revija za sociologiju*, Belgrade, No. 4.
Ammendments to the Constitution of Slovenia (1989), *Borba*, September 28.
Analysis of the reasons for the attack against KONO and JNA, SIV (1989), *Borba*, March 24.
Antonić, Slobodan (1991), Za i protiv konfederalizma (For and against confederalism), *Gledišta*, Belgrade, No. 3-4.
Antonić, Slobodan (1995), Vlada Slobodana Miloševića: pokušaj tipološkog određenja (Slobodan Milošević's rule: attempt at a typological quality) *Srpska politička misao*, Belgrade, No 1.
Aranžman za opšte rešenje (Arrangement for a general resolution) (1991), *Međunarodna politika*, Belgrade, No. 995-997.
Babović, Budimir (1999), Ljudska prava i policija u Jugoslaviji (Human rights and the police in Yugoslavia,) *IGP Prometej*, Belgrade.
Banac, Ivo (1998), Srbi u Hrvatskoj: povijest i perspektive (The Serbs in Croatia: history and prospects) in: Srbi u Hrvatskoj - jučer, danas, sutra (The Serbs in Croatia, yesterday, today, tomorrow), *Croatian Helsinki Human Rights Committee*, Zagreb.
Basta, R. Lidija (1990), Ustav i demoratija - šema tri interpretacije (Constitution and democracy – outline of three interpretations) in: Dva veka savremene ustavnosti (Two centuries of modern constitutionaliity), Belgrade, Serbian Academy of Science and Arts.
Basta, R. Lidija (1998), Uloga ustava u zemljama tranzicije centralne i istočne Evrope (Role of the constitution in countries in transition in Central and Eastern Europe), in: Lavirinti krize (Labyrinths of crisis), S. Samardžić, R. Nakarada and Đ. Kovačević (ed.), Institute for European Studies, Belgrade.

Bebler, Anton (1985), Razvitak jugoslovenske vojne doktrine (Development of the Yugoslav military doctrine), *Politička misao*, Zagreb, No.4.
Bebler, Anton (1991), The Military and the Yugoslav Crisis, *Sudosteuropa*, No.3-4.
Bebler, Anton (1992), The Yugoslav Crisis and the 'Yugoslav People's Army', *Forschungsstelle fur Sicherheitsoikutuj und Konfliktanalyse, ETH Zentrum*, Zurich.
Bebler, Anton (1995), Civil-Military Relations in Slovenia, in: C. P. Danopoulos and D. Zirker (eds): Civil-Military Relations in the Soviet and Yugoslav Successor States, Westview Press, Boulder.
Bekić, Darko (1991), Za regionalni savez o obrani i sigurnosti, (For a regional alliance on defense and security) *Vjesnik*, February 4.
Bjelajac, Mile (1994), Vojska kraljevine SHS/Jugoslavije 1922-1935 (Army of the Kingdom of the Serbs, Croats and Slovenes/Yugoslavia 1922-1935), *Institut za noviju istoriju Srbije*, Belgrade.
Bjelajac, Mile (1999), Jugoslovensko iskustvo sa multietničkom armijom 1918-1991 (Yugoslav experience with a multiethnic army, 1918-1991), *Udruženje za društvenu istoriju*, Belgrade.
Bolčić, Silvano (1987), Interesna dimenzija razvoja (The interest dimension of development), CEKADE, Zagreb.
Borba's barometar (1989), Borba, October 30.
Brioni Declaration (1991), *Međunarodna politika*, Belgrade, No. 995-997.
Brovet, Stane (1989), SSNO Deputy, discussion at the 20th meeting CK SKJ, *VPI*, PU SSNO, Belgrade, No. 3.
Ćavoški, Kosta (2000), Ratne uredbe (War Regulations), u: Ustavnost i vladavina prava (Constitutionality and the rule of law), Kosta Čavoški (ed.), *CUPS*, Belgrade.
Ćosić, Dobrica (1957), Akcija (Action), *Prosveta*, Belgrade.
Ćosić, Dobrica (1988), Uslovi demokratske budućnosti (Conditions for a democratic future), *Književne novine*, Belgrade, No. 766-767.
Cvetićanin, Radivoj (1991), Iza tamnih naočara (Behind the dark glasses), *NIN*, September 20.
Daljević, Milan (1987), SSNO undersecretary, presentation at the Coordinating Committee SK SSRNJ for ONO and DSZ, *VPI*, PU SSNO, Belgrade, No. 2.
Danojlić, Milovan (1992), Dela i nedela nacionalizma (The works and misdeeds of nationalism), *Nedeljna Borba*, June 27-28.
Danopoulos, C. P, Zirker D (1995), Civil-Military Relations in the Soviet and Yugoslav Successor States, Westview Press, Boulder.
Degan Vladimir Đuro (1991), Konfederalizam (Confederalism, *Politička misao*, Zagreb, No. 2.
Deklaracija EZ o Jugoslaviji od 27.08.1991 (European Community declaration on Yugoslavia of 27.08.1991) (1991), *Međunarodna politika*, Belgrade, No.995-997.

Bibliography of Cited Works

Deklaracija EZ o Jugoslaviji, Hag, 06.08.1991 (European Community declaration on Yugoslavia, The Hague, 06.08.1991) (1991), *Međunarodna politika*, Belgrade, No. 995-7.
Deveta konferencija OSKJ u JNA (Ninth Conference of OSKJ in JNA) (1990), *dokumenti, VPI*, PU SSNO, Belgrade, No.1.
Đilas, Milovan (1990), Nova klasa (New class), Narodna knjiga, Belgrade.
Đilas, Aleksa (1990), Osporavana zemlja (Disputed land), *Književne novine*, Belgrade.
Đinđić, Zoran (1988), Jugoslavija kao nedovršena država (Yugoslavia as an incomplete state), *Književna zadruga*, Novi Sad.
Đinđić, Zoran (1988), Komunizam i srpsko pitanje (Communism and the Serbian question), *Knjizevne novine*, Belgrade, October 1.
Diverže, Moris (1966), Uvod u politiku (Introduction to Politics), *Savremena administracija*, Belgrade.
Dizdarević, Raif (1989), speech to the SFRY Assembly, *Vojnopolitički informator*, PU SSNO, Belgrade, No. 6.
Documents for the Ninth Conference of OSKJ in JNA (1989), *SSNO*, Belgrade, November.
Dokument 1 of the SK Slovenia Conference (1988), *Borba*, May 1-3.
Dokuments from the European Community: Declaration on Yugoslaviia of 26.03.1991, Statement on Yugoslavia of 08.05.1991, Declaration on Yugoslavia of 08.06.1991 and Declaration on the situation in Yugoslavia of 05.07.1991 (1991); *Međunarodna politika*, Belgrade, No. 995-7.
Đorgović, Milorad (1991), Šta održava JNA (What maintains the JNA), *Borba*, May 27-28.
Drašković, Vuk (1989), Interview, *Start*, Zagreb, No.1.
Društveni slojevi i društvena svest (Social layers and social consciousness), group of authors (1977), *Centar za sociološka istraživanja IDN-a*, Belgrade.
Đukić, Slavoljub (1992), Kako se dogodio vođa (How the leader happened), *Filip Višnjić*, Belgrade.
Đuretić, Veselin (1985), Saveznici i jugoslovenska ratna drama (The Allies and the Yugoslav war drama), *Balkanološki institut SANU*, Belgrade.
Đurić, Mihajlo (1989), Mit, nauka, ideologija (Myth, Science, Ideology), *BIGZ*, Belgrade.
Ekmečić, Milorad (1989), Stvaranje Jugoslavije 1790-1918 (Creating Yugoslavia 1790-1918), *Prosveta*, Belgrade.
Feher, Ferenc, Agneš Heler, Markuš Đerđ (1986), Diktatura nad potrebama (Dictatorship over needs), *Rad*, Belgrade.
Finer, S.E. (1967), The Man on Horseback, The Role of the Military in Politics, *Pall Mall Press*, London.
Fukojama, Frensic (1990), Kraj povijesti? (The end of history?), *Politička misao*, Zagreb, No. 2.
Gligorov, Vladimir (1985), Politička vrednovanja (Political valuation), *Partizanska knjiga*, Belgrade.

Goati, Vladimir (1986), SKJ, kriza, demokratija (FRY, crisis, democracy), *CEKADE*, Zagreb.
Goati, Vladimir (1999), Izbori u SRJ od 1990. do 1998, Volja gradjana ili izborna manipulacija (Elections in FRY from 1990 to 1998, Will of the people or electoral manipulation) *CESID*, Belgrade.
Golubović, Zagorka (1988), Kriza identiteta savremenog jugoslovenskog društva (Identity crisis of modern Yugoslav society), *Filip Višnjić*, Belgrade.
Gow, James (1992), Legitimacy and the Military, The Yugoslav Crisis, *St. Martin's Press*, New York.
Group of authors (2000), Sanctions now help only Milošević, *Center for Policy Studies*, Belgrade.
Hadžić, Miroslav (1989), Ideološke determinante spoljnopolitičke doktrine SKJ (Ideological determinants of FRY's foreign doctrine), *Međunarodni problemi (International Problems)*, Institut za medjunarodnu politiku i privredu, Belgrade, No. 4.
Hadžić, Miroslav (1990), Sudbina realsocijalizma (The fate of real-socialism) *Vojno delo*, Belgrade, No. 1.
Hadžić, Miroslav (1993), Postsocijalistička transformacija vojske (Post-socialist transformation of the Army), *Sociološke studije*, Institut društvenih nauka, Belgrade.
Hadžić, Miroslav (1995), The Serbian Ending of the Yugoslav Army, in: Serbia Between The Past and The Future, (ed) Dušan Janjić, *Institute of Social Sciences, Forum for Ethnic Relations*, Belgrade.
Hadžić, Miroslav (1996), Armijska upotreba trauma, (The Army's use of trauma) u: Srpska strana rata (Serbian Side of the War), (ed) Nebojša Popov, *Republika*, Belgrade.
Hadžić, Miroslav (1998), The Security profile of the Balkans, in: The Balkans in '97, *Foreign policy papers*, European Movement in Serbia, Forum for International Relations, Belgrade.
Hadžić, Miroslav (1999), Javne ćutnje o Vojsci Jugoslavije (Public hush-up about the Yugoslav Army), u: Ustavna i pravna pitanja jugoslovenske drzave (Constitutional and legal questions of the Yugoslav state), Vesna Petrović (ed), Belgradeski centar za ljudska prava, Belgrade.
Hadžić, Miroslav (1999), Security Ranges of NATO Intervention in Kosovo, *Working Papers 27*, Copenhagen Peace Research Institute.
Hadžić, Miroslav (2001), Critical Security Points of Serbia/FR Yugoslavia, in: Ten Years After: Democratization and Security Challenges in Southeast Europe, *PfP Consortium, National Defense Academy Vienna, Faculty of Philosophy, Institute of Defense, University of Skopje*, Vienna, May.
Heler, Agneš (1984), Teorija istorije (The theory of history), *Rad*, Belgrade.
Heler, Agneš (1993), Interview, *Borba*, June 19-20.
Huntington, P. Samuel (1995), Reforming of Civil-Military Relations, *Journal of Democracy*, Vol. 6, No. 4.

Inđić, Trivo (1998), Nacionalizam - izmedju politicke emancipacije i zloupotrebe (Nationalism – between political emancipation and misuse), in: Lavirinti krize (Labyrinths of crisis), S. Samardzic, R. Nakarada i Đ. Kovačević (ur), *Institut za evropske studije*, Belgrade.

Isaković, Zlatko (1993), From a Cold War to a Peacetime Economy in Central-Eastern Europe: Problems of the Conversion of Military Production, *The Journal of East and West Studies*, Vol.22, No.1, April.

Isaković, Zlatko (1995), International position of Macedonia and security in the Balkans, *Međunarodni problemi*, Belgrade, No.4.

Isaković, Zlatko and C. P. Danopoulos (1995), In Search of Identity: Civil-Military Relations and Nationhood in the Former Yugoslav Republic of Macedonia, in: C. P.Danopoulos and D. Zirker (eds): Civil-Military Relations in the Soviet and Yugoslav Successor States, *Westview Press,* Boulder.

Istorija Jugoslavije (History of Yugoslavia), group of authors (1972), *Prosveta*, Belgrade.

Jazić, Žarko (1991), Jačanje uloge UN u međunarodnoj bezbednosti (Strengthening the role of the UN in international security) *Međunarodna politika*, Belgrade, No. 990-994.

Jones, Ellen (1985), Red Army and Society, A Sociology of the Soviet Military, *Allen and Unwin*, Boston.

Jović, Borisav (1995), Poslednji dani SFRJ Last days of SFRY), *Kompanija Politika*, Belgrade.

Kadijević, Veljko (1988), discussion at the 17th meeting of the Central Committee of the Yugoslav League of Communists, *VPI*, PU SSNO, Belgrade, No. 11.

Kadijević, Veljko (1989), presentation in the SFRY Assembly, December 1988, *VPI*, PU SSNO, Belgrade, No.1.

Kadijević, Veljko (1989), interview on Army Day 1988, *VPI*, PU SSNO, Belgrade, No.1.

Kadijević, Veljko (1989), presentation at the joint session of the Military Council and the Presidency of the Armed Forces Communist Party in the JNA, *VPI*, PU SSNO, Belgrade, No.11.

Kadijević, Veljko (1989), 21st meeting of the Committee of OSKJ in JNA, *VIP*, PU SSNO, Belgrade, No.11.

Kadijević, Veljko (1993), Moje viđenje raspada (My view of the disintegration), *Politika*, Belgrade.

Komitet visokih funkcionera KEBS (Committee of the High Commissioners of OSCE) (1991), Urgent call to cease fire (03.07.91) and the Yugoslav Mission (04.07.91), *Međunarodna politika*, Belgrade, No. 995-7.

Korošić, Marjan (1989), Jugoslavenska kriza (The Yugoslav crisis), *Naprijed*, Zagreb.

Koštunica, Vojislav (2001), Interview, www.politica.co.yu/2001/0711/01_01.htm

Kreč, David, Kračfild Richard, Balaki, S., Igerton L (1972), Pojedinac u društvu (The individual in society) *Zavod za izdavanje udžbenika*, Belgrade.

Kritička analiza funkcionisanja političkog sistema socijalističkog samoupravljanja (Critical analysis of the functioning of the political system of social self-management) (1986), *Naše teme*, Zagreb, No. 7-8.

Krunić, Boško (1988), Introductory words, 17th meeting CK SKJ, *VPI*, PU SSNO, Belgrade, No. 7.

Kučan, Milan (1989), Interview, Komunist, in: *Borba*, October 19.

Kučan, Milan (1989), Interview, Di Prese, in: *Borba*, November 24-26.

Kučuk, Ejub (1993), Ogled o vojnoj profesiji (A look at the military profession), Novi glasnik, *VINC*, Belgrade, No.1.

Lazanski, Miroslav (1991), Ko je izazvao rat (Who incited the war), *Politika*, October 6.

Lazic, Dusan (1999), Spoljna politika Jugoslavije (Yugoslavia's foreign policy), in: Ustavna i pravna pitanja jugoslovenske drzave (Constitutional and legal questions of the Yugoslav state), Vesna Petrović (ed), *Belgradeski centar za ljudska prava*, Belgrade.

Lazić, Mladen (1987), U susret zatvorenom društvu (Going towards a closed society), *Naprijed*, Zagreb.

Lerotić, Zvonko (1986), Još jedanput: od nacionalne individualnosti do načela konsenzusa (Once again: from national individuality to the principle of concensus), *Naše teme*, Zagreb, No.7-8.

Lubarda, Vojislav (1989), Srbofobija kao politika (Serbophobia as politics), *Književne novine*, Belgrade, No. 768, January 15.

Ma Hu Sheng, Razmišljanja na temu uspostavljanja novog međunarodnog poretka (Considerations on the top of establishing a new international order), *Međunarodna politika*, Belgrade, No. 998-1000.

Madžar, Ljubomir (1996), Ko koga eksploatiše (Who is exploiting whom), in: Srpska strana rata (Serbian side of the war), (ed) Nebojša Popov, Republika, Belgrade.

Mamula, Branko (1988), presentation in the SFRY Assembly, December 1987, *VIP*, PU SSNO, Belgrade, No. 2.

Mamula Branko (1988), Lecture in the SKJ Political School, *VPI*, PU SSNO, Belgrade, No. 6.

Mamula, Branko (2000), Slučaj Jugoslavija (The case of Yugoslavia), *CID*, Podgorica.

Mandelbaum, Michael (1999), A Perfect Failure: NATO's War Against Yugoslavia, Foreign Affairs, Vol. 78, No. 5.

Marković, Ante (1989), president of the Federal Government (SIV), presentation at a session of the SK SSRNJ presidency, *Borba*, January 30.

Marković, Ante (1989), president of SIV, presentation before the SFRY Assembly SFRJ, *VIP*, PU SSNO, Belgrade, No. 5.

Memorandum Svetoga arhijerejskog sabora Srpske pravoslavne crkve (Memorandum from the Holy Council of Bishops of the Serbian Orthodox Church) (1992), *Borba*, May 29.

Mićović, Vojislav 1986), Specijalni rat i Jugoslavija (The special war and Yugoslavia), *Rad*, Belgrade.
Mićunović, Dragoljub (1992), Interview, *Borba*, July 20.
Mihailović, Srećko (2000), Politicka i stranacka identifikacija (Political and party identification), in: Javno mnenje Srbije (Serbia's public opinion), S. Mihailović (ed), *Centar za proučavanje alternativa*, Belgrade.
Mihajlov, Mihajlo (1991), Govor ne zaustavlja juriš (Talk does not stop the onslaught), *Borba*, August 17-18.
Mikulić, Branko (1988), president of SIV, presentation in the SFRY Assembly, *Borba*, May 16.
Milić, Vlada (1978), Revolucija i socijalna struktura (Revolution and social structure), Mladost, Belgrade.
Milošević, Slobodan (1989), Godine raspleta (Years of denouement), *BIGZ*, Belgrade.
Milošević, Slobodan (1989), Interview, le Monde, in: *Borba*, July 13..
Mirić, Jovan (1989), Manjina, većina, konsenzus (Minority, majority, consensus), *Naše teme*, Zagreb, No.11.
Mirić, Jovan, Sistem i kriza (System and crisis) (1985), *CEKADE*, Zagreb.
Mirković, Stevan (1988), discussion at the First Conference SKJ, *VPI*, PU SSNO, Belgrade, No.7.
Mišljenje arbitražne komisije EZ od 10. decembra 1991 (Opinion of the EC arbitration committee of December 10, 1991), Izveštaj arbitražne komisije EZ od 15. januara 1992. godine (Report of the EC arbitration committee of January 15, 1992), *Međunarodna politika*, Belgrade, No. 1001.
Mlakar, Mladen (1991), Vjernici uzimaju riječ (The faithful take the floor), *Borba*, January 1-2.
Nacrt zakona o preduzećima (Draft law on enterprises) (1988), *Borba*, October 26.
Naredba Presednistva SFRJ o razoruzanju paravojnih formacija (Order from the SFRY Presidency on the disarming of paramilitary formations) (1991), *VPI*, PU SSNO, Belgrade, No.2.
Nedovršeni mir, Izveštaj međunarodne komisije za Balkan (Incomplete peace, Report from the International Commission for the Balkans) (1998), *Radio B92, Naša Borba*, Belgrade.
Negovanje i vrednovanje tradicija u Vojsci Jugoslavije (Fostering and valuating traditions in the Yugoslav Army) (1993), *VINC*, Belgrade.
Neumann, Franz (1974), Demokratska i autoritarna država (Democratic and authoritarian state), *Naprijed*, Zagreb.
Novi ustavi na tlu bivše Jugoslavije (New constitutions in former Yugoslavia) (1995), Međunarodna politika, Faculty of Law, Faculty of Political Sciences, Belgrade.
Ocokoljić, Stanko (1992), Bezbednost i razoružanje oslobođeni blokovske konfrontacije (Security and the disaarmament of liberated bloc confrontations), *Međunarodni problemi*, IMPP, Belgrade, No.3-4.

Odluka Predsedništva Jugoslavije o reorganizaciji JNA u vojsku Jugoslavije (Decision by the Yugoslav Presidency on reorganizing the Yugoslav People's Army into the Yugoslav Army) (1992), Tanjuga report, *Borba*, May 21.

Odluka Predsedništva SFRJ (Decision by the SFRY Presidency) (1991) 18.07.1991, *VPI, special issue*, PU SSNO, Belgrade, August.

Osnove programa Socijalističke partije Srbije, *SPS* (Basic platforam of the Socialist Party of Serbia) (1993) Belgrade.

Osnovni dokument Slovenije 89 (Basic document of Slovenia 89) (1989), *Borba*, June 24-25.

Pajvančić, Marijana (2000), Ustavnost vanrednog stanja (The constitutionality of a state of emergency), in: Ustavnost i vladavina prava (Constitutionality and the rule of law), Kosta Čavoški (ed), *CUPS*, Belgrade.

Panić, Života (1992), Chief of the Yugoslav Army General Staff, Interview, *Vojska*, September 3.

Pantić, Dragomir (1988), Klasična i svetovna religioznost (Classical and secular religiousness), *IDN*, Belgrade.

Pečujlić, Miroslav, Vlada Milić (1990), Političke stranke u Jugoslaviji (Political parties in Yugoslavia), *Stručna knjiga*, Belgrade.

Perazić, Gavro (1986), Međunarodno ratno pravo (International war law), *VINC*, Belgrade.

Perović Latinka (1996), Beg od modernizacije (Flight from modernization), in: Srpska strana rata (Serbian side of the war), (ed) Nebojša Popov, *Republika*, Belgrade.

Pešec, Mladen (1989), Slom jugoslovenskih elita modernizacije (Collapse of Yugoslavia's modernization elite), *Sociologija*, Belgrade, No.2-3.

Petković, Ranko, SAD, Nemačka i Evropa (The USA, Germany and Europe), *Međunarodna politika*, Belgrade, No. 998-1000.

Petranović, Branko, Zečević, Momčilo (1988), Jugoslavija 1918-1988 (Yugoslavia 1918-1988), thematic collection of documents, *Rad*, Belgrade.

Phelan, Donna (1996), The Agreement on Subregional Arms Control of the 'Dayton Agreement', *Disarmament*, UN, New York, No. 2.

Plan i program političkog obrazovanja i vaspitanja vojnika - mornara u JNA (Plan and program of the political education and training of soldiers-sailors in JNA) (1988), *PU SSNO*, Belgrade.

Podunavac, Milan (1988), Politički legitimitet (Political legitimacy), *Rad*, Belgrade.

Podunavac, Milan (1995), Princip građanstva i priroda političkog režima u postkomunizmu: slučaj Srbija (The principle of a civic society and the nature of the political regime in post-communism: the case of Serbia), in: Potisnuto civilno društvo (Repressed civic society), (ed) Vukašin Pavlović, *Eko centar*, Belgrade.

Podunavac, Milan (1998), Princip građanstva i poredak politike (The principle of a civic society and the political system), *Princip, Faculty of Political Science*, Belgrade.

Popov, Nebojša, Srpski populizam - Od marginalne do dominatne pojave (Serbian populism – from marginal to dominant manifestation), special supplement, Vreme No. 135, Belgrade.

Popović, Milan (1990), Jugoslavija u svetsko-sistemskoj perspektivi (Yugoslavia in world-systemic perspective), *Sociologija*, Belgrade, No. 4.

Posebne mere Predsedništva SFRJ na Kosovu (Special measures of the SFRY Presidency in Kosovo) (1989), *Borba*, February 28.

Pravilnik o ocenjivanju vojnih lica (Rulebook on evaluating servicemen) (1980), *SSNO, Personalna uprava*, Belgrade.

Predlog srpskog crkvenonacionalnog programa (Proposal of a Serbian Church-national program) (1989); Serbian Orthodox Church, *Borba*, July 22-23.

Program IPO starešina i građanskih lica na službi u OS SFRJ (The program of ideological-political education for officers and civilians serving in the SFRY Armed Forces) (1987), *Politička uprava SSNO*, Belgrade, November.

Program PO vojnika – mornara (The political and educational training of soldiers-sailors) (1985), *Politička uprava SSNO*, Belgrade.

Program PO (Soldiers' political and educational training) (1988), *PU SSNO*, Belgrade.

Program IPO za 1989 (The ideological-political program for 1989) (1989), *PU SSNO*, Belgrade.

Puhovski, Žarko (1984), Povijesnost socijalističke realizacije društva (Historicity of the socialist realization of society), *Naše teme*, Zagreb, No. 12.

Puhovski, Žarko (1985), Mijena i povijesnost, u Prijepori oko političkog sistema (Change and historicity, Disputes about the political system), *Naprijed*, Zagreb.

Puhovski, Žarko (1986), Moć i program (Power and program), *Naše teme*, Zagreb, No. 7-8.

Puhovski, Žarko (1990), Socijalisticka konstrukcija zbilje (The socialist construction of reality), in: Napuštanje socijalizma (Leaving socialism), (eds) V. Gligorov, J .Teokarević, *IMRP*, Belgrade.

Pusić, Eugen (1989), Društvena regulacija (Social regulation), *Globus*, Zagreb.

Puzigaća, Milka (2000), Strahovi i raspoloženja (Fears and moods) in: Javno mnenje Srbije (Public opinion in Serbia), S.Mihailović (ed), *Centar za proučavanje alternativa*, Belgrade.

Radinović, Radovan (1990), ONO and DSZ SFRJ, *Naučna knjiga*, Belgrade.

Radinović, Radovan (1990), Promene u savremenom svetu i njihove implikacije na dogradnju koncepcije opštenarodne odbrane i oružanih snaga SFRJ (Changes in the modern world and their implications on expanding the concepts of Total National Defense and armed forces), *Vojno delo, special issue*, VINC, Belgrade, August.

Radinović, Radovan (1991), O vojno-političkim promjenama u Istočnoj Evropi i bezbjednosti Jugoslavije (On military-political changes in Eastern Europe and the security of Yugoslavia), *Vojno delo*, VINC, Belgrade, No. 6.

Rakočević, Živojin (1991), Koreni i geopolitička dimenzija jugoslovenske krize (The roots and geopolitical dimensions of the Yugoslav crisis), *Vojno delo*, VINC, Belgrade, No. 4-5.

Rakočević, Živojin (1991), Zamke i stranputice detanta (The traps and mistaken paths of détente), *Vojno delo*, VINC, Belgrade, No. 1-2.

Redakcijski komentar 'Dubok kadrovski rez' (Editorial comment 'Deep cut in personnel') (1993), *Vojska*, Belgrade, October 14..

Remington, Robin Alison (1995), The Yugoslav Army: Trauma and Transition, in: C. P. Danopoulos and D. Zirker (eds): Civil-Military Relations in the Soviet and Yugoslav Successor States, *Westview Press*, Boulder.

Rice, Condoleezza (1991), Vojska u demokratskom poretku (The army in a democratic system), *Third program*, Belgrade, No. 90-91.

Rokar, Mišel (1990), Kuda ide Evropa? (Where is Europe headed?), *Međunarodna politika*, Belgrade, No. 964.

Rupel, Dimitrij (1991), Slovenija i svet (Slovenia and the world), *Međunarodna politika*, Belgrade, No. 980.

Saglasnost Skupštine Kosova za promene Ustava SR Srbije (Agreement of the Kosovo Assembly to changes in the SR Serbia Constitution) (1988), *Borba*, February 3.

Samardžić, Slobodan (1989), Pred-federalna Jugoslavija: različite zamisli jugoslovenskog federalizma (Pre-federal Yugoslavia: different ideas onYugoslav federalism), *THEORIA*, Belgrade, 2.

Samardžić, Slobodan (1998), Ustavni problemi demokratske transformacije SRJ (Constitutional problems of the democratic transformation of FRY), in: Lavirinti krize (Labyrinths of crisis), S. Samardžić, R. Nakarada and Đ. Kovačević (eds), Institut za evropske studije, Belgrade.

Saopštenja Predsedništva SFRJ i Predsednistva SKJ Communiqué of the SFRY Presidencyand SKJ Presidency) (1988), *VPI*, PU SSNO, Belgrade, No.4.

Šiber, Ivan (1989), Komunisti Jugoslavije o društvenoj reformi 1989. godine (Yugoslav communists on social reform in 1989), *IC Komunist*, Belgrade.

Šimić, Petar (1988), president of OSKJ in JNA, discussion at the First Conference of the Yugoslav League of Communists, *VPI*, PU SSNO, Belgrade, No.7.

Šimić, Petar (1988), introductory remarks at the OSKJ in JNA Conference, *VPI*, PU SSNO, Belgrade, No.8.

Šimić, Petar (1989), discussion at the 20th meeting of CK SKJ, *VIP*, PU SSNO, Belgrade, No.3.

Šipka, Pero, Hadžić Miroslav (1989), Javno mnjenje članova SKJ u JNA o društvenoj reformi i preobražaju SKJ (Public opinion of members of the SKJ in the JNA on social reforms and transformation of SKJ), *Komitet Organizacije SKJ u JNA*, Belgrade.

Slavujević, Zoran (2000), Razmere nelegitimnosti političkog sistema i njegovih institucija (Extent of the illegitimacy of the political system and its institutions), in: Javno mnenje Srbije (Public opinion in Serbia), S. Mihailović (ed), *Centar za proučavanje alternativa*, Belgrade.

Šolević, Miroslav (1989), Interview, *Borba*, February 22.
Srbija i NATO: Srpski diskurs rata i Svetska debata (Serbia and NATO: Serbia's discourse on war and the world debate) (1999), *Nova srpska politička misao*, Belgrade.
Stanković, Donoila, Maltarić Zlatan (1996), Svetska bibliografija o krizi u bivšoj Jugoslaviji (World bibliography on the crisis in former Yugoslavia), *Međunarodna politika i grupa izdavača*, Belgrade.
Stanovčić, Vojislav (1985), Kriza sistema i sistem krize (Crisis of the system and system of crises),inu: Prijepori oko političkog sistema (Disputes about the political system), *Naprijed*, Zagreb.
Stanovčić, Vojislav (1986), Federalizam/konfederalizam (Federalism/confederalism), *Univerzitetska riječ*, Titograd.
Stanovnik, Janez (1989), president of the SR Slovenia Presidency, Interview, Pobjeda, in: *Borba*, April 10.
Statistički godišnjak (Statistical almanac) (1989), *Savezni zavod za statistiku*, Belgrade.
Stavovi CK SK Srbije (Views of the Serbian Communist Party Central Committee) (1989), *Borba*, July 14.
Stavovi Predsedništva SR Srbije (Views of the SR Serbia Presidency) (1989), *Borba*, July 26.
Stobbe, Heinz-Gunther (1996), Denacifikacija u Nemačkoj (Denazification in Germany), in: Srpska strana rata (Serbian side of the war), (ed) Nebojša Popov, *Republika*, Belgrade.
Stojanović, Božo (1998), Jugoslovenska privreda - dirigovana nestabilnost i neefikasnost (Yugoslavia's economy – orchestrated instability and inefficiency), in: Lavirinti krize (Labyrinths of crisis), S. Samardžić, R. Nakarada and Đ. Kovačević (eds), *Institut za evropske studije*, Belgrade.
Stojković, Momir (1991), Novi geopolitički položaj Balkana i Jugoslavije (New geopolitical position of the Balkans and Yugoslavia), *Vojno delo*, VINC, Belgrade, No.6.
Strategija oružane borbe (Strategy of armed combat) (1983), *SSNO*, Belgrade.
Strategijski problemi, godišnjak 88 (Strategical problems, almanac 88) (1988), *COSSIS*, Belgrade.
Strategy of ONO and DSZ SFRJ (1987), *SSNO*, Belgrade.
Šuvar, Stipe (1988), Introductory words at the 17th meeting of CK SKJ, *VPI*, PU SSNO, Belgrade, No.11.
Tadić, Ljubomir (1986), Da li je nacionalizam naša sudbina? (Is nationalismm our fate?), *author's edition*, Belgrade.
Tadić, Ljubomir (1988), Kominterna i nacionalno pitanje Jugoslavije (Comintern and Yugoslavia's national question), *Književne novine*, Belgrade, September 15.
Tadić, Ljubomir (1988), Nauka o politici (The science on politics), *Rad*, Belgrade.
Terzić, Velimir (1982), Slom kraljevine Jugoslavije 1941 (Collapse of the Kingdom of Yugoslavia 1941), *Narodna knjiga*, Belgrade.

Teze Predsedništva CK SK Slovenije o međunacionalnim odnosima (Theses of the CK SK Slovenia Presidency on interethnic relations) (1989), *Borba*, June 30. i July 1-2.
The Military Balance 1990-1991 (1990), London.
Tocqueville, Alexis de (1990), O demokratiji u Americi (On Democracy in America), *Izdavačka knjižara Zorana Stoiljkovića Sremski Karlovci, CID, Titograd.*
Tomac, Zdravko (1985), Neutemeljnost kritika ustavnog modela jugoslavenske federacije (Unfounded criticism of the Yugoslav federation's constitutional model), in: Prijepori oko političkog sistema (Disputes about the political system), *Napijed*, Zagreb.
Tomac, Zdravko (1989), Neka sporna pitanja ostvarivanja i razvoja jugoslavenskog federalizma (Some controversial questions on the achievement and development of Southern Slav federalism); *Naše teme*, Zagreb, No.7-8.
Tomc, Gorazd (1989), Društvena stratifikacija i razvoj nacija u posleratnoj Jugoslaviji (Social stratification and the development of nations in postwar Yugoslavia), *Sociologija*, Belgrade, No. 2-3.
Torov, Ivan (1991), Naoružani arbitri - Armijski prodor u neizvjesnost (Armed arbiters – the Army's penetration into uncertainty), *Oslobođenje*, Sarajevo, September 29.
Uputstvo o praćenju i procenjivanju MPS u JNA (Instructions on monitoring and evaluating MPS in the JNA) (1979), *PU SSNO*, Belgrade.
Uputstvo za praćenje i procenjivanje MPS u TO (Instructions on monitoring and evaluating MPS in TO) (1985), *PU SSNO*, Belgrade.
Ustav Republike Srbije (Constitution of the Republic of Serbia) (1990), *Službeni list*, Belgrade.
Ustav SRJ (FRY Constitution) (1993), in: Zakoni (Laws), *VINC*, Belgrade.
Ustavni razvoj socijalisticke Jugoslavije (The constitutional development of socialist Yugoslavia) (1988), *Eksportpres*, Belgrade.
Vasilijević, Vladan (1991), Na šta je spremna vojska? (What is the Army prepared to do?), *Vreme*, Belgrade, October 7.
Vasović, Vučina (1998), Organizacija vlasti i demokratija (The organization of power and democracy), in: Lavirinti krize (Labyrinths of crisis), S. Samardžić, R. Nakarada and Đ. Kovacević (eds), *Institut za evropske studije*, Belgrade.
Vilić, Dušan, Todorović Boško (1995), Razbijanje Jugoslavije 1990-1992 (The breakup of Yugoslavia 1990-1992), *DIK Književne novine*, Belgrade.
Vojno delo (Military work) (1991), *VINC*, Belgrade, No.1-2.
Vrhovec, Josip (1989), Interview, Večernji list, in: *Borba*, October 16.
Vukotić, Bojana (1996), Jugoslovenski autori o krizi i raspadu Jugoslavije (Yugoslav authors on the crisis and disintegration of Yugoslavia), *Sociološki pregled,* Vol. XXIX, Belgrade.
Vuksanović-Anić, Draga (1993), Stvaranje moderne srpske vojske (Creating a modern Serbian army), *SKZ, VINC*, Belgrade.
Wjatr, Jirzi (1987), Sociologija vojske (Sociology of the army), *VINC*, Belgrade.

Wjatr, Jirzi (1990), Prema novom vojnom identitetu Istočne i centralne Evrope (Towards a new military identity of Eastern and Central Europe), *Politička misao*, Zagreb, No.4.

Woodward, Susan (1997), Balkanska tragedija (Balkan Tragedy), *Filip Višnjić*, Belgrade.

Zaključci 12. sednice CK SKJ (Conclusions of the 12th Meeting of CK SKJ) (1988), *Borba*, January 21.

Zakon o odbrani (The Law on Defense) (1993), in: Zakoni (Laws), VINC, Belgrade.

Zakon o privremenom finansiranju federacije (Law on the provisional financing of the federation) (1988), *Borba*, January 4.

Zakon o Vojsci Jugoslavije (Law on the Yugoslav Army) (1993), in: Zakoni (Laws), *VINC*, Belgrade.

Zbornik radova, Novi svetski poredak i politika odbrane SRJ (Collection of works, New world order and the FRY defense policy) (1993), *FRY Ministry of Defense* Belgrade.

Zbornik radova: O toleranciji, Rasprave o demokratskoj kulturi (On tolerance: Discussions on a democratic culture) (1989), edited and forward by Igor Primorac, *Filip Višnjić*, Belgrade.

Žunec, Ozren (1993), Vojska i demokracija (The army and democracy), *Erazmus*, Zagreb, No. 3.

Žunec, Ozren (1994), Hrvatska u sukobu niskog intenziteta (Croatia in low-intensity conflict), *Erazmus*, Zagrteb, No. 7.

Žunec, Ozren (1995), Okučanski zaključci (Okučani conclusions), *Erazmus*, Zagreb, No. 12.

Žunec, Ozren (1995), Democracy in the 'Fog of War': Civil-Military Relations in Croatia, in: C. P. Danopoulos and D. Zirker (eds): Civil-Military Relations in the Soviet and Yugoslav Successor States, *Westview Press*, Boulder.

Index

Aggression,
   against Serbs 144
   initial 145
   JNA 147 228
   national 263
   NATO, 16 247
   on Croatia 144
   on Slovenia 136
   Serbian Army 18
Aggressor 7, 151, 161, 165, 203, 228
Albanian,
   ethnic 42
Alliance,
   established 15
   military-Serbian 133, 199, 260
Allies
   international 134
   natural 199
   political 13, 72
Anti-reform approach 47
AP, autonomous province 92
Army,
   all Yu-armies 230
   Croatian 77, 98, 147, 227, 230
   inter-Army relations 209
   intra-Army power 217
   model of Party armies 235
   renamed 1
   Republica Srpska 26, 161
   Serbian 1, 4, 8, 110, 127, 147, 157, 218, 226, 261
   Serbo-Chetnik 4, 7

Battle,
   political 41, 57, 107, 177, 236
B-H, Bosnia and Herzegovina 26, 65, 146, 148, 157, 161, 170, 204, 226, 234
Bombing,
   NATO 232, 266
Borders,
   internal 102, 105, 112, 139
Brovet, Stane 20, 67, 111

Center,
   federal 73-74, 197
Centralism 62, 96, 177
Chauvinism,
   nationalism 142
CIA 20
CK SKJ, Central Committee of the League of Communists of Yugoslavia 42
CK, Central Committee 42, 53, 96
Coalition,
   military-political 11, 260
   military-Serbian 108, 135, 199, 260
Command,
   supreme 11, 97, 99, 130, 197, 201, 233-34, 242-46
Commander,
   army 47, 140-41, 159
Communism,
   anti 141, 198, 204

Communist,
  party xi, 179, 181
  Serbo-communist 4, 7, 13, 81, 83, 144-45, 228
  Yugo-communist 4, 81
Community,
  international 22, 106, 122, 133, 139, 147-48, 153, 202, 232-33, 241
Confederation,
  official 178
  Slovenia and Croatia 41
Conflict,
  ethnic 43, 71, 81, 103, 107, 269
  ideological 217
  interethnic 48
  local and regional war conflicts 272
  nationalistic 197
  political 56, 71-72, 176, 178-79, 199, 214
  Serbian-Albanian 230
  territorial 102
Consequences,
  ultimate 85, 189
Conservatism,
  communistic 229
Constitution 31, 41-42, 51, 55-56, 65-66, 74, 78, 92-98, 113-14, 116, 120, 155, 160-61, 185, 195, 197-98, 204, 207, 219, 234, 238, 240-45, 248, 253, 259
Control,
  democratic 206-7, 210, 230, 251
  parliamentary 7, 209, 226, 246
Corps,
  central corps of generals 85
  general 14, 126, 131, 209, 214, 216, 233
  officer 8, 59-60, 69, 86, 145, 198, 206, 211-12, 214-15, 228, 250-51, 258

Crisis,
  Yu-crisis 9, 11-14, 17, 19-20, 24, 166, 170, 175, 177, 258, 260-62, 265-67, 269, 271
Croatia 7-8, 15, 18-19, 22, 26, 29, 40-43, 48, 65-66, 70, 73-74, 76-79, 81-87, 91-92, 94-95, 97-99, 101-2, 104-10, 113-14, 116-19, 122, 124-29, 132, 134-36, 138-61, 169-70, 174-75, 184, 195, 202-4, 215, 226, 231-32, 235-39, 258, 267, 273
Croatian army 77, 98, 147, 227, 230

Defense,
  sector 248
  territorial 90, 101
Democratic reconstitution 46, 239, 248
DEMOS, Democratic Opposition of Slovenia 76
Determination,
  self-determination 65, 75, 77, 95, 105, 139, 149, 152, 177, 201
Diaspora,
  Croats in the diaspora 114
Dilettantism,
  political 8
Drina River 20, 79, 115, 135, 152, 170, 239
DSZ, Social Self-Protection 48, 100, 204, 219

Elite,
  nationalistic 172, 259
  national-republican 218, 261
  republican 40
Enclaves,
  Serbian 143
Enemies,
  mortal 132

Ethnic,
  cleansing 102, 144, 148, 153-54, 169, 226, 269
  conflict 43, 71, 81, 103, 107, 269
  egoism 76
  group xi, 6, 44-45, 47, 75, 95, 105-6, 110, 123, 125, 139, 142, 167, 173, 210, 212, 215-16, 221, 233, 241, 264
  leaders 105, 107, 109, 111, 133, 140
  lines 71, 230
  multiethnic 189, 195, 202, 214, 259, 270
  tensions 71

Fascism,
  antifascism 2, 141
Federal constitution 93, 241, 243
Federalism,
  modern 78, 178
  rigid 257
Federation 46, 84
First World War 1
First Yugoslavia 1, 2, 171, 176-79, 206
Force,
  occupying 4, 138, 203
Formation,
  paramilitary 37, 117, 122, 143, 204, 228, 257
FRY, Federal Republic of Yugoslavia 107, 153, 253, 255

Gazi Mestan, meeting 43
Genocide,
  renewed 115
  repeated 140, 229
Gligorov Kiro 104, 123
Government,
  federal 47, 74-75, 83-84, 99, 107, 109, 115, 135, 180, 242-43, 250

GŠ, General Staff xii, 6, 14, 28, 89-91, 111, 116, 145, 149, 155, 190, 212, 236, 237

Hague, The 20, 145, 233, 234
Hague Tribunal, The 20
Heritage,
  civil-military 206
  political 206
Homogeneity,
  territorial 76

Ideological heritage 61
Ideological postulates,
  JNA 52
  ONO 12
  SKJ 88
Identity,
  national 160, 247
Independence 76
Indoctrination,
  repressive 229
  situational 58
  system 215
  systematic 211
Inflation,
  anti-inflation 40
Institute of Social Sciences xii, 237
Integrity,
  territorial 9-10, 92, 94, 127, 135, 137, 157, 159, 166, 170, 191, 241
Interveners,
  foreign 267, 270
Investigation,
  comprehensive 10
IPO, ideological-political education 58, 88, 220
Izetbegović, Alija 95, 104, 124, 161

JNA, Yugoslav People's Army,
  all-out armed resistance 196
  columns 137
  communist 62-63
  depoliticization 51, 82, 88

ideological entrentechment 59
ideological postulates 52
JNA model 230-31
military and Party leadership 52
misuse of the JNA 228, 258
moral-political state 60
officer corps 211
OSKJ 56, 67, 69, 89
political role 60, 211
political inviolability 48
pro-Serbian transformation 201
radical changes 192
Serbo-communist 228
social and political status 47
top generals xi, 14, 18, 117, 136, 188
Jović, Borisav 19, 29, 156

Kadijević, Veljko 56, 67, 111, 120, 261
KLA, Kosovo Liberation Army 247, 249, 254, 266
KONO, Concept of Total National Defense xi, 16
Kosovo 42-44, 61, 65, 70, 79, 96, 98, 108, 110, 125, 134, 154, 215, 230, 232, 234, 237, 241, 246-50, 254-55, 266-67, 270-72
Koštunica, Vojislav 23, 248

Leaders,
army 13, 35-36, 47, 49, 52-54, 56, 58-61, 81, 83, 85, 138, 151, 190-91, 193, 202
federal 41, 82
federal state 8, 15
military xi, 8, 10-11, 13, 15-16, 18- 21, 23, 26-28, 52, 97, 99, 151-2, 154, 158, 188-96, 198-203, 206, 210, 212, 215, 225, 232-34, 250, 257-60
party 49

republican 50, 73, 81, 90, 102, 103, 107-8, 110, 113, 116, 120, 123, 192, 204, 233
Legality 11, 35-36, 51, 97, 116, 139, 177, 244
Legitimacy 11, 28, 35-36, 41, 56, 72, 77-78, 85, 105, 139, 160, 185, 192, 199, 201, 229, 248
political 177, 185
Local,
warlords 133, 266-69
Loyalty,
personal 206

Macedonia 70, 72, 92, 101, 104, 106, 123, 134, 139, 149, 153, 157, 174, 226, 237, 252, 270
Mamula, Branko 20, 30
Management
concept of socialistic self-management 62
nationalist 174
Maneuvers,
tactical 103, 105
Marković, Ante 74, 84, 92, 109, 125, 193-94, 204
Mediator,
the general's role 80
Militarization,
accelerated 103
Military,
commander 4, 35-37, 47-52, 54-60, 63-4, 67, 72, 80-91, 97, 103, 108, 110-23, 130-31, 134-36, 138-39, 141-43, 145-46, 161
intervention 11, 112, 208, 268
judiciary 209
putsch 51, 67, 83, 117, 195
secret 16, 49, 66
Milošević, Slobodan 18, 22-23, 26-27, 42, 65, 73, 76, 91, 119, 169, 233, 235, 256
Mobilization 121, 126, 139, 143, 146, 157, 159-60, 242-43

Montenegro 1, 28, 42, 63, 65, 70, 73-74, 82, 95-97, 101, 104, 108, 146-47, 174-75, 181, 239-41, 246, 248, 250
Morale,
  combat 209-10, 227, 232-33, 247
MPS, moral-political state 57, 60, 210
MUP, Ministry of Internal Affairs 95, 117, 127-30, 242
Muslim 95, 106, 142, 148, 215

National, patriotic 230
NATO,
  aggression 16, 247
  bombing 232, 266
Negotiations 15, 73, 82, 102-7, 109-10, 120, 123-24, 134, 145, 150, 177, 196
Neo-fascism 15
Nomenclature,
  communist 174-75

Order,
  constitutional 9, 59, 92-93, 99, 108, 118-19, 123, 126-27, 137, 196, 207-8, 210, 242-44
Orientation,
  pro-Serb 139
OS, Armed Forces xii, 30, 49, 52, 56-58, 63, 68, 70, 82, 88-91, 98, 120-21, 130, 160, 207, 210, 220, 226, 243, 277, 281
OSK, Organization of the League of Communists 36, 68
Outbreak of war in Croatia 141

Pacification,
  universal 103
Party,
  model of Party armies 235
  pluralism xi, 54, 97, 240
Peacetime,
  complete 122

Political,
  ambitions 11, 15
  arena 72, 174
  constellation 11, 55, 134, 184, 193
  dissolution 102, 109, 111
  freedom 11
  neutrality 140, 151, 190
  opportunism 36
  parallel institutions 135
  pressure 41, 48, 82, 87, 175, 192
  priority 72
  propagandist 16
  resolution 11, 51
  scene 12, 43, 63, 169, 203
Power-holders 2, 23, 25, 73, 81, 90, 110, 112, 118-20, 169, 191, 227-28
Pretensions,
  territorial 138, 259
Propaganda,
  ideological, political, state, military 72
PU, Political Administration (of the Ministry of Defense) 68
Public
  domestic 8
  foreign 7, 105, 107, 118
  international 7, 144, 195, 199
  local 7

Reason,
  social 171-72, 217
Recomposition,
  territorial and ethnic 139
Referendum,
  Slovenian 41
  Yygoslav 41
Reform,
  anti 46-47
  controlled 45
  economic 41, 62-63
  minded 45-46, 55, 61-62, 195
  prevented 46

Refugees 19, 168, 255, 270
  camps 2
Regime,
  authoritarian 78, 225, 261, 264
  Croatian 118
  defeated 248
  instability 226
  peacetime 226
  political 237
  Serbian 15, 79, 119, 150, 225, 226-28, 261, 267
  socialist 127
Relation,
  civil-military xii, 16-17, 27, 207, 248, 250
  interethnic 51, 110, 185
Religious,
  conflict 169
  ethnic 161
  ethno-war 145
  Islamic 168
  national 18, 26, 170-72, 226-27
Republic
  northern 130, 134
  secessionist 15, 200
  western 42, 72-74, 80, 83, 107, 200
  Yu-republic 7, 14
Republic of Srpska Krajina,
  army 26, 161
Republican,
  armies 67, 81, 83, 90-91, 111, 118-19
  offshoots 133
Resolution,
  Security Council Resolution 1244 248
Revanchism,
  chauvinistic 175
  inter-ethnic 77
RM,
  the Navy 221

RViPVO,
  the Airforce 143

Sacrifices,
  human and material 135
Sanctions,
  international 7, 29, 135
SANU, Serbian Academy of Science and Arts 185
SAO, Serbian Autonomous District 143
Secession 42, 65, 74-75, 77-78, 93, 95, 104-5, 108, 114, 120, 137-39, 152, 170, 229
  public proponent 72
Second World War 7, 167, 169, 175
Semitism, anti-Semitism 141
Separatist,
  potential 72
Serbia 1, 7-8, 15, 17-19, 21-23, 28-29, 31, 41-43, 49-50, 63, 65-66, 70, 73-74, 76-79, 81-85, 91-93, 95-97, 101-2, 104, 106-8, 110, 113-15, 119-20, 123-24, 126, 130, 132, 134-5, 137-8, 142, 146-54, 156-59, 161, 1747-5, 181, 184-85, 197-204, 206-7, 228, 230, 233, 235, 237, 239-44, 246, 248-51, 253-56, 259-60, 266, 268-69
Serbian
  army 1, 4, 8, 110, 127, 147, 157, 226, 261
  national line 203
  pro-Serbian policies 8
Serbo-Chetnik,
  army 4
Serbo-communist,
  army 4, 7
Service,
  security 210, 212, 216, 230
SFRY, Socialist Federal Republic of Yugoslavia 35

Šimić, Petar xi, 222
SIV, Federal Government 41, 193
SK, League of Communists xi, 30, 35-36, 38, 45, 52, 54, 80, 96, 99, 180, 186, 189, 219
SKJ, League of Communists of Yugoslavia 35, 38, 80, 189, 219
SK-PJ, League of Communists – Movement for Yugoslavia 80, 96
Slovenia 7-8, 18-19, 22, 26, 39, 41-44, 48-49, 64-67, 70, 73-76, 78-87, 91-95, 97-99, 101, 104-10, 113-14, 1161-7, 119, 124-27, 132, 134-40, 143, 146-47, 149, 151-52, 154-57, 161, 169-70, 174, 181, 185, 194-96, 200, 203-4, 226, 236, 239, 258, 267, 272
Social,
 conflict 172-3, 182
 distance 173, 217
 mobility 173
 preconditions for war 175
 prosperity 171
 reasons 171-2, 217
 reform 61
 reproduction 172
 sources 172, 174-5
 structure of society 173
 support 11, 142, 190
Socialism,
 anti xi, 39-40, 42, 44-48, 50, 56, 65, 71-73, 79, 85-87, 120, 168-69, 179, 182, 184, 186, 190-93, 195, 199-200, 208-10, 216, 220, 229, 239, 241, 265, 270
Southern Slav peoples 2, 6, 12, 26, 262
Sovereignty 76
Sovereignty,
 authentic 177
SRRN, Socialist Alliance of the Working People 36
SRVS, Alliance of Reserve Army Officers 36

SSNO, Ministry of Defense 36, 66, 81, 88, 204, 212, 221, 250, 255
SSOJ, Union of the Socialist Youth of Yugoslavia 36
State,
 independent 75-76, 91, 104, 123, 135, 149, 155, 267
 national 76
Status,
 client 17, 237, 246
SUBNOR, League of World War II Veterans' Associations 36
SUP, the Police 117-8
Supreme Defense Council 242-44, 251
System,
 multiparty 54, 60, 79

Tactic,
 war 134
Tito, Broz Josip 17, 29, 35, 52, 56, 179, 221, 233
TO, territorial defense 90, 101
Transformation,
 self-transformation 27
Tudjman, Franjo 27, 77, 97, 233

UN Security Council Resolution 757 11
Unitarianism 51, 177-78
Unity,
 ideological-political 58, 60, 88, 219
 moral and political 52, 88
UNPA, UN Protected Area 147
Ustasha 77, 81, 114-15, 141-42, 145

Vatican 20, 154
VJ, Yugoslav Army xii, 6, 8, 14, 16, 23-24, 262-8, 37, 96, 159-60, 207, 226, 236, 239-40, 242-44, 246-48, 250, 254-55, 272
VPI, Military-Political News 37
Vukovar 144, 146, 152

Index

VUR, Chamber of Associated Labor 61

War,
  civil 50, 95, 115, 121, 126-28, 161, 175, 272
  crimes 23, 167, 184, 228, 232, 262, 269
  false 138
  fratricidal 81, 97
  goals 8
  media 44
  prevent 116, 151, 201
  pro 14, 17, 115
  special 4, 10, 60, 86, 94, 127, 210, 220, 231, 262
  Yu-war 6-7, 11, 14, 16-17, 19, 21-23, 26, 29, 165-72, 174-75, 257, 263-69, 271

Warfare,
  regardless 103
Weakness,
  military-political 137

Xenophobia 57, 77, 232, 241

Yugoslav,
  pro-Yugoslav 8, 35
Yugoslavia,
  breakup 8, 38, 115, 148
  four basic variations 74
  political disintegration 74, 86, 169
  recomposition of Yugoslavia 198, 259
  second-and-a-half Yugoslavia 149, 152
  the political configuration 73